Nineteenth-Century
Women Writers
of the
English-Speaking World

Recent Titles in
Contributions in Women's Studies

Nineteenth-Century Women Writers of the English-Speaking World

Edited by
Rhoda B. Nathan

Prepared under the auspices of Hofstra University

Contributions in Women's Studies, Number 69

Greenwood Press
New York • Westport, Connecticut • London

Library of Congress Cataloging-in-Publication Data

Main entry under title:

Nineteenth-century women writers of the English-
  speaking world.

  (Contributions in women's studies, ISSN 0147–104X ;
no. 69)
  Papers given at the Nineteenth Century Women Writers'
International Conference, Nov., 1980, held at Hofstra University.
  Bibliography: p.
  Includes index.
  1. English literature—Women authors—History and
criticism—Congresses.   2. American literature—Women
authors—History and criticism—Congresses.   3. English
literature—19th century—History and criticism
—Congresses.   4. American literature—19th century—
History and criticism—Congresses.   5. Women in
literature—Congresses.   I. Nathan, Rhoda B.   II. Hofstra
University.   III. Nineteenth Century Women Writers'
International Conference (1980 : Hofstra University)
IV. Series.
PR115.N56   1986   820'.9'9287   85–27250
ISBN 0–313–25170–3 (lib. bdg. : alk. paper)

Library of Congress Catalog Card Number: 85–27250
ISBN: 0–313–25170–3
ISSN: 0147–104X

First published in 1986

Greenwood Press, Inc.
88 Post Road West
Westport, Connecticut 06881

Printed in the United States of America

The paper used in this book complies with the
Permanent Paper Standard issued by the National
Information Standards Organization (Z39.48–1984).

10 9 8 7 6 5 4 3 2 1

Contents

Contents

Foreword

The essays in this collection had their origin as papers given at the Nineteenth-Century Women Writers' International Conference in November 1980. The Conference was held under the auspices of the Hofstra Cultural Center, and was organized into panels reflecting the broad areas of general interest expressed in the papers and by the various discussants. With all supplementary oral materials deleted from the final publication, however, it was thought wiser to avoid overlapping classifications and to present the essays alphabetically by author's name.

The published proceedings of the Conference is one of a series of such meetings held at Hofstra University. Others in the series are Eighteenth-Century Women Writers and Twentieth-Century Women Writers.

Acknowledgments

The editor should like especially to thank the following people for their efforts in organizing and coordinating the events of the Conference and in preparing the materials for publication:

Dr. Joseph G. Astman, Professor of Languages and Comparative Literature and Director of the Hofstra Cultural Center.

Ms. Natalie Datlof and Dr. Alexej Ugrinksy, Conference Coordinators.

Dr. Robert N. Keane, Professor of English and Chairman of the English Department and Chairman of the Conference Committee.

Jennifer Kern, Collator of the Author Index and Hofstra Honors English Major and Jo-Ann G. Mahoney, Collator of the Subject Index.

Ms. Marilyn Seidman, Conference Secretary.

Preface

It is worth noting that no novelist ever dedicated a book to George Eliot in her lifetime as a "token of admiration for [her] genius" as Melville did to Hawthorne upon the publication of *Moby Dick*. No one ever greeted Emily Dickinson "at the beginning of a great career" as Emerson did Whitman in recognition of *Leaves of Grass*. All Dickinson received by way of notice was a plea from Thomas Wentworth Higginson, her only mentor, to delay publication.[1] Women like Dickinson were more likely to be pitied than encouraged by their contemporaries, as evidenced from no less a supporter of women's creativity than G. H. Lewes, George Eliot's lifelong companion and inspiration, who wrote in 1853: "If the accident of her position makes her solitary and inactive, or if her thwarted affections shut her somewhat from that sweet domestic and maternal sphere to which her whole being spontaneously moves, she turns to literature as to another sphere."[2] Still, women in the nineteenth century wrote, prolifically and memorably. From their poems, novels, and letters, and from the reliable biographies that recount their contributions, we learn that they were alternately and sometimes simultaneously encouraged, ignored, relegated to the kitchen, and elevated to the salon. They wrote in the parlor, in the attic, in the pantry, and in the bedroom. They wrote in moments snatched from baking the bread and with hands that rocked the cradle.[3] They wrote in secrecy and reigned in public; some served men and others were served by them. Their subjects were the common preoccupations of all writers—matters personal, social, political, and spiritual. They represented no single point of view nor shared any unusual common interest. Although the peripatetic Margaret Fuller, the retiring Brontë sisters, and the sedentary Mrs. Browning led diverse lives, they shared the qualities of devotion to their craft and persistence. They were, to a woman, high-minded and dedicated, remarkable as personalities, and formidable as artists. If any characteristics may be singled out to describe their work as a whole, intensity of commitment and sharp insight should be cited. A large proportion of their work is marked by true excellence. The poetry of Dickinson, the fiction of Austen, Eliot, and the Brontës, and the prose of Margaret Fuller, are acknowledged works of genius by universal standards.

The papers in this collection are not about the "female imagination" or the "feminine sensibility" or the "feminist revolution" of the nineteenth century. They are original and provocative essays dealing with a variety of aspects of the life and literature of nineteenth-century writers of distinction who happened to be women and sometimes wrote from a woman's point of view but always reflected the world in which they lived. Since books by women inevitably mirror the restraints in their lives, the limitations imposed upon their sex are examined as well as are their triumphs of full expression and free creativity. Some of these papers address themselves to the clash between the artist's need to live and work freely and her prescribed societal role. Others outline the conventional education women were given to prepare them for their ordained domestic and cultural position and to disqualify them from active participation in a society that operated very efficiently in the form of a closed circle. Even Emerson, friend to Margaret Fuller and supporter of women's equality in such stirring poems as "Give All to Love,"[4] was guilty of such private observations in his *Journal* as the following entries: "Women generally have weak wills, sharply expressed perhaps, but capricious and unstable" (January 21, 1834), and "Women see better than men . . . quite without any wish to act" (November 17, 1839). The majority of the papers, however, are devoted to detailed analyses of the themes in the literature itself, primarily in the areas of intellectual conditioning, male-female relationships, social imperatives, and spiritual questions. The contributors to this anthology offer a unique dual perspective of the literature and lives of women writers of the nineteenth-century English-speaking world.

Rhoda B. Nathan
Conference Editor

NOTES

1. Dickinson's second letter to Higginson makes reference to his cautious advice: "I smile when you suggest that I delay 'to publish,' that being as foreign to my thought as firmament to fin." June 8, 1862. *The Letters of Emily Dickinson*, 3 vols., ed. Thomas H. Johnson and Theodora Ward (Boston, 1965), p. 405.

2. G. H. Lewes, "The Lady Novelists," *Westminster Review* (London, 1852), 133–34.

3. In a letter to his wife, Higginson records that Dickinson had confided that "she made all the bread, because her father liked only hers." *Atlantic Monthly*, 1871.

4. "Give All to Love," an ostensible love poem, contains the lines: "Free be she, fancy-free; / Nor thou detain her vesture's hem," and ends with "When half-gods go, / The gods arrive." It is clear from the context of the poem's argument that the half-gods are the divinities of romantic love, while the true gods are the deities of the self or the independent soul.

Nineteenth-Century
Women Writers
of the
English-Speaking World

1

The Bride of the White Election: A New Look at Biblical Influence on Emily Dickinson

Peggy Anderson

In his short but momentous essay, "Meditation in a Toolshed," C. S. Lewis discusses the difference between looking "at" the ray of light coming through the crack at the top of a toolshed door and looking "along" the beam of light. When one looks at the light, he is blinded to everything else, but when one looks along the light, he is illuminated. Lewis uses the experience of a young man in love and the scientist who describes romantic feeling in terms of genes and biological urges. The lover is viewing love from inside "along" the emotion rather than from outside, looking "at" the feeling. Says Lewis:

You get one experience of a thing when you look along it and another when you look at it. Which is the "true" or "valid" experience? Which tells you most about the thing? . . . It has been assumed without discussion that if you want the true account of religion you must go, not to religious people, but to anthropologists; that if you want the true account of sexual love you must go, not to lovers, but to psychologists; . . . you must listen not to those who lived inside . . . but to sociologists.[1]

Modern thought, then, sacrifices the thing thought of or the experience discussed to objectivity. Finally, Lewis urges us to look both along and at experience without discounting either.

We have had a great deal of scholarship on Emily Dickinson's poetry that looks at the poetry without also looking along it. The work of John Cody and Rebecca Patterson shows the extremes to which such scholarship may be carried and reveals far more of the scholars' perspectives than the worldview of the poet. Practicing atheists, agnostics, humanists, and those indifferent to spiritual matters have consciously or unconsciously imposed their own biases upon interpretations of her poems, often denying or obscuring her own point of view in-the process. The general assumption is that because Dickinson was not a Christian, only her poems of doubt should be taken literally, while the poems of faith, if they are dealt with at all, are interpreted imaginatively or figuratively. In order to bring some balance to Dickinson studies, I would like to scrutinize her work from the point of view of historic Christianity, dealing mainly with poems that exhibit not just a nebulous religious feeling, but a faith that is demonstrably Christian, using the Bible as the standard for what constitutes a Christian rather than the vague understanding or misunderstanding of avowedly non- or anti-Christians. This paper attempts to show the need for such an approach and to make a small beginning. Assume with me that Emily Dickinson's rejection of Puritanism, the formal church, and baptism did not mean that she rejected Christianity. Indeed, I submit that just the opposite is true, that she rejected the "dimity convictions" which allowed her brother, his wife, and his mistress all to be members in good standing of the church. I also submit that she is not very unorthodox in her faith if one takes the Bible as the criterion instead of the pale thing which New England Puritanism had transmitted to her.

Let us see where looking "at" Dickinson's poetry has brought us. In discussing the influence of Emily Dickinson's reading on her life and work, George F. Whicher quotes her letter to Higginson: " 'For Prose I have—Mrs. Ruskin—Sir Thomas Browne—and the Revelations.' "[2] He then pursues her debts to Ruskin and Browne, but is mute when it comes to " 'the Revelations.' " In the variorum edition of her letters, Thomas H. Johnson and Theodora Ward follow Whicher in commenting on her mention of Ruskin and Browne, but also ignore her reference to the last book in the Bible.[3]

Richard Wilbur, while admitting that "Emily Dickinson also wrote in the meters of hymnody, and paraphrased the Bible, and made her poems turn on great words like Immortality and Salvation and Election," concludes that "those great words are not merely being themselves; they have been adopted for expressive purposes"; his assumption being that she was not a Christian because "at the age of 17 . . . Emily Dickinson found that she must refuse to become a professing Christian."[4] Though it is readily allowed that Emily Dickinson grew artistically, she is often held spiritually to this youthful rejection[5] and her poems of faith are explained away. Charles R. Anderson exemplifies this position in his statement that "many of her apparent assertions of faith are merely part of her strategy of paradox."[6] Indeed, William S. Sherwood stands boldly alone in his tracing of her spiritual journey from early rejection to a later embracing of Christianity, if one discounts J. S. Wheatcroft, who apparently changed his mind from 1963 to 1974. In an article in *Criticism* in 1963, Wheatcroft discusses Dickinson's wearing of white as a sign of her election[7] while his article in *American Transcendental Quarterly* in 1974 states that "she suffers with no hope of consolation" since "the metaphysic of orthodoxy is repudiated by her poetry."[8]

However, "the metaphysic of orthodoxy" is surely affirmed in a number of poems. Poem 608 reads:

Afraid! Of whom am I afraid?
Not Death—for who is He?
The Porter of my Father's Lodge
As much abasheth me!

Of Life? 'Twere odd I fear a thing
That comprehendeth me
In one or two existences—
As Deity decree—

Of Resurrection? Is the East
Afraid to trust the Morn
With her fastidious forehead?
As soon impeach my Crown![9]

Then we have poem 964:

"Unto Me?" I do not know you—
Where may be your House?

"I am Jesus—Late of Judea—
Now—of Paradise"—

Wagons—have you—to convey me?
This is far from Thence—

"Arms of Mine—sufficient Phaeton—
Trust Omnipotence"—

I am spotted—"I am Pardon"—
I am small—"The Least
Is esteemed in Heaven the Chiefest—
Occupy my House"—

If the death of her beloved nephew Gilbert did nothing else, it confirmed in her an assurance of immortality, as her letter 868 to Susan Dickinson makes abundantly clear,[10] and closing with the rapturous "Pass to thy Rendezvous of Light."

Though it is unanimously agreed by Dickinson scholars that the Bible is her chief source, there is little agreement as to how she used it. On the one hand, Charles R. Anderson asserts that she rarely mentions Biblical characters except in the humorous poems;[11] on the other hand, Richard Sewell says that in her letters and poems, she draws from nearly every book in the Bible.[12] Richard Chase says that though she knew the whole Bible intimately,[13] "she was, on the whole, an unbeliever."[14] Allen Tate even calls her work "blasphemous."[15] Anderson also states that Dickinson really didn't believe in heaven[16] or a literal resurrection,[17] despite her use of these Biblical doctrines in many poems. Surely, there are poems where "heaven" is used symbolically or connotatively, but there are a number of poems where Dickinson is presenting the heaven of historical Christianity.

If we assume with Sherwood that "the Biblical tropes in her poetry are there because she believed in the concepts behind them and not because she found them useful tools for structuring and ordering experiences and beliefs for which they were not originally designed,"[18] we will make a start at looking "along" her work. Returning to whether or not she believed in heaven, her poetry shows that she did even before she had come under God's grace, as we see in poem 256:

> If I'm lost—now—
> That I was found—
> Shall still my transport be—
> That once—on me—those Jasper Gates
> Blazed open—suddenly—

We see from this poem that Dickinson has not yet realized that rapturous religious experience brings only a fleeting assurance of heaven and is not the substance of faith. A later poem, 420, contains these lines:

> You'll know it—as you know 'tis Noon—
> By Glory—
> As you do the Sun—
> By Glory—
> As you will in Heaven—
> Know God the Father—and the Son

Because they are parallel constructions, we do not have the liberty to take only the images of "Noon" and "Sun" literally, while leaving the image of "Heaven" for figurative interpretation—we must treat all one way or the other. Here, I see no reason not to take all three literally. If anyone doubts her connecting of nature and supernature, poem 575 shows her attempt to accommodate heaven to items in nature, saying that " 'Heaven' has different Signs—to me— / Sometimes, I think that Noon / is but a symbol of the Place—." She also offers the effects on her of dawn, birds, and sunset as reminders of paradise, but wonders "how Ourself, shall be / Adorned, for a superior Grace— / Not yet, our eyes can see."

For her belief in a literal resurrection, see poems 322, 499, 525, and 664. Poem 322, "There came a Day at Summer's full," is interesting because her delight in the prospect of heaven still hinges on being united with her lover after death; however, the "new Marriage" is not a supernal marriage between the two lovers. Dickinson knew the Scriptures well enough to be aware that in heaven "they neither marry, nor are given in marriage" (Matthew 22:30), but that both would meet at the marriage of the Lamb, freed of earthly bonds and obligations. In 499, she ponders how those in heaven, where according to Revelation 21:4, there is no pain, might view us here on earth:

> Anticipating us
> With transport, that would be a pain

> Except for Holiness—
> Themself—admitted Home—
> Through easy Miracle of Death—
> The Way ourself, must come

Poem 525 discusses the tremendous cosmic and personal import of Resurrection: "What Duplicate—exist— / What Parallel can be— / Of the Significance of This— / To universe—and Me?" Poem 664 is the familiar "Of all the Souls that stand create—."

One fact that becomes apparent the deeper one penetrates Dickinson studies is that she is surely far more conversant with the Bible than are most of the scholars who explicate her poetry. Johnson and Ward mention many Scriptural allusions or quotations in the variorum letters, but their omission of comment on quite a few makes one wonder if they recognized the omitted examples as Biblical.[19] David T. Porter says that the "immortality which Emily Dickinson envisions does not at all times mesh with Christian orthodoxy. It tends, at times, to be an analogue for the ultimate condition of the completed personality."[20] Anyone familiar with the post-Resurrection appearances of Jesus, where he was still himself only so transformed that even Mary Magdalene did not at first recognize him (see John 20:11–18), would have difficulty understanding how this view of immortality is unorthodox or unbiblical. Keeping in mind the poems previously discussed that deal with her belief in heaven and a literal resurrection, let us look at poem 1433, which begins, "How brittle are the Piers / On which our Faith doth tread—" and continues by affirming that God not only authored the bridge of faith, but also "sent his Son to test the Plank, / And he pronounced it firm." The letter in which this poem was enclosed makes it clear that Emily Dickinson sent the lines to Higginson some months after his wife's death to offer encouragement by reminding him that immortality is certain because it was arranged by God and proved by his Son.[21] Thus, we must always keep in mind when reading her poems concerning immortality, that her idea of eternal life is the Christian one, which leaves plenty of room for speculation regarding the mode of life after death, once one has accepted the existence of heaven and a literal resurrection, based on God's grace and Christ's sacrifice.

Another instance of a scholar's lack of knowledge of the Bible surfaces in Anderson's comment on the lines "With Will to choose, or to reject, / And I choose, just a Crown Throne—" from "I'm ceded—I've stopped being Theirs." He doesn't believe that the poem can be dealing with spiritual matters because "choosing" of immortality is "not the way mortals achieve God's grace."[22] However, according to the New Testament, personal choice is exactly the way people receive the grace of God. John 3:16 says "For God so loved the world that He sent His only begotten Son that whosoever believeth in Him should not perish, but have everlasting life." Romans 10:13 states that "Whoever shall call upon the name of the Lord shall be saved." Revelation 3:20 declares, "Behold, I stand at the door and knock: if any man hear my voice, and open the door, I

will come in to him, and will sup with him, and he with me.'' In an earlier
poem, 279, "Tie the Strings to my Life, My Lord," the emphasis is upon
Dickinson's willing submission to divine leadership when she states that she is
"Held fast in Everlasting Race— / By my own Choice, and Thee—.'' This early
poem dramatizes the need of anyone young in the faith for strong support from
God to keep him on the narrow path, while the later poem shows Dickinson's
expanding vision of the Christian life in her awareness of the believer's co-
rulership with King Jesus as promised by the glorified Christ himself in Revelation
3:21: "He who conquers, I will grant him to sit with me on my throne, as I
myself conquered and sat down with my Father on his throne.''

Another poem that suffers from the unfamiliarity of scholars with the Bible
is "God is a distant—stately Lover—.'' Anderson discusses it as an anti-Christian
poem with not "even sound Trinitarian doctrine.''[23] Indeed, it is not the Trinity
being described but the first and second persons of the Godhead, the Father and
Son, so that Anderson's statement is misleading. What Dickinson has done is
offer a clever analogical gloss of St. John, chapter 17, where Jesus prays to his
Father acknowledging their oneness:

Now they have known that all things whatsoever thou hast given me are of thee. For I
have given unto them the words which thou gavest me; and they have received them,
and have known surely that I came out from thee, and they have believed that thou didst
send me. . . . That they all may be one; as thou Father, art in me, and I in thee, that they
also may be one in us; that the world may believe thou hast sent me. (John 17:7, 8, and
21)

In the poem, Miles Standish sends John Alden to woo Priscilla just as God sends
Jesus to woo mankind. Her twist at the end of showing that God covers all bases
in case we should prefer the One sent to the Sender has a sound Scriptural basis.
I John 2:23 states that "Whosoever denieth the Son, the same hath not the Father;
he that acknowledgeth the Son hath the Father also.''

Two rarely-explicated poems are also commentaries on Bible passages. The
quatrain

> To die—without the Dying
> And live—without the Life
> This is the hardest Miracle
> Propounded to Belief.

restates Galatians 2:20 where the Apostle Paul enunciates one of the great mysteries of the Christian life: "For I am crucified with Christ: nevertheless I live;
yet not I, but Christ liveth in me." This essential paradox of Christianity is
summed up tersely in the first two lines, while the poet's reaction in the last
two shows a growing understanding of what Christian maturity means—death
to self. She recognized the reality of this doctrine as a "Miracle," and a hard
one, just the opposite of her statement in poem 499 that physical death is an

"easy Miracle" for the believer. This more difficult doctrine of dying of self is not meant for the skeptic or the vaguely religious, but for the Christian, because it is "Propounded to Belief."

Poem 1055, "The Soul should always stand ajar," is her gloss on Song of Solomon 5:2–6, which reads:

I sleep, but my heart waketh: it is the voice of my beloved that knocketh, saying open to me, my sister, my love.... I have put off my coat; how shall I put it on? I have washed my feet, how shall I defile them? My beloved put in his hand by the hole of the door, and my bowels were moved for him. I arose up to open to my beloved.... I opened to my beloved but my beloved had withdrawn himself and was gone: my soul failed when he spake: I sought him, but I could not find him: I called him, but he gave me no answer.

The poem states that the situation described in the Scripture cannot happen if a soul always leaves its door open a bit, so that "the Heaven," her word for the Biblical beloved, might not try the door and find it locked.

Another factor contributing to a misunderstanding of influences, the Bible included, upon Emily Dickinson is the manner in which explicators defer to or ignore early scholarship. The case of "Mine—by the Right of the White Election!" is a perfect example of too much deference. Higginson and Mabel Todd published it as a love poem[24] despite the religious language. Later, Whicher assumed it to be a love poem, showing that "her lover was hers only 'by the grave's repeal,' which loosed all bonds."[25] Johnson lists it in his category of "poems of 'marriage' and renunciation."[26] Anderson mentions the poem as "an imaginative projection of what it would be like to be betrothed to God,"[27] getting the best of both worlds, as it were. Only the early J. S. Wheatcroft discusses it as a poem affirming her spiritual election.[28]

Though I believe that Wheatcroft's interpretation is correct, Anderson offers the best context for stylistic approach in his comment that "the exclamatory style and the repetition of the rapturous 'Mine' at the beginning of six lines seem to cast this in the mold of rhetoric, the rhetoric of the hymns celebrating heavenly love."[29] Let us examine a particular hymn, "Holy Bible, Book Divine," as a source for the diction:

Holy Bible, book divine,
Precious treasure, thou art mine;
Mine to tell me whence I came;
Mine to teach me what I am;

Mine to chide me when I rove;
Mine to show a Savior's love;
Mine thou art to guide and guard;
Mine to punish or reward[30]

The fourth and final stanza ends with a repetition of the first two lines. Emily Dickinson knew the words as early as 1852, for she says to Susan Dickinson, " 'Precious treasure, thou art mine' " in a letter written in February of that year. The poet enclosed the words in quotation marks as she often did to indicate conscious borrowing.[31] The capitalization and punctuation are exactly the same as in the line of the hymn.

The diction of poem 528 is atypical of Dickinson's usual style. I believe that the choice to depart from her sparse understatement to the exclamatory rhetoric of the hymn was motivated by exhilaration attendant upon her conversion to Christianity in 1862, the probable year of the poem's composition. Tracing the poem to a particular hymn bolsters theological interpretation. I believe that "the Sign in the Scarlet prison— / Bars—cannot conceal!" is the five wounds of Christ in the "Scarlet prison" of his flesh. They are not hidden by the "Bars" of that "prison" because the wounds never healed and are an eternal reminder of the Crucifixion by which Christian election was "Confirmed." The grave was repealed by the Crucifixion. She affirms that her election is not only for eternity, "in Vision," but also has ramifications on this side of the grave, "in Veto!" Indeed, her greatest delight comes in the assurance she feels in her election, saying that it is hers "—long as Ages steal!" This phrase has to do with time, not eternity, and her exultation in spiritual security beginning at conversion carries her far beyond the Puritan concept of merely having a hope of salvation.

Ignoring early scholarship, however, can also lead to misinterpretations of poems. Poem 320, "We play at Paste—," is a case in point. Thomas Johnson assumes it to be a poem stating Dickinson's attitude toward her art.[32] David Porter views it and "I cannot dance upon my Toes—," poem 326, as companion pieces asserting her artistic maturity.[33] There is no evidence that the poet herself or her early editors considered the former to be about art or that the two poems were similar in theme. Dickinson did not place them together in the fascicles,[34] nor did Higginson and Todd publish them together: "We play at Paste—" was published in the 1891 edition, while "I cannot dance upon my Toes—" was not published until 1929. In his *Atlantic Monthly* article discussing the poems Dickinson had sent him over the years, Higginson says of "They play at Paste—" that "it seems a condensed summary of the whole experience of a long life"[35] and he doesn't mention the other poem, though it was in his possession. Obviously, her preceptor did not connect "We play at Paste—" to art, nor did he consider the two poems similar in theme. Surely, the latter poem does concern art, written in defense of her approach to poetry which Higginson had attacked, and dispatched to him in August, 1862. The former, however, is one of the four poems Emily Dickinson sent to him in her first letter, dated April 15, 1862. I believe the poem presents her view of mortal and immortal life. The "paste" and "sands" of this life prepare us for the "Pearl" and "gem" of eternal life. This fits with Sewell's statement that she always considered mortality as preparation for immortality.[36] According to Revelation 21:21, there are twelve gates to heaven, each one a single pearl. The image in the first stanza shows believers dropping off this mortal life of paste as they approach the gates of pearl. The second stanza speaks of "new Hands"—"new" because she had just recently become a Christian and thus the "new creation" of II Corinthians 5:17, "If any man be in Christ, he is a new creation." "Sands" is, of course, a common symbol for time. It is significant that Dickinson uses the plural "we" in this poem instead of the singular "I" of the other. If "We play at Paste—" is about her views on this life and the next, then the plural pronoun helps to universalize the poem and might indicate her identification with fallen human nature prior to conversion and her later awareness of being a part of the mystical body of Christ. Her use of "I" is quite appropriate in the poem discussing her art because the point of that poem is her individuality.

In conclusion, I hope that this paper has established a need for further studies in the area of Biblical influence upon Emily Dickinson. There is the whole complex field of her poems expressing doubt and unbelief to be addressed, but I believe that they can only be treated correctly within a Christian context. St. Thomas's doubt and St. Peter's denial show that her similar feelings are nothing new to the Christian life. Indeed, in poem 1411, she speaks of the "uncertain certainty" of her faith, a statement which merely amplifies the plea of a New Testament Christian to Jesus in Mark 9:24, "I believe; help thou mine unbelief."

NOTES

1. C. S. Lewis, "Meditation in a Toolshed," in *God in the Dock*, ed. Walter Hooper (Grand Rapids, Mich.: Eerdmans Publishing Co., 1970), p. 213.

2. George F. Whicher, *This Was a Poet* (1938; rpt. Philadelphia: Albert Saifer, 1952), p. 208.

3. Emily Dickinson, *The Letters of Emily Dickinson*, 3 vols., ed. Thomas H. Johnson and Theodora Ward (Cambridge, Mass.: The Belknap Press of Harvard University Press, 1958), II, p. 262.

4. Richard Wilbur, "Sumptuous Destitution," in *Critics on Emily Dickinson*, ed. Richard H. Rupp (Coral Gables, Fla.: University of Miami Press, 1972), pp. 48–49.

5. Charles R. Anderson, *Emily Dickinson's Poetry: Stairway of Surprise* (New York: Holt, Rinehart, and Winston, 1960), p. 57; Richard Chase, *Emily Dickinson* (Westport, Conn.: Greenwood Press, 1951), p. 60; Richard B. Sewell, *The Life of Emily Dickinson* (New York: Farrar, Straus and Giroux, 1974), I, 351.

6. Anderson, p. 254.

7. J. S. Wheatcroft, "Emily Dickinson's White Robes," *Criticism*, 5 (1963), 138.

8. J. S. Wheatcroft, "The Holy Ghost in Cages," *American Transcendental Quarterly*, 22 (1974), 104.

9. Emily Dickinson, *The Poems of Emily Dickinson*, ed. Thomas H. Johnson (Cambridge, Mass.: The Belknap Press of Harvard University Press, 1958). All references to poems are to this edition.

10. Dickinson, *Letters*, III, p. 779.

11. Anderson, p. 31.

12. Sewell, II, p. 694.

13. Chase, p. 208.
14. Ibid., p. 163.
15. Allen Tate, "Emily Dickinson," in his *Essays of Four Decades* (Chicago: Swallow Press, Inc., 1968), p. 298.
16. Anderson, p. 254.
17. Ibid., p. 274.
18. William R. Sherwood, *Circumference and Circumstance* (New York: Columbia University Press, 1960), p. 231.
19. Dickinson, *Letters*, I, pp. 145, 146, 147, 156, 195, 215, 277, and 311 for Biblical quotations, paraphrases or allusions not noted by the editors.
20. David T. Porter, *The Art of Emily Dickinson's Early Poetry* (Cambridge, Mass.: Harvard University Press, 1966), p. 18.
21. Dickinson, *Letters*, II, pp. 610–11.
22. Anderson, p. 179.
23. Ibid., p. 180.
24. Emily Dickinson, *Poems*, ed. Mabel L. Todd and T. W. Higginson (Boston: Roberts Brothers, 1890), p. 43, the first poem in the section titled "Love."
25. Whicher, p. 280.
26. Thomas H. Johnson, *Emily Dickinson: An Interpretative Biography* (Cambridge, Mass.: The Belknap Press of Harvard University Press, 1963), p. 82.
27. Anderson, p. 187.
28. Wheatcroft, "White Robes," p. 143.
29. Anderson, p. 184.
30. John Burton, "Holy Bible, Book Divine," in *Nottingham Sunday School Union Hymn Book*, 1st ed. (England, n.p., 1812).
31. Dickinson, *Letters*, I, p. 177.
32. Johnson, *Life*, p. 109.
33. Porter, pp. 10–11.
34. R. W. Franklin, *The Editing of Emily Dickinson: A Reconsideration* (Madison: University of Wisconsin Press, 1967), p. 56.
35. T. W. Higginson, "Emily Dickinson's Letters," *Atlantic Monthly*, 68 (October, 1891), 445.
36. Sewell, II, p. 530.

BIBLIOGRAPHY

Anderson, Charles R. *Emily Dickinson's Poetry: Stairway of Surprise*. New York: Holt, Rinehart, and Winston, 1960.
Burton, John. "Holy Bible, Book Divine." In *Nottingham Sunday School Union Hymn Book*. 1st ed. England: n.p., 1812.
Chase, Richard. *Emily Dickinson*. Westport, Conn.: Greenwood Press, 1951.
Dickinson, Emily. *The Letters of Emily Dickinson*. 3 vols. Ed. Thomas H. Johnson and Theodora Ward. Cambridge, Mass.: The Belknap Press of Harvard University Press, 1958.
Dickinson, Emily. *Poems*. Ed. Mabel L. Todd and T. W. Higginson. Boston: Roberts Brothers, 1890.
———. *The Poems of Emily Dickinson*. 3 vols. Ed. Thomas H. Johnson. Cambridge, Mass.: The Belknap Press of Harvard University Press, 1958.

Franklin, R. W. *The Editing of Emily Dickinson: A Reconsideration.* Madison: University of Wisconsin Press, 1967.

Higginson, Thomas W. "Emily Dickinson's Letters." *Atlantic Monthly,* 68 (October, 1891), 444–56.

Johnson, Thomas H. *Emily Dickinson: An Interpretative Biography.* Cambridge, Mass.: The Belknap Press of Harvard University Press, 1963.

Lewis, C. S. "Meditations in a Toolshed." In his *God in the Dock.* Ed. Walter Hooper. Grand Rapids, Mich.: Eerdmans Publishing Co., 1970, pp. 212–15.

Porter, David T. *The Art of Emily Dickinson's Early Poetry.* Cambridge, Mass.: Harvard University Press, 1966.

Sewell, Richard B. *The Life of Emily Dickinson.* 2 vols. New York: Farrar, Straus, and Giroux, 1974.

Sherwood, William R. *Circumference and Circumstance: Stages in the Mind and Art of Emily Dickinson.* New York: Columbia University Press, 1960.

Tate, Allen. "Emily Dickinson." In his *Essays of Four Decades.* Chicago: Swallow Press, Inc., 1968, pp. 281–98.

Wheatcroft, J. S. "Emily Dickinson's White Robes." *Criticism,* 5 (1963), 135–47.

———. "The Holy Ghost in Cages." *American Transcendental Quarterly,* 22 (1974), 95–104.

Whicher, George F. *This Was a Poet: A Critical Biography of Emily Dickinson.* New York: 1938; rpt. Philadelphia: Albert Saifer, 1952.

Wilbur, Richard. "Sumptuous Destitution." In *Critics on Emily Dickinson.* Ed. Richard H. Rupp. Coral Gables, Fla.: University of Miami Press, 1972, pp. 48–59.

2

Sisters and Survivors: Catherine Parr Traill and Susanna Moodie

Ann Boutelle

Of the many women writers of the nineteenth century, it would be hard to pick out as unlikely and as intriguing a pair as the two sisters, Catherine Parr Traill (1802–99) and Susanna Moodie (1803–85).

Each played a crucial role in the development of the Canadian literary tradition, and each now forms a link in the chain of Canadian women writers, a chain stretching back to Frances Brooke and her 1769 *History of Emily Montague* (the first Canadian novel—and possibly the first "American" novel), and continuing on into the contemporary work of Margaret Atwood and Margaret Laurence. Both sisters, curiously, have found a second literary immortality in the 1970's: Moodie in Atwood's *The Journals of Susanna Moodie* (a poetic sequence); Traill in Laurence's *The Diviners* (a novel). A full century after the creation of their individual (and contradictory) myths, each sister succeeded in becoming one.

They were born in England at the beginning of the nineteenth century—part of one of those astonishing families where everybody seemed to write. Their father, Thomas Strickland, was a gentleman of some means, who allowed all of his nine children access to his substantial library and who took care in supervising his children's education. All of the children "scribbled," and seven out of nine became published authors.

Catherine, one of the younger children, was the first to be published, with a grand total of nine children's books to her credit before her marriage (at the age of thirty) to Thomas Traill, a retired Scottish officer who had been given a grant of land near Peterborough, Ontario. The newly married pair sailed from Greenock in July, 1832. (Samuel Strickland, a brother, had emigrated to the same section a few years before. Susanna and *her* new officer husband—also from Orkney— were soon to follow.) And here, near Peterborough, they proceeded to hack out a farm in the wilderness (or bush): cutting trees, burning brush, leaving the tree stumps to disintegrate while they tilled between them, and erecting shelter. Cut off from civilization, each had to be strong, resourceful, and independent—making do, sometimes, in the most primitive of fashions, struggling daily for survival: "our whole stock of farming implements consists of two reaping-hooks, several axes, a spade, and a couple of hoes. Add to these a queer sort of harrow that is made in the shape of a triangle for the better passing between the stumps."[1] The contrast to the genteel English countryside in which the sisters had been raised could hardly be more marked.

Undaunted, however, Traill was not about to sacrifice her literary career for the sake of survival in a new country. She appears to have managed both with supreme ease. Only four years after her arrival in Canada, her *Backwoods of Canada* was published. Based on letters written to her mother and friends, the book details the experience of emigration: the departure of the boat, the voyage across, the arrival to face cholera, and the journey to the interior.

The work is remarkable not only for the vivid and sharp description of terrain, weather, farm implements, plant life, Indian neighbors, and practical skills (maple-sugaring, for example), but also for the implicit portrait of the author. Traill comes across as a relentlessly formidable lady: capable, confident, always in control, without a shred of self-pity or a backward glance. Less than one page is devoted to her own bout with cholera (which almost proved fatal); the book radiates energy, efficiency, and pride: "It has ever been my way to extract the sweet rather than the bitter in the cup of life, and surely it is best and wisest so to do."[2] Every word she writes reflects this determinedly optimistic and purposeful outlook.

The woman who was to produce nine children (no mean trick, considering her late start) presents her first-born in this volume as a speedy and presumably easy *fait accompli*. On the second of November, 1833, she gives a first reference to "my baby," then slides quickly into a description of the tea-chest (lined with black bearskin) in which the baby rides. Mother, bread-maker, gardener, writer, she impresses constantly with her seemingly inexhaustible supply of energy: "You say you fear the rigours of the Canadian winter will kill me. I never enjoyed better health, nor so good, as since it commenced."[3]

Even more amazing is the one passion to which she gives full rein: her interest in botany. An amateur, yet highly knowledgeable and active botanist, Traill found herself in a kind of made-to-order paradise. A nineteenth-century Eve, naming the plants in Eden, she finds in the rich profusion of the surrounding plant life an unexpected and intoxicating pleasure. Dried specimens are eagerly sent off to a professor at Edinburgh University. Pages and pages of *The Backwoods* are indulgently devoted to the plant life. Her description is sharply accurate, occasionally lyrical, and never forgetful of the practical aspects:

The wood-cress, or as it is called by some, ginger-cress, is a pretty white cruciform flower; it is highly aromatic in flavour; the root is white and fleshy, having the pungency of horse-radish. The leaves are of a sad green, sharply notched, and divided in three lobes; the leaves of some of them are slightly variegated; the plant delights in rich moist vegetable mould, especially on low and slightly swampy ground; the flower-stalk is sometimes naked, sometimes leafed, and is crowned with a loose spike of whitish cruciform flowers.

There is a cress that grows in pretty green tufts at the bottom of the waters in the creeks and small rivulets: it is more delicate and agreeable in flavour than any of the land-cresses; the leaves are of a pale tender green, winged and slender; the plant looks like a green cushion at the bottom of the water . . . it makes a very acceptable salad in the early spring, and at the fall of the year.[4]

Traill's *Canadian Settler's Guide* (1855) is a companion-piece to *Backwoods*, which had been intended for women of her own class who might follow. The *Guide*, however, is addressed to the less capable, less organized emigrants— the unprepared who had left in desperation, without means to get themselves started, and without any knowledge of what to expect. Traill provides for them a comprehensive and detailed handbook. The table of contents is alphabetized (typical of Traill's control and practical approach) and gives a good picture of her range: Ague, Apples, Beer, Bees, Borrowing, Bread-making, Buckwheat, Cakes, Carpets (Homemade), Canada (Letters from), Candle-making, Cheese-making, Coffee and Tea (Substitutes for), Corn, Curing of Fish, Curing of Meat, Dairy, Dysentery, Dyeing Wool, Fish, Fire, Fruits, and so on. A survival manual (potentially still useful if our own society should fall apart), the book is written in a sturdy and clear prose. The only rhapsodic passages are again those concerning plants and flowers.

To Susanna Moodie, however, the Canadian flora offer little consolation. The differences between the sisters' reactions are so great that it is hard to believe that they are even related, let alone that they lived close to each other and experienced the same Peterborough bush. They might as well be in two different universes.

Roughing It in the Bush (1852) is Moodie's record of the toils, dangers, and difficulties of the first few years. Where Traill gives encouragement and practical advice, Moodie serves up a plateful of terror. Beset by constant calamities and disasters, she is never in control. Her book is designed as a warning to emigrants, attempting to scare them off and to counterbalance the frequently fraudulent claims of the land companies. The final paragraph of the work forms the triumphantly depressing conclusion:

If these sketches should prove the means of deterring one family from sinking their property, and shipwrecking all their hopes, by going to reside in the backwoods of Canada, I shall consider myself amply repaid for revealing the secrets of the prison-house, and feel that I have not toiled and suffered in the wilderness in vain.[5]

Meanwhile, Moodie's estimate of the personal sacrifice entailed is relentlessly blunt:

For seven years I had lived out of the world entirely; my person had been rendered coarse by hard work and exposure to the weather. I looked double the age I really was, and my hair was already thickly sprinkled with grey. I clung to my solitude. I did not like to be dragged from it to mingle in gay scenes, in a busy town, and with gaily dressed people. I was no longer fit for the world.[6]

The causes of this sudden aging are abundantly described. Terror stalks through her world. Moodie is surrounded by a hostile and violent nature, a world of fire and ice, with wolves about to descend the chimney. The human neighbors offer no support. Indeed, they themselves are as much a threat as the wolves: drunkards, borrowers, people who beat horses, men with crazy brothers, potential axe-murderers. While Moodie's nose remains above the water, at any moment it could be submerged. She is scared even of the cows:

The red heifer . . . came lowing to the door to be milked, but I did not know how to milk in those days, and, besides this, I was terribly afraid of cattle. Yet, as I knew that milk would be required for the tea, I ran across the meadow to Mrs. Joe, and begged that one of her girls would be so kind as to milk for me. My request was greeted with a rude burst of laughter from the whole set.

"If you can't milk," said Mrs. Joe, "It's high time you should learn. My girls are above being helps."

"I would not ask you but as a great favour; I am afraid of cows."

"*Afraid of cows!* Lord bless the woman! A farmer's wife and afraid of cows."

Here followed another laugh at my request; and, indignant at the refusal of my first and last request, when they had all borrowed so much from me, I shut the inhospitable door, and returned home.

After many ineffectual attempts, I succeeded at last, and bore my half-pail of milk in triumph to the house.[7]

This triumph, however, is short-lived. On her next attempt:

I had just finished milking, and with a brimming pail was preparing to climb the fence and return to the house, when a very wild ox we had came running with headlong speed from the wood. All my fears were alive again in a moment. I snatched up the pail, and, instead of climbing the fence and getting to the house, I ran with all the speed I could command down the steep hill towards the lake shore; my feet caught in a root of the many stumps in the path; and I fell to the ground, my pail rolling many yards ahead of me. Every drop of milk was spilt upon the grass. The ox passed on.[8]

Moodie is obviously far more human than Traill, but with an irresistible tendency to dramatize. The work is as much fiction as biography. She copes with her terrors by exaggerating them and writing them down—to humorous or thrilling effect—and she supplies a sense of constant danger for the unwary and the helpless. This makes for splendid reading, as the reader can hardly wait for the next disaster to strike.

Journeys are cold and long. Fallen trees block their passage. The food at the only available inn is cold and inedible. And the children are asleep (as if, in their innocence, spared from full knowledge of the dreadful world they are entering) when they meet up with a typically grotesque group:

> The man was blear-eyed, with a hare-lip, through which protruded two dreadful yellow teeth that resembled the tusks of a boar. The woman was long-faced, high cheekboned, red-haired, and freckled all over like a toad. The boy resembled his hideous mother, but with the addition of a villainous obliquity of vision which rendered him the most disgusting object in this singular trio.[9]

These appalling creatures are a grotesque version of what the Moodies will become: human beings distorted by experience, made ugly, animal-like.

With frightfully severe winters and with plagues of black flies in the summer, the elements are at constant war with the vulnerable family. There are no less than two fire sequences, one in winter, one in summer. In each, Moodie is on her own, without her husband's help. In the winter fire, babies are put into drawers, hastily covered with blankets, and set outside in the snow. Gunpowder, meanwhile, is about to explode. In the summer fire, the hired help carelessly and without warning burns the fallow. As a wall of flame surrounds the house, the lake hovers Tantalus-like in the distance. The children are again helplessly and innocently asleep, but a providential rain saves them all at the last moment.

All this is a little unbelievable. If Moodie were as helpless and incapable as she presents herself, she would never have survived. Traill, meanwhile, is giving helpful hints about how to prevent fires and how to put them out—tin or iron nailed down below the stove, throwing salt on a fire, wrapping a child tightly: "In cases of emergency, it is folly to fold one's hands and sit down to bewail in abject terror: it is better to be up and doing."[10]

And so these two writers present us with two very different types of women, despite the overlapping of background and experience. One is a strong role model, courageous, inspiring, instructing: "I aimed at no beauty of style. It was not written with the intention of amusing, but simply of instructing and advising."[11] The other appears determined to present herself as a hysteric—and writes a book which both amuses and terrifies. The truth undoubtedly lies somewhere in between: Moodie is stronger than she dare admit; Traill weaker.

For each, however, writing plays a central and crucial role: for Traill, a means of educating and helping; for Moodie, a means of personal psychological survival.

And most importantly, each defines the self as much through the role of writer as through the role of woman. They point the way, not only for their companions in the nineteenth century, but also—in our day—for ourselves.

NOTES

1. Catherine Parr Trail, *The Backwoods of Canada* (Toronto: McClelland and Stewart, 1966), p. 70.

2. Ibid., p. 114.

3. Ibid., p. 72.

4. Ibid., p. 83.

5. Susanna Moodie, *Roughing It in the Bush* (Toronto: McClelland and Stewart, 1962), p. 237.

6. Ibid., p. 237.

7. Ibid., p. 227.

8. Ibid., p. 129.

9. Susanna Moodie, *Roughing It in the Bush, or Life in Canada* (New York: George P. Putnam, 1852), II, 9–10.

10. Catherine Parr Traill, *The Canadian Settler's Guide* (Toronto: McClelland and Stewart, 1969), p. 204.

11. Ibid., p. xviii.

3

The Novels of Mary Jane Holmes: Education for Wifehood

Lucy Brashear

Tedious as it is to read the soap-opera novels of the American literary ladies of the nineteenth century, at that time their books were outselling those of Hawthorne, Melville, and Twain. Little wonder that Hawthorne called them "a d——d mob of scribbling women."[1] One of his rivals, Mrs. Mary Jane Holmes, wrote thirty-nine novels between 1854 and 1905, four of which were best-sellers, and by conservative estimates sold over two million hardback copies.[2] Although critics classify her fictional genre as novels of manners,[3] sentimental[4] or domestic,[5] socially speaking, they are courtesy books, lineal descendants of the works of Fanny Burney and Jane Austen. In the tradition of her predecessors, Holmes used her novels to advise young women to conform to the manners and morals prescribed by society if they were to be victorious in winning the coveted title of wife.

For the readers of romance, Holmes's books never disappoint: every heroine makes an enviable match with a handsome suitor, who is older and wiser than she. Educated at an Ivy League school (preferably Yale) and independently wealthy, he is a Byronic hero from whom all vestige of sexual irregularity has been scrupulously expunged. Spinsterhood or an unhappy marriage, that is, one in which the husband drinks, gambles, or teaches music, is embarrassing proof that a woman has been inattentive to the most pressing consideration of her life, or, even worse, is being penalized for past transgressions. Although Holmes buries her advice under a thin veneer of mawkish claptrap, it is clear that a woman who follows the rules governing acceptable female decorum and trains herself for a career of marriage will be bountifully rewarded with material blessings bestowed by a rich husband, but the woman who fails to do so will be punished with poverty, the trademark of the spinster or the sign of an unfortunate alliance.

Haunted by the spectre of indigent spinsterhood, marriageable women—even twin sisters or best friends—compete to become Mrs. Dr. Van Buren or Mrs. Senator Woodhull. To assist these contenders, Holmes's courtesy book novels offered reliable homilies illustrating effective methods to market one's salable assets of beauty and charm. Holmes's plot formula rarely varies: an impoverished but well-born young girl develops to physical loveliness and emotional maturity after enduring a ritualistic period of learning to humble her spirit and refine her manners. Her painful preparation for marriage is bountifully rewarded by what Holmes labels a "brilliant match."

Although Fred Lewis Pattee speaks for many critics when he says that Holmes's women, similar to others in the popular fiction of this time, were always "snow-white or coal-black,"[6] Nina Baym divides them into "a trio of female types: diabolic, angelic, and human."[7] Holmes, however, does not view women according to their innate natures, as these critics argue, but rather by their ability or inability to be educated for wifehood.

This thesis is peculiarly evident in Holmes's symbolic treatment of hair. Although traditionally light and dark hair signifies virtuous characters as opposed to evil ones, Holmes's heroines do not conform to this standard. Brown hair, preferably auburn or chestnut, indicates Holmes's ideal woman, untutored as of yet in the role she must follow but capable of learning. In contrast, most of Holmes's blondes are innocent naives who never mature to responsible womanhood. Either they die young or they remain perpetual children because of an inherent physical, mental, or emotional disability, such as blind Alice of *Marian Grey*,[8] mad Nina of *Darkness and Daylight*,[9] or flighty Lilian of *Mildred*.[10] Occasionally, fair-haired women are used as foil characters, mature and responsible, but they never command reverential awe as do the brown-haired heroines.

Although auburn is the desirable hue, black hair frequently signifies an unblemished heroine, whose mysterious aristocratic background must be disclosed or her forceful personality tempered before she can be acknowledged ready for marriage. Edith Hastings, for example, of *Darkness and Daylight*, is a "black-eyed, black-haired, black-faced little girl," who "possessed a spirit as proud as that of her high born mistress" (p. 11). The reader knows, however, that Edith's marriage to the wealthy Arthur St. Claire is a *fait accompli* when Edith discovers that she is really an heiress and at the same time happily subdues her passionate nature. (Throughout her long literary career Holmes remained oblivious to her peculiar penchant for unusual causal relationships.) Although raven hair is reserved for Holmes's wicked or misguided women, they are not irredeemable. Julia, in *Sunshine and Tempest*,[11] who has frequently wronged her sister, confesses her sins and assumes a new life, chastened by experience. She has learned, but too late.

Any change in hair, such as the color or length, is a symbolic gesture of the gravest import. The golden hair of the innocent and childlike Fanny in *Sunshine and Tempest* turns to light brown after marriage and motherhood. A reader may relax, comforted in the knowledge that with additional age and experience, Fanny's hair will darken to a rich auburn. In the same book the wicked but beautiful Julia disavows her femininity when her long flowing black hair is cut. 'Lena Rivers, like Julia, also fears that the loss of her hair will rob her of womanhood. Although dangerously ill, 'Lena begs her attendants not to cut her hair: "take everything else, but leave me my curls. Durward thought they were beautiful, and I cannot lose them."[12]

Philosophically, Holmes's educational curriculum for the training of young women for marriage was founded on three objectives: improve the physical appearance, mold the personality, and develop social and academic skills. In a woman's trip to the altar, her first and most important step was to undergo metamorphosis and assume those physical attributes that society (as interpreted by Holmes) considered essential to beauty, namely, regular features, a white complexion, rich auburn hair—flowing in soft waves or coiled in braids—large brown or blue eyes, chubby arms, small hands and feet, and a soft, low voice. Sometimes this transformation called for radical measures: in *The English Orphans* Mary Howard suffers two protruding teeth to be extracted without benefit of novocaine,[13] her rotund friend Jenny painfully diets to win the love of Willy (p. 230), and Marian Grey considers "poulticing" to eliminate freckles (p. 15). Holmes never permits her readers to forget that ugly girls need not despair. In *Dr. Hathern's Daughters*, the maid Julina Smith migrates to Paris, acquires new teeth, bleaches her hair, and then marries a rich old man.[14] Unfortunately Julina's drugstore blonde hair was an imprudent choice for it marks her as a woman who is not to be trusted. While titian or excessively curly hair held no symbolic meanings for Holmes, in her book *Marian Grey* it is "prescribed by fashion as harried and unbecoming" (p. 5). Frederic Raymond speaks not just for Holmes but for all of society when he says that "a woman with red hair cannot be handsome" (p. 271). In a frenzy of masochism Marian hysterically tries to tear out her corkscrew curls, but during a serious illness her hair is sheared away and obligingly reappears as auburn waves (pp. 116–42). Such is the miraculous reward for a life of virtue.

Although Holmes preferred to dress her heroines in virginal white adorned by a single flower in the hair, her ingenues quickly learn the value of a fashionable wardrobe if they are to make an impressive conquest. Hidden away on the banks of the Chicopee, these Cinderellas emerge as belles at Saratoga and Newport by way of the chic modistes of New York and Boston. With newly acquired tastes they gauge the width of a lace ruffle, distinguish between seemly and meretricious jewelry, and choose harmonious color combinations, which would never be confused with the garish attire of menial workers. Above all, they are clean: hair shines and cosmetics are shunned as public notice of a faded beauty.

It is not enough that a woman be beautiful, however; she must also be young. Lida Gibson, of *Sunshine and Tempest*, who is scarcely out of puberty, accepts spinsterhood with resigned cheer, saying, "I have reached the advanced age of twenty-two without ever having had an offer, so I have given up in despair and am looking forward to a long life of single-blessedness'' (p. 210). As Holmes herself grows older, her young ladies do not despair so soon as Lida. By the time of *Marian Grey* (1863), spinsterhood is reckoned at the ''dreaded age of thirty'' (p. 326).

Although Holmes never deviated from the belief that a woman must be beautiful or become so if she is to place first in the field, she emphasized just as fervently the second division of her educational trivium—the need to recognize and avoid certain personality traits ascribed to the ''general mother'' Eve and expatiated upon by the patriarchs of the church: pride, arrogance, hypocrisy, deceit, cruelty, vanity, shrewishness, and garrulousness. Holmes added a few of her own: her wicked women are shamelessly ignorant of the criminality of such activities as bribing postal officials to steal letters or misrepresenting facts to gain access to someone else's fortune. These women are all punished, however, not by the law, but by a higher law which dooms them to consumption, factory work, loss of beauty, or most heinous of all—spinsterhood.

In the preface to one of Holmes's best-sellers, *'Lena Rivers*, she cites ''high temper'' as an admirable characteristic of women (p. iv), for example, Alice of the ''Old Red House,'' who fights ''like a tiger'' for Frank[15] or the autobiographical Mary Jane of ''The Gilberts,'' who squelched the proud Adaline with a scornful remark.[16] Holmes may give lip service to ''high temper,'' but her heroines, like spirited horses, are eventually broken. In *Ethelyn's Mistake*, the heroine confesses, ''My old hot temper is not all subdued, though I hope I am a better woman.''[17] It is disquieting to contemplate the degree of sadism and masochism underlying this obsession for women to be subdued, a subject Holmes delicately sidesteps. Although wife-beating occurs in both *Darkness and Daylight* (p. 142) and *Rosamond*,[18] Holmes indicates that the abused wives in these novels required stronger discipline than a mere reprimand to check their ''high tempers.''

Like females in a scene drawn from Elizabethan drama, Holmes's heroines are tested to demonstrate allegiance toward their masters. In her version of *Jane Eyre—Darkness and Daylight*—Holmes's heroine, Edith Hastings, resists Arthur's deliberate trap to measure Edith's level of feminine curiosity and guards the key entrusted to her rather than use it to discover the secret of the mysterious room. To quote Holmes's imitable phraseology, ''Edith was the soul of honor'' (p. 94).

The price for learning to discipline the spirit and become submissive was high—the loss of self-esteem. In a society that elevated women to saints or reduced them to devils, a low self-image was considered the complement of pride, and thus, a sign of female virtue. A woman had visibly conquered her rebellious nature when she became all things to all people. Holmes's heroines, similar to many politicians' wives today, were automatons who charted out a survival course which demanded total repression of their feelings and desires in exchange for the security and reflected glory inherent in their social positions.

Regeneration is complete when ''high temper'' becomes sublimated in acts of charity. As Lady Bountiful, the formerly fractious woman visits the homes of the destitute and sick, replenishing their supplies from her little basket. No reader would be so ignorant as to assume that Lucy Harcourt, the golden-haired beauty of *The Rector of St. Mark's*, would be a good wife to the eligible young clergyman, Arthur Leighton. Uncomfortable in the presence of her indigent neighbors, "Lucy grew sick and faint" at the "poverty,—squalid, disgusting poverty, visible everywhere."[19]

Although beauty and personality required immediate attention, farsighted guardians saw to the training of their young charges in respect to social graces and academic studies as well. For example, the wealthy Mrs. Conway of *Maggie Miller* imported a governess from England to teach her granddaughters "how to *sit* and how to *stand*, how to *eat* and how to *drink*."[20] Housekeeping chores such as cooking, baking, and cheese-making were also expected of these young women, but it comes as no surprise that none of Holmes's heroines practice these tasks after their wealthy marriages. More to their tastes are the genteel occupations of needlework, painting, dancing, singing, and, in particular, piano playing. No matter that the fire is out and the cupboard bare, money must be found to pay for music lessons. Frequently a secret benefactor bestows a piano on a beautiful but destitute girl with the implied understanding that she demonstrate symbolically her readiness for marriage by acquiring instant musical dexterity. In order for 'Lena Rivers to please Durward, she "redoubled her exertions, practicing always five, and sometimes six hours a day" (*LR*, p. 218). It is a truism with Holmes that her most talented pianists enjoy the most successful marriages.

As to academic preparation, Holmes's men study for the law or medicine at Yale, Harvard, Amherst, and Andover; whereas her women attend Charlestown Seminary or Madame Duvant's fashionable school. Vital as are beauty and personality, it is understood that a prudent woman would not subscribe to Lilian's theory in *Mildred* that once she is married it won't matter that her husband learns she is a "putty head" (p. 108). Marian Grey sets a better example when she says, "I'll go away to school, and maybe, after a good many years are gone, you won't be ashamed of me, though I shall never be as beautiful as Isabel" (*MG*, p. 86). Poor girls who are subsidized by a guardian are frequently trained to be teachers or governesses. For example, Mrs. Greenleaf, in the short story "Bad Spelling," insists that her "poor relation" Mildred be taught geography, history, arithmetic, and grammar as teacher preparation, but that her privileged daughter Arabella "study French, Italian, music, painting, dancing, and the 'old poets.'"[21] Just as Holmes reflected nineteenth-century admiration of piano skill, she also revealed the importance of good grammar, spelling, and penmanship. Several of her young ladies are disappointed in their marriage hopes as a result of their inability to spell. When Arabella's father faces bankruptcy, she loses not only a fiancé but also a teaching position. To reinforce the moral, Holmes predicts that Arabella will never "rise higher than her present practice—that of a *plain* sewer" (p. 125).

Not all of Holmes's heroines are seminary educated, however. Her favorite heroine is the unwanted, unlovely orphan, who is befriended by a wealthy young benefactor, learning her lessons in reading and subduing her temper directly from him. Maggie Lee, along with other Holmes heroines, is educated at the feet of her guardian "on a low stool, her accustomed seat at his side."[22] Less obvious is the example that a woman should occupy a position inferior to that of the male closest to her. Vital as Holmes considered learning, however, she never lets her readers forget that most men were of the same mind as Mr. Thornton, whose experience with two wives had taught him that "Your superior women do not always make their husbands happy" (*Mildred*, p. 113).

The most important part of a woman's education, however, was not learned from a book but rather instilled by society, namely, the necessity to marry one's kind. As far as Holmes is concerned, Romeo and Juliet would have lived happily ever after if they had just married their own. In nineteenth-century America, color was the taboo primeval as illustrated in the bizarre story "Glen's Creek."[23] Orianna, a young Indian woman, desperately tries to scrub away her dark skin after the man she loves says to her, "Hang it all, Orianna, why were you not white!" (p. 303). When little dying Charlie prays to God to "make Orianna white" (p. 304), his prayer is answered and Orianna is discovered to be a missing white child whose skin was stained with walnut dye by her foster mother, an Indian woman. This tale is particularly revealing, for Holmes's message is explicit: in respect to marriage, white must be whiter than white.

All of Holmes's books end with the heroine's possession of the coveted marriage license, proof that her education for wifehood has been successfully completed. By pandering to the sentimental platitudes of her readers, Holmes developed a large audience which she sought to edify in respect to social decorum in much the same way that Harriet Beecher Stowe used her novel *Uncle Tom's Cabin* as a forum to present a humanitarian approach to the issue of slavery. But the comparison stops there. It is ironic that while Stowe was speaking out for the right of blacks to determine their own lives, Holmes was reinforcing the traditional concept that the destined role for a woman was to serve a husband. And just as ironical, both succeeded. Rational people, both in the North and in the South, eventually recognized the validity of Stowe's premise in respect to race, but were paradoxically blind to its application to women as well. A hundred years has not erased this peculiar double vision: there are still women who fear spinsterhood in much the same way as did Holmes's young Anna Livingston, who said, "I wouldn't be an old maid for the world—I'd run away first!" (*LR*, p. 127). Although readers no longer easily translate Holmes's Latin definition of marriage as the "*ultima thule* of a woman's hopes" (*Rec. of SM.*, p. 293), unfortunately many agree with the spirit of it and subscribe implicitly to her educational theories requisite for a "good match." A century separates Mary Jane Holmes from the present-day Marabel Morgan and her "total woman" creed, but philosophically they are sisters under the skin: both have shrewdly exploited their narrative skills to keep alive a belief in women's servitude, an idea which may well have succumbed decades ago were it not for the popular books of Holmes and a still continuing "mob of scribbling women" who see themselves as evangelists of marriage.

NOTES

1. "To William D. Ticknor," January 19, 1855, *Letters of Hawthorne to William D. Ticknor*, int. John Cotton Dana (Newark, N.J.: The Carteret Book Club, 1910), I, p. 75.

2. Sarah G. Bowerman, "Holmes, Mary Jane Hawes," *DAB* (1932); Frank Luther Mott, *Golden Multitudes* (New York: The Macmillan Company, 1947), pp. 125–26, 308, 320, 321.

3. Helen Waite Papashvily, *All the Happy Endings* (New York: Harper and Brothers Publishers, 1956), p. 149.

4. Herbert Ross Brown, *The Sentimental Novel in America 1789–1860* (Durham, N.C.: Duke University Press, 1940), p. 297.

5. Donald A. Koch, ed., *Tempest and Sunshine and The Lamplighter* (1854; rpt. New York: The Odyssey Press, 1968), pp. vii, ix–xiii.

6. Fred Lewis Pattee, *The Feminine Fifties* (New York: D. Appleton-Century Company, 1940), p. 125.

7. Nina Baym, "Portrayal of Women in American Literature, 1790–1870," in *What Manner of Women*, ed. Marlene Springer (New York: The Gotham Library: New York University Press, 1977), p. 228.

8. Mary Jane Holmes, *Marian Grey* (New York: Carleton, 1877).

9. Mary Jane Holmes, *Darkness and Daylight* (New York: Carleton, 1868).

10. Mary Jane Holmes, *Mildred* (New York: Carleton, 1877).

11. *Tempest and Sunshine*, ed. Koch.

12. Mary Jane Holmes, *'Lena Rivers* (New York: G. W. Dillingham Co., 1897), pp. 349–50.

13. Mary Jane Holmes, *The English Orphans* (New York: Carleton, 1883), pp. 102–3.

14. Mary Jane Holmes, *Doctor Hathern's Daughters* (New York: G. W. Dillingham Company, 1895), p. 451.

15. Mary Jane Holmes, "The Old Red House Among the Mountains," in *The Homestead on the Hillside and Other Tales* (New York: Carleton, 1865), p. 251.

16. Mary Jane Holmes, "The Gilberts," in *Homestead*, p. 165.

17. Mary Jane Holmes, *Ethelyn's Mistake* (New York: Carleton, 1869), p. 376.

18. Mary Jane Holmes, *Rosamond and Other Stories* (New York: Hurst and Company, n.d.), pp. 79–80, 90.

19. Mary Jane Holmes, *Westlawn and The Rector of St. Mark's* (New York: Carleton, 1874), p. 333.

20. Mary Jane Holmes, *Dora Deane and Maggie Miller* (New York: G. W. Dillingham, 1888), p. 223.

21. Mary Jane Holmes, "Bad Spelling," in *Rosamond*, p. 115.

22. Mary Jane Holmes, "Maggie Lee," in *Rosamond*, p. 131.

23. Mary Jane Holmes, "Glen's Creek," in *Homestead*.

4

Lewis Carroll and the Education of Victorian Women

Morton N. Cohen

We are all aware that Charles Lutwidge Dodgson, better known as Lewis Carroll, nurtured all his mature life a special preference for the female of the species. The preference was special because it was a preference not for all females, but for young girls. Even in Victorian times—some would say particularly in Victorian times—the idea of an unmarried Oxford don, however respectable, pursuing friendships with pre-pubescent girls offended some sensibilities.

But now, more than three quarters of a century after Dodgson's death, when virtually all those young friends of his have also died, we should be able to look at the evidence coolly and clinically. The record of these friendships is formidable, not only because Dodgson himself kept diaries and wrote mountains of letters, but because those little girls collectively left behind yet another treasure trove of memorabilia—their own personal reminiscences. But nothing in these private documents reveals any greatly guarded secrets; there lurked behind the features of that benign Oxford cleric no sinister Mr. Hyde. The evidence makes us realize that, ho hum, nothing scandalous entered into those relationships. They were all open and free, something that both parties greatly enjoyed. No sordid details await us, nothing will titillate the prurient. Dodgson did not possess wandering hands, he made no attempt upon the chastity of those young female friends.

Psychoanalysts have a good deal to say, of course, about the Reverend Charles Dodgson's suppressed desires, and we may ourselves be certain that the man regarded any sexual promptings that he may have felt as inspired by the devil. So genuine and devout a Christian was he that he chained his natural instincts and allowed them, at least those that were sexual, no conscious expression. The result is that in his life we find idealized relationships, where purity and beauty are worshipped, where young girls become young angels and, when they mature, young goddesses. Sex does not enter at all. Dodgson wants to admire the girls aesthetically, he enjoys their companionship, he seeks to contribute to their intellectual and social development, and, perhaps most of all, he tries to amuse them.

For that is, after all, the aim to which he devoted much of his life, helping his young friends in every possible way. He wrote his two great children's classics to amuse the most famous of those young girls, and he wrote dozens of other works in order to entertain hundreds, thousands of other young friends, both seen and unseen, the world over. The young girls he actually knew and cared for he aided in a multitude of ways. He supervised their careers, he gave them spiritual guidance, he took them on outings to London, he received them as house guests at the seaside, he bought them railway tickets, he gave them books and other presents, he took them to the theater, he fed them and clothed them, he photographed them, he paid some of their dentists' bills, he told them stories, and, most relevant for our purpose, he tutored them in mathematics and logic, he arranged for them to have lessons in elocution, he paid for them to get instruction in French, music, and art, and he took a constant interest in cultivating their talents and in helping them to cultivate their minds.

Because a hundred years or so have passed since Dodgson engaged in all this tutelage, and attitudes have changed enormously in that time, we ought perhaps to remind ourselves what standard attitudes Dodgson's contemporaries held towards women, young or mature. True, Dodgson lived in an age of chivalry, when, at least in polite circles, gentlemen treated ladies with mannered courtesy. Often, womanhood was idealized, even idolized. This worship of the female, we know, was an extension of attitudes that prevailed during the Romantic Period that regarded women as closer to heaven's angels than to earth-bound men.

But that was not the whole story. All Victorians, even those who idolized women, saw them as the "weaker sex," requiring protection and support. Those famous lines from Tennyson's *The Princess* capture the Victorian assessment of woman's place in the universe:

> Man for the field and woman for the hearth:
> Man for the sword and for the needle she:
> Man with the head and woman with the heart:
> Man to command and woman to obey;
> All else confusion.

Perhaps even more striking is that some of the medical authorities and scientists of the time pronounced the female inferior. Sir Almroth Wright, who invented the anti-typhoid inoculation and was one of the greatest pathologists of his time, as late as March 28, 1912, argued in *The Times* (London) that a woman's physiology, her "hyper-sensitivity," her "innate unreasonableness," her periodic "loss of proportion" made her unfit to vote. In earlier Victorian days the notion of woman as a weaker vessel was even more deeply rooted. The female body was capable of bearing children, but not of performing any other chores requiring physical prowess or endurance; to subject it to "manly" tasks would be to abuse it. Similarly, if one strove to educate the female mind, if one, as it were, subjected it to mental exercise for which the female brain was unfit, one would tax it beyond endurance and it might shatter. Women were, for the Victorians, quite distinct from men: they functioned differently, their purpose on earth was different, and one had a clear duty to recognize, protect, and even encourage that difference. Only by keeping woman in her place, in the home, as a mother, as a supervisor of the servants, a keeper of keys, a social butterfly— only in these ways were the true and natural functions of both woman and man fulfilled.

In most matters, Charles Dodgson was a man of his time. In spite of his great gifts of imagination, he did not often, as a person, transcend Victorian structures. True, he had a mind of his own and indeed decided major issues for himself. In the face of a dictum of Samuel Wilberforce, Bishop of Oxford, proclaiming the theater a form of godless entertainment, Dodgson was courageous enough, for instance, to insist openly that the English theater offered wholesome and uplifting experiences, and he attended theatrical performances and often took his young friends to them. Dodgson also had the courage to depart from the "high church" fold of his father and earlier progenitors because he found high church formality and ceremony too elaborate for his simple tastes. He was more comfortable as a broad churchman and he became one.

These examples attest to an independent man who thought for himself and made significant decisions either with or against the tide, according to his own lights. And yet, in examining Dodgson's whole life, one must conclude that he did not often break new ground, nor did he frequently break with convention. He was, in the main, in religion, in politics, even in art, conventional.

We should not be surprised, then, to find that in his attitudes to women he tends to accept past standards, to hold the line, to resist change. In his general attitude to work, for example, and in particular to the studies of mathematics and logic, he is stern. He believed in a carefully thought out and disciplined approach, he would not compromise and he would not be compromised on the requirements he set for himself, for his colleagues, or for his students. He regularly opposed lower standards of admission to Oxford and lower standards for passing examinations. He showed compassion for the unqualified and for those who failed to make the grade, but before any of them received Dodgson's "seal of approval," they simply, each and every one, had to climb the steep cliffs of Higher Mathematics on their own.

Of course, most of Dodgson's pupils—certainly all of his official ones—were men, the men of Oxford. When we ask about Dodgson's attitude towards women and women's education—how he stood on the issue of opening the gates of Oxford to women, to granting them degrees, to accepting them as equals—when we ask these questions, knowing the man and his time, we have every right to expect a conventional reply: a woman's mind, like her body, is inferior to a man's, women are not capable of higher education and granting them university educations would be contrary to their best interest and to the best interest of society. Certainly, that is the sum and substance of conventional Victorian attitudes.

But on examining Dodgson's record on the subject of women's education, we come in for some surprises. We cannot cast him as a champion of change— it would have violated his character if he took a liberal stance on these issues— but, on the other hand, he is not a dyed-in-the-wool Victorian.

As we know, higher education for women began, more or less, at Queens College in London in 1848, but Queens was a *college* only in name and offered women separate and far-from-equal education. Queens College apart, real education for women in England still had to arrive at the established male universities. Of these, Cambridge first allowed women to sit for examinations, and that landmark was passed in 1868, when Dodgson was thirty-six years old. At Cambridge, too, in 1869, the first important woman's hall was established, if not as part of the university itself, certainly on the fringe: Newnham Hall, later Newnham College. And in 1873, again at Cambridge, the hall that would become Girton College was founded. Oxford, you see, lagged behind.

Although women could attend lectures and take examinations at the University of Oxford from 1875, no hostels for women existed there until 1878, when the earliest women's halls, Lady Margaret Hall and Somerville College, opened. From time to time, the women of Oxford struggled fiercely against the iron gates of the University, but they made slow progress. Not until 1894 were all University examinations in arts and music open to women. But no woman could yet earn an Oxford degree.

Actually, the question of degrees for women first became a real issue in 1896, two years before Dodgson's death, and he took a genuine interest in the debate. In March of that year, Congregation, the University governing body, was to vote on whether Oxford should grant degrees to women. In the months before the crucial vote, newspapers were full of articles and letters stating arguments for and against the proposal. People in Oxford, and it seems from the widespread material that appeared on the subject, people everywhere in England, took one side or another and believed, in each case, that he or she had something new or freshly persuasive to say on the subject. The letters columns in *The Times* were largely devoted to the debate, public meetings were held and reported in the press, and a good many dinner tables groaned under the fists of pundits all too eager to pronounce on the merits or, more likely, the demerits of degrees for women.

Now, we have seen that Dodgson was not an adventurous trail blazer, and I should add, too, that when on April 29, 1884, twelve years earlier, the University, by a large majority vote, admitted women to additional examinations, Dodgson recorded in an unpublished passage of his diaries that he had voted "*non-placet.*"[1] In the crucial vote on March 13, 1896, the vote was overwhelmingly

(215 to 140) against giving Oxford degrees to women, and, no doubt, Dodgson voted with the majority. But, although in 1884 he was opposed to giving women access to more Oxford examinations and in 1896 to awarding women Oxford degrees, he certainly did not oppose giving women higher education. Quite the contrary. After the vote was taken and the women lost, Dodgson composed an essay on the subject and, like some of the other quieter souls in the Oxford community, he took the trouble to publish his views privately. His pamphlet, *Resident Women-Students*, consists of merely four pages and is dated four days after the crucial vote in Congregation.[2]

Characteristically Dodgson frames the issues involved as logical propositions. He begins thus:

In the bewildering multiplicity of petty side-issues, with which the question, of granting University Degrees to Women, has been overlaid, there is some danger that Members of Congregation may lose sight of the really important issues involved.

The following four propositions should, I think, be kept steadily in view by all who wish to form an independent opinion as to the matter in dispute.

The first proposition is that "One of the chief functions, if not the chief function, of our University, is to prepare young Men . . . for the business of Life. Consequently"—and here Dodgson presents his second proposition— "The first question to be asked . . . is 'How will it affect those for whose well-being we are responsible?' " He then puts his third proposition, that any scheme for admitting women students as full-fledged members of the University will eventually make residency at the University compulsory. Consequently—and now we have his fourth proposition— "Any such Scheme is certain to produce an enormous influx of resident Women-Students." Considering that three thousand undergraduate men were then enrolled at Oxford, Dodgson predicts that before long, an influx of some three thousand young women students would occur. "Such an immigration," he goes on, "will of course produce a rapid increase in the size of Oxford, and will necessitate a large increase in our teaching-staff and in the number of lecture-rooms." Then he asks this question: "Will the mutual influence, of two such sets of Students, residing in such close proximity, be for good or for evil?" Dodgson recalls at this point that he often discussed the issue with his old late friend Henry Parry Liddon, Canon of St. Paul's Cathedral, and that Liddon had expressed "most warmly and earnestly, his fears as to the effect . . . flooding Oxford with young Women-Students would have on the young Women themselves."

Dodgson does not go on to say that he agreed with Liddon on this or on any other particular. Instead, he proceeds to offer a solution to the problem. "Surely, the real 'way-out,' from our present perplexity," he wrote, is for Oxford, Cambridge, and Dublin to "join in a petition to the Crown to grant a charter for a Women's University. Such a University," he continues, "would very soon attract to itself the greater portion of young Women-Students. It takes no great time to build Colleges; and we might confidently expect to see 'New Oxford,' in the course of 20 or even of 10 years, rivaling Oxford, not only in numbers, but in attainments. At first, perhaps, they might need to borrow some teachers from the older Universities; but they would soon be able to supply all, that would be needed, from among themselves; and Women-Lecturers and Women-Professors would arise, fully as good as any that the older Universities have ever produced.''

He adds one last paragraph showing that he is aware that his proposal is not new and that one strong argument against it is that ''it is *not* what the Women themselves 'desire.' '' But he rejects that argument as logically weak. Like the proper Victorian he was, Dodgson insists that ''Even men very often fail to 'desire' what is, after all, the best thing for them to have.''

Dodgson's position, his propositions, and his proposals are not remarkable either for the man or for his time. They reflect, in fact, precisely the sort of person he was—not a great educational reformer, he was not in the forefront of social change. But having said that, we must add that he was at core a decent human being with sensitive feelings and a ''sensible'' outlook on life. What is remarkable about the man is not that he opposed making Oxford available to women students, but that he opposed their admission to degrees only on social, and not on intellectual grounds. He makes it quite clear that he has a deep respect for the intellectual potential of women and that women, in his view, were capable of the highest intellectual accomplishments. Indeed, had he believed otherwise, he would not have spent as much of his time and energy as he did in tutoring individual girls. Actually, even while Dodgson opposed opening Oxford to women, he spent much of his effort educating females, and he did that in three distinct ways.

One way was on a personal one-to-one basis. He gave individual instruction to a good many growing children throughout the years. He either went to their homes or they came to his rooms at Christ Church, and he took great pains with their instruction. He also carried on individual ''correspondence courses'' in letters, setting problems for his pupils to solve, correcting answers they sent him, and trying to explain their errors when they went wrong. Toward the end of his life, he conducted a long correspondence with one of his sisters, herself a woman of some age by then, instructing her in formal logic.[3]

The second way that Dodgson taught young girls was by inventing games and puzzles and by writing texts for them. Many of his writings are mathematical or logical games and exercises created for his young friends. Among his published works that fall into this category are *Castle-Croquet*, *Court Circular*, *Doublets*, *The Game of Logic*, *Lanrick*, *Mischmasch*, *Syzygies*, and *A Tangled Tale*. Some of these games appeared in print first in ladies' or girls' periodicals, as set exercises for readers to solve. Readers' answers were printed in subsequent weeks' issues and prizes were awarded. Respondents often became correspondents of Dodgson's, and in fact that is how he made some of his fastest friends.

The books that resulted when Dodgson assembled these periodical exercises between hard covers were usually dedicated to one or another of his child friends.

The third way that Dodgson taught young girls was in a more formal school setting. He often took the opportunity, when he met schoolteachers or head mistresses socially to inquire whether they would like to have him come and give logic lessons to any of the girls at their schools. The result was that classes were especially arranged for girls and even mistresses who wanted to take logic lessons. One of Dodgson's most interesting triumphs took place at the distinguished Oxford High School for Girls where over a number of years he gave what amounted to "mini-courses" in logic. The school "adopted" him as a special friend, and the girls wrote about him affectionately both in memoirs they left behind and in the school magazine they published regularly during the years while he was there. Dodgson also gave logic lectures at Oxford colleges for women, notably at Lady Margaret's Hall and at St. Hugh's.

By all accounts, Dodgson was a great success at these lectures, in spite of the notorious and troublesome stammer that kept him from taking up regular parish preaching. And his special gift seemed to lie in his allowing Lewis Carroll to take over from Charles Dodgson. New claims have been made recently for Dodgson as an innovator in the history of mathematics and logic.[4] I am not equipped to judge how valid these claims are, but I know that Dodgson brought to his works in mathematics and logic, as to his classroom teaching of these subjects, an imagination and inventiveness that we do not normally associate with such "dry" subjects. The exercises he invented, the paradoxes he posed, the examples he supplied are all couched in drama and suspense and infused with an intrinsic laughter and sense of fun, a quality of real life. In all, he made mathematics and logic live for his students as they never lived before. No wonder that professional mathematicians and logicians the world over readily smile as they recognize Dodgson's "Barber-Shop Paradox" or his "Paradox of Achilles and the Tortoise." These problems and many more bear the genius of humor and creativity characteristic of the *Alice* books.

So it was in those classrooms when Charles Dodgson drilled his female students in the strict exercises and arguments of higher mathematics: he drew them into interesting situations, he inspired them to use their own imaginations, he aroused their interest and made them laugh at his examples. Of course he adored the rows of young females hanging on his every word; no doubt, the very nature of his audience sparked him on to new creative heights. But, all the same, he never lost his sense of proportion about the relationships, nor did he ever think that what he was doing was at all ordinary. Writing to a friend in his early days of lecturing at the Oxford High School for Girls, he reported: "*Every* afternoon, oddly enough, I have an engagement, as I have taken to giving lectures, on my Game of Logic, to young people. . . . Girls are *very* nice pupils to lecture to, they are so bright and eager."[5] In turn, the students appreciated him. "When Mr. Dodgson stood at the desk in the sixth-form room and prepared to address the class," one of his pupils wrote in later years, "I thought he looked very tall and seemed very serious and rather formidable . . . [but] as he proceeded I think the facts became rather more and more fanciful and the fancies more fantastic."[6] Another student remembered that "the girls adored him; he entertained them with written games on the blackboard. He was perfect with children," she added, "and there were always tribes of little girls attached to him. He made everyone laugh."[7] And yet one more girl's testimony must be given. Enid Stevens, one of his all-time favorites, was an Oxford High School student. "I never realized," she wrote after Dodgson's death, "—as I do now—what jewels were being poured out for my entertainment. I know now that my friendship with him was probably the most valuable experience in a long life, and that it influenced my outlook more than anything that has happened since; and wholly for good."[8]

Charles Dodgson may not have done much to advance women's entrance to the sacred halls of Oxford University, to secure them degrees there, but he influenced many a female's own education in his time, and who can doubt that he has had an enormous influence in shaping women's minds in general and, incidentally, men's. The two great English classics he wrote have, indeed, made Alices of us all. He wrote many other books for the instruction and amusement of girls, and he devoted his entire life to instructing and entertaining young females. "And so you have found out that secret," he once wrote to his friend Ellen Terry, "one of the deep secrets of Life—that all, that is really *worth* the doing, is what we do for *others*?"[9] Dodgson profoundly believed that maxim, and he did more for young girls than for any other group.

Dodgson's name will not enter scholarly tomes devoted to the struggle for women's rights. But many women in the world have benefitted from his having trod the face of the earth and inhabited those rooms at Christ Church. But perhaps, for our purpose today, we ought to recognize one thing about Dodgson that was not true of most Victorian males. Over and over again, he shows a deep respect for female intelligence, and nowhere does he make any distinction whatsoever between a good "male mind" and a good "female mind." For Charles Dodgson, a good mind was a good mind. In that one regard if in no other, he was ahead of his time and transcended its prejudices.

In 1920 Oxford University got round to giving women degrees. This past summer, I sat at High Table at Christ Church with women dons noticeably present. And one day, the Porter said as he handed me my mail, "Yes, the last bastion has crumbled. We are to have thirteen ladies here in October." For the first time in history, last month women were admitted to study in that masculine holy of holies, Christ Church.

Charles Dodgson has been dead for eighty-two years now, but I like to think of his spirit still hovering over Tom Quad, and I believe that, in his wisdom and with his whimsicality, he is concocting some special rhymes to celebrate the first thirteen women to become full members of Christ Church. I don't think that, now, he would disapprove.[10]

NOTES

1. Dodgson's manuscript diaries are in the British Library.

2. It is reprinted in *The Complete Works of Lewis Carroll* (London, 1939), pp. 1068–70.

3. For a record of this correspondence, see Lewis Carroll, *Symbolic Logic*, ed. William Warren Bartley III (New York and London, 1977).

4. See the editor's introduction in ibid.

5. Morton N. Cohen, ed., *The Letters of Lewis Carroll*, 2 vols. (New York and London, 1979), p. 680.

6. E. M. Rowell, "To Me He Was Mr. Dodgson," *Harper's Magazine*, CLXXXVI (February, 1943), 319–23.

7. Ethel Sidgwick, *Oxford High School, 1875–1960*, ed. V. E. Stack (Abingdon, Berkshire, 1963), pp. 56–57.

8. "Mrs. Shawyer's Reminiscences," *The Diaries of Lewis Carroll*, 2 vols., ed. Roger Lancelyn Green (New York and London, 1954), pp. xxiv-xxvi.

9. *The Letters of Lewis Carroll*, p. 813.

10. For background material for this essay, I have also drawn on the following works: Vera Brittain, *The Women at Oxford* (London, 1960); Walter E. Houghton, *The Victorian Frame of Mind, 1830–1870* (New Haven and London, 1957); and Josephine Kamm, *Hope Deferred* (London, 1965).

5

Emily Dickinson and Her Mentor in Feminist Perspective

Tilden G. Edelstein

Most twentieth-century literary critics and scholarly admirers of Emily Dickinson's poetry have been embarrassed by her long and momentous association with Thomas Wentworth Higginson. Soon after publication in 1862 of Higginson's *Atlantic Monthly* article, "Letter to a Young Contributor," Dickinson mailed some of her poems to him, asking if "they breathed" and what was "true." For the next twenty-five years her literary relationship with Higginson was among the few she had with anyone. She continued to send him letters and poems; he repeatedly wrote to her and twice visited Emily Dickinson in her Amherst home. Invited to participate at her funeral ceremony in 1886, Higginson read some lines about immortality from Emily Brontë, whose books Dickinson long had admired. Coediting, in later years, the very first three volumes of Dickinson poetry to be printed, he also helped introduce her work to the public through an extensive number of his articles and reviews.[1]

My book *Strange Enthusiasm: A Life of Thomas Wentworth Higginson*, published in 1968, has been considered the first scholarly biography of Higginson; I revised it slightly for a 1970 paperback edition.[2] This symposium has given me the opportunity to review what I had written about Dickinson and Higginson. I do so in the context of the Dickinson scholarship published since the 1960's and seek to review this important relationship utilizing some of our recently acquired understanding of nineteenth-century women's culture by twentieth-century scholars. I especially wish to incorporate the views of some feminist Emily Dickinson scholars for exploring the relationship between the poet and Higginson.

The high estimate of Dickinson poetry dominated literary criticism by the 1960's. Even the title of George F. Whicher's pivotal biography, *This Was A Poet* (1938), indicates it had been necessary as late as the 1930's to argue for her poetic genius. (A formidable critical trio, Allen Tate, Ivor Winters, and R. P. Blackmur, repeatedly had denied it.) Richard Chase and Henry Wells, among others, also helped establish the incontrovertible quality of her poems.[3] Increasing attention to Emily Dickinson's life, however, stimulated continuing skepticism about her poetic accomplishments based upon the ludicrous assumption that acknowledging the quality of her poetry required accepting the good health of her psyche. This assumption led to viewing her as if almost every act was a deliberate and rational effort to produce great poetry. Richard Chase, for example, argued that Dickinson, happily, was no emotionally starved and repressed female who championed reform causes as did Henry James's neurotic Olive Chancellor in *The Bostonians*. It was irrelevant, according to Whicher, that women were excluded from Amherst College because the poet readily imbibed the town's educational atmosphere.[4] Present in Whicher's writing and in others of this and previous generations was the familiar stereotype of the wholesome domestic female who found happiness and fulfillment with cake recipes, and learning without access to institutions of higher education. Her association with Higginson, for these male scholars and literary critics, was viewed as a disaster. Portrayed as a critical barbarian, he became the repugnant representative for the narrow literary taste of Dickinson's contemporaries. According to Whicher, Higginson was unable to distinguish Emily Dickinson from Queen Victoria and Lucy Stone.[5] And neither the queen nor the women's rights reformer were much different from Olive Chancellor in Whicher's view.

The scholarship of the 1960's, however, revealed new tolerance of Higginson. He had been a militantly radical abolitionist and a lifelong and renowned feminist: two causes no longer dismissed by scholars as nineteenth-century zealotry. Additionally, it had become obviously worthwhile to try to understand why Emily Dickinson turned to Higginson and not to a more outstanding nineteenth-century literary luminary. Thomas H. Johnson, who edited her poetry and letters for Harvard University Press, conceded that Higginson's championing of women's rights and women writers might have moved Dickinson initially to confide in him; Theodora Ward, who had served as Johnson's editorial assistant, argued that Dickinson had decided, after reading his books and articles, that Higginson was great. Still, past scorn for Higginson did not disappear: Charles Anderson fully developed the theme of the 1930's about Dickinson's flawless judgment and personality. She consciously toyed with Higginson, according to Anderson, always recognizing his tremendous personal and literary limitations.[6]

Looking back at what I wrote in the 1960's, it is evident that as a Higginson biographer and an historian committed to the importance of extensively examining manuscript and published evidence, I had been disturbed to learn that while Emily Dickinson's letters, poems, and snippets had been repeatedly read and discussed, Higginson's work virtually was ignored by twentieth-century literary scholars and critics. Perusal of Higginson sources had been limited largely to the three extant letters he wrote to Dickinson and an article about her he published late in life. Dickinson scholars apparently lacked the stamina and / or curiosity to read Higginson's voluminous published writings—and surely not his readily available manuscript journals and diaries. Having read all of Higginson's writings, I can understand the good taste of Dickinson scholars and literary critics, but fastidiousness aside, we must remember that Emily Dickinson appears to have read everything by Higginson available. Indeed, there was an enormous amount available: some sixty published articles in 1862, when she first wrote to him; and there would be thirteen books and innumerable articles and book reviews by the time of her death.[7]

An accurate context for their relationship only can be provided by examining these writings and rich biographical detail of Higginson's life. Especially central for our understanding of the similarities and differences between the two people is the nature of Higginson's support for the women's rights movement and his private and public encouragement of women writers; even more crucial are his images of women and women writers.

Some of the findings which distinguished my book from the previous work about the Higginson-Dickinson relationship establish that Higginson wrote about many subjects for which Dickinson cared deeply: nature, children, women, renunciation, religion, death, and immortality. When his conceptions of these subjects proved to be far different from hers his work still remained for Dickinson a useful source of information. Most important to her were the numerous empirical details about nature which reflected Higginson's formidable botanical knowledge.[8] Higginson's work provided the textbooks for this non-matriculating Amherst resident.

The biographical context in which she wrote to him helps explain why she initially did so, as well as illuminate the recurrent incongruousness of their continuing relationship. At the time Higginson wrote "Letter to a Young Contributor," especially inviting women to write poetry and submit it for publication, he stressed poetic privacy and the life of renunciation, reflecting his own severe but temporary isolation from the world. Soon, however, he would return to vigorous public activity as the colonel of the first black regiment in the Civil War, a regiment of South Carolina freed slaves. Symptomatically, on the day he received Dickinson's first letter and poems, he had publicly endorsed gymnasium exercise for women.[9] While literary critics can debate Higginson's impact on Dickinson's poetry and its publication, it remains certain that he had absolutely no success in converting her to a physical fitness program. She also was unconverted to another Higginson commitment. When he received a stomach wound in battle, Dickinson wrote to him that she viewed war as "an oblique place."[10]

After Higginson's two visits to Dickinson's Amherst home, dramatically evidencing some of their differences, it could be expected that the relationship would remain of peripheral but haunting importance to him. Her views about poetry, and even more markedly, about people and social issues, violated almost everything Higginson believed and acted upon. Yet a mutual attraction remained, and she kept sending him letters and poems to which he continued to respond. One of his short stories contains a mysterious and elusive heroine named Emilia, and his novel also presents an Emilia, but this time she is a composite of both Emily Dickinson and Margaret Fuller. While not called "half cracked," Emilia experiences motionless trances and ultimately dies at sea. Furthermore, Higginson's willingness to edit the Dickinson poems for publication after her death, and yet title and bowdlerize them, reveal the continuing ambivalence—the acceptance and rejection—of their relationship.[11]

Since my Higginson biography appeared, Richard Sewell and John Cody have published significant Dickinson biographies. A recent essay by Adrienne Rich represents a growing trend toward relating Dickinson's poetry and life to the feminist perceptions of the 1970's.[12]

Sewell has published the most comprehensively researched Dickinson biography. While showing an admirable mastery of a wide range of manuscript and monograph material, he repeats Whicher's simplistic view that Higginson mindlessly "exuded health and buoyancy" because he believed all causes were just. But Sewell is too sound a scholar to ignore that Higginson and Dickinson were "so close in some ways."[13]

John Cody's psychoanalytical analysis—however correct some critics may be about its excessively rigid Freudian structure—notably treats Emily Dickinson's life as less than idyllic. Her psychic tensions can be described and analyzed differently from Cody but only hagiography can continue to ignore them. (Indicative of the decline of Dickinsonian biographical eulogy is John Walsh's effort to show that Dickinson often was debilitated by mental illness as well as a plagiarizer from Elizabeth Barrett Browning.) Both Walsh and Cody state that because of his views about nurturing female potential Higginson was an excellent person for Dickinson to seek out.[14]

Rich returned to part of the 1930's theme reiterated by Anderson in the 1960's but did so from a feminist perspective: Dickinson's life was "deliberately organized on her terms." The poet, she argues, had to translate "her own unorthodox, subversive, sometimes volcanic propensities into a dialect called metaphor" with rhetorical flourish, which raises unanswerable counterfactual conjecture: imagine what would have been the result if Jonathan Edwards or William James had been women. Such feminist issues also were raised in the 1970's by Elsa Greene who suggests that nineteenth-century women were expected to inspire poems, not write them. The inferior status of nineteenth-century women, not Dickinson's psyche, she asserts, was the crucial issue: by simply "choosing the vocation of poetess, Emily Dickinson risked psychic and social penalties." Rebecca Patterson adds: "She was the victim of an age that mutilated its gifted women."[15]

What also emerges, it now can be argued, is that Higginson's feminism and Dickinson's relationship to it deserve more exploration than either I, or Dickinson scholars and literary critics, have given it. First, it must be recognized and emphasized that the women's rights movement of the 1850's and 1860's had no literary figure, male or female, as well known as Higginson. Emerson, Thoreau,

Harriet Beecher Stowe, Melville, among others, refrained entirely from public advocacy of feminism. Hawthorne opposed feminism altogether. (One may only conjecture that Margaret Fuller was prepared to fill the role of public advocate, but she died in a shipwreck in 1850.)

The seventies and eighties were no different. Higginson was an articulate and consistent advocate of women writers. He had long supported education for women: as early as 1850 he taught poetry to female factory workers in Newburyport, Massachusetts, stressing the need to nurture "the culture of the mind." Among eighty-nine signatories of a petition calling for the first national women's rights convention, he suggested that women not only needed civil rights, but also needed more than just opportunities for visiting, gardening, novel reading, crocheting, and baking an occasional sponge cake. Calling for the enfranchisement of women in an 1853 article, he compared their plight to the disfranchised black majority in South Carolina. Even before the publication of "Letter to a Young Contributor," the *Atlantic Monthly* published his "Ought Women to Learn the Alphabet," which argued that once women were educated they could not be expected to limit their activities to polite conversation. As William Chafe has noted in *Women and Equality*, the antebellum women's rights movement challenged almost every assumption about women's "place" and advocated the elimination of the "double standard in morality, education, and the economy."[16]

Dickinson, as a conscientious reader of his articles and books, was familiar with Higginson's advocacy of women's rights, including, of course, the encouragement of female writers. But just as Higginson's literary views would prove to be different from hers, so too was the extent of his feminism. Higginson believed and practiced the view that intellectuals must be social activists and must write and speak explicitly about all vital public issues. He was different, therefore, from Emerson, Thoreau, Melville, Hawthorne, and others—including Emily Dickinson. Most suggestive from today's perspective is that Higginson's view of feminism stressed the need to develop the whole woman, the mind and the body. He was especially eloquent in repeatedly demanding that women's minds and their bodies must cease to be corseted by the restrictions of stereotypes and prejudices. They must have the opportunity to use their minds and also must be encouraged to exercise their bodies.[17] Statues, not women, belonged on pedestals. This idea of developing the whole woman left Higginson and Dickinson far apart. His invitations to her, furthermore, to attend literary gatherings of men and women, invitations which she rejected, exemplified how he viewed female emancipation in contrast to how she viewed her life and role as a poet. "An artist," he noted in "A Plea for Culture," can afford to be poor but not to be companionless."[18] Other women writers took his advice. He stressed the educated, psychologically stable, physically healthy woman; she was a relatively isolated poetic genius filled with psychic tensions. As a spokesman for women's rights and advocate in behalf of women writers Higginson enticed Dickinson to begin and maintain their relationship. But just as their mutual interest in nature, children, renunciation, religion, death, and immortality proved to be illusory, even more crucial was the dissimilarity of her view of herself as a female poet and Higginson's.

Perhaps most revealing is that all those twentieth-century Dickinson literary critics and scholars who have decried her choice of Higginson have been unable to suggest a nineteenth-century person who would have been a realistic substitute. What remains true is that Higginson was the best male literary critic, who also was a feminist, produced by nineteenth-century America—and Emily Dickinson was its best poet. The incongruousness of their relationship reveals much about nineteenth-century American culture and its response to innovative poetry and emerging feminist ideology.

NOTES

1. *Atlantic Monthly*, 9 (1862), 401–11; Dickinson to Higginson, April 15, 1862, in Thomas H. Johnson and Theodora Ward, eds., The *Letters of Emily Dickinson* II (Cambridge, Mass., 1958), p. 403. The fullest accounts of their relationship are in Tilden G. Edelstein, *Strange Enthusiasm: A Life of Thomas Wentworth Higginson* (New Haven, 1968), pp. 250–51, 342–52, and in Richard B. Sewall, *The Life of Emily Dickinson*, II (New York, 1974), pp. 532–76.

2. Edelstein, New Haven, 1968; New York, 1970.

3. Richard Chase, *Emily Dickinson* (New York, 1951); Henry Wells, *Introduction to Emily Dickinson* (New York, 1947); Klaus Lubbers, *Emily Dickinson: The Critical Revolution* (Ann Arbor, 1968), pp. 173–75.

4. Chase, p. 73; George F. Whicher, *This Was A Poet* (New York: Scribner's, 1938), p. 39; Elsa Greene, "Emily Dickinson was a Poetess," *College English*, 34 (1972), 65.

5. Lubbers, p. 6; Whicher, p. 120.

6. Johnson, *Emily Dickinson, An Interpretive Biography* (Cambridge, 1955), pp. 80–86; Theodora Ward, *The Capsule of the Mind: Chapters in the Life of Emily Dickinson* (Cambridge, 1961), p. 189; Charles Anderson, *Emily Dickinson's Poetry: Stairway of Surprise* (New York, 1960).

7. A full list of Higginson's more than 500 titles can be found by consulting the following: Winifred Mather, *A Bibliography of Thomas Wentworth Higginson* (Cambridge, 1906); Mary Thacher Higginson, *Thomas Wentworth Higginson* (Boston, 1914); also see footnoted references to previously unlisted items in Edelstein, *Higginson*.

8. Edelstein (1968), p. 342; Sewall, II. p. 568.

9. *Atlantic Monthly*, 9 (1862), 401–11; Edelstein (1968), pp. 250–51; *Worcester Spy*, April 17, 1862; Higginson to Brander Matthews, January 6, 1892, Matthews MSS, Columbia University.

10. John E. Walsh, *The Hidden Life of Emily Dickinson* (New York, 1971), p. 149; Edelstein (1968), pp. 250–51.

11. Ibid., pp. 343–44, 308, 313; Thomas Wentworth Higginson, "The Haunted Window," *Atlantic Monthly*, 19 (1867), 429–31; Thomas Wentworth Higginson, *Malbone: An Oldport Romance* (Boston, 1870).

12. John Cody, *After Great Pain: The Inner Life of Emily Dickinson* (Cambridge,

1971); Adrienne Rich, "Vesuvius at Home: The Poems of Emily Dickinson," *Parnassus*, 5 (1976), 49–74.

13. Sewall, II, p. 547.

14. The most critical assessment of Cody is Simon A. Crolnick, "Emily Dickinson and the Psychobiographer," *Literature and Poetry*, 23 (1973), 68–81; Walsh, pp. 137, 141.

15. Rich, pp. 52, 53; Greene, pp. 63, 66, 67; Rebecca Patterson, "Emily Dickinson's 'Double Tim': Masculine Identification," *American Imago*, 28 (1971), 362.

16. Edelstein (1968), pp. 124, 125, 148–49; "Woman and Her Wishes," *Woman Rights Tract No. 4* (Newburyport, Mass., n.d., also published in *Una*, June, 1853); *Atlantic Monthly*, 3 (1859), 150; William Chafe, *Women and Equality: Changing Patterns in American Culture* (New York, 1977), p. 37.

17. Thomas Wentworth Higginson, "Saints and Their Bodies," *Atlantic Monthly*, 1 (1858), 585, 586, 590–91, 594; Thomas Wentworth Higginson, "Gymnastics," *Atlantic Monthly*, 7 (1861), 299, 300–301; Edelstein (1968), pp. 250–51.

18. *Atlantic Monthly*, 19 (1867), 33.

6

Henry James and the Artist-Heroine in the Tales of Constance Fenimore Woolson

Mary P. Edwards Kitterman

In *A Literature of Their Own*, Elaine Showalter examines the "double critical standard" which nineteenth-century English literary critics assumed as they wrote about novels by women writers. "We tend to forget," she suggests, "how insistently Victorian reviews made women the target of *ad feminam* criticism."[1] In a chapter titled "The Double Critical Standard and the Feminine Novel," she outlines the characteristics attributed to female and male writers by this method:

If we break down the categories that are the staple of Victorian periodical reviewing, we find that women writers were acknowledged to possess sentiment, refinement, tact, observation, domestic expertise, high moral tone, and knowledge of female character; and thought to lack originality, intellectual training, abstract intelligence, humor, self-control and knowledge of male character. Male writers had most of the desirable qualities: power, breadth, distinctness, clarity, learning, abstract intelligence, shrewdness, experience, humor, knowledge of everyone's character, and open-mindedness.[2]

Critics involved in this "masculine critical hegemony"[3] included those writing for all of the major British periodicals—*Blackwood's*, *Westminster Review*, *Gentleman's Magazine*, *National Review*, *North British Review*, and *Cornhill Magazine*, to cite a few. As we study the evidence Showalter presents, startlingly enough, it appears that even a critic like G. H. Lewes, Victorian liberal and companion to George Eliot, judges the work of women writers according to a scheme of "masculine" and "feminine" traits. Lewes concludes, for example, that

. . . we may be prepared to find women succeeding better in *finesse* of detail, in pathos and sentiment, while men generally succeed better in the construction of plots and the delineation of character.[4]

Likewise, when we turn to the American literary scene, the same kind of criticism prevails. To look, for instance, at early reviews by Henry James is to find what one contemporary Jamesian scholar has characterized as "slashing attacks on women's fiction."[5] Conventionally considered as a writer who "understood women" and created realistic and sympathetic feminine portraits,[6] as a critic, James, to the contrary, seems enthralled by the criteria of the "double critical standard." His later critical essays, as well as his early reviews, indicate that from the beginning to the end of his long life and career, he never once questioned his fundamental premise about creative power: to James it was clear that the masculine imagination was innately superior to the feminine. Women writers, however, demanded attention from James, sometimes as competitors in the literary marketplace, sometimes as friends, for women were engaged in an attempt to redefine the nature and role of the woman artist, to free her from the limitations which Victorian culture imposed. Even the most popular women writers, like Ouida and Marie Corelli, took their work seriously, while some of the literary women who were James's close friends, like Mrs. Humphry Ward, Vernon Lee, and Constance Woolson, were as dedicated to the art of fiction as was James himself. In fact, it was this very commitment to art which complicated their friendships with James. On the one hand, like a Jamesian character in Woolson's story "A Florentine Experiment," James became "partly priest, partly pedagogue."[7] For these dedicated women writers, James was the celebrant at the high altar; his books were holy, and it was he who could guide the developing woman artist. On the other hand, James was the woman writer's severest critic. For example, in 1877, he wrote,

George Sand invites reperusal less than any mind of equal eminence. Is this because after all she was a woman, and the laxity of the feminine intellect could not fail to claim its part in her?[8]

In his correspondence and conversations with his friends who were women writers, however, James did not wish to appear ungentlemanly, so he would envelop his harsh judgments in a haze of seeming compliments. In *A Backward Glance*, Edith Wharton records such an instance; Mrs. Wharton's husband, Edward, had asked James about her latest work:

"Oh, yes, my dear Edward, I've read the little work—of course I've read it." A gentle pause, which I knew boded no good; then he softly continued: "Admirable, admirable; a masterly little achievement. . . . Of course so accomplished a mistress of the art would not, without deliberate intention, have given the tale so curiously conventional a treatment. Though indeed, in the given case, no treatment *but* the conventional was possible: which might conceivably, my dear lady, on further consideration, have led you to reject your subject as—er—in itself a totally unsuitable one."[9]

Mrs. Wharton called this combination of gallantry and savagery James's "terrifying benevolence."[10]

Ultimately, James's patronizing attitudes were destructive. In the face of such opposition, only the strongest-willed women writers can endure, let alone mature. Adrienne Rich alludes to this in her essay, "When We Dead Awaken":

I am suggesting that the specter of this kind of male judgement, along with the active discouragement and thwarting of her needs by a culture controlled by males, has created problems for the woman writer: problems of language and style, problems of energy and survival.[11]

Sexually biased male criticism directed toward the inadequacies of the feminine mind becomes restrictive and depressing—disastrous, if not fatal—for both the personal and professional life of the woman writer. An examination of Henry James's tales and criticism about women writers which is juxtaposed against a reading of works both by and about nineteenth-century women novelists who were his friends discloses such a figure in the carpet. In particular, if James's friendship with Constance Woolson is viewed from the context of his characteristic attitudes toward women writers, the artist-heroine in Woolson's own tales becomes a central figure for those interested both in the effects of the double critical standard and in the James-Woolson relationship itself. Four of her stories focus on the interaction between a confident, dominant man (most often an artist or critic) and a woman artist / critic who aspires to go beyond the conventional feminine roles. In each case, the male figure is a Jamesian type. Taken together, the stories create a paradigm which attests to the force of the double critical standard.

James's earliest reviews of novels by women writers set the tone for his later complex friendships with Mrs. Ward, Vernon Lee and Constance Woolson. Written between 1864 and 1866, these essays read like a handbook of advice to women writers and exemplify the young James's preconceived ideas about the limited potential of a woman's mind. "Like all women," James wrote, Miss Braddon "has a turn for color" (*Notes and Reviews*, p. 115),[12] and like those of all women, Mrs. Gaskell's "men are less successful than her women" (*NR*, p. 158). Why women novelists try to portray male characters at all actually seems to mystify James. D.M.M. Craik's *A Noble Life* (1866) becomes a case in point, as he writes,

Since, indeed, the history of a wise man's soul was in question, a wise man, and not a woman something less than wise, should have undertaken to relate it. . . . Such a feat was doubtless beyond Miss Muloch's powers—as it would indeed have been beyond any woman's. (*NR*, p. 170)

Louisa May Alcott's *Moods* (1865) also prompts James to similar comments. Further, Alcott's impossible male characters are linked in James's mind to her limited opportunities for observation: "If Miss Alcott's experience of human nature has been small, as we should suppose, her admiration of it is nevertheless great'' (*NR*, p. 58). However, it also appears that the woman writer who seems to have had experience is as damned as Miss Alcott, who had had little. James is incensed when Miss Braddon ''knows much that ladies are not accustomed to know, but that they are apparently very glad to learn'' (*NR*, p. 115). Even in his discussion of George Eliot, James insists on the double critical standard:

In our opinion, then, neither ''Felix Holt'', nor ''Adam Bede'', nor ''Romola'', is a master-piece. . . . They belong to a kind of writing in which the English tongue has the good fortune to abound—that clever, voluble, bright-colored novel of manners which began with the present century under the auspices of Miss Edgeworth and Miss Austen. George Eliot is stronger in degree than either of these writers, but she is not different in kind. She brings to her task a richer mind, but she uses it in very much the same way. With a certain masculine comprehensiveness which they lack, she is eventually a feminine—a delightfully feminine writer. (*NR*, p. 207)

Some fifteen years before he was to meet Constance Woolson, then, James's basic premises about the feminine imagination had been enunciated. His tales, ''Greville Fane'' (1892) and ''The Next Time'' (1895), as well as his later essays about George Eliot and George Sand, were only to create and perform variations on these early themes. In the former, the popular woman novelist who succeeds in the literary marketplace becomes an object of ridicule as her art is contrasted with that of a subtle and refined masculine intelligence, while in the latter, James definitively concluded that neither Eliot nor Sand was masculine enough for real greatness.[13] In addition, James's story ''The Velvet Glove'' (1909) reflects the complications which arose in both his imagination and his life when a serious male writer or critic became involved with a woman writer on a social basis: the difficulties which present themselves in such a situation jeopardize the male writer's professional integrity as well as his personal priorities.

The woman writer who most complicated James's life seems to have been Constance Woolson (1840–94). While Miss Woolson appears in none of James's tales about women writers, she does seem to figure in several others. She was first drawn to James out of admiration for his fiction: she appreciated his technique, and she felt that his writing voiced her own deepest feelings.[14] In the story of their friendship, however, the lines between the professional and the personal seem to blur. Thus, after reading accounts of their relationship, it is tempting to see Woolson's intimacy with James as the germ of many of his tales. For example, in a recent article by Woolson scholar Rayburn Moore, she is linked to tales like ''The Jolly Corner'' (1908) and ''The Bench of Desolation'' (1909) which portray a ''poor, sensitive gentleman'' who is ''involved romantically with an equally sensitive but more aware woman.''[15] She is also certainly associated with one of James's masterpieces, ''The Beast in the Jungle'' (1903), for the idea of that tale originated in her notebooks (included in *Constance Fenimore Woolson*, ed. Clare Benedict), which James had read after Woolson's death in 1894.[16] Even the last line of James's final tale, ''A Round of Visits''

1910), seems to echo her name, for the narrator of the story holds himself responsible for the suicide of a friend.

During the seventies, Miss Woolson was "the most 'unconventional' feminine writer that had yet appeared in America."[17] As Anne Douglas Wood has noted, "Constance Fenimore Woolson, a descendant of James Fenimore Cooper and a friend of Henry James, began her own career in declared hostility to her rhapodical sisters."[18] She started writing in earnest at the age of thirty, following her father's death in 1869. Her stories of northern Michigan (such as "The Lady of Little Fishing") and her sketches of Southern life (such as "Rodman the Keeper" and "King David") were so successful that Harper and Brothers wrote in 1877 asking whether or not it would be possible for her to send all she wrote to their house (*CFW*, II, 23–24). Recent studies of Woolson focus on those stories set in the Carolinas, the mountain regions of Tennessee, and northern Florida in order to emphasize her role as a local colorist who "attempted to capture in her work the uniqueness of the places about which she wrote—to value their differences rather than to urge their conformity with the rest of the nation."[19] She was particularly interested in picturing Northerners who had come below the Mason-Dixon line following the Civil War, for as Evelyn Helmick suggests, "Miss Woolson's major theme in all her southern work is the contrast between the northern and southern temperaments."[20]

Miss Woolson had two literary advisors throughout the seventies: the poet and critic E. C. Stedman, and the poet Paul Hamilton Hayne. Her correspondence with these men seems to prefigure her early relationships with Henry James, for they both encouraged her professional aspirations and acted as valued literary friends. However, Woolson had reservations about some of their perceptions, as evidenced in jottings from her notebooks. Commenting on Stedman's Victorian Poets, she wrote,

VICTORIAN POETS. MRS. BROWNING.
Mr. Stedman does not really believe in woman's genius. His disbelief peeps through every line of the criticism below, whose essence is— "She did wonderfully well for a woman." (*CFW*, II, 93)

One of our earliest feminist critics, Woolson was preoccupied with the nature and role of the woman artist. She saw herself as different from other literary women; Jay Hubbell's edition of the Woolson-Hayne letters makes it clear that she often wondered where her artistic theories would lead her.[21] For instance, in 1875 she reflected, "I have the idea that women run too much into mere beauty at the expense of power; and the result is, I fear, that I have gone too far the other way; too rude; too abrupt."[22] This correspondence also lists her favorite authors—George Eliot, George Sand, Charles Reade, Charlotte Brontë, and Dumas père—and cites her favorite novel, *The Mill on the Floss*.[23]

In 1879 she reviewed James's *The Europeans* for the *Atlantic*; she admired James's substance and style and defended his fiction against its detractors. As a feminist critic, however, Woolson faulted James for his mishandling of the character of the baroness, charging that the author had dwelt on the irregularities of the woman's physical features to the detriment of his presentation of her personality:

Mr. James might have stated that her face was irregular, judged by rule, but he should have dwelt upon what beauties she *did* have, so that they would make a vivid impression; just as, in real life, they would have domineered vividly over her lacks, if she had entered the room where we were sitting. She is *his* creation; *we* don't know her. He should have answered for her in this respect, and started us fairly. (*CFW*, II, 60)

Devastated by her mother's death in 1879, Woolson left America and travelled abroad. In 1880, she met James. Some of her letters from the period attest to their developing friendship; one of these paints the portrait of James which reappears in her tales:

Mr. James is 36; rather taller than John Hay, and with a larger frame, a beautiful regular profile, brown beard and hair, large light grey eyes, from which he banishes all expression, and a very quiet, almost cold, manner. . . . He was very kind to me. He has many acquaintances in Florence and he was constantly invited out to lunch and dinner parties; yet with all this, he found time to come in the mornings and take me out; sometimes to the galleries or churches, and sometimes just for a walk in the beautiful green Cascine. (*CFW*, II, 185)

Volumes II and III of Leon Edel's biography of James carefully detail their subsequent meetings: one-fifth of *The Middle Years* is devoted to the significance of their relationship, and Edel must be credited with having pieced together evidence for and accounts of the months spent by James and Miss Woolson in ancient villas on Bellosguardo in 1887, as well as their rendezvous in Geneva in 1888, and their visits in England in 1892. Edel also speaks of their plan to collaborate in the writing of a play, and of James's pledge, after Miss Woolson had gone back to Italy, "of a yearly visit."[24] However, since almost all of the Woolson-James correspondence "was destroyed by them as soon as letters were answered,"[25] the deepest emotions of either party can only be inferred.

Five of Constance Woolson's short stories seem to reflect her personal and professional interaction with James: one of them, "A Florentine Experiment" (1880) has a setting reminiscent of their early days spent in exploration of Florence; the other four deal with the question of the woman writer. The first of the latter group was "Miss Grief" (1880), the story of an American writer who has been unable to publish and who feels that she has been "racked," "stabbed," and killed by "literary men" (*For the Major and Selected Short Stories*, p. 40).[26] In Rome, she seeks out the story's narrator, a young Jamesian type, who agrees to befriend Miss Grief. After reading her manuscript, he plans to make certain emendations which he feels will make her play popular. He is astonished at Miss Grief's response, for she insists, "There shall not be so much as a comma altered'' (p. 134). The narrator still determines to "help" Miss Grief secretly, but he becomes chagrined when, after setting out to alter, piece, condense, and lengthen, he cannot succeed in completing anything "that approached, in truth, Miss Grief's own work just as it stood" (p. 138). Trying to remove an unwanted character from her story, for example, the narrator finds "that to take him out was like taking out one especial figure in a carpet; that is, impossible, unless you unravel the whole" (p. 139). (James's own story, "The Figure in the Carpet," is dated 1896.) When the story ends with Miss Grief's death, the narrator ponders, "She, with the great power, failed—I, with the less, succeeded" (p. 143). The tale seems to anticipate some of James's own work; as John Dwight Kern, one of Woolson's biographers, suggests:

The sketch is wholly a study of character and of artistic method in the manner later made famous by James. The death of "Miss Grief" is essentially the martyrdom of an artist who refuses to compromise her principles for the sake of popular success.[27]

Kern's argument, however, is only partially valid, for while the subject and style of the story may be called Jamesian, James was never to imagine that a woman writer could have greater power than a male writer or that a woman writer would sacrifice everything for her art.

Two years later, Woolson published "The Street of the Hyacinth" (1882), another story about a woman artist. Miss Grief had been an older woman, forty-three when she died, but Ethelinda Faith Macks was only twenty-two. She had come to Italy from America in order to pursue her ambition to become a greater painter. As an art student, Ettie had been most impressed by the articles in the magazines and papers by the expatriated American art critic, Raymond Noel (as Woolson had been drawn to James). Confident and frank, Miss Macks approaches Noel and makes several requests of him:

. . . first: I would like your opinions of all that I have done so far. . . . Second: I want your advice as to the best teacher. . . . Third: I should be glad if you would give a general oversight to all I do for the next year. (*FM*, p. 148)[28]

Noel is amused by Ettie and finally agrees because he is sure that he can act solely as mentor:

If she had shown the faintest indication of knowing how much she was asking, if she had betrayed the smallest sign of a desire to secure his attention as Raymond Noel personally, and not simply the art authority upon whom she had pinned her faith, his disrelish for various other things about her would have been heightened into utter dislike. (P. 151)

In the ensuing five weeks, Noel decides that Ettie has no talent, but he does not want to be the one to tell her so. His thoughts resemble those found in James's criticism of women novelists:

It was one of Raymond Noel's beliefs that, where women were concerned, a certain amount of falsity was sometimes indispensable. There were occasions when a man could no more tell the bare truth to a woman than he could strike her: the effect would be the same as a blow. (P. 155)

Noel's standards for judging the quality of a work of art also seem Jamesian. Miss Macks insists that it is "the subject, the idea, that is the important thing," and that "execution is secondary" (p. 164), but the great art critic disagrees. Noel measures an artist by applying the same "test of execution" suggested by James in "The Art of Fiction."[29]

After a two year absence from Italy, Noel returns to find the aspiring young painter much changed. Ettie had abandoned her high hopes, had worked as a governess, and then had begun a day school in her parlor. She had been angry with Noel and explains her feelings to him: "My hopes were false ones, and had been so from the beginning; you knew that they were, yet you did not set me right" (p. 170). Convinced of her mediocrity as a painter, Ettie admits that she has been in love with Noel. However, although Noel now begins to court her, she refuses to marry him because of his previous condescending attitudes. Finally, as the building in which she lives is to be demolished, she capitulates and accepts his proposal, partly in order that she may continue to care for her elderly mother. Like many Victorian women, Ettie had not been exceptional enough to create a new role for herself.

Constance Woolson had often pondered the nature of the feminine mind. Was it capable of greatness? Her thoughts remind us of those later expressed by Virginia Woolf: education, freedom, and experience were essential to the development of a creative woman's mind.[30] In 1890, Woolson had met Brugsch Bey and had commented to her old teacher, Linda Guilford:

I could see that he did not believe that women could be very profound students in anything, though, of course, he did not actually say so to me. I think we can be, only our education must begin a hundred years before we are born. I mean that it will take several generations of study and training before our girls can equal our boys in scholarship, or, rather, before our women can equal our men. . . . I think the feminine mind inferior to the masculine at present, simply because our girls have not for centuries been solidly educated as boys have been. . . . Girls do so much need a more thorough education. I seldom hear my own sex talk long without noticing the lack of broad, reasonable, solid views. But . . . training is all that is needed.[31]

Woolson's conclusions foreshadow those proposed by Julia A. Sherman's recent study on *Sex-Related Cognitive Differences* which suggest that "the cogent question appears to be not 'Are women as intelligent as men?' but 'Do we want women to be as intelligent as men?' "[32]

As a part of her own educational and artistic regime, Miss Woolson left Italy and travelled to Switzerland or the Black Forest each summer. On her first such

ojourn in 1880, she had written to Katherine Mather to describe her projected
ip:

am going to Coppet soon to see the house of Mme. de Stael, or rather, to stand there
ast for its association with her and Madame Recamier . . . (*CFW*, II, 225).

Like Mrs. Browning, Margaret Fuller, and Marie Corelli, Constance Woolson
admired Mme. de Stael, and her third story about women artists, set at Coppet
self, is titled "At the Chateau of Corinne" (*Harper's New Monthly Magazine*,
5, 1887). It is the tale of Katherine Winthrop, an American poet, and John
Ford, an American who pities women writers. Interestingly, the description of
ohn Ford's eyes matches the one Woolson had given of James's eyes: "Ford's
eyes were grey, without much expression, unless calmness can be called an
expression" (p. 781).[33] The controversy between the two has to do with Mrs.
Winthrop's art. Ford declares that "Corinne was an inordinate egoist" (p. 787),
while Mrs. Winthrop defends Mme. de Stael as a "woman of genius" (p. 787).
Ford, an advocate of the cult of true womanhood,[34] insists that no womanly
woman would want such a title:

'A woman of genius! And what is the very term but a stigma? No woman is so proclaimed
by the great brazen tongue of the Public unless she has thrown away her birthright of
womanly seclusion for the miserable mess of pottage called 'fame.' '' (p. 787)

After reading one of Katherine Winthrop's poems, Ford goes on to deliver a
polemic against women writers:

We do not expect great poems from women any more than we expect great pictures; we
do not expect strong logic any more than we expect brawny muscle. A woman's poetry
is subjective. . . . Her mental realm is not the same as that of man; lower, on the same
level, or far above, it is at least different. And to see her leave it, and come in all her
white purity, which must inevitably be soiled, to the garish arena where men are con-
tending, where the dust is rising, and the air is tainted and heavy—this is indeed a painful
sight. Every honest man feels like going to her, poor mistaken sibyl that she is, closing
her lips with gentle hand, and leading her away to some far spot among the quiet fields,
where she can learn her error, and begin her life anew. (p. 789)

This lecture exhibits the typical Victorian attitude toward women artists and also
sounds reminiscent of James's own criticism of novelists like Miss Braddon or
Ouida. Katherine Winthrop, as might be expected, is angered by these remarks
and Ford leaves Switzerland. Apparently, however, the widowed Mrs. Winthrop
does not take her literary talent seriously enough, for some time later, upon
Ford's return, she becomes convinced by his arguments. Realizing that Ford is
"narrow" and "prejudiced," that he would "keep women down with an iron
hand," she is still moved by something very like a mist in the grey eyes she
had always thought too cold (p. 796). She agrees to marry him and to abandon

her writing. Ford makes it clear; she must only show him her true nature, her "sweet . . . gentle, womanly side" (p. 798); no pretensions to genius may remain if she is to have a home and family.

Unlike Katherine Winthrop, Constance Woolson felt that the "only way in which she could fulfill her soul destiny" was as a literary artist.[35] Her final story of art and artists is about a male writer who is unable to develop his great potential because of his responsibilities as a husband and a father. "In Sloane Street" (1892) seems to anticipate James's treatment of the same subject in "The Death of the Lion" (1894) and "The Next Time" (1895). The psychological novelist, Philip Moore, is an American who has been traveling abroad with his wife Amy and their two children. Now quartered in London, they also have a traveling companion with them, Gertrude Remington, Moore's next-door neighbor from childhood on. Moore's wife is critical of Gertrude's appearance:

You'd be a great deal more attractive and comfortable to look at, Gertrude, if you had a few cozy little habits, nice homelike little ways. . . . A tall thin woman in a tailor-made gown, with her hair dragged tightly back from her face, and all sorts of deep looks— why, naturally, all men are afraid of her.[36]

Amy also doubts Gertrude's taste in literature: why must Gertrude read Le Maitre and Marie Bashkirtseff? Like most other people, Amy herself prefers popular three-decker novels that sell in thousands and thousands.

Philip, however, writes analytical novels; although Amy cannot imagine why anyone would write them, Woolson justifies both her fiction and James's by having Gertrude suggest "that persons who write analytical novels, and those also who like to read them, are interested in the study of character" (p. 474). In spite of Gertrude's understanding and sympathy for him, Philip is suspicious of exceptional women. For example, although he had once (like James) appreciated George Eliot's books, her "first two, perhaps," that was "ages before the flood" (p. 474). Now, with maturity, Philip asserts,

Women can't write. And they ought not to try. Children's stories—yes, they can write for children, and for young girls, extremely well. And they can write little sketches and episodes if they will confine themselves rigidly to the things they thoroughly know, such as love stories, and so forth! But the great questions of life, the important matters, they cannot render in the least. How should they? And when in their ignorance they begin, in addition, to preach—good heavens, what a spectacle. (p. 474)

Once again, it is as if Henry James were speaking. The story concludes when the characters are all back in America. Gertrude is left alone in Massachusetts as Constance Woolson was alone, finally, in Italy. Philip and Amy set off for a new life in Washington, sacrificing the art of fiction on the altar of the good life. It seems ironic that a story which attacks women like Amy Moore should have appeared in *Harper's Bazaar: A Repository of Fashion, Pleasure, and nstruction.* Gertrude Remington must have been amazed and chagrined to find erself among those pages of fashions from Worth and coiffures by Lentheric.

Miss Grief and Miss Remington seem most reminiscent of Constance Woolson, who was proud, independent, and committed to her work, yet sometimes lonely and unsure of her artistic powers in a culture which belittled the woman artist. The more traditionally feminine role had its appeal, but marriage seemed to preclude serious writing. Once in a while, these tensions between the "woman" and the "artist" appear in Woolson's correspondence. At the birth of a niece, she had written, "Oxford and rooms and writing a novel are poor things compared to a baby."[37]

She created no more stories related to her friendship with Henry James because of her death which came unexpectedly on January 24, 1894. Although her family explained her death as "the result of an accident during delirium caused by a severe and prolonged attack of influenza,"[38] it seems more likely that Constance Woolson committed suicide. After having sent her nurse out of the room for some milk, she either fell or jumped from her second-story window in Venice. According to her sister, Miss Woolson had "suffered from periodical fits of acute depression" for many years (*CFW*, II, xiv). Woolson's own journals and letters give the same impression. In particular, these depressions seem related to the death of a loved one (her father and her mother, for instance) or to her work. With regard to the latter, Woolson often commented on the strenuous nature of the literary life. Writing about George Eliot, she had said,

As to what you allude to—the tone of her letters and journals—to me all that seems but the bodily weariness of such constant literary toil; and (alas!) the melancholy which seems to me to belong to all creative work in literature. (*CFW*, II, 28)

In another letter to a relative, she discussed the same matter, emphasizing the exhaustion she felt at the completion of a work:

I don't suppose any of you realize the amount of time and thought I give to each page of my novels. . . . It takes such entire possession of me that when, at last, a book is done, I am pretty nearly done myself (*CFW*, II, 52).

Like Virginia Woolf, Constance Woolson "usually felt depressed after finishing a book,"[39] and like Woolf, Sexton, and Plath after her, she apparently felt that the complicated professional and personal life of a literary woman was too difficult to pursue.

Feeling implicated, James could not face Miss Woolson's funeral, although he later helped Clara Benedict, her sister, as she packed up the literary remains. In a letter dated 1907, Mrs. Benedict referred to that time: "What he did for us during those awful weeks made several people who never liked his writing, change their opinion entirely—they then read between the lines."[40] Reading between the lines has now become a preoccupation with those informed about his literary friendship. Clearly, Woolson's tales of women artists reflect the complexities of her relationship with James. In addition, most critics agree that James's later works are haunted by the idea "of some friendship or passion or bond—some affection long desired and waited for, that is formed too late."[41] What better witness to the vitiating power of the double critical standard? James's attitudes toward women writers had injured his disciple, and they had also turned against the mind from which they had come and had wounded the master.

NOTES

1. Elaine Showalter, *A Literature of Their Own: British Women Novelists from Brontë to Lessing* (Princeton: Princeton University Press, 1977), p. 73.

2. Ibid., p. 90.

3. Ibid., p. 31.

4. As quoted in Showalter, p. 87 ("The Lady Novelists," *Westminster Review*, n.s. II [1852]: 133).

5. Alfred Habegger, *Gender, Fantasy, and Realism in American Literature* (New York: Columbia University Press, 1982), p. 290.

6. Mary Doyle Springer, *A Rhetoric of Literary Character: Some Women of Henry James* (Chicago: University of Chicago Press, 1978), p. 2.

7. *Atlantic Monthly*, 46 (October, 1880), 510.

8. Henry James, "George Sand" (1877) in *French Poets and Novelists*, ed. Leon Edel (New York: Grosset and Dunlap, 1964), p. 181.

9. Edith Wharton, *A Backward Glance* (New York: Charles Scribner's Sons, 1933), pp. 180–81.

10 Ibid., p. 181.

11. Adrienne Rich, "When We Dead Awaken" (1971); reprinted in *Adrienne Rich's Poetry*, eds. Barbara C. Gelpi and Albert Gelpi (New York: W. W. Norton and Co., Inc., 1975), p. 92.

12. Henry James, *Notes and Reviews*, ed. Pierre de Chaignon La Rose (Cambridge, Mass.: Dunster House, 1921). All further references to these reviews from this volume will be to this edition and will be cited by page number in the body of the paper.

13. See Henry James, "George Eliot's *Middlemarch*," in *The Future of the Novel*, ed. Leon Edel (New York: Vintage Books, 1956). See also Henry James, "George Sand's 'Mademoiselle Merquem,' " rpt. in *Literary Reviews and Essays*, ed. Albert Mordell (New York: Grove Press, 1957); idem, "George Sand," in *French Poets and Novelists*; idem, "George Sand, 1897," in *Notes on Novelists* (New York: Charles Scribner's Sons, 1914); idem, "George Sand, 1899," in *Notes on Novelists*; idem, "George Sand, 1914," in *Notes on Novelists*.

14. Miss Woolson's reverent view of James's fiction is unreservedly expressed in the few letters to James which still exist. These manuscript pages are in the collection at the Houghton Library at Harvard University and may be examined on request.

15. Rayburn Moore, "The Strange Irregular Rhythm of Life: James's Late Tales and Constance Woolson," *South Atlantic Bulletin*, 41 (1976), 87.

16. "To imagine a man spending his life looking for and waiting for his 'splendid moment.' 'Is this my moment?' 'Will this state of things bring it to me?' But the moment never comes." Constance Woolson's notebooks are included in the volume arranged and

edited by her niece, Clare Benedict, *Constance Fenimore Woolson* (London: Ellis, 1930). This quotation is from page 144. All further references to this volume appear in the text of the paper.

17. Fred Lewis Pattee, *The Development of the American Short Story* (New York: Harper and Brothers, 1923), p. 250.

18. Ann Douglas Wood, "The Literature of Impoverishment: The Women Local Colorists in America, 1865–1914," *Women's Studies: An Interdisciplinary Journal*, 1 (1972), 4.

19. Anne Rowe, *The Enchanted Country: Northern Writers in the South, 1865–1910* (Baton Rouge: Louisiana State University Press, 1979), p. 57.

20. Evelyn Helmick, "Constance Fenimore Woolson: First Novelist of Florida," in *Feminist Criticism: Essays on Theory, Poetry, and Prose*, ed. Cheryl L. Brown and Karen Olson (Metuchen, N.J.: The Scarecrow Press, Inc., 1978), p. 242.

21. Woolson's correspondence with Hayne is in the William R. Perkins Library, Duke University. It has been quoted extensively and presented by Jay B. Hubbell in *The New England Quarterly*, 14 (1941), 715–35. The quotations in this paper are from this edition of the letters.

22. Hubbell, p. 718.

23. Ibid., pp. 724–25.

24. The most relevant passages in Edel's account of the friendship between James and Woolson occur as follows: III, 193 ff.; III, 249 ff.; III, 317–19.

25. Rayburn S. Moore, *Constance Fenimore Woolson* (New York: Twayne Publishers, Inc., 1963), p. 147.

26. Constance F. Woolson, "Miss Grief," in *For the Major and Selected Short Stories*, ed. Rayburn S. Moore (New Haven: College and University Press, 1967). All further references to the story will be from this edition and the citations will appear in the body of the essay.

27. John Dwight Kern, *Constance Fenimore Woolson* (Philadelphia: University of Pennsylvania Press, 1934), p. 140.

28. Constance F. Woolson, "The Street of the Hyacinth," in *For the Major and Selected Short Stories*, ed. Rayburn S. Moore (New Haven: College and University Press, 1967). All further references to the story will be from this edition and the citations will appear in the body of the essay.

29. See *The Future of the Novel*, p. 10.

30. See Virginia Woolf, "The Intellectual Status of Women," in *The Diary of Virginia Woolf, 1920–24*, ed. Anne Olivier Bell (New York: Harcourt Brace Jovanovich, 1978), pp. 339–42 (Appendix III).

31. Linda Guilford, MSS No. 484, "Notes in Memory of Miss Woolson." This manuscript is in the Western Reserve Historical Society in Cleveland, Ohio, and may be examined on request. Rights to reproduction belong to the Western Reserve Historical Society.

32. Julia A. Sherman, *Sex-Related Cognitive Differences* (Springfield, Ill.: Charles C. Thomas, Publisher, 1978), p. 172.

33. Constance F. Woolson, "At the Chateau of Corinne," *Harper's New Monthly Magazine*, 75 (1887), 778–96. All references to this story are to this edition and the citations will appear in the body of the essay.

34. The definitive essay on this issue is Barbara Welter's "The Cult of True Wom-

anhood, 1820–1860,'' *American Quarterly*, 18 (1966), 151–75. The virtues of true womanhood are piety, purity, submissiveness, and domesticity.

35. Guilford manuscript, p. 6.

36. Constance Woolson, "In Sloane Street," *Harper's Bazaar*, 25 (June 11, 1892),
473–78. All references to this story are to this edition and the citations will appear in the
body of the essay.

37. Guilford manuscript, p. 6.

38. Henry Mills Alden wrote two articles in memory of Constance Woolson. The first
appeared soon after word of her death had arrived (*Harper's Weekly*, 38 [February 3,
1894]). This essay speculates about reasons for her suicide. The second appeared a week
later (February 10, 1894) and gave the family's explanation.

39. Moore, *C. F. Woolson*, p. 37.

40. Clare Benedict, ed., *The Benedicts Abroad* (London: Ellis, 1930), p. 2.

41. Henry James, *The Notebooks of Henry James*, ed. F. O. Matthiessen and Kenneth
B. Murdock (New York: George Braziller, Inc., 1955), pp. 182–83.

BIBLIOGRAPHY

Alden, Henry Mills. "Constance Fenimore Woolson." *Harper's Weekly*, 38 (February
        3, 1894), 113–14, 38 (February 10, 1894), 130.
Benedict, Clare, ed. *The Benedicts Abroad*. London: Ellis, 1930.
———. ed. *Constance Fenimore Woolson*. London: Ellis, 1930.
Brown, Cheryl L., and Olson, Karen, eds. *Feminist Criticism: Essays on Theory, Poetry,
        and Prose*. Metuchen, N.J.: The Scarecrow Press, Inc., 1978.
Edel, Leon. *The Life of Henry James: The Untried Years (1843–1870)*. New York: J. B.
        Lippincott, 1953.
———. *The Life of Henry James: The Conquest of London (1870–1881)*. New York:
        J. B. Lippincott, 1962.
———. *The Life of Henry James: The Middle Years (1882–1895)*. New York: J. B.
        Lippincott, 1962.
———. *The Life of Henry James: The Treacherous Years (1895–1901)*. New York: J. B.
        Lippincott, 1969.
———. *The Life of Henry James: The Master (1901–1916)*. New York: J. B. Lippincott,
        1969.
Gornick, Vivian, and Moran, Barbara K., eds. *Woman in Sexist Society*. New York:
        New American Library, 1971.
Guilford, Linda. "Notes in Memory of Miss Woolson." Unpublished manuscript. MSS
        No. 484, February 28, 1894. Western Reserve Historical Society, Cleveland,
        Ohio.
Habegger, Alfred. *Gender, Fantasy, and Realism in American Literature*. New York:
        Columbia University Press, 1982.
Hubbell, Jay B., ed. "Some New Letters of Constance Fenimore Woolson." *New England
        Quarterly*, 14 (1941), 715–35.
James, Henry. *The Art of the Novel: Critical Prefaces*. Ed. Richard P. Blackmur. New
        York: Charles Scribner's Sons, 1934.
———. *The Complete Tales of Henry James*. 12 vols. Ed. Leon Edel. New York: J. B.
        Lippincott Co., 1961–64.

————. *French Poets and Novelists*. Ed. Leon Edel. New York: Grosset and Dunlap, 1964.

————. *The Future of the Novel*. Ed. Leon Edel. New York: Vintage Books, 1956.

————. *Literary Reviews and Essays*. Ed. Albert Mordell. New York: Grove Press, 1957.

————. *The Notebooks of Henry James*. Eds. F. O. Matthiessen and Kenneth B. Murdock. New York: George Braziller, Inc., 1955.

————. *Notes and Reviews*. Cambridge, Mass.: Dunster House, 1921.

————. *Notes on Novelists*. New York: Charles Scribner's Sons, 1914.

————. *Theory of Fiction*. Ed. James E. Miller, Jr. Lincoln: University of Nebraska Press, 1972.

Kern, John Dwight. *Constance Fenimore Woolson*. Philadelphia: University of Pennsylvania Press, 1934.

Moore, Rayburn S. *Constance Fenimore Woolson*. New York: Twayne Publishers, Inc., 1963.

Moore, Rayburn S. "The Full Light of a Higher Criticism: Edel's Biography and Other Recent Studies of Henry James." *South Atlantic Quarterly*, 63 (1964), 86–93.

————. "Review of *Henry James: The Treacherous Years*." *American Literary Realism*, 3 (1970), 273–75.

————. "The Strange Irregular Rhythm of Life: James's Late Tales." *South Atlantic Bulletin*, 41 (1976), 86–93.

Pattee, Fred L. *The Development of the American Short Story*. New York: Harper and Brothers, 1923.

Rich, Adrienne. *Poetry*. Eds. Barbara Gelpi and Albert Gelpi. New York: W. W. Norton and Co., 1975.

Richardson, Lyon N. "Constance Fenimore Woolson: 'Novelist Laureate' of America." *South Atlantic Quarterly*, 39 (1940), 18–36.

Rowe, Anne. *The Enchanted Country: Northern Writers in the South, 1865–1910*. Baton Rouge: Louisiana State University Press, 1979.

Sherman, Julia A. *Sex-Related Cognitive Differences*. Springfield, Ill.: Charles C. Thomas, Publisher, 1978.

Showalter, Elaine. *A Literature of Their Own*. Princeton: Princeton University Press, 1977.

Springer, Mary Doyle. *A Rhetoric of Literary Character: Some Women of Henry James*. Chicago: University of Chicago Press, 1978.

Wharton, Edith. *A Backward Glance*. New York: Charles Scribner's Sons, 1933.

Wood, Anne Douglas. "The Literature of Impoverishment: The Women Local Colorists in America, 1865–1914." *Women's Studies*, 1 (1972), 3–40.

Woolf, Virginia. *The Diary of Virginia Woolf, 1920–24*. Ed. Anne Olivier Bell. New York: Harcourt Brace Jovanovich, 1978.

Woolson, Constance Fenimore. "At the Chateau of Corinne." *Harper's*, 75 (1887), 778–96.

Woolson, Constance Fenimore. "A Florentine Experiment." *Atlantic*, 46 (1880), 502–30.

Woolson, Constance Fenimore. *For the Major and Selected Short Stories*. Ed. Rayburn S. Moore, New Haven, Conn.: College and University Press, 1967.

Woolson, Constance Fenimore. "In Sloane Street." *Harper's Bazaar*, 25 (June 11, 1892), 473–78.

7

Nineteenth-century Women Cook Book Authors

Lucille Fillin and Walter Fillin

Nineteenth-century women cook book authors did not write about *Twenty-five Ways to Cook a Carrot* or *How to Lose Ten Pounds in Ten Days*. They were highly educated, idealistic and strongly motivated women who lived by the ethic of plain living and high thinking. Although they carried on their traditional roles in household and family life, they had wider interests in the world outside the kitchen. They used their literary gifts to write about other subjects in addition to cooking. They did battle for a variety of causes and convictions. They were to become an inspiration for feminists of a later era.

Contemporary cook books are the end results of a long evolutionary process in the field of culinary literature. A study of the Bible reveals many references to food and feasting and to famine as well. In ancient Greece the most treasured manuscript was that of Athenaeus in his *Diepnosophist* or *The Banquet of the Learned*. The author describes these occasions, the basis of which were lively philosophical and poetic discussions along with the flowing wines. There was just as much food for the soul as for the stomach and the cooks were considered great artists and honored as such. In early Rome a similar manuscript was written by Apicius in his *De Re Coquinaria*, describing the sumptuous feasts and the entertainment. The guests were male, the only women present being the dancing girls and courtesans. The food was brought from the far corners of the Empire, fish from distant seas, kept alive in buckets of sea water, fruits from North Africa served along with copious quantities of wine and honey. Desserts were chilled concoctions prepared with ice and snow, brought down from the Alps by relays of slaves.[1]

One of the earliest printed cook books, published in Latin in the era of the Gutenberg Press, was Platina's *De Honestata Voluptate* or *On Honest Indulgence and Good Health*. The author, whose real name was Bartolomeo de Sacchi di

Piadena, was librarian to the Vatican and wrote of medical matters, such as the importance of play and pleasure as necessary for good digestion and of the cooking secrets of the Pope's kitchens. Ancient texts such as Platina's, which combine health references in addition to food or cookery, are often found in great medical libraries.

In medieval England, the physicians responsible for the health and welfare of the ruling families set down their own regulations for use in diet and disease. Chamberlains, stewards, and cooks, whose function was to provide for the thousands of guests to the royal court, wrote their rules for the menus and for the elaborate entertainment—hence the phrase "on a royal scale."

Other fascinating manuscripts, available to scholars, are the household books and diaries kept by women of upper-class families. These hand-written volumes were passed from mother to daughter through successive generations.

In an exception to this practice, Gulielma Penn, too ill to accompany her husband, William Penn, and their children on their venture to the New World, gave her notebooks to her oldest son.[2] Recently these have been transcribed and published as *Penn Family Recipes*, the original title being *My Mother's Receipts for Cookereys and Preserving and Chyrurgery*.

In the case of women as cook book authors, the eighteenth century saw their flowering and by the nineteenth century their works were accepted and used by a wide audience.

As for the women writers whose cook books were coming into print, Dr. Samuel Johnson reflected the masculine attitude of his time. Boswell, his devoted amanuensis, took down the words "women can spin very well, but they cannot make a good cookery book . . . I could write a better one myself."[3] (He never did.) He was referring to Hannah Glasse's *The Art of Cookery Made Plain and Easy*. It is to be noted that Dr. Johnson, a famous traveler and gourmandizer, devoured many a meal prepared by women skilled in cookery.

Hannah Glasse's book of 1747 (our copy is dated 1774) provides us with insights into the culinary and social customs of her time. Her work is a prototype of other household books and gives an indication of the many family tasks which fell into the province of the housewife. She was an experienced cook with some education and wrote in detail of the skills and knowledge necessary for the management of a household. There are hundreds of recipes or "receipts" for meat and game (much of these baked into pies, as a form of preservation) and for fish, poultry, and puddings. There are directions for the distillation of medicinal drinks, termed "cordials," and for the making of cosmetics. Included are "A Cure for the Bite of a Mad Dog," "A Water to Ward Off the Plague," "A Liquor for a Child Who Has the Thrush," "How to Make Paco-Lilla or Indian Pickles," and some useful advice for the captain of a sailing ship—a sauce that will keep for one year and a note on how to save beef drippings from the rats: "turn the bowl upside down."

The housewife was master of many skills: the care and laundering of clothing, management of the dairy, preservation of fruits and vegetables, bottling of jams and jellies, and the salting and pickling of meat and fish for winter use. She supervised the orchard, the poultry-run, the brew-house and the still-room. In addition, she was required to play the part of doctor, nurse, and veterinarian.

Mrs. Glasse objected to the new and fashionable practice prevalent among the aristocracy, that of importing French chefs into English households. She sets forth her strong feelings in the preface:

I have heard of a cook that used 6 pounds of butter to fry 12 eggs. When everyone knows, that understands cooking, that 1 / 2 a pound is full enough, but then it would not be French. Such is the blind folly of this age that they would rather be imposed on by a French booby than give encouragement to a good English cook.

Her book and those of her contemporaries, Mrs. Raffald, Mary Kettilby, and Eliza Smith, sold very well. They were reissued well into the nineteenth century in England and in America. Mrs. Smith's book, *The Compleat Housewife* or *The Accomplish'd Gentlewoman's Companion* (1753)[4] was pirated (no copyright existed) and altered in colonial America. Hers was a popular title, printed and sold by the firm of William Parkes, editor of the *Williamsburg Gazette* in Virginia. He added remedies from the slave quarters and an entire section taken from Mrs. Harrison's *Housekeepers Pocket Book—Every Man His Own Doctor* (London, 1755).

The first truly American cook book was written by Amelia Simmons (1796) and printed at her own expense in Hartford, Connecticut. It was entitled *American Cookery by an American Orphan—For American Orphans*. Her hope was to give the female orphan an opportunity to learn a respectable and independent trade. Beyond that, her book achieved a greater end. It was the first to present American recipes as differing from the English and to note the use of native American Indian foods such as cornmeal, Indian pudding, crookneck squash, Johnny-Cake or Journey cake, to be carried by the traveller in his saddle bag, pickled watermelon rind ("American" citron), and cranberries to be served with roast turkey. Very few copies of Amelia Simmons's book survive. It should be noted here that cook books are subject to hard usage in the kitchen and are rarely preserved as first editions. Our copy is a private edition printed as a "Christmas Keepsake" by the West Virginia Pulp and Paper Company in 1963.

In early nineteenth-century America, sex was no barrier to authorship. In New England, for example, it seemed quite natural for women to write. They had at hand a source of inspiration—the Lyceum, where they could attend lectures by philosophers, poets, transcendentalists, and advocates of abolition, of temperance, and of higher education for women. Women's suffrage, however, was not at first a popular cause. In the early years of the century, it was considered unladylike.

Lydia Maria Child was the popular author of the day. She was a poet, a novelist, and the editor of a successful periodical, *The Juvenile Miscellany*. When she wrote her cook book *The American Frugal Housewife: Dedicated to*

Those Who Are Not Ashamed of Economy in 1892, she did so out of dire necessity. The Childs, both ardent abolitionists, needed money to subsidize David Child's experiments in raising a crop of sugar beets on his barren, rocky New England farm. His dream was to substitute beet sugar for the cane sugar produced by slave labor. Many years of back-breaking toil and much money went into this futile experiment.

The American Frugal Housewife was an instantaneous success and by 1850 it had gone through thirty-two editions. It appealed to all classes of society. Among the suggestions included were: Do not waste any food—use it to the last morsel, bones for the stock pot, scraps of bread for pudding. The turkey, for example, must be used right down to the carcass, for broth, and the feathers made into fans and feather dusters. Bottles were not to be thrown away—the author was an early advocate of ecology. Bits of orange and lemon peel added to brandy could give a delicious flavor, worn out clothing was to be cut into strips and woven into blankets. Every scrap of string and paper should be saved and reused. Sugar, when purchased, came in purple wrappers. These wrappers, thrown into the dye pot, would give color to a worn out cotton dress. Mrs. Child adds a dissertation on the evils of extravagance and on the wasting of money on frivolous amusements, citing in particular those mothers who took their elegantly attired daughters to fashionable spas in order to attract wealthy husbands.

In 1833 Mrs. Child expressed her convictions on abolition in a pamphlet entitled *An Appeal in Favor of That Class of Americans Called Africans*. Her exhortations met with disapproval in her own community. She then left for New York City to work for William Lloyd Garrison on the staff of his *National Anti-Slavery Standard*. She resigned after a disagreement over his editorial policies. A contract to write articles for a newspaper, *The Boston Courier*, gave her the opportunity to earn her keep as a reporter. With her young friend Margaret Fuller,[5] who was employed on the staff of Horace Greeley's *Tribune*, she explored the teeming slums of lower New York and was appalled by what she saw. She and Miss Fuller brought their findings to public attention in their newspaper articles. These articles led to a campaign for public reform. An example of the disparate outlook of the two women is revealed in their visit to the Women's Prison on Welfare Island. Miss Fuller gave lectures on philosophy to the inmates while Mrs. Child brought them clothing and warm blankets.

Mrs. Child also wrote many anti-slavery articles and pamphlets, a book, *The History of Conditions of Women in Various Ages and Nations*, a primer, *The Freedman's Book* (to teach former slaves to read), and a book of poetry, *Flowers for Children*, with the well-remembered lines, "Over the river and through the woods to Grandmother's house we go."

Miss Eliza Leslie of Philadelphia was told by a publisher to stick to poetry, but she proceeded instead to write a series of popular cook books. Since many refugees from France had come to settle in the United States, Americans were becoming aware of the delectable cuisines of France. In 1827 the Del Monico family opened its first café in New York. Located in the Wall Street area, it played a major part in educating the businessman in the glories of French food and wine. Miss Leslie capitalized on this trend in her book *Domestic Cookery Chiefly Translated from Sulpice Barue* (1832). Our copy, the fourth edition, is dated 1836.

Bibliographers never bother to dig too deeply into the existence of a chef called M. Barue. He may have been a clever figment of the author's imagination. The use of a man's name, particularly that of a Frenchman, lent an air of authenticity to her work and no doubt helped sales. The book was a great success and includes elegant recipes such as Blanquette de Veau, Boeuf à la Mode, Mushroom and Green Bean Purees, Cornichons, and, of course, French Pastry.

A friend of ours still treasures his copy of Miss Leslie's *Directions for Cookery in its Various Branches* of 1849. His great-grandmother had received it as a bridal gift in that year. Most earlier cook books were devoted to New England foods, but in this volume Miss Leslie extends her range into the recipes of regional America. This author introduces her readers to the bounty of the South in Lady Baltimore Cake, Crab Fritters, Coconut Pie, Carolina Punch, and Mint Julep. The mysteries of New Orleans Gumbos and their use of West Indian and African spices are explained in great detail.

A note about recipes, or receipts as they were then termed: most recipes stem from a heritage of agricultural and culinary knowledge. Newcomers to this country brought with them the tastes of their native lands. Many of their dishes were incorporated into later nineteenth-century cook books, with the addition of regional products as well. Hannah Glasse and her contemporaries borrowed freely from earlier English cooks and Mrs. Beeton borrowed freely from Hannah Glasse. Miss Leslie and her contemporaries used the recipes of their forebears and, with flamboyant imagination, of French cooks as well. Miss Leslie's writings might exemplify the practice of borrowing, but in modern times, James Beard, a well-known expert in the field of gastronomy, considers Miss Leslie's newer recipes an important contribution to nineteenth-century culinary Americana.

Christianity in the Kitchen (1861) was Mrs. Anna Peabody Mann's contribution to nineteenth-century cooking lore. She was one of the famous Peabody sisters of Salem and a highly principled woman.[6] A fierce warrior in the battle for temperance, she believed that excessive drinking was the cause of bad morals and criminal acts. She was also deeply concerned with the daily diet of the American public.

"There's Death in the pot" (2 Kings 4:40) was her watchword. She was convinced that many foods were poisonous. She took her cue from an earlier work, *A Treatise on the Adulterations of Food and Culinary Poisons* by Frederick Accum. Adulteration of foodstuffs was a common practice at the time. Mrs. Mann presents a long list of foods which she considered poisonous. Flour, for example, was adulterated with plaster of Paris by unscrupulous millers, confectionery painted with prussic acid in the coloring, vinegar might contain oil of vitriol which eats through the lining of the stomach. Cayenne pepper might be colored with poisonous red lead. Bottled fruits and vegetables were to be purchased with caution as they were often processed with salts of copper. These were but a few of the foodstuffs considered to be indigestible and, therefore, "Unchristian!" "Make your own bread; do not trust the baker, as he might substitute saleratus or baking soda for yeast." She tells her readers to shun the making of cakes by standard recipes since these called for leavening agents which might be deleterious to health. She provides as an alternative a laborious recipe for Snow Cake. Part of the instructions read: "take 20 eggs and beat them for three hours." This was hand beating, with no mechanical helpers at the time.

As the wife of Horace Mann, a strong advocate of temperance, Anna Mann passed along his principles to her readers. However, in the recipe for Calf's Foot Jelly (good for an invalid) she includes a pint and a half of Madeira wine and a teacup full of brandy. Mrs. Mann wrote the book in an effort to help her husband out of his financial difficulties. He was the first president of Antioch College, "The Athens of the West," but the school was on the verge of bankruptcy. The sale of the book was to bring in funds. The book, however, was not a success, with few copies being sold. Today it is very scarce.

While Mrs. Horace Mann was issuing her dire warnings to America, Eliza Acton, in England, was concerned with similar problems. In *The English Bread Book* (1857) she presented her findings from a more scholarly point of view.

The rapid industrialization of England included the mechanization of grain mills. People were being deprived of a daily loaf of decent bread, a good nourishing loaf of bread to strengthen a man's life. The country woman still baked her own bread, with the local water mills grinding wheat and other grains. In the industrial towns and cities commercial millers and bakers were taking over. The flour available to the general public had most of its nourishing whole wheat kernels extracted, ostensibly catering to the public taste for fluffy white breads. Flour was being adulterated with harmful additives.

Miss Acton presents documented studies of grains grown in other countries and of the milling processes used in England and abroad. She approved of the French system of constant supervision of bakers, as controlled by the ancient Syndicat des Boulangers. Products not meeting their standards were not allowed on the market. Idwal Jones in *Chef's Holiday* (1952) tells an interesting story about the Syndicat's controls. He asked a baker how the regulations were enforced and was told "after they hung a few offenders in the Middle Ages, things got better." Miss Acton urged that English wheat be properly ground without the removal of the nutritive components. The remainder of the book includes directions for baking many types of bread, local and foreign. The reader could find a wide range of recipes for Surrey Cottage Bread, Scotch Bannocks, Newcastle Brown Bread with caraway seeds, French Bread and German Pumpernickel.

Eliza Acton succeeded in her hopes of bringing to public attention the problems of milling and baking. English housewives took her warnings to heart and went on to bake bread at home, using more healthful ingredients.

Eric Quayle in *Old Cook Books* tells us that Eliza Acton had early hopes of becoming a poet. When she presented a full-length manuscript to Thomas Longman, the British publisher, he told her, ''Nobody wants poetry now. Go home and write me a cookery book''—a far cry from the advice given to Eliza Leslie in Philadelphia. The Longmans published Miss Acton's first cookery book, and some of her later works as well, to the mutual satisfaction of all concerned. Miss Acton wrote other well-known books: *Modern Confectionery* (c. 1826) and *Modern Cookery in All Its Branches* (1845).

Poetry and cooking went hand in hand for Emily Dickinson. She was the family bread-baker and brought to that homely task all the facets of her vivid imagination. In a letter to a schoolmate, Abiah Root, dated 1845, she wrote: ''I am going to learn to make bread tomorrow. So you can imagine me with my sleeves rolled up, mixing flour, milk, saleratus, etc., with a good deal of grace. I advise you, if you don't know how to make the staff of life, to learn with dispatch.'' In another letter of 1850, she wrote, ''Twin loaves of bread have just been born into the world under my auspices—fine children, the image of their mother.''[7]

Emily Dickinson took the recipe for the favorite Rye and Indian Bread from her mother's copy of Lydia Child's *The Frugal Housewife*. She made cakes, puddings and wine jelly as well, and often sent her friends gifts of Federal Cake and Chocolate Caramels. These were accompanied by little poems, notes and flowers from her garden. For the neighboring children at play she liked to fill a basket with glazed gingerbread cookies and let it down by rope from the window of her attic bedroom.

She had no objection to the use of liquor and made excellent currant and raspberry wines. Later-day admirers have assembled the recipes from notes and manuscripts into a little book entitled *Emily Dickinson—Profile of the Poet as Cook—With Selected Recipes*.[8]

In England the most popular author of the nineteenth century was Mrs. Isabella Beeton, who wrote *The Book of Household Management*. She was one of many children in a large and lively family. All twenty-one were well accustomed to participating in social activities as they lived at the Epsom Downs Race Track, where her stepfather was clerk of the course. Upon her marriage to Samuel Beeton, the publisher of *English Woman's Domestic Magazine*, she became a career woman in her own right, sharing the duties of writing and publishing. She travelled to Paris to bring back the first fashion color plates for subscribers and soon after began to write articles of domestic interest. At the urging of her husband she began work on a cook book. The monthly parts, twenty-four in number, were first printed in a series in the magazine and later published in their entirety in book form in 1861. Charles Dickens used the same procedure when he published his stories, chapter by chapter, in his magazine *Household Words*.

Mrs. Beeton's book contains 1,112 pages, copiously illustrated with woodcuts and color plates. It was an immediate success, reprinted in many editions over the next sixty to seventy years. It was the customary gift for the English bride. Many of these young women carried it to remote corners of the empire as a tie to the homeland, and tried to adapt their domestic mores to Mrs. Beeton's rules in India, Asia, and Africa. Anthony Burgess calls the book "solid grub to feed an Empire." Steven Marcus[9] considers it the best description of the Victorian household in its full flower. The author's great-niece, Nancy Spain,[10] recalls that it was escapist reading in the underground shelters during the blitz of World War II.

Household Management contains hundreds of recipes for good English food, many of these sent in by readers of the magazine and carefully tested by Mrs. Beeton. There are recipes for Steak and Kidney Pie, Christmas Plum Pudding, Scones, Crumpets, Yorkshire Pudding, Syllabub, Flummery, Pickled Beef, Potted Shrimp, Toad in the Hole, Bubble and Squeak, and special directions for the making of Benevolent Soup to feed the poor at the kitchen door. Does the fork go to the right or left of the plate? ask Mrs. Beeton; a menu for sixty persons for an After the Ball Supper, ask Mrs. Beeton; to set a bone fracture, to bring down a fever, cure convulsions, plan a picnic for forty, or serve a Formal Dinner à la Russe for fifty persons, ask Mrs. Beeton; to cure the ringworm, to carve a haunch of mutton, Mrs. Beeton explains, she knows. She consulted with members of the legal profession before setting down her dicta on legal memoranda to guide her female readers. She explains how to keep a budget and how to pay bills, and gives instructions for the writing of a will. The property rights of married women, or lack of these rights, at the time, were given due consideration. It should be noted as well that a husband had the right to beat his wife, but only with a stick no wider than the width of his thumb.

A fascinating section of the book is devoted to The Duties of the Domestic Staff. The author visited the homes of the well-to-do and the establishments of royalty in order to observe the manner in which they were run. The reader is given exact instructions as to the duties of the butler, the housekeeper, the cook, the valet, the coachman, the chambermaid, the scullery maid, the children's nurse, the sick-nurse, and many others. As an example, "The Duties of the Footman": In the morning hours, he is expected to rise early in order to get through his dirty work before the family is stirring—boots and shoes polished (with directions given for making the polish), knives and forks cleaned, lamps trimmed, the master's clothes brushed, the furniture rubbed over—so that he may put aside his working dress, tidy himself and appear in a clean jacket to lay the cloth and help to serve breakfast to the family. To the less affluent readers the book must have provided a thrilling glimpse into the life of the upper-class household in Victorian England.

It is quite astonishing to discover that Isabella Beeton accomplished her massive task of writing and research in a very short life span. She died in childbirth, at the birth of her fifth child, at the tender age of twenty-nine. The writers of the television series *Upstairs-Downstairs* surely must have conferred with the spirit of Isabella.

It is useful to pause at this point to consider the daily life of women in the nineteenth century. Cooking was done over an open hearth with a separate side oven for baking. The work was drudgery, consuming most hours of the day.

Food was cooked in heavy iron pots and three-legged trivets. Wood stoves did not come into use until the 1840's. There was little or no provision for running water in the kitchen, no proper refrigeration, and no decent lighting. The Industrial Revolution, with all of its new mechanical innovations, had made few inroads into the household.

It took two thoughtful women, advanced for their time, to dwell on the plight of the housewife and to suggest helpful improvements. These were Catherine Beecher, Principal of the Hartford Female Academy, and her sister, Harriet Beecher Stowe. The book on which they collaborated was *The Principles of Domestic Science as Applied to the Duties and Pleasures of the Household* (1870). The authors set forth practical ideas for the construction and heating of the house in order to provide more leisure time for women. The hours saved could then be used for doing "good works"—for helping the poor and other morally uplifting activities.

The Principles was an unusual work for its time, with its chief emphasis not on cookery, but on the health and hygiene of the family. Some of the chapter headings are: "Scientific Domestic Ventilation," "Cleanliness," "Giving in Charity," "Health of Mind," "Care of the Ignorant, the Homeless, the Helpless and the Vicious." To contemporary readers one appealing suggestion is that of doing away with all window curtains, to save the time wasted in washing and ironing and to substitute climbing plants in their stead. This custom now prevails in Soho and other artistic quarters. The sisters Beecher suggested a better kitchen arrangement to save steps for the housewife. They made an architectural rendering for a "Continuous Working Surface,"[11] cupboards centering about the sink and providing extra work space, with supply areas within easy reach. These built-in sections were to be used for storage of everyday necessities—flour, cornmeal, sugar, and cleaning supplies. An adaptation of this plan came into popular use with the commercial manufacture of the Hoosier Cabinet. This was a feature of American kitchens well into the 1930's. The cottage which Harriet Beecher Stowe built to demonstrate her innovations still stands, near Mark Twain's Gothic mansion in Hartford, Connecticut. Even though constructed in 1875, the Stowe cottage contains the basis for our modern kitchen.

Catherine Beecher had written *A Treatise on Domestic Economy, for the Use of Young Ladies at Home and at School* (1846). She was an early feminist and a leader in the battle for the improvement of education of women. She felt that the use of the term "domestic economist" was more fitting than "housewife." Her work commanded great respect and, as a result, courses in domestic economy were incorporated into the curriculum of many new Midwestern Universities.[12] Kathleen Smallzried in *The Everlasting Pleasure* (1956) says "Catherine Beecher was midwife to the domestic scientist and pall bearer to the compleat woman, or accomplish'd gentlewoman as described by E. Smith."

Mary Hooker Cornelius's *The Young Housekeeper's Friend* (1859) is much the same as other nineteenth-century cook books, but it has a special literary association. Scholars with an interest in Louisa May Alcott[13] know that she did not care much about food but followed the Spartan diet of her early days at Fruitlands, an unsuccessful experiment in communal living. Her meals consisted mainly of cold water, apples, boiled rice and graham meal. In *Little Women*, a semi-autobiographical story, the March family lives in a state of high-minded poverty, similar to the life advocated by Lydia Maria Child. When Meg, a new bride, notes that the currant bushes in the garden are ripe, she opens her copy of Mrs. Cornelius and attempts to follow the instructions for making currant jelly. She spends long hours on a hot summer afternoon trying to make the jelly. The resulting failure and the mess in the kitchen can be attributed to Meg and not to Mrs. Cornelius. There is not much other mention of food in *Little Women*. Our copy of *The Young Housekeeper's Friend* is bound with the pages interleaved with blank ruled foolscap for the reader's notes and comments.

Early observers of the American scene had taken note of the drearier aspects of American gastronomy, as did Mrs. Trollope in her *Domestic Manners of the Americans* (1836) and Charles Dickens in his *American Notes* (1842). Both authors were critical of American food and manners and their books had in turn been greeted with a storm of protest in the American press. Lizzie Borden, an inadvertent food critic, firm of mind and strong of conviction, breakfasted that fatal Friday morning on the cold indigestible remains of the previous Sunday's roast mutton, and then:

> Lizzie Borden took an axe
> And gave her mother forty whacks
> And when she thought that she was done
> She gave her father forty-one.

Lizzie was tried for murder and acquitted—surely "justifiable homicide."

One of the first California cook books is an unusual one, entitled *What Mrs. Fisher Knows about Old Southern Cooking* (1881). It was published and distributed by The Women's Co-Operative Printing Office of San Francisco. The author was a highly esteemed black cook who catered the banquets tendered by notable families of the city. San Francisco, at that time, was a place where great fortunes were made, and often lost, in railroads and in gold and silver mines. Mrs. Fisher lists the names and addresses of her patrons, many of whom are well-known to readers of California history, even today.

The book is drawn from Mrs. Fisher's knowledge of Southern cooking and of the best ways to prepare Green Turtle Soup, Oyster Gumbo, Terrapin Stew, Quail, Pickles, Sauces, Pastries, and Biscuits. In her preface, the author explains that she has never learned to read or write, but has dictated the book in order that it might be published. It is signed Mrs. Abby Fisher, late of Mobile, Alabama.

In 1876 Miss Juliet Corson opened her New York Cooking School in a small house off the Bowery. Her ambition was to improve the health and eating habits of the general public. Her background is most interesting. Reared in affluence and educated in Latin and Greek, she was cast adrift at the age of sixteen, when her father remarried. She went on to become secretary to the Women's Educational and Industrial Society, where poor young women were trained for jobs in business and domestic work. When asked to set up a cooking program, Miss Corson read cook books, studied nutrition, and took lessons from a well-known French chef, M. Biot.

At her school she taught the daughters of factory workers at a nominal fee, to do plain cooking and charged a larger amount to teach the young women of wealthier families. She stressed the principles of cooking and menu planning and took her students to the public markets where they were taught to select the freshest fruits, vegetables, beef and poultry. At the school she stressed the preparation of dishes such as Ragout of Beef, fish filets, and light and digestible breads.

When the Railroad Strike of 1877 occurred, with its attendant unemployment, she wrote and distributed free of charge 50,000 copies of a pamphlet, *Fifteen-Cent Dinners for Workingmen's Families*.[14] Newspapers in other cities took up the cause. The *Baltimore Daily News* distributed 1,000 copies in one week, and the *Philadelphia Record* printed the pamphlet as well.

As an interesting sidelight, the Socialists of that era were furious with Miss Corson, accusing her of collusion with the capitalists by showing that workers could do well on lower wages.

Miss Corson was the author of several cook books: *A Textbook for Cooking Schools* (1877), *The New Family Cookbook* (1885), and a pamphlet, *Family Living at $500 a Year*. She edited a successful magazine, with a circulation of 20,000, entitled *American Cookery Devoted to Reform in the Kitchen and to the Refinement of the Table*. Its contents include her rather pious stories and her own recipes. When she asked her readers in other parts of the country to send in their recipes, the results made for an early compendium of regional American cookery. There were Bean Dishes and Chowders from New England, Gumbo and Sweet Potato Pie from the South, Saratoga Potatoes (potato chips), and from the Western states, Venison Steaks and Bear's Paws in Cream Sauce.

Toward the end of a busy life she gave popular lectures in many cities and was hailed as "A Culinary Crusader" at the Chicago-Columbian Exposition of 1892–93.

In Philadelphia, Mrs. Sarah Tyson Rorer, author and teacher, established the Philadelphia Cooking School in 1883.[15] Aside from her culinary abilities she had a wealth of experience in the new field of nutrition. As a young woman she had studied chemistry with hopes of becoming a pharmacist. (The Philadelphia College of Pharmacy was admitting women students as early as 1876.) Her ambitions were deflected by marriage and by the birth of an invalid son. She then undertook a serious study of nutrition and diet and applied this knowledge to the improvement of her family's health.

When her talents were recognized by the leaders of the New Century Club, an organization sponsoring the cultural activities of women, Mrs. Rorer was asked to give lectures and demonstrations in cooking. Later, she was invited by the dean of the Women's Medical College to conduct classes for the medical students and nurses. This course included the preparation of an invalid diet of gruel, beef tea, eggnog, and khoumis (a form of fermented milk). Under the sponsorship of the eminent physician, S. Weir Mitchell, she was invited to teach at the Jefferson College of Medicine and to prepare special diets, geared to the needs of individual patients. These diets were useful in the treatment of diseases such as tuberculosis, nephritis, and anemia. Her pioneer efforts led to the inclusion of a course on diet in disease in the medical curriculum.

In her spare hours, Mrs. Rorer found time to teach classes in cooking at the Bedford Mission. Social workers then felt it their duty to obliterate all traces of foreign heritage in their immigrant students and to Americanize them as quickly as possible. This they considered a patriotic duty. Mrs. Rorer took a more liberal approach. She soon realized that the factory girls, newly arrived from Poland, Germany, Italy, Austria, and Hungary, had a great culinary heritage of their own to offer. She taught them plain and economical cookery, and in turn learned to prepare their national dishes. She imparted this new knowledge to the students at the Philadelphia Cooking School where she had a clientele of wealthier American students. She failed in one aspect of her indoctrination—none took kindly to the use of garlic.

Cook books flowed from her pen as water from a tap. There are at least twenty. Some of these are: *The Philadelphia Cookbook* (1886), *Home Candy Making* (1889), *How to Cook Vegetables* (1891) published by the Burpee Seed Company, *How to Use a Chafing Dish* (1894), *Good Cooking* (1896), *Cereal Foods and How to Cook Them* (1899), and *Ice Creams, Water Ices and Frozen Puddings*.

In addition to her other accomplishments, she was a successful journalist, writing for Finley Acker's magazine *Table Talk*. The publisher was interested in pure foods, and refused to publish advertisements for liquors, immoral literature, lotteries, and fraudulent schemes. Mrs. Rorer was asked to edit a column called "Housekeeper's Inquiries." Her column became so popular that it generated an enormous number of new subscribers. She answered questions on cooking, diet, and all aspects of housekeeping. When unsure of her answers, she consulted Isabella Beeton's *Book of Household Management*.

Mrs. Rorer was invited to participate in the Chicago-Columbia Exposition as director of the Corn Kitchen, sponsored by the commercial producers of grains, cereals, and corn. She demonstrated the use of Indian corn in all of its aspects: in bread, in cereals, in puddings, in hominy grits, and in waffles. She had a glimpse of Chicago society when she was entertained by Mrs. Potter Palmer, the "Mrs. Astor of the Middle West."

At the culmination of her career she was appointed Domestic Science Editor of *The Ladies Home Journal*, a post she held for many years. If everything else about her is forgotten she will be remembered for her dictum "Every American should eat a salad a day—at least 365 days a year."

In Boston, Maria Parloa was a familiar figure in the field of cooking, giving private classes for housewives. She wrote several cook books, her first, *The Appledore Cookbook With Receipts for Plain and Rich Cooking* (1872), includes a recipe for "Snow Pancakes" which calls for a cup of fresh clean snow (difficult to find today) with a topping of maple syrup.

Her second book was *Camp Cookery or How to Live in Camp* (1878). At that time, New England families spent their vacations in the wilderness in Maine or New Hampshire, giving each campsite its own fanciful Indian name. There the family slept in open air in tents, fished, picked wild berries, and searched for suitable salad greens in the fields. In the evenings it was the custom to gather around the fire, sing popular songs and listen to Indian legends. Miss Parloa gives instructions for making the fire and for cooking fish, corn, and other edibles over the grill. To extend a primitive food supply, each family brought along several cases of canned food from S. S. Pierce in Boston. The book gives detailed instructions for comportment in camp and for the proper attire for ladies—long bloomers, cotton middy-blouses and water-proof boots.

When the Boston Cooking School opened under formal charter, in 1879, Miss Parloa was invited to become an instructor. She wrote *The New Cook Book and Marketing Guide* (1881), the first practical approach to the problems of budgeting.

Mrs. D. A. Lincoln took over as superintendent of the school, and was a forceful influence in the culinary field. In addition to her work at this private school she managed to introduce a course in domestic economy into the curriculum of the Boston Public School system. For this purpose she wrote *The Boston School Kitchen Text Book for Use in Public and Industrial Schools* (1894). In the book there is a photograph of the earliest class of twenty-four little girls dressed in white aprons with white caps to cover their hair, standing in front of twenty-four small stoves, probably preparing toast and cocoa.

Outstanding among her books is *The New Boston Cookbook* (1887). It contains the first comprehensible guide to the use of weights and measure, and advocates the use of a standard glass measuring cup, new on the market, for accurate measurement of liquid and dry ingredients. Among other things, the book includes a recipe for Gateau à la Princess Louise (Queen Victoria's daughter); and with some disapproval, a recipe for Frog's Legs, "popular only with the French."

Mrs. Lincoln was one of the first women to realize that there were profits to be derived from the promotion of packaged foods and kitchen equipment. She was commissioned by the Peerless Stove Company to write *The Peerless Cook Book* (1886) for use with their new stove and did a second edition which included recipes to be used with their chafing dish. Sunday night supper was a fashionable social event, centering about the use of the chafing dish. The hostess could prepare, before the eyes of her guests, such delectable dishes as Welsh Rarebit, Lobster à la Newburg or Creamed Curried Chicken.

She also wrote other testimonials for ice cream freezers, gelatins, baking powder, and flour. Mrs. Lincoln wrote in glowing terms about these items and suggested that they had her stamp of approval.

Fannie Merritt Farmer took over the operation of the Boston Cooking School in 1891 and under her tutelage the school achieved great renown. Born in 1857, she was crippled by disease, possibly poliomyelitis, while in high school. She then devoted herself to family chores and to cooking. At the age of twenty-eight she decided to attend the Boston Cooking School, then under the supervision of Mrs. Lincoln. She felt that the study of food preparation might lead her into a career, and concentrated on the study of nutrition and diet for the sick.

In 1896, she wrote *The Original Boston Cooking School Cookbook*, and published it at her own expense in an edition of 30,000 copies. In order to defray the printing costs, she solicited advertisements to be included in the book. Manufacturers of commercial products placed great credence on the approval of the school and their advertisements proved profitable. Some of the companies who bought space were Hub Kitchen Ranges, Knox's Gelatine, Walter Baker Chocolate and Cocoa Company, and George's Genuine Codfish.

The author had a scientific approach to her subject. She gave the chemical composition and the nutritional value of all foods used in the family diet. Careful attention was given to the presentation of recipes. Readers were enabled to tell at a glance the necessary ingredients and the quantities to be used. Each recipe is followed by explicit directions for preparation, by the time needed for completion of the dish, and by the oven temperature. She demanded exactitude and, in fact, was known as "The Mother of the Level Measure."[16] The book covers all phases of cooking, recipes for the chafing dish, preserving, canning, and food for the sick. It appealed to a multitude of readers—from the novice to the experienced cook. Several million copies were sold by the 1930's. To more critical cooks, however, Fannie Farmer had become a little pedantic. In later years the sales were eroded by the emergence of Mrs. Rombauer's *The Joy of Cooking* and other twentieth-century classics.

In reviewing the lives and works of these nineteenth-century women cook book authors, we find that many of them led more varied lives than writers of today. Their books reflected a philosophy of life and a serious interest in the world about them. They were deeply involved in their battles for abolition, the temperance movement, housing reform, improvement of public health, the care and feeding of the poor, and higher education for women. Some of them lived to see the realization of their dreams, others did not.

They are women to be admired.

NOTES

1. Betty Wason, *Cooks, Gluttons and Gourmets.* (Garden City, N.Y.: Doubleday, 1962).

2. Evelyn A. Benson, *Penn Family Recipes* (York, Pa.: George Shumway, 1966).

3. James Boswell, *The Life of Samuel Johnson*, vol. 2 (London: J. M. Dent and Sons; New York: E. P. Dutton & Co., 1906).

4. Eleanor Lowenstein, *Bibliography of American Cookery Books, 1742–1860* (Worcester, Mass.: Antiquarian Society, 1972).

5. Helen G. Baer, *The Heart is Like Heaven—The Life of Lydia Maria Child.* (Philadelphia: University of Pennsylvania Press, 1964).

6. Louise Hall Tharp, *The Peabody Sisters of Salem.* (Boston: Little Brown and Co., 1950).

7. Thomas H. Johnson and Theodora Ward, eds., *The Letters of Emily Dickinson*, vol. I (Cambridge: The Belknap Press of Harvard University Press, 1958).

8. Guides at The Dickinson Homestead, *Emily Dickinson, Profile of the Poet as Cook* (N.Y.: Houghton Mifflin, 1976).

9. Steven Marcus, *Beeton's Book of Household Management* (London: Jonathan Cape Ltd., 1971). Facsimile copy reviewed in *New York Times Book Review*, Dec. 14, 1969.

10. Nancy Spain, *Mrs. Beeton and Her Husband* (London: Collins, 1948).

11. Siegfried Giedion, *Mechanization Takes Command* (New York: W. W. Norton and Co., 1969).

12. Lyman Beecher Stowe, *Saints, Sinners and Beechers* (Indianapolis: The Bobbs-Merrill Co., 1934).

13. Madeleine B. Stern, *Louisa May Alcott* (Norman: University of Oklahoma Press, 1950).

14. Meryle Evans, "A 19th Century Culinary Crusader," *The New York Times*, January 3, 1979.

15. Emma Seifrit Weigley, *Mrs. Sara Tyson Rorer, The Nation's Instructress in Dietetics and Cookery* (Philadelphia: The American Philosophical Society, 1977).

16. Florence Fabricant, "Fannie Farmer's New Cookbook," *Americana Magazine* (March / April, 1980).

BIBLIOGRAPHY

Accum, Frederick. *A Treatise on Adulterations of Food and Culinary Poisons, etc.* London: Longman, Hurst, Rees, Orme and Brown, 1820.

Acton, Eliza, and Hale, Mrs. S. J. *Modern Cookery in All Its Branches*. Philadelphia: John E. Potter Co., 1860.

Acton, Eliza. *The English Bread Book for Domestic Use*. London: Longman, Brown, Green, Longman and Roberts, 1st Edition, 1857.

Aresty, Esther B. *The Delectable Past*, New York: Simon and Schuster, 1st Printing, 1964.

Axford, Lavonne Brady, comp. *English Language Cookbooks 1606–1973*. Detroit: Gale Research Co., 1976.

Baer, Helene G. *The Heart is Like Heaven—The Life of Lydia Maria Child*. Philadelphia: University of Pennsylvania Press, 1964.

Beard, James. *American Cookery*. Boston: Little Brown and Co., 6th Printing, 1970.

Beecher, Catherine E. *A Treatise on Domestic Economy for the Use of Young Ladies at Home and at School*. New York: Harper and Bros., 3rd Edition, Revised 1846.

Beecher, Catherine E., and Stowe, Harriet Beecher. *Principles of Domestic Science; as Applied to the Duties and Pleasures of Home*. New York: J. B. Ford and Co., 1879.

Beeton, Isabella. *The Book of Household Management*, London: S. O. Beeton, 1st Edition, 1861.

Benson, Evelyn Abraham, comp. *Penn Family Recipes—Cooking Recipes of William Penn's Wife Gulielma*. York, Pa.: George Shumway, 1st Edition, 1966.

Bitting, Katherine Golden. *Gastronomic Bibliography*, Ann Arbor: A. W. Bitting, 1939. Rpt., Gryphon Books, 1971.

Boswell, James. *The Life of Samuel Johnson*, vol. II. London and Toronto: J. M. Dent and Sons; New York: E. P. Dutton and Co., 1906.

Brooks, Van Wyck. *New England Indian Summer*. New York: E. P. Dutton, 1940.

Child, Lydia Maria. *The American Frugal Housewife: Dedicated To those Who Are Not Ashamed of Economy*. New York: Samuel S. and William Wood, 22nd Edition, 1838.

Corson, Juliet. *American Cookery. A Monthly Cookbook Devoted to Reform in the Kitchen and to the Refinement at the Table*, vol. I, nos. 1–12 (January–December). Royal Baking Powder Co., 1876.

Corson, Juliet. *Family Living on $500. A Year*. Franklin Square, N.Y.: Harper and Bros., First Edition, 1888.

Cornelius, Mary Hooker. *The Young Housekeeper's Friend*. Boston: Thompson, Brown and Co., 1871.

Clutterbuck, Lady Maria (Mrs. Charles Dickens). *What Shall We Have For Dinner?* London: Bradbury and Evans, 1852.

David, Elizabeth. *English Bread and Yeast Cookery*. London: Allen Lane, 1st Edition, 1977.

Dickens, Charles, *American Notes*. London: Chapman and Hall, 1842.

di Paidena, Bartolomeo de Sacchi. *Platina*. Venice, 1475 Facsimile: Malincrodt Chemical Works, St. Louis, Mo., 1967 as #V—Collection of Food Classics.

Evans, Meryle. *A 19th Century Culinary Crusader. The New York Times*, January 3, 1979.

Fabricant, Florence. "Fannie Farmer's New Cookbook." *Americana Magazine*, March / April, 1980.

Farmer, Fannie Merritt. *The Boston Cooking School Cook Book*. New American Library, Facsimile of 1896 Edition, 1974.

Feret, Barbara L. *Gastronomical and Culinary Literature*. London: The Scarecrow Press, Inc., 1979.

Fillin, Lucille, and Fillin, Walter. *Cook Books—A Special Collection*. Hempstead, N.Y.: Hofstra University Library, 1976.

————. *Encyclopedia of Collectibles—Cookbooks*. Alexandria, Va.: 1978.

Fisher, Mrs. Abby. *What Mrs. Fisher Knows About Old Southern Cooking*. San Francisco: Women's Co-Operative Printing Office, 1881.

Flower, Barbara, and Rosenbaum, Elizabeth. *The Roman Cookery Book—The Art of Cooking by Apicius*. London: George G. Harrap and Co., Ltd., 1974.

Freeman, Sarah. *Isabella and Sam—The Story of Mrs. Beeton*. Coward, McCann and Geoghegan, Inc., 1st American Edition, 1978.

Giedion, Siegfried. *Mechanization Takes Command*, New York: W. W. Norton and Co., 1969.

Glasse, Hannah. *The Art of Cookery Made Plain and Easy*. Edinburgh: Alexander Donaldson, 1774.

Glozer, Liselotte F., and Glozer, William K. *California in the Kitchen. 1870–1932*. Privately Printed, 1960 (500 copies).

Guides of the Dickinson Homestead. *Emily Dickinson—Profile of the Poet As Cook—With Selected Recipes*. Amherst, Mass.: Dickinson Homestead, 3rd Printing, 1977.

Hazlitt, W. Carew. *Old Cookery Books and Ancient Cuisine*. London: Elliot Stock, 1902.

Huggett, Frank E. *Life Below Stairs—Domestic Servants in England From Victorian Times*. London: Book Club Associates, 1977.

Johnson, Thomas, and Ward, Theodora, eds. *The Letters of Emily Dickinson*, vol. I. Cambridge, Mass.: The Belknap Press of Harvard University Press, 1958.

Jones, Evan. *American Food—The Gastronomic Story*. New York: E. P. Dutton, 1st Edition, 1974.

Kettilby, Mary (and by Several Hands). *A Collection of About 300 Receipts in Cookery, Physick and Surgery*. London: Richard Wilkin, 1st Edition, 1714.

Leslie, Miss Eliza. *Domestic French Cookery*. Philadelphia: Carey and Hart, 4th Edition, 1836.

Lincoln, Mrs. D. A. *Mrs. Lincoln's Boston Cook Book: What To Do and What Not To Do In Cooking*. Boston: Roberts Brothers, 1st Edition 1887.

Linscott, Robert N., ed. *Selected Poems & Letters of Emily Dickinson*. New York: Doubleday / Anchor, 1959.

Lowenstein, Eleanor. *Bibliography of American Cookery Books, 1742–1860*. Worcester, Mass.: Antiquarian Society; Corner Book Shop, N.Y., 1972.

Mankowitz, Wolf. *Dickens of London*. New York: Macmillan Publishing Co., Inc., 1st American Edition, 1976.

Marcus, Steven. *Beeton's Book of Household Management. New York Times Book Review*, December 14, 1969.

Oxford, Arnold Whitaker. *English Cookery Books to the Year 1856*. London: The Holland Press, 2nd Impression, 1977.

Parloa, Maria. *Mrs. Parloa's New Cook Book. A Guide To Marketing and Cooking*. Boston: Estes and Lauriat, 1881.

Parloa, Maria. *Camp Cookery. How To Live In Camp*. Boston: Graves, Locke and Co., 1878.

Pennell, Elizabeth Robins. "Good Old Hannah Glasse—Another Cookbook." G. P. Putnam's Sons, *The Critic Magazine* (September, 1904).

Quayle, Eric. *Old Cook Books—An Illustrated History*. New York: E. P. Dutton, 1st Edition, 1978.

Raffald, Elizabeth. *The Experienced English Housekeeper*. Manchester: J. Harrop, 1st Edition signed by the author, 1769.

Rorer, Mrs. S. T. *Good Cooking*. Curtis Publishing Co., Philadelphia: Doubleday & McClure Co., 1898.

Simmons, Amelia. *American Cookery*. Reprint of Hudson and Goodwin 1796 Edition by West Virginia Pulp and Paper Co., 1963.

Simon, Andre L. *Bibliotheca Gastronomica*. London: The Holland Press, #234 / 750, 2nd impression, 1978.

Smallzried, Katherine Ann. *The Everlasting Pleasure*, New York: Appleton, Century, Crofts, 1st Edition, 1956.

Smith, Eliza. *The Compleat Housewife or Accomplish'd Gentlewoman's Companion*. Facsimile of Combination of 15th Edition (1753) and 18th Edition (1773), Literary Services and Production Ltd., London, 1968.

Spain, Nancy. *Mrs. Beeton and Her Husband*. London: Collins, 1st Edition, 1948.

Stark, Lewis M. *The Whitney Cookery Collection*. New York Public Library Bulletin, 1959.

Stern, Madeline. *Louisa May Alcott*. Norman: University of Oklahoma Press, 2nd Printing, 1971.

Stowe, Lyman Beecher. *Saints, Sinners and Beechers*. Indianapolis: Bobbs Merrill Co., 1934.
Tharp, Louise Hall. *The Peabody Sisters of Salem*. Boston: Little Brown and Co., 1950.
Thomas, Lately. *Del Monico's—A Century of Splendor*, Boston: Houghton Mifflin Co., 1st Printing, 1967.
Trollope, Mrs. Frances. *Domestic Manners of the Americans*. Barre, Mass.: Imprint Society, 1969.
Vicaire, Georges. *Bibliographie Gastronomique*. Paris: P. Rouquette et Fils, 1st Edition, 1890.
Wason, Betty. *Cooks, Gluttons and Gourmets. A History of Cookery*. Garden City, N.Y.: Doubleday and Co., Inc., 1st Edition, 1962.
Wilson, Edmond. *Patriotic Gore*. New York: Oxford University Press, 1962.
Weigley, Emma Seifrit. *Sarah Tyson Rorer, The Nation's Instructress in Dietetics and Cookery*, vol. 119. Philadelphia: The American Philosophical Society, 1977.

8

Jane Eyre and Poverty

Barbara T. Gates

Charlotte Brontë's critics are no longer intimidated by her disclaimer, "I cannot write books handling the topics of the day; it is no use trying."[1] Although Brontë is rightly viewed primarily as a novelist of character rather than as a social novelist, the topics of her day are certainly not absent from the pages of her novels, even in relatively apolitical works like *Jane Eyre*. Their presence has, in fact, been noted in a number of recent studies[2] and has led to such reassessments as Terry Eagleton's Marxist reading, which shows us Jane Eyre as a nineteenth-century "outcast bourgeoise" achieving "independence vis-à-vis the upper class" while humanizing Rochester in the bargain.[3] One can hardly disagree that part of Jane's individual struggle is to find her niche in the middle class by this means. I would further suggest, however, that Jane must also come to understand her position vis-à-vis Victorian poverty, and that concern with poverty, as with the other social questions that arise in this novel, becomes an important index to character for Brontë. Only slowly and painfully does Jane acquire both experience of the fine line that divides her genteel poverty from the more abject sort, and knowledge of just what factors stand between the Victorian poor and starvation: the Poor Laws, crime, and various forms of private charity.[4] As *Jane Eyre* progresses through its three volumes, a seemingly independent Jane is forced to realize the inevitability of interdependence, most significantly by arriving at a state of utter poverty in Morton and on the moors. It is only after this chastening experience and the subsequent months of running her own charity school that Jane finally earns union with the even more severely chastened Rochester. Thus development of character unifies this novel, as it does all of Charlotte Brontë's books, but attention to poverty sheds light on both character and morality in *Jane Eyre*.

This can be seen from the outset, where Jane is reminded of her poverty first by John Reed and then by the servants of the Reed household. In chapter 1, John humiliates Jane, telling her, "You have no money: your father left you none; you ought to beg, and not live here with gentlemen's children like us,"[5] while in the next chapter, Miss Abbot scolds that Jane is "less than a servant" for she does "nothing for her keep" (p. 9) and Bessie warns that if the Reeds were to reject Jane, she would have no recourse other than the poorhouse. Later we find that such reproofs are not new to Jane but have been part of her life since her "first recollections of existence" (p. 10). They also represent typically Victorian attitudes toward poverty. For John, as for many Victorians, money implies gentility. Increased emphasis on wealth toward mid-century had actually caused increased scorn toward the poor, an attitude reflected in mid-century novels. Walter Houghton reminds us that Tom Brown at Oxford found poverty "a disgrace to a Briton, and that, until you know a man thoroughly, you must imagine him to be the owner of unlimited ready money,"[6] and John Reed gives us a younger and crueler version of the same notion. Miss Abbot's rather different rebuke—to work, not to beg—is of course grounded in the Victorian work ethic, the same ethic that helped in the drafting of the unpopular 1834 New Poor Laws,[7] which Bessie indirectly refers to. Able-bodied people ought, even as children, to be equal to earning their own keep. If not, the workhouse was the fitting establishment for them. Probably through Bessie, her only friend, Jane develops an early horror of the workhouse and through Miss Abbot, a tendency to relegate all non-workers to the status of paupers.

At this stage of her life Jane herself parrots the attitudes toward poverty found at Gateshead. In talking to Mr. Lloyd about her prospects, she admits that she fears poverty as something "connected with ragged clothes, scanty food, fireless grates, rude manners, and debasing vices" (p. 20) and hesitates to flee Gateshead for such degradations, even if her flight might be to other relations. Ironically, it is just after this declaration that Jane learns of the circumstances of her own father's death: a case of typhus caught while serving as a curate ministering to the poor. Transmitted to Jane's mother, this typhus is what has left Jane an orphan; but the implications of such a spread of disease, and the interrelationship of poor and non-poor that it signifies, are still lost to Jane. As she has just said to Lloyd, she is not "heroic enough to purchase liberty at the price of caste" (p. 20). Thus Jane remains in the Reeds's power and is sent off to Mr. Brocklehurst to be kept humble and made useful, according to Mrs. Reed's wishes.

At Lowood, for the first time subject to institutionalized, private charity rather than to toleration by rich relatives, Jane puzzles over the tablet above the door. She cannot put together the word "institution" in Lowood Institution, and the verse "let your light so shine" from Matthew 16 which follows it on the inscribed tablet. It takes Helen Burns to explain the meaning of "charity-school," and months of hardship and no little humiliation by the mean-minded, evangelical Brocklehurst before Jane absorbs her new situation and learns to cope with it. Meanwhile, she must hear Brocklehurst forbid curly headed girls to wear curls in "an evangelical, charitable establishment" (p. 55) and witness at first hand a typhus epidemic not unlike the one which destroyed both of her parents. It is nonetheless this shattering epidemic that prompts the eventual "regeneration" of Lowood into something more of a model for private charity in Victorian times, just as it is this regenerated Lowood that gains Jane's first approval of a benevolent institution. Her description of the new school indicates a place where the inscription from Matthew might be more fitting and gives us the very type of a mid-Victorian, associated charity:

Several wealthy and benevolent individuals in the county subscribed largely for the erection of a more convenient building in a better situation; new regulations were made; improvements in diet and clothing introduced; the funds of the school were entrusted to the management of a committee. Mr. Brocklehurst, who, from his wealth and family connections, could not be overlooked, still retained the post of treasurer; but he was aided in the discharge of his duties by gentlemen of rather more enlarged and sympathizing minds. (p. 72)

Associated charity had become prevalent in Brontë's day and was distinguished from many earlier philanthropic efforts by the active involvement of larger numbers of patrons.[8] Thus at Lowood Brocklehurst eventually found even his office of inspector "shared by those who knew how to combine reason with strictness, comfort with economy, compassion with uprightness" (p. 72). Far from suffering under the aegis of such a foundation, Jane grows there, for six years as a pupil, then for two more as a teacher. In this situation she can accept her condition of genteel poverty, hampered neither by the cruelty and condescension of the Reeds nor by the penuriousness and malice of Brocklehurst. Having attained the "industrious, working, respectable poverty" that she had once described to Mr. Lloyd, Jane is seen by Bessie as quite "genteel enough" a young lady (p. 80) before she leaves for Thornfield.

At Thornfield, Jane continually lives up to this image. In volume two, nearly all of which encompasses the Thornfield story, she is little troubled by her earlier fears of destitution. Rochester may tease her about having literally survived such a place as Lowood and by labelling her care for Adele as a "charitable purpose" and as "benevolent acts" (p. 114), but he never really makes sport of her onetime poverty. Thus Jane can more readily accept her still humble role of governess, though it galls her when she compares herself with Blanche Ingram, and ultimately, it prompts her well-known outburst to Rochester: "Do you think, because I am poor, obscure, plain and little, I am soulless and heartless?" (p. 222). Yet governessing really has given Jane a sense of identity and self-respect that enables her to face the dying Mrs. Reed with compassion and with considerable character. When Mrs. Reed levels the old Gateshead insults at Jane, even to the point of telling her that she "would as soon have been charged with a pauper brat out of a workhouse" (p. 204) as with a beggar like Jane, Jane listens as patiently to this as to Mrs. Reed's concern over her own comparatively mild fall from wealth. In terms of Jane's apprehension over poverty, then, the Thornfield section of *Jane Eyre* functions as a bridge between the other two volumes of the novel. Until the end of this volume, Jane does not have to face the kinds of humiliation which beset her in childhood, or when she does face them, as in seeing Mrs. Reed, they are powerless to hurt her deeply simply because they do not apply to her current state.

The morning after Rochester's proposal, Jane's security with respect to future poverty reaches its zenith. Carried away with joy and the prospect of her new status, she runs down the walk and gives all the money in her purse to a beggar-woman and her son, "pale, ragged objects both" (p. 226). Her action is of course premature, but it tells us a great deal about Jane. Freed from financial worry herself, she is not indifferent to the needs of strangers as she was not to those of Mrs. Reed. But at this stage when a sense of security envelops Jane, it also tends to reinforce her feelings of independence and make her morally priggish. We can see this particularly well in her conversations with Rochester, whom she sees as her master by rank but her moral inferior. When, for example, prior to his proposal he asks her whether a "wandering and sinful, but now rest-seeking and repentant man" may hope for attachment to a gentle woman like herself, she replies:

a wanderer's repose or a sinner's reformation should never depend on a fellow-creature. Men and women die, philosophers falter in wisdom, and Christians in goodness: if any one you know has suffered and erred, let him look to higher than his equals for strength to amend, and solace to heal. (p. 192)

Taken aback by this rather uncharitable advice, Rochester tries to query Jane about the instruments of God's workings—other human beings—but Jane has no further reply. Having newly found her own independence from the Reeds and from charitable institutions of whatever sort, Jane is not prepared to admit her own need for aid from others.

Nor, certainly, is she willing to be "kept" by Rochester, who now inundates her with gifts. "The more he bought me," Jane tells us, "the more my cheek burned with a sense of annoyance and degradation" (p. 236). All this buying betokens possessiveness, and to be owned by a prospective husband turns out nearly as humiliating as to be treated as a charity case. Thus Jane aches for a literal "independency" and resolves to write to Uncle Eyre in Madeira. Refusing to play Danae to Rochester's Zeus, she insists that his regard, not showers of gold, are what she wants.

Jane is no doubt right to reject this side of Rochester but probably wrong not to see that she is applying middle-class decorum and false pride in her genteel poverty to his accustomed aristocratic behavior. Rochester need not purchase Jane's love, for she has already given it to him; nevertheless, like all persons in Brontë's world, Jane cannot live wholly on her own. Brontë will therefore subject her to the most severe test of her self-sufficiency, turning her once again from "an ardent, expectant woman" to "a cold, solitary girl" (p. 260) at the end of the second volume, after the announcement of Rochester's intended bigamy. Provided with only a small parcel, which she subsequently loses, and the few shillings left after her generosity to the beggars at Thornfield, Jane sets out for a transforming encounter with real destitution. Since people are not to be appealed to for charity, Jane turns first toward nature to support her in her need. Throughout the Thornfield section of the novel, Jane has shown a simplified Wordsworthian attitude toward nature; "Nature must be gladsome when I was so happy" (p. 226), she says just before she offers her shillings to the beggars. In volume three, however, she finds that poverty, not happiness, is the natural state of affairs. The Christian God resides not in nature but in humankind, just as Rochester had suggested.

Thus Jane's real trials begin with her gnawing hunger on the moors.[9] Unequal to a life lived wholly in nature and now acknowledging herself to have "a human being's wants" (p. 286), Jane follows the sound of a church bell into the town of Morton and there stands "in the position of one without a resource: without a friend, without a coin" (p. 287). In quite different circumstances from those of volume one, she is no longer a child with a child's appeal to sympathy. Instead she is faced with a series of unpleasant and degrading encounters as she searches for a morsel of food to sustain her and comes closer and closer to beggarhood. With a Morton shopkeeper she thinks first of barter, of offering her gloves or handkerchief for a roll. Finding herself too embarrassed to go through with her intentions, however, she winds up asking what sort of employment is available in Morton, a hope that carries her next to the door of a householder, then on to the parsonage. Lack of success at each stage in her search for work eventually leads her back to the shopkeeper and to her first appalling apprehension of how a genteel-looking young woman, desperate for food, must appear to an outsider. The shopkeeper will not take Jane's gloves because she suspects Jane, probably of trafficking in stolen goods. It is the humiliation of this realization that finally forces Jane into active begging, first for bread from a farmer and then for pig-food, the leftovers from a child's breakfast.

All of these encounters painfully humble Jane before she arrives at Moor House and call forth her old ideas of poverty, formed at Gateshead. She is now truly the beggar that John said she should have been all along; she sees that she is less than a servant after all; and she is still as determined as ever to avoid the workhouse at all costs. Confronted, she thinks, with the imminent prospect of death, she observes that it is "far better that crows and ravens . . . should pick my flesh from my bones, than that they should be prisoned in a workhouse coffin and moulder in a pauper's grave" (p. 290). Jane does not, however, blame those who reject her, since she still maintains her stiff-necked notions of independence. "What claims had I to importune her?" (p. 287), she remarks when rebuffed by the shopkeeper. Only when she arrives at Moor House at the complete end of her resources and is rejected by Hannah, not only as a vagrant but also as a poser in collusion with housebreakers, does she find herself altogether at the mercy of others and willing to accept charity without a murmur. If the proposal of Rochester was the zenith of her prospects, this, then, is their nadir. In her words, "a pang of exquisite suffering—a throe of true despair—rent and heaved my heart. Worn out, indeed, I was; not another step could I stir. I sank on the wet door-step: I groaned" (p. 295).

Brontë lets Jane sink into this mire of despair—which is surely a nineteenth-century Slough of Despond—only to chasten her and let her rise once again, having shed a part of her former pride along with her wet clothes. Jane has learned poverty of spirit at this stage of her progress. Yet Richard Benvenuto[10] is quite right not to find an entirely new Jane resurrected after this baptism through poverty, for Brontë is too good a psychologist ever wholly to take away Jane's spirit, or starchiness, or love of lecturing. Jane soon begins once more to "know herself," as she tells the reader just after she crosses the threshold of Marsh End. She can still think of poverty as degradation, associated with the dirt and disorder that pervaded her clothes when she came to the middle-class home of the Rivers. Nonetheless, as soon as she can she puts on her "own things, now clean and dry," and goes down to the kitchen to read servant Hannah two lessons that she herself has learned: first, that the poor may indeed have a right to importune others, and second that poverty is no fair gauge of immorality, let alone of criminal intent. When Hannah finds that Jane is resentful of her attitude toward Jane's begging and asks that Jane not think too hardly of her, she gets a very fiery retort:

But I do think hardly of you . . . and I'll tell you why—not so much because you refused to give me shelter, or regarded me as an impostor, as because you just now made it a species of reproach that I had no 'brass' and no house. Some of the best people that ever lived have been as destitute as I am; and if you are a Christian, you ought not to consider poverty a crime. (p. 301)

Here for the first time Jane comes closer to seeing that all people are caught up in one another's poverty, as in one another's lives, and that she herself can be as much in need of their relief as they of hers. This is a hard realization for Jane but one she must work through before eventual reunion with Rochester.

The Rivers, however, do help Jane to learn this and also to reestablish a sense of her own worth. With them Jane discovers the difference between compassion and charity, a distinction she makes clear in a conversation with St. John. She owes his sisters, she tells him, for "their spontaneous, genuine, genial compassion," as large a debt as she owes him for his "evangelical charity" (p. 308). For Jane, compassion confers a sense of independence, whereas charity implies debt. Such a distinction is not lost on St. John, who feels the sting of Jane's comparison and is goaded into finding some means of employment to help her attain independence.

Jane's new school for the poor, suggested by St. John and supported by the Olivers, thus becomes the testing ground for her new sense of self and her different attitude toward poverty. Jane's situation will be humble but not ignoble, and rather more in keeping with her desire for autonomy than was governessing. It is, however, a drop on the social scale and this fact still shames Jane:

I felt desolate to a degree. I felt—yes, idiot that I am—I felt degraded. I doubted I had taken a step which sank instead of raising me in the scale of social existence. I was weakly dismayed at the ignorance, the poverty, the coarseness of all I heard and saw round me. But let me not hate and despise myself too much for these feelings: I know them to be wrong—that is a great step gained; I shall strive to overcome them. (p. 360)

Here we see that Jane has not been transformed overnight from pride and prejudice to compassion toward ignorance and poverty, but that she has certainly been made aware of her own narrowness of viewpoint. Slowly she will earn the regard of her poor scholars as she learns to prize them more highly, so that ultimately she recalls this part of her life with a heart swelling with thankfulness rather than sinking in dejection (p. 322). Yet Jane's tempering of ambition and growing increase in compassion are precisely what create difficulties when St. John asks her to step over into the life of a missionary. At this point she is no longer threatened by poverty, for the Eyre legacy has become hers and, through gratitude, the Rivers' as well, since fair-minded Jane immediately wishes to share her wealth with her kin. But she is not prepared to surrender herself and become a nineteenth-century Mother Teresa to the poor of India. The village school has allowed her to follow in the footsteps of Miss Temple and to bring light into the lives of young, British peasant girls, if not orphans. This mission pleases her, to be sure, but leaves no taste for the further regenerating of the race that St. John counsels her toward.

Instead Jane must make her way back toward Rochester and find another way to use the compassion hard won since Thornfield. This time she is followed by the lessons of poverty, but not by its spectre, and "softens" the account of her "three days of wandering and starvation" (p. 387) in order not further to hurt the already anguished Rochester. Poverty has outlived its usefulness in Brontë's plot but remains strong in the memory and actions of Jane. Having been humbled and made dependent by destitution, as Rochester has been by fire, Jane has learned the folly of her earlier statement that "a wanderer's repose or a sinner's reformation should never depend on a fellow-creature." People can indeed be the "instruments" of one another's salvation, as Rochester had intimated, and Jane is now ready to be Rochester's. Because he has obvious need of her, she can with all honesty say to him, "I love you better now, when I can really be useful to you, than I did in your state of proud independence, when you disdained every part but that of the giver and protector" (p. 392). Yet because Jane has learned the final lessons of poverty at the home of the Rivers sisters, Rochester will not feel in her love what he calls a "sacrifice." Jane knows how to give love without requiring dependence and to accept it without tempering her own sense of self-respect. She has become an independent woman not only financially, as she tells Rochester, but in other ways, too, is now her "own mistress" (p. 389).

With this in mind and with a vivid recollection of Jane's chastening through her trials in Morton, it is interesting to recall Mrs. Rigby's now infamous review of *Jane Eyre* and to ponder what Rigby could have had in mind when she said:

Altogether the autobiography of Jane Eyre is preeminently an anti-Christian composition. There is throughout it a murmuring against the comforts of the rich and against the privations of the poor, which as far as each individual is concerned, is a murmuring against God's appointment—there is a proud and perpetual assertion of the rights of man, for which we find no authority either in God's word or in God's providence.[11]

Surely Charlotte Brontë's intentions must have been quite opposite to what Mrs. Rigby imagined. Jane is learning about Christian charity with regard to poor relief even as she scolds Hannah for insensitivity on this subject. In fact, what Jane learns from poverty will take her through a pattern of Victorian conversion, not rebellion, a pattern that both she and Rochester need to experience before their final reunion at Ferndean. Jane indeed begins by asserting her right to autonomy, but like so many other personae in Victorian literature, she must die to that old need and eventually find a new self, in this case one still self-reliant but not divorced from a need for others. Abject poverty is Brontë's means of humbling her protagonist sufficiently for Jane to be required to find that new self, in effect reborn from the marshes near Morton. As a consequence, the Jane we find at the end of the novel is an individual who has learned of the inter-connectedness of human life and of the need for dependence and compassion as well as for independence. Her turning has encompassed what Jerome Buckley finds at the center of the Victorian conversion: a new birth involving "the crucial insight into a reality, human or divine, beyond the old self-absorbed life."[12] She was moved from poverty to humility to charity, and the story she tells is both of a woman's liberation and of the social and self-imposed limits to liberty which all the Brontë sisters knew.

The novel *Jane Eyre* may not, then, be preoccupied with the topics of its day, but it is occupied with them. Since they intimately concern the novel's main characters, topics like poverty are used to relate private and social aspects of the novel. Charlotte Brontë is neither a Dickens nor a Mrs. Gaskell, but she likes to improve her already good characters for the betterment of others. After her three days on the moors and in Morton, Jane touches her school-girls, Rochester, and even Hannah in a way that she has never touched anyone before. This is not large-scale social reform, to be sure; yet it does imply that people can achieve increased awareness of both their own blindness and the pain and ignorance of others, and that they can act in private but significant ways to relieve that blindness and pain. In Brontë, social regeneration comes through individual regeneration. Since all human beings are related—a lesson which Jane Eyre learns through poverty and Charlotte Brontë stresses through coincidence—one person's gain in charity offers hope for others.

NOTES

1. Letter to George Smith, October 30, 1852, *The Brontës: Their Lives, Friendships nd Correspondence*, 4 vols., ed. T. J. Wise and J. A. Symington (Oxford: Shakespeare Head Press, 1932), IV, pp. 13–14.

2. For a summary of such studies see Herbert J. Rosengarten, "The Brontës," in *Victorian Fiction: A Second Guide to Research*, ed. George H. Ford (New York: Modern Language Association of America, 1978), pp. 185–86.

3. Terry Eagleton, *Myths of Power* (London: Macmillan, 1975), p. 32.

4. See Geoffrey Best, *Mid-Victorian Britain, 1851–1875* (New York: Schocken, 972), pp. 120–33.

5. All quotations from *Jane Eyre* are from the third edition (New York: Mershon, 848); here p. 10. Subsequent references will be included in the text.

6. Walter E. Houghton, *The Victorian Frame of Mind, 1830–1870* (New Haven: Yale University Press, 1957), pp. 184–85.

7. The Reverend Patrick Brontë was violently opposed to the New Poor Laws and in 1837 made an eloquent and fiery speech against them. Reported in *The Times*, February 27, 1837, the speech could hardly have escaped the notice of Brontë's own daughter.

8. See Best, *Mid-Victorian Britain*, pp. 133–35.

9. I am wholly in agreement with Jennifer Gribble, who believes that "nature is for ane no mere escape from the pressures of social living but a means by which she comes to understand more surely and deeply what her social experience teaches" ("Jane Eyre's magination," *NCF* 23 [1968], 293).

10. Richard Benvenuto, "The Child of Nature, the Child of Grace, and the Unresolved Conflict of *Jane Eyre*," *ELH* 39 (1972), 620–38. Benvenuto, who discusses Jane's attitude toward poverty in the introduction to his essay, does not believe that Jane grows through understanding destitution.

11. Elizabeth Rigby, "Vanity Fair and *Jane Eyre*," *Quarterly Review* (December, 1848), reprinted in *The Brontës: The Critical Heritage*, ed. Miriam Allott (London: Routledge and Kegan Paul, 1974), p. 109.

12. Jerome Hamilton Buckley, *The Victorian Temper: A Study in Literary Culture* (New York: Vintage, 1951), p. 105.

9

Once More to the Attic: Bertha Rochester and the Pattern of Redemption in *Jane Eyre*

Gail B. Griffin

In the memories of women who love books, the first encounter with *Jane Eyre* is lodged in a special place. We forget now how many times we have read it; after a while we internalize it; it becomes our own story, our personal myth. In our minds we relive it over and over again: leaving Gateshead in the cold, pre-dawn darkness; glowing in the light of public exoneration at Lowood and finding peace and dignity in that unlikely place; wandering the great corridors of Thorn-field—but always stopping at the attic door, waiting to hear that low, joyless laugh and feel the shiver down the spine once more. All *Jane Eyre* lovers have been strangely drawn to Bertha Mason Rochester, reacting first in delicious terror to the monster who laughed at the keyhole and appeared in bedrooms in the middle of the night; then, more wisely, responding with pity for the hopeless victim, lost to the sun, running back and forth across the attic on all fours; then, finally, as we become more sophisticated readers, we were fascinated by the rich psychological texture of Jane's relationship to her mad double, whose laughter suddenly, unexpectedly echoes through the third story like a nagging reminder to Jane of something almost forgotten and an eerie warning of something to come.

Finally, in recent years, the girls once mesmerized by Jane's story, now grown into literary critics, have trouped in turn upon Bertha's attic room. Our inchoate sense of some link, some communion between the two Mrs. Rochesters has been amply substantiated. Adrienne Rich's important essay of 1972, "Jane Eyre: The Temptations of a Motherless Woman," discusses Bertha briefly as Jane's double and as a figure of warning, representing the result of a liberated female imagi-nation in nineteenth-century society.[1] Elaine Showalter's 1977 book, *A Literature of Their Own*, treats Bertha in more detail in the context of women's madness, dealing with her as the incarnation of Jane's repressed sexuality.[2] Both works confront Rochester's complicity in his wife's insanity, and Rich addresses his hypocrisy in incarcerating his wife for the lustful " 'propensities' "[3] which he possesses in acknowledged abundance. In a fine, short article, Karen Mann has placed Jane and Bertha together in the web of male-dominated economic structures.[4] But Bertha did not receive the treatment she deserved until 1979, when Sandra M. Gilbert and Susan Gubar discussed in depth her role as Jane's dark doppelganger in their book on nineteenth-century female writers whose title, *The Madwoman in the Attic*, pays tribute to Bertha. With sensitivity and careful attention to detail the authors explore Bertha's diverse roles in Jane's saga: her striking similarity to Jane as well as her striking opposition; her monitory role as warning and example; her enactment of Jane's subconscious desires and repressed anger; her relationship to the child Jane, incarcerated in the Red Room and driven to something like madness.[5] Gilbert and Gubar demonstrate that Jane's "confrontation, not with Rochester but with Rochester's mad wife Bertha, is the book's central confrontation."[6]

This important truth having been documented, what remains to be said? I think that the puzzle is not yet complete, that Bertha's place in the vast and intricate design of *Jane Eyre* is not fully traced. Two important points have yet to be made, one concerning Bertha's function in Jane's personal quest, and the other having to do with Bertha's relationship to Rochester, a relationship slighted by these critics in favor of her doubling with Jane. And yet to understand Jane's suffering and redemption requires an understanding of Rochester's, in which Bertha is crucial; and the whole pattern of sexual struggle and liberation in the novel is incomplete without the figure of Bertha at its center, Jane on one side, Rochester on the other.

Adrienne Rich prepares our way with her interpretation of the moon in *Jane Eyre* as a Great Mother goddess, providing the maternal guidance Jane desperately seeks and occasionally finds in other women. This goddess actually speaks to Jane in a dream the night before she leaves Thornfield: " 'My daughter, flee temptation!' " to which Jane responds, " 'Mother, I will' " (p. 181).[7] Diana and Mary Rivers, Rich tells us, are incarnations of this goddess in her dual aspects, as their names suggest.[8] But the earlier mother-figures are also involved in this lunar network. Maria Temple's first and last names certainly link her with the Mother goddess, and even Helen Burns bears the name of a female literary archetype, something of a goddess. These two important role models are related to the symbol of the moon, which begins to appear in Jane's life when she arrives at Lowood. At Gateshead the moon is conspicuously absent: in the terrifying Red Room episode, Jane wishes for the eerie light on the wall to be the moon, but it is not (p. 14); as she leaves Gateshead, "[t]he moon [is] set, and it [is] very dark" (p. 35). Miss Temple literally breaks upon Jane's benighted consciousness like a full moon from behind a cloud, and she is consistently described in lunar terms: as having "a pale and large forehead" (p. 36), a "white forehead" (p. 62), "whiteness [in] her large front" (p. 40), "beaming dark eyes" (p. 62) with "a benignant light in their irids" (p. 40), "a complexion, if pale, clear'' (p. 41), and ''something of serenity in her air'' (p. 63). Helen Burns, who assures Jane that Miss Temple '' 'is above the rest' '' (p. 44), is also a moonchild. Jane often remarks upon the light in her eyes, like Miss Temple's; and on one occasion, when Helen is in trouble with one of the teachers, the connection grows more explicit: ''such spots are there on the disc of the clearest planet; and eyes like Miss Scatcherd's can only see those minute defects, and are blind to the full brightness of the orb'' (p. 59). Finally Jane is drawn within the lunar circle, one night when she is alone with Helen: ''Some heavy clouds, swept from the sky by a rising wind, had left the moon bare; and her light, streaming in through a window near, shone full both on us and on the approaching figure, which we at once recognized as Miss Temple'' (p. 61). This sorority of the moon gives Jane the fundamental strength to overcome the ghosts of the past and the demons of the future. To Thornfield she brings a painting of the Evening Star—Venus, another female Goddess—as a woman rising into the night sky, bathed in moonlight (p. 110).

At Thornfield the moon, consistently referred to as ''she,'' gazes maternally down upon important events: Jane's first meeting with Rochester (p. 97), her return to Thornfield that evening (p. 102), his proposal of marriage (p. 225), during which, he later tells her, she '' 'glowed in the moonlight' '' (p. 230), absorbing something of the goddess herself. Rochester betrays the spirit of the moon in his fairy-tale version of his marriage to Jane, recited for Adele's benefit: he plans to '' 'take mademoiselle to the moon' '' (p. 234), in defiance of natural law, where they will live in isolation. Interestingly enough, Adele objects thoroughly to this proposal, verbalizing what is in Jane's heart.

The moon appears at three other critical points at Thornfield, each time preceding the intrusion of Bertha into Jane's life. A bright moon wakes her just before Bertha's attack on her brother, Richard Mason (pp. 180–81); the night of Bertha's entry into Jane's bedchamber is dark, but Jane dreams of wandering through the ruins of Thornfield '' 'on a moonlight night' '' (p. 248) and wakes to see Bertha; and finally, on the night before the wedding and Jane's discovery of Bertha's reality and identity, the moon is a constant, active presence, first ''blood-red and half overcast'' (p. 243), then disappearing within the clouds (p. 244), then appearing again (p. 244), then finally shining ''peacefully'' (p. 251). The changeability of the moon corresponds to Jane's confusion on this night of foreboding: '' 'I cannot see my prospects clearly tonight' '' (p. 245), she tells Rochester.

The moon on this night is not the serene maternal goddess—or perhaps she is another aspect of that goddess: ''Her disk was blood-red and half overcast; she seemed to throw on me one bewildered, dreary glance, and buried herself again instantly in the deep drift of cloud'' (p. 243). In fact, she strongly resembles Bertha herself as she first appears by Jane's bedside after tearing the veil. Just so does Bertha momentarily emerge from the gloom to glance down at Jane in the candlelight and then disappear into her attic darkness. Bertha is the third moon-figure in the novel, the only one at Thornfield, and considered in this light her significance expands. Elaine Showalter observes that the "periodicity of Bertha's attacks suggests a connection to the menstrual cycle,"[9] a connection strengthened by this association with the moon, particularly a "blood-red" moon. The moon is an ambivalent symbol, traditionally signifying female chastity but also female inconstancy, unchastity, sexual aggressiveness, the temporary insanity associated with menstruation in Charlotte Brontë's age. Bertha is called "the lunatic," a term which, of course, derives from the moon, so it is appropriate that it be her symbol. In fact, then, Bertha is the dark side of the moon whose bright side is Miss Temple; both are aspects of womanhood in Jane Eyre—the serenity and the rage, the dignity and the torment. The female dichotomy so dear to the male literary imagination—the angel and the whore, the fair and dark heroines—is reappropriated, and the symbol of the moon, enclosing this dualism, is thus recast in distinctively female terms.

Bertha, then, enters the ranks of the mother-figures Rich sees as guiding Jane's quest. There are two indications, one more direct than the other, that Brontë sees her in this light. The first has to do with Bertha's name. The names of four of the chief characters in the novel are versions of the traditional four elements composing all of creation: Air (Jane Eyre), water (St. John Rivers, linked by first name as well as last), fire (Helen Burns), and earth, contained in the word "Bertha." This quartet of elements was usually divided into pairs of opposites: fire and water, earth and air. The fire and water figures, Helen and St. John, certainly belong together as emblems of a spirituality Jane deeply admires but cannot fully accept. The air and earth figures, Jane and Bertha, are thus doubled once again. This elemental opposition usually denoted the separation of spirit (air) and body (earth), divine and mundane, and this is certainly one aspect of the Jane-Bertha relationship, if Bertha represents Jane's submerged sexuality. But in a novel as full of the power of nature—also defined as a maternal "she"— as this one, "earth" certainly has other connotations: growth, renewal, fertility. Bertha is an Earth Mother figure, highly sexual and capable of the destruction that is inseparable from creation and new birth. For Bertha's name also conspicuously contains the word "birth," more directly suggesting that she is another mother figure for the orphan Jane. Bertha is at once the angry orphan of Jane's past,[10] imprisoned within the "disciplined and subdued character" (p. 73) that leaves Lowood, but also one of the maternal spirits creating Jane's future— helping Jane give birth to herself.

Jane believes this new self to be on the verge of birth the night before the wedding: "Mrs. Rochester! She did not exist; she would not be born till tomorrow, some time after eight o'clock A.M.; and I would wait to be assured she had come into the world alive before I assigned to her all that property" (p. 242). The new self, as she fears, is stillborn, precisely because Mrs. Rochester *does* exist. That night, in Jane's dream of Gateshead, the maternal moon spirit takes human form and its voice admonishes her to flee temptation. But has not this spirit, in one of its incarnations, already issued this warning? For two nights earlier, the preternaturally strong and murderous Bertha enters Jane's room but nakes no move to harm her rival; instead, she tears the bridal veil asunder. As vell as an enactment of Jane's subliminal desire,[11] this is surely a maternal varning from one Mrs. Rochester to another, from one who has been sold in narriage to one who has felt that she is about to be bought, like a "slave" (p. 36) or a " 'jewel' " (p. 238). The torn veil signifies broken union but also leared vision, since the veil is meant to protect the bride from the world and o hide the world from the bride's innocent eyes. Bertha tries to tell Jane what Rochester will not, but what another mother figure, Mrs. Fairfax, has also tried o communicate. Jane is soon on her way to her next foster-mothers, the Rivers isters.

It is interesting that Bertha's odd gentleness to Jane is reciprocated. Upon first nearing Bertha's laugh, Jane calls it, among other things, "tragic" (p. 94). When Rochester proposes, Jane's concern is whether she can accept " 'without fearing that anyone else is suffering the bitter pain I myself felt a while ago' " p. 231): her empathy creates a hypothetical Bertha. She even enacts Bertha's death in her dream before their first confrontation. Finally, in her long discussion with Rochester after the secret is out, Jane's language in referring to Bertha is n marked contrast to his own. Whereas he calls her a hag, a demon, a fiend, Jane calls her " 'your wife' " (p. 267) and " 'that unfortunate lady' " (p. 265), granting her both status and dignity. " '[She] cannot help being mad,' " Jane admonishes. It is, of course, this power of empathy, Jane's ability to turn her own suffering into a medium of moral vision, that Rochester lacks. In their final interview, Jane repeatedly sees herself in Bertha's place—as the discarded plaything (p. 274), as a madwoman (p. 279). Jane is not Bertha's rival, but her only defender. It is Rochester who perceives them as rivals; where Jane sees similarity and kinship, he sees polar opposition, and this false perception of the two women in his life is at the root of his moral failure and his suffering.

Bertha shares with Rochester nearly as rich a psychological interrelationship as she shares with Jane. In the first place, there are suggestions of physical similarity between husband and wife: Bertha is of a "stature almost equalling her husband" (p. 258); he is described as dark and swarthy, like Bertha, in fact, he calls himself " 'blackaviced' " (p. 176) and Jane describes Bertha's face as " 'blackened' " (p. 249). Both are slightly androgynous: Jane remarks upon Bertha's "virile force" (p. 258), while in Rochester's gypsy episode he explores a female identity remarkably reminiscent of Bertha: " 'a shockingly ugly old creature . . . almost as black as a crock' " (p. 169), the footman calls her, and Jane confirms that her face is "all brown and black" (p. 172). Blanche announces that " 'we have a genuine witch in the house, who is in close alliance with the old gentleman' " (p. 170). " 'I'm sure she is something not right!' " exclaim the young ladies (p. 171). To Jane, who addresses her as " 'mother' " (p. 172), the gypsy confides that she has " 'an acquaintance with . . . Mrs. Poole' " (p. 174).

Among other things, this scene is Rochester's enactment of the Bertha within him, a creature he fears intensely, as is clear in his description of the disastrous marriage, in which he is at great pains to draw fine lines between Bertha's " 'debauchery' " and his own " 'dissipation' " (p. 274). " 'Any enjoyment that bordered on riot,' " he explains to Jane, " 'seemed to approach me to her and her vices, and I eschewed it' " (p. 274). He is terrified of becoming like her. It is this inner Bertha from which he has been running these ten years, during which he has attempted to deny it by locking it in an attic and rationalizing away his marriage. " 'Let her identity, her *connection with yourself*, be buried in oblivion' " (p. 273), he has told himself (italics mine).

But just like the real Bertha, the interior Bertha keeps breaking out, incendiary and dangerous. During the final interview, as Jane is imagining herself and calling herself a madwoman, Rochester is showing similar symptoms: "His voice was hoarse; his look that of a man who is just about to burst an insufferable bond and plunge headlong into wild license. I saw that in another moment, and with one impetus of frenzy more, I should be able to do nothing with him. The present—the passing second of time—was all I had in which to control and restrain him" (p. 266). Later, a "wild look raised his brows"(p. 278). And when Jane returns to Thornfield, she is told by the innkeeper that after the fire, Rochester " 'grew savage—quite savage. . . . He never was a wild man, but he got dangerous' " (p. 376).

The more Rochester tries to deny Bertha, to lock her in the past, the more she comes to represent his past itself. She is often referred to as a ghost, and her third story has "the aspect of a home of the past: a shrine of memory" (p. 92). "What crime was this," Jane wonders, "that lived incarnate in this sequestered mansion?" (p. 185). Much later, Rochester insists on another semantic distinction: " 'Mind, I don't say a crime: . . . my word is *error*' " (p. 191). But the novel bears Jane out: Bertha is the incarnation of his crime, for which he pays dearly. In a Victorian novel the past is never to be denied, and certainly not in this one; both Jane and Rochester must confront painful pasts, represented for each of them by Bertha. The past becomes the future, then, their inescapable destinies, of which they both speak in terms suggestive of Bertha. Rochester describes his thus: " 'I was arranging a point with my destiny. She stood there, by that beech-truck—a hag like one of those who appeared to "Macbeth" on the heath of Forres. "You like Thornfield?" she said. . . . "Like it if you can!" ' " (p. 125). Certainly, Bertha is the "hag" who renders Thornfield unlikable for him. A few pages later, Jane uses another metaphor from Bertha's world: "My thin crescent-destiny seemed to enlarge" (p. 129). She then remembers how Rochester's destiny "had risen up before him" (p. 129), and almost immediately she hears Bertha's laugh at the door and discovers the fire. Later, on the confused eve of the wedding, the moon "[shuts] herself wholly within her chamber," again like Bertha, and Jane muses, "I imagined my fortune and passed its meridian, and must now decline" (p. 244). For both of them, Bertha is the ghost of an angry past and the unavoidable shape of the future. Ostensibly the impediment between them, she is in fact their strongest link.

Subconsciously Rochester sees Bertha as his demon, his evil self; consequently, he seeks an angelic self to save him. After incarcerating Bertha, he tells us, " 'My fixed desire was to seek and find a good and intelligent woman whom I could love: a contrast to the fury I left at Thornfield' " (p. 273). Womankind thus divides in his mind into the two familiar opposed types: demons like Bertha, and the ideal woman for whom he searches, " 'the antipodes of the Creole' " (p. 274). His own base and better instincts he projects outward upon the world of women, and, failing to find his ideal, he decides that all women are Berthas. He returns to England " 'sourly disposed against all men, and especially against all *woman*kind' " (p. 275). The story is a familiar one: his own self-division and self-hatred ultimately result in misogyny. Jane, listening quietly, understands this; she hears the tale of rejected mistresses— " 'I tired of her in three months. . . . I was glad to . . . get decently rid of her' " (p. 274)— and realizes that she, too, as his mistress, would eventually be discarded as falling short of the ideal. The problem lies not with the mistresses strewn across Europe, but with Rochester himself, with the dipolar archetypes of his own devising.

Jane, of course, has stumbled into this psychodrama in the role of Bertha's opposite: " 'a very angel,' " he calls her (p. 228). From the first she refuses to play: " 'I am not an angel . . . and I will not be one until I die: I will be myself. Mr. Rochester, you must neither expect nor exact anything celestial of me' " (p. 228). Helen Burns was an angel—almost—but Helen is dead, and while Jane has absorbed wisdom from her, she can never be like her. In fact, one of the most powerful impulses of the book is the triumph of the human, the decidedly un-angelic; the human triumph of Jane Eyre and Edward Rochester, as against the angelic triumph of Helen Burns and St. John Rivers. Rochester's attempt to fit Jane to his mental constructs, then, violates both the book's humanism and Jane's individual humanity. His refusal to allow her this humanity— his insistence that she be an angel, or a "doll," or a member of his " 'seraglio' " (p. 236)—is the real cancer in the initial relationship, the real impediment to matrimony, the one Jane senses well before she is aware of Bertha.

As an angel, Jane knows, she is in a perilous position. In the kind of imagination that divides women into opposing types, it is easy to slip from one category to the other: " 'Don't turn a downright Eve on my hands!' " Rochester warns (p. 228), citing the archetypal evil woman. In addition, the categorizing imagination finds ready scapegoats in the women chosen to represent aspects of itself; it becomes easy to pass the buck. Pleading with Jane to remain with him, Rochester calls her " 'my sympathy—my better self—my good angel' " (p. 277). As Bertha is supposed to have damned him, Jane is now expected to save him, and in refusing for the sake of her own moral salvation, she "turns a downright Eve" on him, becoming, in his mind, his corruptor: " 'Then you snatch love and innocence from me? You fling me back on lust for a passion— vice for an occupation?' " (p. 279). Jane immediately refuses responsibility for his future moral decay. But in Rochester's psychodrama he is torn between two female forces, representing his good and evil selves, and the good angel is now "flinging" him, helpless, into the arms of lust—that is, the Bertha within.

In reality, as I have tried to show, the opposing angel and demon are in sympathy—and in league. They are cooperating for Rochester's salvation. In her first appearance in the story, Bertha brings fire to Rochester's bed and Jane the flood to quench it; both are, Biblically speaking, manifestations of a vengeful God but forces for redemption and cleansing, forces at once destructive and recreative. The account of Rochester's reaction to the incident suggests this collaboration and its Biblical overtones:

> "Is there a flood?" he cried.
> "No, sir," I answered; "but there has been a fire. . . ."
> " . . . Who is in the room beside you? Have you plotted to drown me?
> " . . . Somebody has plotted something. . . ." (p. 131)

It is Bertha's fire which ultimately succeeds where Jane's milder baptism has failed, but to the extent that Bertha is Jane's alter-ego and agent, the fire is Jane's as well, especially since she has already dreamed it. Rochester has hoped for a " 'final re-transformation from India rubber back to flesh' " (p. 116); this metamorphosis comes only when he has acknowledged the humanity of both Jane and Bertha. He realizes his crime in attempting to dupe Jane into a position which would cost her integrity and self-respect; and he realizes Bertha's humanity and her relationship to him to the extent that he risks his life to save her, the impediment to his happiness, whom more than anything he has wished dead.

Blind, Rochester can finally see the maternal moon that has watched over Jane—a significant enlargement of his perception. They both see it in its final appearance in the novel, on the night Jane refuses Rivers and hears Rochester's voice (pp. 369, 393). The illumination is at last mutual. The mutilation Rochester suffers is only in the most superficial sense a castration, as it is so often interpreted. It is indeed the loss of a certain kind of false masculinity, the kind that impedes humanity. Jane and Bertha bring Rochester what is for Charlotte Brontë the saving gift: suffering, enough to change India rubber to flesh, enough to tap the reserves of empathy that can admit him to the human family.

In the gypsy episode Jane looks at Rochester in his disguise, which we have already seen to resemble Bertha, and realizes that "her accent, her gesture, and all were familiar to me as my own face in a glass" (p. 177). Later she wakes in the night to see Bertha for the first time, as a reflection in a mirror,[12] dressed in white and wearing the veil, a demonic version of Jane, the secretly mad bride. At two important points in the novel—in the Red Room and on the morning of her wedding—Jane fails to recognize herself in the mirror. But she sees herself in these two others, and they in her. The three of them are deeply involved with each other, a three-way mirror reflecting a shared existence. Bertha is the catalyst in this delicate psychic chemistry. In her the anger, the madness, the sensuality, the suffering of Jane and Rochester meet. And fittingly, she is the critical agent in the redemption of both. Having acknowledged her, they can live, and she can die.

NOTES

1. Adrienne Rich, "Jane Eyre: The Temptations of a Motherless Woman," *Ms.* (October, 1973). Reprinted in *Lies, Secrets, and Silence* (New York: Norton, 1979), pp. 89–106. For other treatments of Bertha's warning role, see Richard Chase, "The Brontës, or Myth Domesticated," in *Forms of Modern Fiction*, ed. William V. O'Connor (Minneapolis: University of Minnesota Press, 1948), pp. 102–13; and Peter Grudin, "Jane and the Other Mrs. Rochester: Excess and Restraint in *Jane Eyre*," *Novel*, 10 (1977), 145–57.

2. Elaine Showalter, *A Literature of Their Own* (Princeton: Princeton University Press, 1977), pp. 118–22.

3. Charlotte Brontë, *Jane Eyre* (New York: Mershon, 1848), p. 293. Subsequent references come from this edition and will appear parenthetically.

4. Karen B. Mann, "Bertha Mason and Jane Eyre: The True Mrs. Rochester," *Ball State University Forum* 19, no. 1 (1978), 31–34.

5. Sandra M. Gilbert and Susan Gubar, *The Madwoman in the Attic: The Woman Writer and the Nineteenth Century Literary Imagination* (New Haven: Yale University Press, 1979), pp. 336–71.

6. Gilbert and Gubar, *Madwoman in the Attic*, p. 339.

7. Rich, "Jane Eyre," pp. 101–102.

8. Ibid., p. 103.

9. Showalter, *Literature of Their Own*, p. 120.

10. Gilbert and Gubar, *Madwoman in the Attic*, p. 360.

11. Ibid., p. 359.

12. Grudin, "Jane," 151.

10

Christina Rossetti: A Reconsideration

Robert N. Keane

Christina Rossetti has been regarded by many as Britain's finest poet, yet her work has seldom been studied for its own sake. During her lifetime she was hailed as "the Queen of the Pre-Raphaelites" by Edmund Gosse and "the Jael who led us to victory" by Algernon Swinburne, tributes suggesting that her poetry played a key role in the Pre-Raphaelite movement. Later Victorian critics presented her as a poet of nun-like piety whose lyrical talents made her the rival of Mrs. Browning as the leading woman poet of her time. Early twentieth-century critics embroidered on her reputation for disappointment in love and quiet piety *en famille*. More recent scholars have probed her poetry for a secret love affair or made her a champion of feminist creativity. In the last few years, however, there has been some movement toward studying her poetry for its own sake.

In the light of this new, healthier trend, it might be useful to point out some of the long-standing problems in Rossetti scholarship and to suggest some of the directions that future criticism may follow.

The first difficulty in studying Rossetti's work is in dealing with the widespread influence of her family on her life and writing. Throughout her days Christina was part of a close-knit family and protected by its members. As is often the way with Italian families, she was closest to her mother and sister, but she also shared the artistic interests of her brother and participated, in a peripheral fashion, in the activities of the Pre-Raphaelite Brotherhood. When she began to publish her poems commercially, Dante Gabriel served as advisor and illustrator. Later William Michael became her editor and continued so after her death. In fact, William is the fosterer and preserver of the literary reputations of all his family, notably his father, his brother, and his younger sister. William wrote biographies; edited letters, journals, and poems; and in general forwarded and protected his family's reputation. Though truthful, he is reserved and protective; what William says can generally be trusted, but what he does not say—and what he excised from the manuscripts he published—leaves ample room for conjecture.

Mackenzie Bell's life of Christina, written shortly after her death, is the work of a family friend assisted by William. The latter wrote a lengthy memoir of his sister as an introduction to his edition of her poetical works in 1904. Both biographies are honest and accurate but reveal little of the genius behind the poetry. The appreciative biographies by Cary (1900), Sandars (1930), and Zaturenska (1949) add nothing to the facts in Bell and William Rossetti. Only R. D. Waller's study of the *Rossetti Family* (1932) breaks any new ground.

William's editing of his sister's poetry is very perplexing. As modern scholars have noted, he altered the texts without explanation, did not offer variants, gave only the scantiest annotation, and chose to omit manuscript poems in his possession. His arrangement of the poems is also confusing. He starts with "Long Poems" and "Juvenilia" and then categorizes poems by subject matter, ending with "Italian Poems." Within each category he follows chronology but breaks this pattern to retain certain later volumes as published. Yet the poems in Christina's volumes of 1862, 1866, and 1881, her best-known books, are scattered among the categories. The effect of all this is to defeat an orderly reading of the poetry. Though William may have been a capable biographer and editor by Victorian standards, his work hardly meets the needs of modern scholarship.

The next problem in studying Rossetti and her work is presented by the major distortion woven into the chief modern biography, that by Lona Mosk Packer (1963). In a work of wide-ranging scholarship, Packer has vitiated her achievement by structuring her book around the thesis that Rossetti's work was inspired by her secret love for the poet-artist, William Bell Scott. Offering only circumstantial evidence, Packer bends every interpretation of the poetry toward her central theory, unbalancing her book and blocking out alternate interpretations.

Another difficulty in achieving a balanced view of Rossetti's work is presented by the new wave of feminist criticism. Seeking to redress the imbalance of centuries, feminist critics often overstate their case. Rossetti must certainly be understood in her role as a woman, and Jerome McGann's recent review in *Victorian Studies* makes valuable suggestions in this direction, but Rossetti hardly saw herself "as a fragile, vainly costumed lady, no ruler of nature at all but a tormented servant" as Sandra Gilbert and Susan Gubar portray her in *The Madwoman in the Attic*. In another extreme interpretation, some critics suggest that "Goblin Market" represents a rejection of male sexual subjection in favor of lesbian sisterhood.

In a more promising development, recent critics have inclined toward the careful study of Rossetti's texts without undue biographical emphasis. But to study the text, one must have a good text to work from. That need is being answered by the issuance of the first volume of a projected three-volume scholarly text of Rossetti's poetry by Rebecca W. Crump of Louisiana State University.[1] Crump presents the volumes as Rossetti first published them, starting with the

Goblin Market and *Prince's Progress* volumes of the 1860's. Unpublished poems and juvenilia will be placed in the third volume of the edition. Crump is also the editor of an edition of *Maude*, an early prose tale by Rossetti. Mention might also be made of Gwynneth Hatton's edition of the unpublished poems with extensive introduction and notes, a doctoral dissertation from St. Hilda's College, Oxford (1955). The availability of well-edited texts will give encouragement to the reconsideration of Rossetti's work on its own merits.

As the means become increasingly available, it is interesting to speculate on the direction that the re-evaluation of Rossetti's work might take. The prime need would seem to be a study of the writer's poetic craftsmanship. Essays by Nesca Robb (1948), C. M. Bowra (1949), Lionel Stevenson (1972), and others barely begin the task. A full-scale assessment of the poet's work is what is needed. This is not an easy undertaking since Rossetti produced over a thousand poems, most at a high level of competence on a narrow range of subjects with few long works as guideposts. The poet achieved her mature style by twenty and thereafter produced poems at a fairly regular rate. Thus the critic finds it hard to trace development or change in style as the poet's career progresses. One approach might be to categorize the poems by content and form. One might use such categories as love, seasons, death, religion, and children. But the difficulty with this system, as demonstrated by the 1904 *Works*, is that categories overlap: love with season, love with death, religion with death, and so on. However, the study of these overlaps shows Rossetti's cast of mind. Love is generally defeated by time as the fruitful seasons must eventually lead to winter and death. The realization of this fact leads on to religion as the only surety beyond the grave. Chronologically Rossetti wrote more secular poetry in the early part of her career and turned increasingly to religion in later years.

Rossetti's central motif is the impermanence of life's temporal cycle set against the final surety of Christianity's eternal cycle. Earth's seasons offer all too brief a span; spring all too soon ends in autumn and winter, whereas heaven's cycle begins with the autumn of life's unfulfillment but ends in the spring of God's salvation. The following lines from "If Only" superimpose the earthly and heavenly cycles as spring becomes the Easter of salvation:

> My tree of hope is lopped that spread so high;
> And I forget how Summer glowed and shone
> While Autumn grips me with its fingers wan,
> And frets me with its fitful windy sigh.
> When Autumn passes then must Winter numb,
> And Winter may not pass a weary while,
> But when it passes Spring shall flower again:
> And in that Spring who weepeth now shall smile,
> Yea, they shall wax who now are on the wane,
> Yea, they shall sing for love when Christ shall come.
>
> (*Works*, ed. Rebecca W. Crump, p. 181)

In the temporal cycle, spring is birth and death at the same time:

> There is no time like Spring that passes by,
> Now newly born, and now
> Hastening to die. (*Works*, p. 35)

By contrast winter may seem to be death, but his symbolism bodes forth life. In "The Months: A Pageant," the opening poem of her fourth volume of poetry, Rossetti presents a sequence of the months, ending with December who gleefully supplants a joyless November:

> Dimmest and brightest month am I;
> My short days end, my lengthening days begin;
> What matters more or less sun in the sky,
> When all is sun within? (*Poetical Works*, William Michael Rossetti, p. 54)

December then proceeds to deck the house for Christmas and concludes his song with:

> Then Spring her snowdrop and her violet
>   May keep, so sweet and frail;
>   May keep each merry singing bird,
> Of all her happy birds that singing build:
> For I've a carol which some shepherds heard
>   Once in a wintry field. (*Poetical Works*, pp. 54–55)

December makes it clear in this poem that Spring's new flowers represent but an evanescent joy whereas the Christmas child offers an eternal hope. But to earn this new life, man must learn to renounce the impermanent natural world. Any hope, such as earthly love, that puts its faith in the natural is doomed to the despair of nature's oncoming winter, as seen in "Fata Morgana" and "A Pause of Thought." The Eden of innocence is inexorably lost, as in "Shut Out," and man must come to terms with death.

The strongest tie on earth that draws man to the temporal is sexual love, the desire of individuals to share their feelings and propagate their kind. Rossetti's own experience with love would seem to have been unfulfilling, and her poetry emphasizes the defeat of love far more than its triumph as we see from the narrative poems. Often the bridal union is interrupted by a third party—a ghostly lover or a discarded love or even a sister—as in "The Hour and the Ghost," "Love from the North," "Maude Clare," "Cousin Kate," "Noble Sisters," and "Sister Maude." Or the lovers may fail one another as they do in "Jessie Cameron," "An Apple Gathering," and "The Prince's Progress." The lovers may have to look beyond this life as in "The Convent Threshold" and "Monna Innominata." The happy domesticity that ends "Goblin Market" is atypical of Rossetti's work, and critics have played down this seeming commitment to married felicity.[2] On the other hand, the temptation toward the goblin fruit of earthly love and sensual living is much more central to Rossetti's point of view.

Shorter poems often depict the lovers separated by the grave. Even Rossetti's well-known poem of fulfillment, "A Birthday," is followed in the *Goblin Market* volume by three poems on the death of love: "Remember," "After Death," and "An End," the last an allegory on the death of love himself:

> Love, strong as Death, is dead.
> Come, let us make his bed
> Among the dying flowers:
> A green turf at his head;
> And a stone at his feet,
> Whereon we may sit
> In the quiet evening hours. (*Works*, p. 38)

Many of these poems set forth the relationship of the dead beloved in the grave and the living lover, or would-be lover, above. In some instances, death proves the fidelity of love; in others the dead or dying beloved dismisses her lover and suggests that forgetting may be the best solution for both of them. Often, as in "Sound Sleep" and "Rest," no memory breaks the perfect sleep of death as Rossetti's maidens await the trumpet of judgment. Or the beloved may yearn to dream in death, thereby to relive what life has let pass by, as in these lines from "Echo":

> Yet come to me in dreams, that I may live
>   My very life again tho' cold in death:
>   Come back to me in dreams, that I may give
>   Pulse for pulse, breath for breath:
>   Speak low, lean low,
> As long ago, my love, how long ago. (*Works*, p. 46)

Rossetti's professedly religious poems center on Christ's generous suffering in his desire to redeem the wayward soul. The weak and fearful soul leans heavily on the Redeemer's superabundant mercy and aid. But salvation is not guaranteed, and the soul must endure a lonely battle against temptation, sin, and despair in a transitory world, waiting until the end comes and the heavenly vision is vouchsafed. No mystic like Emily Brontë, Rossetti clung to her faith through many trials.

Rossetti's powerful command of verbal rhythm is shown in the lines quoted from "Echo" and in the shifting cadences and sound orchestration of "Goblin Market." Primarily a lyric poet, Rossetti ranges ably across the standard meters, using a variety of stanza forms, line lengths, and rhyme schemes. While using iambic pentameter in sonnets and hexameter in a few poems, she favors tetrameter with trimeter for variation. She can follow a standard meter and then, when the mood of the poem calls for it, alter the metric movement, as she does in the final stanza of a poem on "Summer":

> Before green apples blush,
> Before green nuts embrown,
> Why, one day in the country
> Is worth a month in town;
> Is worth a day and a year
> Of the dusty, musty, lag-last fashion
> That days drone elsewhere. (*Works*, p. 143)

Though Rossetti's prevailing mood is melancholy or meditative, she has her lighter moments. A contrast to her melodramatic balladry is offered in the sprightly denial of " 'No, Thank You, John' " or the coy teasing of "Winter: My Secret." "I tell my secret? No indeed, not I," the speaker jests in the latter poem. The secret is private, or maybe there is no secret at all; and winter is no time for telling:

> Today's a nipping day, a biting day;
> In which one wants a shawl,
> A veil, a cloak, and other wraps:
> I cannot ope to every one who taps
> And let the draughts come whistling thro' my hall;
> Come bounding and surrounding me,
> Come buffeting, astounding me,
> Nipping and clipping thro' my wraps and all.
> I wear my mask for warmth: who ever shows
> His nose to Russian snows
> To be pecked at by every wind that blows?
> You would not peck? I thank you for good will,
> Believe, but leave that truth untested still. (*Works*, p. 47)

Thus, in a teasing mood, Rossetti uses winter as a symbol of the world's harshness and wraps herself for warmth in the clothing of poetic imagination. The cautious questioner is put off till a warmer season when:

> Perhaps my secret I may say,
> Or you may guess. (*Works*, p. 47)

The command of rhythm and symbol here bespeak Rossetti's mastery of her craft and her ability to adopt various moods.

Three other aspects of Rossetti's career need further study: her relationship to the Pre-Raphaelite movement, her place as a religious poet, and her position among other women poets of the century. While much has been made of Rossetti's love affairs, there has been no close study of her imaginative affinity with her brother, Dante Gabriel. The Rossetti children were part of a close family, and like the Brontës, they wrote stories and poems and drew pictures to illustrate this work. The three youngest were able poets by their mid-teens and often competed in writing sonnets to each other's rhyme words.

As a young artist will, Dante Gabriel used his family as models for his early sketches and paintings. Christina became his icon for purity and piety, and hers is the face of the Virgin Mary in his first two exhibition oils and many later works. For love in its profane modes, Dante Gabriel turned to Elizabeth Siddal, Fannie Cornforth, and Jane Morris. Significantly, Christina always kept aloof from these more earthly icons.

Christina shared in the Pre-Raphaelite Brotherhood by contributing poems to *The Germ*, the group's short-lived magazine. In the 1850's Dante Gabriel and his friends wrote and illustrated ballads; Christina quietly followed this trend on her own. Throughout their lives brother and sister shared a continuing interest in ballads and sonnets. Dante Gabriel's *House of Life* sonnet series bears interesting comparison to Christina's "Monna Innominata." The two poets often dwelt on the theme of separated lovers, but the parting for Dante Gabriel is that of earthly yearnings while Christina offers a more spiritual dimension. Yet the conclusion of "The Convent Threshold," after its striking heavenly vision, comes quite close to that of Dante Gabriel's "Blessed Damozel":

> If now you saw me you would say:
> Where is the face I used to love?
> And I would answer: Gone before;
> It tarries veiled in paradise.
> When once the morning star shall rise,
> When earth with shadow flees away
> And we stand safe within the door,
> Then you shall lift the veil thereof,
> Look up, rise up: for far above
> Our palms are grown, our place is set;
> There we shall meet as once we met
> And love with old familiar love. (*Works*, p. 65)

In this poem, as in "Echo" and many others, Christina almost seems to be commenting, by comparison and contrast, on her brother's poetry. Much of Christina's experience of the outer world comes through her association with her brother. Though Christina was never "the Queen of the Pre-Raphaelites," her works and face are part of the movement. Many of her poems contain strong pictorial imagery, and Pre-Raphaelite artists used both her poems and her face in their art. Her close connection with the movement and her brother in particular deserves thorough study.

Religion is at the core of most of Rossetti's work. She remained true to the Anglican faith of her mother and sister throughout her life, but lacking mysticism or simple piety, she struggled with a sense of her own unworthiness. Inwardly she was inspired by the Bible, books of prayer, and the religious poets of the sixteenth and seventeenth centuries; outwardly she followed her mother's High Anglicanism but stayed clear of Roman attractions. In later life she engaged in the activities of the Society for the Promotion of Christian Knowledge. Conrad

Festa and John O. Waller have recently studied some of the Anglican influences on her work, notably that of the Reverend William Dodsworth, and Jerome Bump has shown her influence on Gerard Manley Hopkins. But much more needs to be done in this direction.

Similarities between Rossetti and other female poets of her time have been pointed out by critics from the nineteenth century on. Mackenzie Bell discusses her in relation to Elizabeth Barrett Browning in his early biography. Both the Brownings were touchstones for the Pre-Raphaelites, and Rossetti herself suggests comparison to Barrett Browning in the headnote to "Monna Innominata." Morton Dauwen Zabel has compared her to Emily Dickinson, and others have suggested parallels to Emily Brontë. Feminist critics are drawing attention to Rossetti, and it is to be hoped that a balanced appraisal can be arrived at.

Christina Rossetti's work has received increasing attention in recent years, and Crump's edition of the poetry will greatly assist the poet's rising reputation. Though religion and family dominated Rossetti's life and work, her skill as a poet should take priority. In a sense, Christina Rossetti gave her life to her family, her soul to God, and bequeathed her poetical genius to the generations of mankind.

NOTES

1. The standard edition of the *Works* is being edited by Rebecca W. Crump for Louisiana State University Press; volume one was issued in 1979 and is used herein for most textual quotations. The fullest bibliography is by Crump, *Christina Rossetti: A Reference Guide* (New York: G. K. Hall, 1976). See also William Michael Rossetti, *The Poetical Works of Christina Georgina Rossetti* (London: Macmillan, 1904). See also William E. Fredeman, *Pre-Raphaelitism: A Bibliocritical Study* (Cambridge, Mass.: Harvard University Press, 1965). For a commentary on recent scholarship, see Jerome J. McGann, "Christina Rossetti's Poems: A New Edition and a Revaluation," *Victorian Studies*, 23 (Winter, 1980), 237–54.

2. Miriam Sagan, "Christina Rossetti's 'Goblin Market,' " *The Pre-Raphaelite Review*, III (May, 1980), 66–76. See also Germaine Greer's introduction to her edition of *Goblin Market* (New York: Stonehill, 1975); and, more recently, Dorothy Mermin, "Heroic Sisterhood in *Goblin Market*," *Victorian Poetry*, 21 (Summer, 1983), 107–18.

11

The Price of Love: Gaskell versus Eliot

Coral Lansbury

It is always tempting for women today to reach back and claim the famous women of the past as friends and allies, to see the same struggles being fought, and our present tragedies of a measure with their own. We seek continuity and we require that continuity to conform with our own sense of radical tradition. Yet, in many cases, this falsifies the condition of the past and distorts the circumstances of the present. For example, despite the admonitions of Elaine Showalter, it has recently become a critical commonplace to regard George Eliot as a feminist and a crusader for the rights of women. Felicia Bonaparte has stated in her recent work that "Eliot was a great feminist, and her novels, although they never stoop to mere propaganda, urge a relentless war against the conditions by which women's lives have been restrained and wasted."[1]

This is questionable. I would suggest instead that Eliot fully accepted the contemporary definition of woman's emotional nature and compounded this with an obsessional dread of the woman who deliberately chose a single life. When these attitudes are maintained by an extraordinary intellect with a determinist vision, the result is tragic paradox. It is rather like Karl Marx who averred that the quality he admired most in women was their weakness while holding to the ideal of an egalitarian society.

Women are born to love in Eliot's fictional world, but equally so, the woman does not exist who is neither diminished nor destroyed by love. Consider the evidence: Janet in *Janet's Repentance* (and let us pause to note how often repentance is to become a descriptive term for women who have sought love); Maggie Tulliver for whom love leads to death, Hetty Sorrel paying a savage price for love, Romola betrayed by love, Esther Lyon's sacrifice of a fortune in order to marry a poor man, and Dorothea, that finer and more spiritual Esther, who is given the choice between marriage and the power to accomplish great work in the world, and who dwindles into an unseen force for good as the wife of Will Ladislaw.

It is a mistaken assumption to see George Eliot as a radical nonconformist because she lived with George Henry Lewes without marriage lines. No one lamented her condition more than Eliot and insisted that she was indeed a conventional wife in all save legal and religious sanction. Her situation was dictated by circumstance, not choice. Certainly, it is unwise to draw parallels between Eliot and George Sand, who despised the institution of marriage. Eliot's acceptance of conventional marriage is revealed in the exchange between Eliot and Elizabeth Gaskell when the latter had just learned the identity of the author of *Scenes from Clerical Life*. Gaskell wrote with her customary frankness: "I never was such a goose as to believe that such books as yours could be a mosaic of real and ideal. I should not be quite true in my ending, if I did not say before I concluded that I wish you were Mrs. Lewes. However that can't be helped, as far as I can see, and one must not judge others."[2] George Eliot's response to this letter was remarkable. To their common friend, Barbara Bodichon, she wrote: "I have had a very beautiful letter from Mrs. Gaskell, and I will quote some of her words, because they do her honor, and will incline you to think more highly of her."[3] Far from being pained by Gaskell's bluntness, Eliot responded with unusual warmth, and with a sense of gratitude only equalled by her effusive thanks to her brother when he wrote to congratulate her on marrying John Cross. Isaac Evans had, of course, refused to acknowledge his sister's existence after she set up house with Lewes. George Eliot was happy to be the legal wife of John Cross and rejoiced in the marriage.

A distinction can be drawn here between Eliot and Gaskell. For Eliot, a heroine's acceptance of marriage entailed sacrifice, and often a subsequent repentance. And we must exclude here the Celias and Lucys and Tessas who are too stupid to know real pain, too worldly to experience spiritual loss. When Esther Lyon decides to marry Felix Holt, it is expressed in this fashion:

> There was something which she now felt profoundly to be the best thing that life could give her. But—if it was to be had at all—it was not to be had without paying a heavy price for it, such as we must pay for all that is greatly good. A supreme love, a motive that gives a sublime rhythm to a woman's life, and exalts habit into partnership with the soul's highest needs, is not to be had where and how she wills: to know that high initiation, she must often tread where it is hard to tread, and feel the chill air, and watch through darkness. It is not true that love makes all things easy: it makes us choose what is difficult. (Ch. 49)

There is here a conflation of mundane and spiritual love that would have offended both Gaskell's practical and religious temperament. Eliot's heroine renders supreme love to the man; Gaskell warns continuously against making an idol of any human being, reserving worship for God alone. The majesty of Eliot's language, resonant with Biblical cadence, too often conceals a certain blindness, shall we call it, "a spot of commonness" where love and marriage are concerned.[4]

Having had long experience as a wife and mother, Gaskell did not regard marriage as an idyllic state requiring a devotional disposition on the part of a woman. When Gaskell's heroine makes a good marriage, the head and heart are joined, rather like Margaret Hale deciding to marry John Thornton in *North and South*. Quite simply, she proposes to him in terms of a commercial transaction:

If you would take some money of mine, eighteen thousand and fifty-seven pounds, lying just at this moment unused in the bank, and bringing me in only two and a half percent.—you could pay me much better interest, and might go on working Marlborough Mills. (Ch. 52)

How different it is when Esther voluntarily gives up her share of the Transome estate, requesting a mere 200 pounds a year, in order to make Harold Transome a rejected but rich suitor, and Felix Holt a poor and happy husband.

It cannot be denied that George Eliot was a passionate and loving woman, but, like her heroines, she was always subject to the emotional domination of men. When she describes Philip Wakem in *The Mill on the Floss*, we are told that he was "by nature half feminine in sensitiveness, he had some of the woman's intolerant repulsion towards worldliness and the deliberate pursuit of sensual enjoyment" (bk. 5, ch. 3). This femininity is emphasized by Wakem's physical frailty—he is a cripple in effect. Eliot's women can never be accused of feeling like men, if only because they are more spiritual and sensitive. This is not the case with Gaskell—her women are often most admirable when they are least feminine in any conventional sense. The sharp Mr. Preston is reluctantly forced to admire Molly Gibson in *Wives and Daughters* when she calmly threatens him with blackmail—either he returns Cynthia's letters or she will take the whole story to Lady Harriet. It is the moment when he "perceived that Molly was . . . unconscious that he was a young man, and she a young woman" (ch. 44). Or Mary Barton ordering her lover Jem to leave her when she realizes that her father has returned to die, saying that she will send for him when she needs him, but not to approach the house until she gives him word. Again, there is the contrast between Tom Tulliver commanding his sister not to see Philip Wakem again, and her reluctant acceptance of his authority, and Gaskell's Maggie in *The Moorland Cottage* who will not give up her lover, even though it will save her brother Edward from a charge of forgery. Maggie Tulliver obeys her brother with the bitter reproach: " 'you are a man, Tom, and have power, and can do something in the world.' " To which Tom replies, " 'Then, if you can do nothing, submit to those that can' " (bk. 5, ch. 3). But not even a brother's threats of violence and a mother's tears can make Gaskell's Maggie reject the man she loves. She answers them both simply: " 'I cannot give up Frank,' said she in a low, quiet voice."

Mr. Browne threw up her hands, and exclaimed in terror—

"Oh, Edward, Edward! go away—I will give you all the plate I have; you can sell it—my darling, go!"

"Not till I have brought Maggie to reason," said he in a manner as quiet as her own, but with a subdued ferocity in it, which she saw, but which did not intimidate her. (Ch. 9)

There is no appeal to the ways of the world and society here, simply the conviction that it is often a woman's duty to deny the assumed moral authority of a man.

For a married woman Gaskell led an unusually independent life, traveling alone and taking charge of her own money. This was not the case with George Eliot, who tended to experience the world of emotion through men like her father and her brother, John Chapman, Dr. Brabant, Herbert Spencer, and George Henry Lewes. Intellectually she was free, prepared to debate every issue of the day, but emotionally she was bound to the customary view of woman's role in society.

Women must yield to male authority in Eliot's novels because they are incapable of resisting their sexual and emotional needs. Yet, this submission always involves a sense of pain and loss, and the pain becomes anguished when women like Romola and Dorothea seek spiritual as well as emotional fulfillment in a man. Because man is inherently flawed and society reflects that nature, Eliot's women struggle vainly to assert a spiritual ideal against masculine oppression. John Stuart Mill insisted that if women were given the vote, a new spirituality and purity of intention would shape politics and society. Eliot could not accept this optimistic view, for her society was too corrupt for redemption, and woman's spiritual strength would always be crippled by her sexuality. To Barbara Bodichon's distress she was opposed to women's suffrage and told Edith Simcox "that she cared for the womanly ideal, sympathized with women and liked for them to come to her in their troubles, but while feeling near to them in one way, she felt far off in another; the friendship and intimacy of men was more to her."[5]

The essential irony here is that Eliot was in her own self the denial of her stated opinions and her fictional women. Few of us, like Dr. Johnson, have the honesty of our own contradictions, and fewer still are ever aware of those contradictions. Eliot frequently said that it was woman's work to guide, to prepare, and show the way, but it would be men who completed the task and the journey. No woman, as she wrote in the prelude to *Middlemarch*, could find spiritual fulfillment and moral authority in contemporary society

for these later-born Theresas were helped by no coherent social faith and order which could perform the function of knowledge for the ardently willing soul. Their ardour alternated between a vague ideal and the common yearning of womanhood; so that the one was disapproved as extravagance, and the other condemned as a lapse.

It would seem then that Dorothea's tragedy was to be born in a time when it was futile for a woman to aspire to the role of St. Theresa. The very notion was as absurd as those aristocratic Victorian gentlemen pretending to be medieval knights and riding into the mud of the Eglinton Tournament. Spiritual aspiration in the Victorian woman relegated her to an historical anachronism, in Eliot's opinion. Herein lies the ambiguity and the sophistry in Eliot's vision of women.

When Eliot was writing *Middlemarch*, the world was still resounding to the name of a woman whose spirituality rivaled St. Theresa and whose practical social reforms were far more varied and extensive. That woman was Florence Nightingale, and for Elizabeth Gaskell she was a living saint. In a letter to Catherine Winkworth she described Nightingale as another St. Elizabeth of Hungary, a Joan of Arc, and her customary Yorkshire caution was swept up into a paean of praise: "I never heard of anyone like her—it makes one feel the livingness of God more than ever to think how straight He is sending His spirit down into her, as into the prophets and saints of old."[6]

George Eliot and Elizabeth Gaskell both met Florence Nightingale. Gaskell described a tall, dark-haired woman of great beauty and rare intellect who could be the model for Dorothea. But whereas Gaskell was rhapsodic in her praise of Nightingale's beauty and dedicated life, Eliot is reticent to the point of withdrawal. To Sara Hennell she wrote: "I had a note from Miss Florence Nightingale yesterday. I was much pleased with her. There is a loftiness of mind about her which is well expressed by her form and manner."[7] Gaskell recalled every detail of Nightingale's appearance down to the white drapery about her head and her black shawl, concluding that "you may get *near* an idea of her perfect grace and lovely appearance. She is like a saint."[8]

Of course, there was a price to be paid if a woman desired to move the world in the years before the Married Women's Property Act, and Gaskell knew it. A woman had to remain single if her money and her identity were not to be swallowed up by a man. If a woman desired a public life her sexuality had to be sublimated in her work. Nightingale was not so different from St. Theresa in this regard. This was the sacrifice Gaskell recognized in Nightingale's life and she paid tribute to it. She would not have anyone think of Nightingale as an old maid, a woman whose celibacy was imposed upon her by a lack of male regard. Rather, Gaskell took pains to note: "I believe there is no end to the offers she has had—for nine years Mr. M. Milne was at her feet, but Parthe says she never knew her to care for one man more than another in any way at any time."[9] Gaskell saw Nightingale as a solitary: "She has no friend—and she wants none. She stands perfectly alone, half-way between God and His creatures."[10] And to the end, Gaskell praised "this extraordinary creature" even though she felt a little chilled by Nightingale's singular dedication and sympathized with the family of ducks that had suddenly found a wild swan in their midst.

Eliot's reaction to the fame of Florence Nightingale was strange—it was almost as though she desired this remarkable woman to die, because her very existence confounded and disturbed some deep conviction she held about the nature of women. Even as Gaskell was writing in awe of Nightingale and naming her saint and genius, Eliot responded to a letter from Sara Hennell:

Thank you for sending me that authentic word about Miss Nightingale. I wonder if she would rather rest from her blessed labors, or live to go on working? Sometimes, when I read of the death of some great, sensitive human being, I have a triumph in the sense that they are at rest; and yet, along with that, such deep sadness at the thought that the rare nature is gone forever into darkness, and we can never know that our love and reverence can reach him, that I seem to have gone through a personal sorrow when I shut the book and go to bed.[11]

There are some extraordinary transpositions of gender and tone in this passage. Once dead, the Nightingale's "blessed labors" at an end, Eliot would then feel a sense of triumph, and, it should be noted that in the concluding lines Nightingale has become male and all is resolved into a closed book. The transition from life to art, mediated by Eliot's emotional response, is remarkable. Is there any need at this point to speak of women's fear of success and the efforts that so many women make to evade the responsibilities of success?

The Victorians accepted a single life as a prerequisite for the rare woman choosing public life. A single woman possessed authority and income that was denied a married woman. Far from seeing marriage as a woman's goal, Gaskell appreciated the diversity of women's natures. In her novels a woman is often most admirable when she refuses marriage. Poor Ruth in the novel of that name achieves a measure of dignity when she rejects Bellingham's proposal, even though the marriage would give her instant respectability and legitimize her child. Eliot could never accept this. There is a point in *Middlemarch* when Dorothea finds herself a widow possessed of a great fortune and the opportunity to work for the new hospital in Middlemarch. But Dorothea, who resembles Nightingale physically and contemplates a similar career, chooses instead to marry Will Ladislaw. And with that marriage, love is satisfied but the money and all the good it can do is sacrificed. "Her finely-touched spirit had still its fine issues, though they were not widely visible. Her full nature, like that river of which Cyrus broke the strength, spent itself in channels which had no great name on the earth" (finale). Surely the language here cannot conceal the futility and despair of this statement. And who is Cyrus in Dorothea's life? Is the man who can break the course of a mighty river Will Ladislaw, or is it the transference of women's frailty to an assumed male dominance.

Gaskell appreciated that not only could a woman live alone; women could also live together in rich contentment. Cranford is a utopia of women, and elderly women at that. This vision of women is given depth in *The Gray Woman* where two women become husband and wife and care for a child. Amante is not a Rosalind, a woman masquerading as a man; she is husband and father, protector and friend. Eliot could never see beyond the authority of men to a condition of society where women need not be sacrificed for love. The sustaining friendship of women was alien to her nature and reluctantly she confessed to Barbara Bodichon: "Yes. Women can do much for the other women (and men) to come. My impression of the good there is in all unselfish efforts is continually strengthened. Doubtless many a ship is drowned on expeditions of discovery or rescue, and precious freights lie buried. But there was the good of manning and furnishing the ship with a great purpose before it set out."[12]

Always the emphasis upon preparation, not conclusion, on the aspiration and never the goal. Yet, by her own work, Eliot confounded all these intimations of weakness. Society was moved by her writing, and her novels helped to shape a new fictional universe. She possessed the intellect of a philosopher and the language of her poet, but throughout her life she professed a view of women that was essentially commonplace. It is not the first occasion, and it will not be the last, when a woman has undervalued herself and her sex in the market of the world.

NOTES

1. Felicia Bonaparte, *Will and Destiny Morality and Tragedy in George Eliot's Novels* (New York, 1975), p. viii.

2. J.A.V. Chapple and Arthur Pollard, eds., *The Letters of Mrs. Gaskell* (Manchester, 1966), p. 592.

3. Gordon S. Haight, ed., *The George Eliot Letters* (New Haven: Yale, 1954–78), III, p. 226.

4. For example, whereas Gaskell warns against devotion and the worship of any individual, Eliot argues that a woman's devotion for a man is too often tarnished by feminine capriciousness. Thus in "Westward Ho! And Constance Herbert," *Westminster Review* LXIVC (July, 1855), reprinted in *Essays of George Eliot*, ed. Thomas Pinney (New York, 1963), pp. 135–36, Eliot states: "We are inclined to think that it is less frequently devotion which alienates men, than something infused in the devotion—a certain amount of *exigeance*, for example, which, though given in small doses, will, if persevered in, have a strongly alterative effect."

5. *George Eliot Letters*, I, p. 299.

6. *Letters of Mrs. Gaskell*, p. 307.

7. *George Eliot Letters*, I, p. 206.

8. *Letters of Mrs. Gaskell*, p. 306.

9. Ibid., p. 320.

10. Ibid., p. 319.

11. *George Eliot Letters*, II, p. 61.

12. Ibid., VI, 290.

12

A Second Look at *The Belle*

Howard N. Meyer

The one-person play, *The Belle of Amherst*, subtitled "A Play Based on the Life of Emily Dickinson," opened April 28, 1976, and was a success on Broadway. The performance of Julie Harris was an acting tour-de-force and gave credibility to the playwright's portrait sketch. Public Television perceived a ready-made subject for mass culture and taped a performance that was a hit when first telecast (December 29, 1976) and that will be repeated from time to time.

The play consisted of a narrative in which the actress, taking the audience into her confidence, as it were, described in random order some highlights of the poet's life and a good deal of her daily routine. There were also brief and pretended (we hear only one side) dialogues with a variety of persons. Part of the play was based on excerpts from her letters, part on some of the poems, and part invented by playwright William Luce. The whole was well received by the public and most of the critics.

Differences in biographical interpretation are not unusual. One of Emily Dickinson's principal biographers, Richard B. Sewall, ruefully admitted, "The whole truth about Emily Dickinson will elude us always." A revival and broadening of the interest in the work of a poet of rare genius is commendable. But distortions deliberately contrived for dramatic effect that cheapen her character and defame a neglected American hero go beyond the bounds of artistic license.

To give the play a semblance of dramatic structure—and to generate a bit of audience excitement—a particular event is chosen as central and crucial. The conventions of creation of tension in the first act and its resolution in the second

The author appreciates the instigation of Anna Mary Wells and Tillie Olsen and suggestions from Ms. Wells.

are observed by building up to and supposedly showing what happened at and after Emily Dickinson's meeting with Thomas Wentworth Higginson in 1870.

This was, in fact, an event of significance in the sense that it furnished the occasion for the best first-hand description of the poet as a person. This was left us by Higginson, to whom she sent letters over a period of two dozen years that have been an invaluable source for every biographer—a source, indeed, for many of the lines of the play, though neither the program nor the 1976 published version credits Higginson.

There could not have been a falser rendition of the prelude to and content of this meeting than that given by Mr. Luce. The play is wholly untrue in its depiction of the object and nature of the encounter; quite unfair in the creation of a stuffy "Professor Higginson," shown as unconditionally and devastatingly discouraging in his verdict on her work, a verdict supposedly sought and given by virtue of his authority as editor of the *Atlantic Monthly*.

To attempt to give full credit to Thomas Wentworth Higginson as a neglected American hero is beyond the scope of this chapter. But it is important to record at the outset that he never was a "professor" of anything anywhere. One cannot discern any object in the invention of the title save to appeal to the average American middle-brow audience's latent anti-academic hostility. Nor was he ever editor of the *Atlantic*, with authority to accept or reject anything. He was a frequent and valued contributor in the periodical's early years. He was a "freelance," as Moncure Conway said,[1] and not only as a writer; he was one, in the original sense of the phrase: a brave and independent spirit whose lance was at the ready to serve every cause he deemed to be worthy.

That these were the crucial causes of the nineteenth century, abolitionism, feminism, environmentalism, anti-imperialism, is extremely relevant to his friendship with Emily Dickinson. It was because of his writings and his well-known activism in these spheres that she (who from other evidence can be characterized as a kind of radical recluse), chose him to be her pen pal, her audience, the sounding board for her verse, a comrade with whom she could commune in her self-chosen isolation from a community with whose inhabitants she chose not to mix.

There had been eight years of friendly and intimate intercourse by correspondence that preceded that 1870 meeting at Amherst. Its service to her morale was such that she described it as having saved her life. The meeting itself had the value, if we accept her own metaphor, of a blood transfusion. In writing to thank him for coming she said: "The vein cannot thank the artery, but her solemn indebtedness to him, even the stolidest admit, and so of me who try, whose effort leaves no sound."[2]

That meeting was followed by a continued correspondence that ended only with her death. After a second visit in December, 1873, she wrote to thank him and to send a New Year's gift. He replied, "Each time we seem to come together as old and tried friends; and I certainly feel that I have known you long and well, through the beautiful thoughts and words you have sent me. I hope you vill not cease to trust me and to turn to me; and I will try to speak the truth to ou and with love."[3]

When she passed away, Colonel Higginson (as he was known to the public or his brief career as leader of the first regiment of black ex-slaves permitted o fight for their own people's freedom), was called by the family to deliver the ulogy. He was then pressed into service to find a publisher willing to put some of her poetry, posthumously controlled by a family to whom she had been eluctant to entrust it, into print. This service he cheerfully and successfully performed, though his own publisher, Houghton, Mifflin (who, ironically, published Luce's play), declined.

Nothing that has been sketched in the previous paragraphs is to be found in *The Belle of Amherst*, nor even hinted at. It served the purpose of the playwright o set up Higginson solely as the target of a scheming, ambitious Emily, plotting only to manipulate the 1870 meeting as a stepping stone to publication and then o fame. It is intolerable to one who knows the facts—even as little as can be found in her own letters to him—to hear the Julie Harris version of Emily Dickinson say, in the syllables of 1950's teenage talk, "When he reads my poems, won't he go wild?"[4] and "I want him to see that I'm different. Not just a country poetess sending little verses to the city editor—but really inspired!"[5]

As false as the Act I prelude is to Emily Dickinson's nature (and to the pre–1870 correspondence with Higginson), is the Act II version of the sisters scheming for the meeting and the dialogue (we hear Emily's supposed side only), at the meeting itself. We have Higginson's record of the meeting, confirmed by her letters; it is necessary to say that it is sheer invention as presented in the play and while it is false and unfair to Higginson, it is even worse, demeaning and degrading to have her say to him

Why has it taken eight years? O, I know you've been so busy. And then, you *were* away in the—the war—the *Civil* War, wasn't it? . . .

But now, to the real purpose of your visit! I've been waiting to hear from your own lips—what you are planning for my poems.[6]

Then, after the out-of-character stage direction, "Emily shuffles through many more papers, spilling some on the floor and scrambling to pick them up,"[7] she is made to say as she thrusts one poem at her visitor:

It wasn't what I would have chosen. But perhaps for publication, it's more appropriate—more appealing to the reading public. Now I have many more . . . over a thousand you've never read! Enough for several volumes I should think. Oh, and I prefer morocco-bound.[8]

And so on, culminating in another false-to-life stage direction from which we learn of his response: "Emily finally sits back. Then slowly, she leans forward. What she is hearing from Higginson is shocking. Her mouth falls open. She clutches the arms of the chair"[9] and protesting, conveys to us the dimensions of his supposed condemnation. Then, as the stage direction once more prompts, she "stops, her hand is midair. She is crushed."[10]

Then, so that the audience shall not underestimate the gravity of the offense falsely imputed to Higginson by Luce, she turns, and is made to recite a poem which was in fact, written in response to a completely different occasion:

> A great Hope fell
> You heard no noise
> The Ruin was within . . . [11]

Short of quoting the full length version of what really took place, the readiest refutation is found in the words of two scholarly biographers, neither a partisan of Higginson. Thomas H. Johnson, later to edit the definitive Belknap edition of *The Poems of Emily Dickinson* (1955), wrote, in his biography, of the meeting, "His coming had allowed her to discharge the greatest debt of gratitude she was ever to feel and her letters to him thereafter are without urgency though their relative number during the remaining fifteen years of their correspondence greatly multiplies." And Richard B. Sewall, the biographer most complete, observed that her sister

Vinnie's remark that Emily was always on the lookout for the rewarding person, by whom she meant someone who could listen without apparent bewilderment and respond approximately in kind, applied to a very few people. . . . Certainly Higginson, from Emily's point of view, must have been one of the most rewarding.

It is a great pity that not one dramatic critic had enough education to soundly criticize this distortion of our literary history. Too bad that when published, plays are not reviewed, as books are (or should be) by persons who know something of the subject. Higginson, in oblivion still, after two decades in which the militancy he stood for in favor of justice in race relations, and the fight for feminism that he helped launch were both revived, can afford to sustain the slight inflicted on him. But the picture of Emily Dickinson as a scheming exhibitionist, a kind of Mailer or Capote-type of individual, is so intolerable that one shudders to read it and regrets that it will be heard over and over again.

NOTES

1. Moncure Daniel Conway, *Autobiography: Memories and Experiences* (Boston and New York: Houghton, Mifflin Co., 1904), I, p. 277.

2. Thomas Wentworth Higginson, *Carlyle's Laugh and Other Surprises* (Boston and New York: Houghton, Mifflin Co., 1909), p. 276 (originally published in *Atlantic Monthly*, October, 1891).

3. Thomas H. Johnson and Theodora Ward, eds., *The Letters of Emily Dickinson*, 3 vols. (Cambridge, Mass.: The Belknap Press of Harvard University Press, 1958), II, p. 519.

4. William Luce, *The Belle of Amherst* (Boston: Houghton, Mifflin Co., 1976), p. 39.
5. Ibid., p. 38.
6. Ibid., p. 46.
7. Ibid.
8. Ibid., p. 47.
9. Ibid., p. 48.
10. Ibid.
11. Ibid.

13

'Michael Field' (Edith Cooper and Katherine Bradley) and Their Male Critics

David J. Moriarty

'Michael Field' is the pseudonym used by Edith Cooper and Katherine Bradley, whose unique collaboration amounts to a staggering twenty-five "tragedies," a masque, and eight volumes of verse. In addition, the British Museum collection contains a number of unpublished manuscripts, extensive correspondence, and detailed journals, excerpts of which have been edited and published under the title *Works and Days* by Sturge Moore.[1] Male critics, inclined to note prolific nineteenth-century men writers, regardless of their talents, have ignored or misrepresented these two women more often than not, but what is as disconcerting, feminist critics have ignored them as well, despite the fact that they worked in a genre which is, even today, dominated by men as critics, writers, and producers. Without question Katherine Bradley's and Edith Cooper's experience serves as a protocol for the rediscovery of not only the nineteenth-century woman writer, but all those writing against the accepted societal and cultural grain.

Katherine (b. 1846) and her niece Edith (b. 1862) were born sixteen years apart in the mid-nineteenth century into prosperous Birmingham merchant families, which allowed them the means and the leisure time to pursue their writing, in addition to providing them access to the limited opportunities available to the women of that time for higher education, without which their collaboration would have been impossible.

Neither woman had an early formal education, but Katherine, who acted as her niece's companion and tutor during Edith's formative years, managed to attend the summer session at Newnham College and to go abroad briefly to study at the College de France in Paris, where a love affair with a French friend's brother came to an abrupt end at his untimely death, an experience that propelled Katherine into a state of moral and religious confusion. Upon her return to England, she sought out the counsel of John Ruskin, whose "religion of art"

was appealing to those many Victorians afflicted with a similar sense of dou
in such matters.

In the lengthy correspondence between the two that ensued, Katherine a
dresses Ruskin reverentially as "Master,"[2] while Ruskin's salutations progre
from being detached and formal to a more familiar and patronizing addres
revelatory of his attitude toward women. For example, Ruskin's initial lette
begin "My Dear Madam," but this immediately becomes "Dear Miss Bradley,
then "My Dear Miss Bradley" and "Dear Miss Catherine [sic]." Indeed, thoug
Ruskin was clearly impressed by her letters and continued the corresponden
regularly over many months, eventually welcoming her as a "companion"
the Guild of St. George, a society founded by Ruskin to foster his eccentr
economic ideas, his intimacy betrays a patriarchal stance and a refusal to tre
Katherine as an adult and an equal. There are many examples of this attitude
the letters. After Katherine had sent him a copy of her first volume of lyric
The New Minnesinger (1876), Ruskin responded, "Some of the best poetry
modern times is by women (Mrs. Browning, Miss Ingelow, Miss Proctor)" b
teasingly undercut this a few days later with, "How much too serious my li
is to be spent in reading poetry (unless prophetic). But I did accidently open tl
Minnesinger and liked a bit or two of it—and I don't think I threw it into tl
wastepaper basket." Finally, when Katherine admitted to reading some contem
porary "atheistic" philosophers, Ruskin's attitude toward women, an attitud
Edith was to characterize years later as "a speckled silliness" (*WD*, p. 115
comes to the fore as he replies lividly, "you must be called a false disciple. . .
When you called me master—I understood that if in anything you would obe
me . . . in the choice of books." Calling Katherine "too stupid" and "a doubl
feathered little goose" for reading "these miserable modern wretches," Ruski
concluded his letter of December 28, 1877, with a bizarre yet revealing imag

Suppose a child whom I had sent on a perfectly safe road, deliberately jumped off in
a ditch—wallowed there with the pigs without telling me—got torn by their tusks—an
then came to me all over dung and blood—saying, "I didn't care"—what could I do
or say?

Katherine's independent choice of reading matter had severed the master
disciple relationship, and Ruskin, in another letter two days later, sternly e
communicated her from the Guild, "I have at once to put you out of the S
George's Guild—which *primarily* refuses atheists—not because they are wicke
but because they are fools," and although Ruskin had tempered his tone but n
his attitude when, in another letter less than a fortnight later, he advised, "giv
up all metaphysical reading at present, be content with history—poetry," th
correspondence soon ceased.

In 1878 when the two women went to Bristol to study the classics and ph
losophy at University College, they championed such causes as antivivisectio
and women's rights in the Debating Society and adopted the style of the Ne

Woman, aesthetic, colorful, freely flowing, at a time when corsets and bustles were the conventional fashion.[3] Because of their "careless hair and untidy feet," a Mary Sturgeon's phrase (*Michael Field*, p. 22), they were fascinating figures or those at Bristol, and yet their close personal relationship excluded intimacy with others, a seclusion to be maintained throughout the rest of their lives. It was at Bristol that the women made the decision to live together and collaborate in their art for the remainder of their days, a decision formalized in a dedicatory poem written when Edith was seventeen and Katherine thirty-two. According to Sturgeon, the poem is an exchange of marriage vows,[4] a promise to unite as poets and lovers against the conventional world, "The world was on us, pressing sore; / My love and I took hands and swore, / Against the world, to be / Poets and lovers evermore, / . . . Indifferent to heaven or hell." The radical mission the women set for themselves in the poem is reinforced by the form, since it is an extreme variation of that most conventional of forms, the sonnet.

During the 1880's, after a period of extensive travel in Germany and Italy, the women returned to Bristol and published over the next few years a series of poetic dramas based upon legendary and historical matter. The accession to Ruskin's counsel to concentrate on history and poetry is only apparent here, since each of these plays contains, hidden beneath the historical veneer, a contemporary and feminist message, often inspired by their reading of the "miserable modern wretches" like Nietzsche.[5]

For example, *Callirrhoe* (1884), received with much critical acclaim (*MF*, p. 17), though based on an ancient Greek legend quite clearly reveals the influence of Nietzsche's *Birth of Tragedy* as it contrasts the conflict between the Apollonian concept of rational order and what Nietzsche saw as the more modern idea, Dionysian rage, madness, and self-destruction (*MF*, p. 31). It was in the legend of Callirrhoe that the women also found a precise metaphor for their mission as tragic poets in the mad priestesses, the Maenads, who officiated at the Dionysian rites.[6]

The volume drew the notice of Robert Browning, and the women wrote divulging their true identities, Edith explaining to Browning in a letter of May, 1884, the unique nature of their collaboration, describing *Callirrhoe* as "like a mosaic work—the mingled, various product of our two brains. . . . if our contributions were disentangled and one subtracted from the other, the amount would be almost even."[7] Katherine, writing a few months later, in a letter dated November 7, 1884, cautioned Browning to keep their identities secret: "we have many things to say that the world will not tolerate from a woman's lips. We must be free as dramatists to work out in the open air of nature—exposed to her vicissitudes, witnessing her terrors: we cannot be stifled in drawing-room conventionalities" (*WD*, p. 6).

Browning, with good intentions, promoted their work and announced in public at a dinner party in the spring of 1885, attended and reported on by Arthur Symons, in his article "Michael Field," "I have found a new poet."[8] Symons's own curiosity about this 'Michael Field' was aroused, and though he did not meet the women until years later, he almost immediately wrote a favorable review of their work, pronouncing *Callirrhoe* a play that proved them genuine poets. On their most recent volume, containing *The Father's Tragedy* (1885), Symons concluded "that it gave one a sense of the outraged Earth" (Symons, p. 1585). *The Father's Tragedy*, a play that turns upon the generational clash between father and son, Symons succinctly described as "literally the father's annihilation" (Symons, p. 1591), a correct assessment of the work, which calls for an end to patriarchal tyranny and for mutual love and understanding between the generations.[9]

The attentions of the likes of Browning and Symons had uncovered the secret of 'Michael Field,' and when it became generally known that it was Katherine and Edith who were writing these plays with themes "the world will not tolerate from a woman's lips," not surprisingly, their subsequent work received more hostile scrutiny (*MF*, p. 29 and *WD*, p. xvi). The first to feel the conventional critics' wrath was *Brutus Ultor* (London: G. Bell and Sons, 1886), a play couched in the familiar Shakespearian form and delineating the struggle between the noble Brutus, champion of freedom and "the outraged Earth," and the evil Sextus, the aptly named, tyrannical and misogynistic rapist of the piece, which ironically was intended for a wider audience than the previous plays (*MF*, p. 118) and which contains a more overt feminist message.

For example, the conflict between the protagonist and antagonist is almost coincidental to a discussion of the role of women in the revolutionary process as the idea of women's fulfillment in motherhood is challenged in favor of women's active participation in the overthrow of tyrannous convention. Brutus is eulogized at the close because he has recognized women's potential beyond motherhood: "He felt the wrongs / Of women as they'd natures of their own / And use beyond child-bearing" (*BU*, p. 76).

The next play, *Canute the Great* (1887), despite the nominal male main character, is most notable for a rather explicit love scene between two women, which forms the core of the drama (Act III, scene iii),[10] and this theme of lesbian love is integral to *Long Ago* (1889), a volume of lyrics in imitation of Sappho.[11] Although the life experience of Katherine and Edith is sufficient to explain their interest in the poetess of Lesbos, Sappho was a fascinating figure for many during the *fin de siècle*. Indeed, a cult of Lesbos had developed at this time, one aspect of a general interest in sexual inversion at the close of the last century,[12] but since most of the followers of this cult were male, the lesbian is most often treated merely as a vehicle for male fantasies.

One must be aware of this to understand Arthur Symons' vehement objections to this work. Symons, one of the instigators of the Decadent Movement in England, found the poems too chaste, "enfeebled by alterations, . . . colorless and bloodless" (Symons, p. 1590). Though Symons admitted that Edith and Katherine had "at their finest, . . . something fierce, subtle, strange, singular— which can become sinister" (Symons, p. 1587), in other words "decadent," the women never regarded their love as such. What is strange is that Symons, inding nothing decadent in these love lyrics, chose to denigrate them on false grounds. Calling the work a "sacreligious [*sic*] attempt . . . on the unsurpassable genius of Sappho" (Symons, p. 1589), Symons objected because "What they actually did was to take a few lines from the Greek of Sappho; then attempt to translate those lines; then to add variations on these themes of their own inventing" (Symons, p. 1589). This last aspect is what most disturbs Symons, that the women used Sappho's poetry as a departure point to examine "themes of their own inventing," based on their personal experience, rather than limiting themselves to translating the Greek lyrics, which leads Symons to absurdly suggest that Swinburne had come nearer to the essence of lesbian love because he had limited himself to a close translation of Sappho's Greek and had striven "to cast his spirit into the mould of [Sappho]."[13]

The plays the women wrote during the 1890's, from what Symons calls "their second dramatic period—when they were almost ignored—when they came to a certain extent into contact with the so-called Decadent Movement,"[14] are among their most significant. Upon close examination they can hardly be termed decadent, and yet Symons persisted in his attempt to make the women conform to the decadent mythology, which requires that the artist be "almost ignored," ignored by the general public while admired by the chosen few.[15]

The Tragic Mary (London: G. Bell and Sons, 1890), for example, warrants comparison with Swinburne's treatment of Mary Stuart in his *Bothwell*, in which the character is studied as a decadent witch woman. 'Michael Field,' on the other hand, draws Mary Stuart with a sympathy that humanizes the character, stripping away the symbolic overtones of the *femme fatale* image and allowing the reader to examine Mary as the queen held captive—a figure that recurs often in their dramas.[16] The reality is that Mary, like Shaw's St. Joan, is exploited and finally abandoned by her abusers, becoming the exemplum of the politically exploited woman. This is the tragic irony of the character for the women, not, as it is for Swinburne, that Mary loses her lover Bothwell. Oscar Wilde recognized this when he wrote to the women, "Your queen is a splendid creature, a live woman to her finger tips. I feel the warmth of her breath as I listen to her. She seems closer to flesh and blood than the Mary of Swinburne's *Bothwell*."[17]

Stephania, a Trialogue (London: Elkin Mathews and John Lane, The Bodley Head, 1892) is significant on two counts: first, the "trialogue" form and simple suggestive language closely resembles that used by the Flemish symbolist, Maeterlinck, for his innovative *Pelleas et Melisande*,[18] published in the same year, making *Stephania* one of the first examples of a *genuine* symbolist drama produced in England; second, the main character is again without the extremes of idealization and / or harlotry with which the decadents, in their misogynistic vision, usually associated the *femme fatale*.[19] The point of the play is to expose the reality that the symbolic role of the temptress is not congenial to women. Indeed, as Stephania observes, it can be a rather tedious burden:

> O God, how tedious is the harlot's part,
> The mimic vanity, the mimic rage,

The waiting upon appetite! I loathe
My gems, my unguents, all the fragrant lights
I scatter on my hair. To dress for him,
To garnish infamy, to give one's face
The vermeil of a flower! I have such need
Of rest, to lay the cerecloth over him!
A lethargy falls on me like a hell
Pressed inward—ah, I have such need of sleep,
The Change, the peace! (*Stephania*, p. 91)

A *Question of Memory*, performed at the Opera Comique in London on the evening of October 27, 1893, was a singular event in the women's lives. Not only is it their one "realistic" prose drama and their only play produced on stage, but it is the only drama in which the women employed a relatively contemporary setting and common, rather than noble, characters, making it an important departure from the rest of their canon. Staged under the auspices of J. T. Grein's Independent Theatre, which was formed to offer the audience drama not available in the commercial theaters of the day,[20] this play is one of the mere handful of native-born dramas presented by the Independent, a fact that illustrates both the uniqueness of A *Question of Memory* and the bankrupt condition of the British drama at the time.

By employing a stream of consciousness prose for the dialogue, as well as an unconventional ending, where two men and a woman decide to live together, the women upset the critics accustomed to stock dialogue, characters, and the conventional resolution of the common melodramatic fare, and the reviews were either unenthusiastic or patronizing, causing Edith to record in the journal, "We wake to the surprise of finding every morning paper against us. . . . The evening papers are worse than the morning. They are like a lot of unchained tigers. We are hated, as Shelley was hated, by our countrymen, blindly, ravenously" (*WD*, pp. 181–82).

The review which appeared in the *London Times* is one of the milder ones. After noting the women's inexperience in "the practical work of the stage," and that the work was unfit for the ordinary theater—strange criticism when one considers the number of women whose plays were performed on stage during the nineteenth century—the *Times* critic continues, "there is a deal of excellent material in it of a somewhat inchoate description, and on the part of the Independent Theatre, . . . its production was a wise measure."[21]

William Archer, credited with popularizing Ibsenism in England, and a critic usually open to the "new drama," began his review as the *Times* critic had ended his, with praise not directed at the women for their daring play, but at the Independent for producing it: "The Independent Theatre would have been false to its mission had it refused its hospitality to such a singular piece." Then Archer went on to express his reservations:

The authors . . . write a curious short-winded prose. . . .

. . . In the first, second, and fourth acts there is scarcely a single natural sequence of thought, feeling, and expression. The dialogue is always flying off at unexpected tangents, and trying to obtain subtlety by means of incoherence. The authors have observed, quite justly, that feeling *is* incoherent—or rather, that consciousness is like a swirling stream, in which the unexpected and apparently irrelevant objects are always floating to the surface for a moment and then disappearing again, in obedience to laws which we can not formulate. . . . Dialogue . . . is not the dialogue of life, but a world evolved from the playwright's inner consciousness.

Archer has defined the stream of consciousness style well, but he has missed the significance of this experiment in adapting it for the drama because he has been conditioned by his taste for Ibsen to expect "the dialogue of life," realistic dialogue, in a play with realistic setting and based on a real occurrence. Archer cannot be excused, however, for his concluding remarks on the unconventional ending— "there is an idea concealed in the . . . casuistry of the last act; but I own it eluded me,"[22]—since anyone familiar with Ibsen's plays should be aware that it was with precisely such "casuistic situations" that he often ended his dramas in order to shock the audience's conventional expectations.

A Question of Memory was beset with problems even before its performance, when friction developed in rehearsals between Acton Bond, the male lead, and the producer, Herman de Lange. As Alice Grein, wife of the theater group's founder, reconstructs the situation, this personality conflict was so severe that the production was in jeopardy, and the women, without any experience in mounting a stage production, were caught in the middle, but when de Lange recommended drastic, and perhaps warranted, alterations in the script, the women resisted and found themselves allied with Bond, at which point Grein himself had to step in to prevent the situation from completely deteriorating.[23]

Grein played his own part in compromising the play's potential for success by choosing François Coppee's *Le Pater* as the second play on the bill. Obsessed with the idea of presenting a play in a foreign language with an English cast, Grein insisted on Coppee's French verse drama, even though, as Alice Grein points out (J. T. Grein, *The Story of a Pioneer*, p. 134), "There was admittedly a justification in the complaint of Michael Field, who feared that the impression on the audience might be weakened by repetition" (both plays containing a climactic scene that involved a shooting). Grein's only concession was to place the women's play first on the program, a departure from the practice of presenting the major production after the curtain raiser, so that their shooting might occur first. According to Alice Grein, "The evening ended with cheers not unmixed with hisses" (pp. 135–36), many of which were directed at the Coppee play that the *Times* critic, quoted above, dismissed tersely and disapprovingly as "on a communistic theme." Given the entire experience, neither Katherine nor Edith, as Alice Grein notes, "were concerned in writing another play for the stage" (p. 136).

The women reverted, instead, to writing closet dramas, with remote historical settings, yet not without contemporary overtones. *Attila, My Attila* (London: Elkin Mathews, 1896) is the first of a series of plays set during the decadence of the Holy Roman Empire.[24] A good part of the play is set in Byzantium, which was associated in *fin de siècle* mythology with the corrupt aristocratic order of the nineteenth century, ripe to be swept away by the invading barbarians, who with their destruction will bring liberation and a new order.[25]

Philippe Jullian, yet another critic who tries to claim the women as decadents, regards this play, along with Yeats's Byzantium poems, as fine examples of the Byzantine style, a style which he points out was popularized by Sarah Bernhardt in various roles that he claims capture "the crimes and splendours of Byzantium."[26] Indeed, the women note in their journal that "Honoria was conceived with Sarah Bernhardt before us all the while."[27]

Honoria, the main character of the play, is, like Byzantium, where East intersects with West, an identity of opposites. She is, in fact, a very contemporary type, that of the "New Woman," which began to emerge in real life and on the stage during the 1890's. The women have cleverly transposed this type from the symbolic intellectual and aesthetic decadence of the late nineteenth century to its source, the last days of the Roman Empire. As they indicate in their preface to the play, "Honoria [who] sought to give freedom to her womanhood by unwomanly audacities . . . [is the] New Woman of the 5th century."[28]

Honoria, of patrician birth, rebels against the boring prospects her status has in store for her, seduces one of the household slaves, and finds herself a pregnant teenager. Upon discovery of her condition, the family is shocked, primarily because she has stooped to the level of a common slave as a means to liberation. The child is done away with; the slave is banished to the salt mines, and Honoria is sent off to the relatives in Byzantium.

The second act begins fourteen years later and reads like a latter-day suburban housewife's nightmare as Honoria, now a mature woman, has been held captive by the relatives through the intervening time, but during this period, she has conjured another fantasy of escape, fantasizing that Attila, that Third World force, will liberate her. The play ends fraught with the irony the authors guaranteed in their preface as the family, heavy-handed throughout and concerned with the conventional proprieties, to discourage Honoria's potential for realizing her latest fantasy, redeems Eugenius from the salt mines and forces her to consummate their marriage. Just as this has been completed, Honoria receives the news that the Hun has been murdered on his marriage bed by a young woman who has been compelled to marry him.

Though the play seems an exercise in the black humor of which the decadents were fond, an ability to mock their own symbols and fantasies, it is not only this. The women have successfully combined this decadent mythology of Byzantium with a satiric view of the nineties' type of the New Woman and her potential for liberation through fantasy. And in the process they have managed to evolve from the old form of tragedy its modern counterpart, black comedy, since Honoria is no tragic heroine in the traditional sense. Too involved in her fantasy of escape and lacking self-realization, Honoria's circumstances do not evoke the conventional catharsis of pity and fear but merely reinforce the reader's own anxiety. In this sense, she is a truly evolutionary and modern character, so caught up in her own self-absorption and self-indulgence, and unable to effect her own liberation, that she represents the modern character in the throes of the contemporary dilemma, paralyzed by self-pity. That this is more precisely a black comedy rather than a traditional tragedy is evidenced by the heavy irony throughout the black humor, emphasized in the outrageous title, *Attila, My Attila*.

A review of the play that appeared in *The Athenaeum* of April 11, 1896 (no. 3572, p. 487), is an odd one. It begins by noting that the characters and matter have been taken directly from Gibbon's *The Decline and Fall . . .*, without "departure from historical fact . . . , every incident . . . being supported by authority," an important observation for it disarms the reader tempted to dismiss the characters and plot as incredible. Equally important is the reviewer's acceptance of the fact that Honoria is meant to represent the rebellious and contemporary "New Woman." "As a womanly estimate of a woman, the character of 'little Honoria' commands a certain amount of acquiescence," indicates the critic. "We might otherwise be disposed to assign to temperament rather than to mutiny a species of aberration not known among ladies of imperial rank." The suggestion that the play, which the reviewer, lacking our present-day terminology, dubs "an historical ironical tragedy of much power," might be "one on which the Independent Theatre might cast its eyes," reveals this critic's awareness of the ironic and contemporary overtones of the drama. Since the Independent as a rule spurned historical costume drama in favor of more contemporary plays with topical themes and characters, and had, in fact, presented a number of plays in which the New Woman had received serious consideration,[29] the reviewer's comment carries the implication that the group might now be ready for an ironic, satiric treatment of the type.

Though it is difficult to determine if the reviewer is being ironic with such remarks as "in some forms, at least, of dramatic work the competition of women is to be feared," which is immediately undermined by the observation, "There is, however, to speak seriously, much that is genuine and gripping in the play," it is not difficult to discern the sex of the author of such remarks in this unsigned review. Is he being "genuine," a word he uses twice to describe the play, with the contention, "It is a pity that the crudeness elsewhere observable should extend to the language"? Carefully couching his comments in noncommittal either / or phrasing, he puzzles, "We do not know whether to laugh or be shocked when the loving Eugenius addresses to Satyrus, the eunuch, so purely a John Bullish a curse as 'Damn your eyes.' " Is he implying that we should laugh, allowing the women their ribald joke at the expense of the eunuch, the kind of thing often appreciated in a Shakesperean play, or is he indicating that such bawdiness is shocking?[30]

Equally odd is the reviewer's concluding statement, "we do not quite know what to say, except that we think of Aphra Behn, when we are informed in the last act that *coram populo*—the *populus* including ourselves—the marriage of Eugenius and Honoria has been 'consummated.' " Although the consummation seems necessary to develop the play's ironic ending, the reader does not quite know what to think of the reviewer's interesting evocation of Aphra Behn, the accomplished woman dramatist of the bawdy Restoration period, ignored and discredited during the Victorian era for her "coarseness." Is the critic implying an intriguing comparison with Behn's plays, or is he merely objecting that all such untowardness is inexcusable in women playwrights?[31]

By leaving the reader both options, the reviewer is a perfect example of the ambivalent male critic, who, when faced with a work by women, the obvious merits of which can easily be seen, must still accede to his readership, disinclined to accept from women what they might from men. Thus, this critic succeeds, perhaps unintentionally, in damning the play with "feint" praise.

In 1898, persuaded by their artist friends Charles Shannon and Charles Ricketts to move from their "bourgeois house" at Reigate, which they had maintained for ten years, to the more fashionable Richmond, popular with artist and writer types, the women acquired "The Paragon," a small Georgian style house, which they furnished with things "antique," "Japanese," and "aesthetic," a taste cultivated by those in the elite artistic circles of the 1890's. In effect, the move to Richmond served to further insulate the women from the vagaries of the conventional world, which they felt had denied them deserved recognition, and "The Paragon," extensively described by Sturge Moore in his preface to *WD*, pp. xvii-xix, became their refuge from this world, their palace of art.

Though they continued to hold out the hope that their work would be appreciated in another place by another generation, making this hope explicit in a note to the American edition of their earlier collection of poems, *Underneath the Bough* (1898), where they wrote in the singular person of 'Michael Field,' "For some years my work has been done for 'the younger generation'—not yet knocking at the door, but awaited with welcome. Meanwhile, readers from further England—if they will pardon my so classing them—have given me that joy of listening denied to me in my own island,"[32] still in private they were bitter and disillusioned, particularly Katherine, upon whom the adverse criticism had begun to take its toll. The spirit of two women against the conventional world, announced in their dedicatory sonnet, had been dampened in Katherine, who wrote to the noted alienist, Havelock Ellis, "want of due recognition is being its embittering, disintegrating work, and we will have in the end a cynic such as only a disillusioned Bacchante can become" (*MF*, p. 30).

Both women were well aware that the greater part of the cold and negative reception of their later work was due to their gender, and Katherine entered this cynical observation in the journal, "If women seek to learn their art from life, instead of what the angels bring down in dishes, they simply get defamed" (*WD*, p. 202). By the end of Victoria's reign, Katherine's cynicism had hardened, as evidenced by her attack on the illusions of the Victorian era, a summation that reveals an abandonment of some of the causes so enthusiastically supported earlier. Reaction had indeed set in when Katherine wrote in 1901:

> The great illusion of the Victorian age is the illusion of progress. . . .
> Growth of suburbs, growth of education among the poor, an unmitigated evil—extension of franchise and growth of free trade, unmitigated disasters—the growth of Trade Unions, the damnation of the future.
> The growth of sentimentality towards crime; and of sciencecraft (the priestcraft of the Victorian age), insidious, berotting influences.
> The synthesis of the reign—Imperialism.
> The great virtue to be cultivated— ''hardiness''. . . . [33]

Escape from cynicism was afforded when both women converted to Roman Catholicism in 1907. The concept of the sacrificial transubstantiation appealed to conventional mode, their earlier frame of reference for their role as poets, as Maenad priestesses presiding over the creation of tragic poetry through self-effacement and divine madness. The message was now to be translated via Christian mysticism.

After converting, they devoted their efforts to religious verse, though they did publish a number of dramas anonymously,[34] which received a critical respect denied most of their previous attempts (*MF*, p. 29), an experience that only reinforced the fact that the hostile reception accorded some of the earlier works was a response to women writing in a genre dominated by male writers and critics.

The rhythm of their collaboration was not even disrupted, in a macabre sense, by death, and Edith, who died of cancer on December 13, 1913, was quickly followed by Katherine, who died of the same disease on September 26, 1914. Of the plays that were published posthumously, *In the Name of Time* (London: Poetry Bookshop, 1919) contains, according to Mary Sturgeon, the essential philosophy behind all their work, ''a philosophy of change serving a religion of life,'' as the women project through their protagonist Carloman, in reality the rebel son of Charles Martel but in essence Everyman, their ''supreme symbol of freedom.'' The play combines a call for the loosening of the old bonds with a recognition of the difficult struggle involved. Carloman's mission is to seek what he calls ''the Great Reality,'' and his life becomes a series of confrontations with the established order, while his quest is marked by failure and futility.[35] Finally, thrown in prison, he discovers that ''the Great Reality'' consists of ''Fellowship, pleasure / These are the treasure,''[36] and it is in confinement that he formulates the ''philosophy of change serving a religion of life.''

> The God I worship. He is just *to-day*—
> Not dreaming of the future,—in itself
> Breath after breath divine! Oh, He becomes!
> He cannot be of yesterday, for youth

> Could not then walk beside Him, and the young
> Must walk with God: and He is most alive
> Wherever life is of each living thing.
> Tomorrow and tomorrow, those todays
> Of unborn generations.[37]

These lines capture for Mary Sturgeon the women's message: "a worship of life, a belief in the joy of fellowship, and a vision of change as the vital principle of living." "It is," Sturgeon concludes, "simply the freedom of love."[38]

Though many major Victorian figures recognized their genius, one finds more recent critics, like Austin Clarke, dismissing the women in ignorance of their work as "two spinster ladies, [who] steadily wrote a series of historical tragedies in five acts and in blank verse."[39] Other critics similarly treat the women as freaks when they quibble over whether they were "decadent." If such is not "wholly irresponsible," as Mary Sturgeon contends, it may be irrelevant, given Richard Gilman's examination of the term.[40] Any attempt to make them conform to the myth of decadence, like Symons and Jullian do, is to misrepresent them. Though they employed decadent motifs, they adapted these to "themes of their own inventing," "fellowship," "a worship of life," and "the freedom of love," themes not readily identifiable with decadence.

The superficial trappings of decadence may be present—the unconventional life style, with lesbian overtones; the fascination with Roman decadence; the ultimate submission to the authority of the Roman church—yet much of this must be regarded for what it was, both for them and for their *fin de siècle* counterparts: a pose, a mask, a disguise. In this sense, the women exemplify the "drowning theory" of Annis Pratt, who writes, "The drowning effect, . . . to drown out what they are actually saying about feminism, came in with the first woman's novel and hasn't gone out yet." Pratt continues, "Many women . . . have even succeeded in hiding the covert or implicit feminism in their books from themselves. . . . As a result we get explicit cultural norms superimposed upon an authentic creative mind in the form of all kinds of feints, ploys, masks, and disguises imbedded in plot structure and characterization."[41]

If one fails to see through such a disguise, one becomes mired in false paradoxes. Theodore Maynard, the Catholic poet and essayist, senses the paradox of 'Michael Field' when he writes that the women "left a heritage not only of poetry but of paradox. There had been successful literary collaborations before . . . but no collaboration in which the identity of the artists was so completely sunk as in the case of these two ladies. . . . " Maynard, however, goes on to chase the false paradox, so intent on absolving the women as Catholic poets, when he argues, "Here were souls who, though they had been by circumstance and choice decadents of the decadents, never . . . committed in all their lives a really serious sin. . . . "[42]

The real key to the paradox of Katherine and Edith lies not in whether they lived blameless lives, but in their unique collaboration, which for Mary Sturgeon stands "as a robust denial that women are incapable of greatness in art and comradeship," and represents a discovery of "the secret of psychological truth," "a great capacity for life," "an immense love of liberty, and hatred of every kind of bondage," and "a prevailing love of freedom, which takes many forms and is apparent everywhere." All of this is accompanied, according to Sturgeon, by "the fragmentary, the suggestive and often complex wisdom" of the collaboration.[43]

And yet Sturgeon also misses the real paradox and ultimate reason for the women's obscurity, that these poets of liberty never succeeded in breaking through the confines of their passionate devotion to each other. They wrote of their collaboration as a marriage; it is implicit in their dedicatory sonnet and is made explicit by Katherine, whose entry in the journal compares their work with that of the Brownings, each of whom wrote separately. From this Katherine concludes, *"we are closer married"* (*WD*, p. 16), indicating an even greater exclusivity than that of the conventional monogamous relationship, since it extends through life and vocation to art.

Indeed, this exclusivity encompassed not only their reclusive life, but their art as well. Choosing to write in a genre, not often attempted by women, and not popular in an age which preferred prose melodrama, the women discovered the "historical, ironical tragedy," or black comedy, the symbolist drama, and stream of consciousness dialogue. Making their plays "hard reading," in the words of Maynard, who also points out that by publishing their plays in prohibitively priced volumes and in limited editions, they guaranteed themselves "but a few readers"[44] the women again accord with Pratt's "drowning theory." They recognized full well the need for concealment, which explains their use of the male pseudonym, and which gives reason why, after their real identities were known, their work took on a more complex, less traditional, more innovative tenor.

In reference to their art and life, the women often use the imagery of confinement, suffocation, and claustrophobia, images that are related to the captive woman figure that reappears throughout their work. Sandra Gilbert and Susan Gubar, in the Preface to their study of the nineteenth-century woman writer, metaphorically titled *The Madwoman in the Attic*, observe:

Both in life and in art, we saw, the artists we studied were literally and figuratively confined. Enclosed in the architecture of an overwhelmingly male-dominated society, these literary women were also, inevitably, trapped in the specifically literary constructs of what Gertrude Stein was to call "patriarchal poetry." For not only did a nineteenth-century woman writer have to inhabit ancestral mansions (or cottages) owned and built by men, she was also constricted and restricted by the Palaces of Art and Houses of Fiction male writers authored. We decided, therefore, that the striking coherence we noticed in literature by women could be explained by a common, female impulse to struggle free from social and literary confinement through strategic redefinitions of self, art, and society. (Pp. xi-xii)

As early as a letter, dated November 23, 1884, to Robert Browning, Katherine recognized the need to escape from the stifling confines of the conventional Victorian drawingroom and redefine the self, art, and society according to the feminine ideal. Turning her own paradox, she wrote, "We hold ourselves bound in life and literature to reveal—as far as may be—the beauty of the high feminine standard of *the ought to be*. . . . By that I mean we could not be scared away, as ladies, from the tragic elements of life" (*WD*, p. 22).

Yet it is the tragic element of their own lives that—permitted an economic independence not afforded many Victorian women, which enabled them to escape the stifling drawingrooms for a "room of their own"—they insured their obscurity. In retreating to this room to create their "mosaics," they allowed it to become a Palace of Art and, like Tennyson's "Lady of Shalott" and the captive women in their own dramas,[45] in seeking to express in their art the experience of life denied to so many women, they came to be prisoners of their art. Confusing their dramas with the experience of life, their art became their life. After the performance of *A Question of Memory*, for example, Edith noted in the journal, "I am a woman, and to bring out a play is experience of life—just what women feel so crushingly that they need. You men get it like breathing" (*WD*, p. 184).

Concurrent with this substitution of art for life experience is the strong identification with one's characters, embodying those fantasies denied one in real life. As Edith reflected toward the end of her life, "I am an artist to the fingertips and I must bring the whole of my life to art, express it in terms of art. . . . I explain the strong physical identification I have with my characters" (*WD*, p. 312–13). When such an artist, who has only vicariously experienced life from the tower of art without participating in it directly, is confronted by one who has, there is a feeling of bitter envy, accompanied by the notion that the vicarious experience of life through art is a suffocating existence. Katherine's reflections on Olive Schreiner, the successful novelist of *The Story of an African Farm* (1883), reveal this.[46] Of Schreiner, one who has experienced life first hand in the African territories, Katherine writes:

Olive Schreiner home from the Cape, after years of brute, wild life in Africa. The ambassador pays his respects to her, Watts asks to paint her (he is refused), she goes the round of the great. Lovers from Africa come after her—to sink on their knees as soon as they land. . . . Meditating on all this I am filled with jealousy; this woman has been worshipped—she has known solitude—she has walked naked in the open air, she has handled politics, she has set one up and put down another.

I have lived . . . , neither breathing nor being breathed upon. (*WD*, pp. 193–94).

We are the ones living "those todays / Of unborn generations" envisioned in the final lines of the women's final drama, and it would seem appropriate not to end on a note of suffocation, but upon breathless fantasy. Imagine that we have climbed that difficult stairway and, having knocked on the attic door, we discover that it is opened and that we have been awaited with welcome, we of "the younger generation." Imagine that we are greeted with these, the final lines from "Fellowship," a poem which appeared in the American edition of *Underneath the Bough*, and which, though specifically written by Katherine for Edith, expresses what both women sought to achieve, their image of themselves and their mission, their hope for what they would be for "the younger generation."

> O friends, so fondly loving, so beloved, look up to us,
> In constellation *breathing* [emphasis added] on your errand arduous. . . . Now faded
> from . . . sight
> We cling and joy. It was thy intercession gave me right
> My fellow, to this fellowship—O Henry, my delight!
>
> Fellowship, pleasure / These are the treasure. . . .

NOTES

1. *Works and Days*, excerpts from the women's journals, in twenty-six large volumes covering each year from 1883 to 1914, ed. T. Sturge Moore and D. C. Moore (London: John Murray, 1933), contains observations of activities, correspondence, and drafts of poetry and is a valuable source of biographical information; cited in the text as *WD*. Another valuable source is Mary Sturgeon's literary biography, *Michael Field* (London: G. G. Harrap, 1922; rpt. Freeport, N.Y.: Arno Press, 1975), the only book-length treatment of the women's lives and work; cited in the text as *MF*. Sturgeon is one of the few who has read extensively the women's work and thus she has a good overall perspective of their concerns, themes, and intentions, generally lacking in subsequent critics. Biographical information for this text is taken from these two sources, unless otherwise cited.

2. Cf. undated letter, addressed "My Dear Master," quoted in *Works and Days*, pp. 162–63. This correspondence, covering roughly the period between June, 1875, and January, 1878, has been quoted at length in *Works and Days*, pp. 143–72. Subsequent citations of these letters in the text are from these pages. For an assessment of the place and proper pursuits of women in the Pre-Raphaelite and Arts and Crafts movements, both heavily influenced by Ruskin, see Anthea Callan's *Women Artists of the Arts and Crafts Movement, 1870–1914* (New York: Pantheon Books, 1980).

3. The women might very well have been imitating in their dress Elizabeth Siddal, wife of Dante Rossetti, the Pre-Raphaelite poet-painter. Philippe Jullian writes in his *Dreamers of Decadence*, a study of the nineteenth-century roots of symbolism, translated by Robert Baldick (New York: Praeger, 1971), p. 141, that Siddal, "renouncing corsets, crinolines, heels, and false chignons, became the 'New Woman.' Her simplicity offered a deliberate contrast to vulgar overdressing while her casual stance, her full neck and her flowing hair showed the way toward the line of an *Art Nouveau* arabesque."

4. Mary Sturgeon, "Michael Field," *Studies of Contemporary Poets*, rev. ed. (London: G. G. Harrap 1920), p. 351. This poem, the final lines of which are quoted in the text, was printed in *Underneath the Bough* (London: G. Bell and Sons, 1893), a collection of love lyrics the women had written for each other over the years. A revised and enlarged second edition was published in the same year.

5. Jullian, pp. 140–41, describes the women's "decadent" activities during their stay in Florence, Ruskin's favorite city:

In the name of Walter Pater, a despotic lesbian called Vernon Lee reigned there over a court of more or less Botticellian characters in a neo-Platonic atmosphere. . . . Two of her female friends, an aunt and niece who called themselves "Michael Field," devoted their time to putting the Primitives into sonnets [collected in *Sight and Song* (London: Elkin Mathews and John Lane, The Bodley Head, 1892)]. These ladies had countless imitators who hung around the Ponte Vecchio looking for some Beatrice, or else for a page, preferably disguised as a character from Rossetti.

Sturgeon, *Michael Field*, p. 30, indicates that, in addition to Nietzsche, the women also read during this period: Flaubert, Ibsen, Hegel, Heine, Tolstoy, and Whitman. Subsequently, they adeptly translated some of Baudelaire's poems from *Fleurs du Mal*, and, in 1891, caught up in the Wagnerian fad, they made a special trip to Germany to attend performances of his music dramas, a trip which is recorded in *Works and Days*, pp. 54–65.

6. Michael Field, *Callirrhoe and Fair Rosamund* (London: G. Bell and Sons; and Clifton: J. Baker and Son, 1884). *Callirrhoe* is based on an ancient Greek legend of a woman who avenges her husband's murder. *Fair Rosamund*, the second play in the volume, is a reworking of one of Swinburne's earliest verse dramas, *Rosamund* (1860), and it features the confrontation between the wise-politic woman, Elinor of Acquitaine, wife of Henry Plantagenet, and Henry's naive mistress, Rosamund, the first of a number of so-called *femme fatale* figures treated with sympathy by the women in their plays. Though it is not surprising to find the women, particularly in their early dramas, imitating Swinburne's themes, plot structure, and language, since Swinburne was, at the time, considered one of the foremost tragic poets on the English scene, the women depart markedly and significantly from Swinburne in drawing their female characters. Sandra M. Gilbert and Susan Gubar, in their study of the nineteenth-century woman writer, *The Madwoman in the Attic* (New Haven and London: Yale University Press, 1979), p. 454, discover this Maenad motif in George Eliot's 1871 verse drama, "Armgart." Quoting lines describing Armgart, "it must have leaped through all her limbs— / Made her a Maenad—made her snatch a brand / And fire some forest, that her rage might mount / Leaving her still and patient for a while," Gilbert and Gubar conclude that Armgart's Maenad fury reveals a recognition "that her art legitimizes passionate assertion of self that would otherwise be denied her."

7. Letter quoted in *Works and Days*, p. 3. Two years later in a letter to Havelock Ellis, the pioneer psychoanalyst in England, Katherine struck the same note: "the work . . . is a perfect mosaic: we cross and interlace like a company of dancing summer flies; if one begins a character, his [*sic*] companion seizes and possesses it; if one conceives a scene or situation, the other corrects, completes, or murderously cuts away." Quoted in Sturgeon, *Michael Field*, p. 47. Sturgeon in "Michael Field," *Studies of Contemporary Poets*, p. 351, speculates on the exact nature of this unusual collaboration, and citing both internal evidence and the testimony of those who knew them, concludes that Katherine was the initiator, lyricist, and conceiver of protagonists, while Edith was generally the critic, constructing and shaping the verse, plot, and characters.

8. Arthur Symons, "Michael Field," *Forum*, LXIX (1923), 1584. This article is subsequently cited in the text as Symons.

9. Michael Field, *The Father's Tragedy, William Rufus, and Loyalty or Love* (London: G. Bell and Sons; and Clifton: J. Baker and Son, 1885). The subplot of *The Father's Tragedy* contains an attack on the commonly held Victorian idea that matrimony was essentially an economic transaction. While the two patriarchs negotiate the transaction, the two individuals for whom the marriage is being arranged are repelled by one another,

with the implication that such a marriage would be, just as Blake and Shelley perceived such, a form of prostitution. *William Rufus* has no literal female characters but functions on a symbolic level as the encounter between the tyrannical patriarch, usurping the peasants' land for his own pleasure, and the Earth Mother, who avenges this rape of the land when Rufus is killed in a hunting mishap as his arrow glances off an oak tree, rebounds, and strikes him dead. As Sturgeon points out in *Michael Field*, p. 131, the plot is developed from the idealistic perspective of the younger generation, and the bulk of it was written by Edith when she was sixteen or seventeen.

10. Michael Field, *Canute the Great and A Cup of Water* (London: G. Bell and Sons and Clifton: J. Baker and Son, 1887). In their preface to *Canute the Great*, p. 5, the women indicate that the protagonist evidences the evolutionary struggle of the tragic figure, alienated from his gods, his forefathers, and his dreams, and whose hopes are not founded on past experience, nor his ideals on memory. Paralleling Canute's attempt to efface his past is Edith's effort to escape the domination of her husband, Edric, another misogynistic "heavy." After she bungles an attempt on Edric's life, Edith drifts into madness, during which an apparition of her husband haunts her by repeating the formula: "Wives obey your husbands." She is consoled and lifted out of her madness by Elgiva, after which follows the love scene between the two women. According to Sturgeon, *Michael Field*, p. 148, *A Cup of Water* was developed from a projected theme of D. G. Rossetti, and which, upon superficial reading, seems a delightful idyll of a rustic lass who falls in love with the handsome prince. The play, however, conceals another attack on marriage without love, the free soul fettered by convention, the treatment of women as chattel, and the impulse toward adultery fostered by such conditions. The prince turns out to be married; Cara is forced to marry another whom she does not love.

11. Michael Field, *Long Ago* (London: G. Bell and Sons, 1889). Only one hundred copies of this volume, with the intentionally ironic title, were initially printed, undoubtedly due to the sensitive theme.

12. Jullian, *Dreamers of Decadence*, p. 111.

13. Symons, p. 1589. Symons's article is a direct response to Sturgeon's book, which was written a year earlier. Perhaps because Sturgeon does not regard the women as decadents, Symons attacks her observations that the early plays, as well as *Long Ago*, contain Nietzschean overtones (p. 1589). Although he admits to his enthusiasm for their work early on, the entire article seems an effort to revise that enthusiasm and denigrate their subsequent work, praised by Mary Sturgeon. Symons indicates that the women's plays lack "construction" and "complexity" (p. 1587), and there is a great deal of self-promotion by Symons, who notes that it was he who introduced the women to Verlaine, took them to a rare public lecture by Walter Pater, and favorably reviewed their early plays. Symons even finds space in this short article to quote from one of his own translations of Sappho's Greek (cf. pp. 1585–89). Though Symons's assessment has a right to stand with Sturgeon's more favorable one, it must be noted that in the many years which intervened between Symons' acquaintance with the women and the article's appearance, he had lost touch with the women and their work, while he had published a number of pieces, most notably "Gabriele D'Annunzion" in *Studies in Prose and Verse* (1904), which reveal a deep-seated misogyny. Having suffered a severe mental breakdown in 1908, requiring an extensive stay in an asylum, Symons's mental state remained unstable in subsequent years. All of this makes him a less than reliable source for an evaluation of the women's work.

14. Symons, p. 1588. Symons's classic article "The Decadent Movement in Litera-

ture'' first appeared in *Harper's New Monthly Magazine* for November, 1893, and was an important step in codifying the principles and confluence of *fin de siècle* decadence and symbolism.

15. In addition to Symons and Browning, the women attracted the respect and recognition of many notables of the period: George Meredith, George Moore, Oscar Wilde, W. B. Yeats, Swinburne, J. T. Grein, and the painters Charles Shannon, Charles Ricketts, as well as Selwyn Image, who did the designs for their play *The Tragic Mary*. Cf. Sturgeon, *Michael Field*, p. 38 and *Works and Days*, Sturge Moore's Preface, p. xvii, and pp. 195, 263, etc. Lionel Johnson, a prominent nineties poet, thought enough of 'Michael Field's' poetry to select some for inclusion in A. H. Miles's influential, multivolume anthology, *Poets and Poetry of the Century* (London: Hutchinson and Company, 1891), vol. VIII *The Contemporary Poets*.

16. This figure occurs in *Attila, My Attila* (1896), *Queen Mariamne* (1908), *The Tragedy of Pardon* (1911), a version of the Tristan and Isolde legend, and *Deirdre*, published posthumously in 1918, based on the popular myth of the Celtic Twilight.

17. Letter of August 13, 1890, quoted in *Letters of Oscar Wilde*, ed. Rupert Hart-Davis (New York: Harcourt, Brace and World, 1962), p. 272. The *femme fatale* figures drawn by the women have a depth of character and a vitality decidedly lacking in the cold, mysterious figures of the male dramatists, which explains the strong irony that flows through the women's plays, generated by such conflict of perspective. As women they were well aware of this irony, arising from the reality of their own experience, contradicting the way this experience was interpreted by the masculine vision. Such a conflict is, of its very nature, tragic, another reason why these women are obsessed with the tragic form and characters. Whereas Swinburne's women are symbols of mystery, evil, and death, those of these women playwrights are real, live beings. For example, the reader of *The Tragic Mary* cannot, as he can in Swinburne's play, accept Bothwell's charge that Mary has played the temptress.

18. As Jullian points out in *Dreamers of Decadence*, p. 184, many of Sarah Bernhardt's best roles were transvestite. The women had seen Bernhardt in the role of Pelleas in the Maeterlinck play, as this entry in *Works and Days*, p. 245, describing her performance, indicates:

She comes, an elfin travesty of man, thin in limb, broad in hip and shoulder—the red-gold wig resting where epaulets usually rest. Under the big wig, eyes of the everlasting Lilith and lips of Lilith when she was hanging on the Apple-tree. Yet this being acts Pelleas till sex is forgotten as an accident—and the ideal lover remains, très male, tempers her effulgent feminine power—gives a sense of mass to her passion.

19. Cf. Jullian, p. 104.

20. Cf. William Archer, *The Old Drama and the New* (London: W. Heinemann, 1923), p. 308. Nicolaas Schoonerwoerd in *J. T. Grein, Ambassador of the Theatre* (Assen, The Netherlands: Van Gorcum, 1963), p. 103, observes that though Grein, a Dutchman, had every intention of presenting English-made plays, there were few available that were suitable for the Independent's purposes. Among those listed by Schoonderwoerd as performed by the Independent are a play by Arthur Symons, a translation from the French of de Banville by John Gray, a play by Andre Rafflovich, a Polish exile, Shaw's first play to be performed, *Widowers' Houses*, and John Todhunter's Ibsen-type play, *The Black Cat* (pp. 128–29). It should be noted that the last two playwrights were Irishmen.

21. "The Independent Theatre," *The London Times*, October 28, 1893, p. 6, col. 5.

22. This review is reprinted in William Archer's *The Theatrical 'World' for 1893* (London: W. Scott, 1894), pp. 251–55. In their "Preface" to *A Question of Memory* (London: Elkin Mathews and John Lane, The Bodley Head, 1893), n. p., the women indicate that the play was based on a real incident reported in the press, which took place during the Hungarian uprising against the Austrian occupation in 1848. Ferencz, a rebel, is captured by the Austrians, who threaten to shoot his mother, sister, and lover, if he does not reveal the site of the rebel ambush. His mother and sister, who support the cause, willingly die, but his lover pleads for life, and he is about to reveal the location to save her life, when Ferencz's memory goes blank and his sweetheart is also executed by the Austrians. Upon his return to his native village after his release, Ferencz meets Stanislaus, another rebel, who confesses that he has given the Austrians the information on the threat that his lover would be shot. The play ends with the two men and Elizabeth, Stanislaus's lover, proposing to live together. The symbolic and ironic overtones of the incident can be detected in this brief summary of the plot, since the irony seems the reason the women chose to write their play. By combining a realistic setting and a real event with symbolic potential, together with the stream of consciousness dialogue, they were attempting to present what the French critic Augustin Filon in his *The English Stage* (London: J. Milne, 1897), p. 291, has pointed out the progressive British audiences of the day were demanding, that "realism will be symbolic or non-existent."

23. 'Michael Orme,' pseudonym for Alice Augusta (Greeven-Grein), *J. T. Grein, The Story of a Pioneer, 1862–1935* (London: J. Murray, 1936), pp. 133–36. Archer, in his comment in *The Theatrical 'World' for 1893*, p. 255, that, "The acting was much stronger on the female than on the male side," confirms the impression that Bond was a bad actor with a big ego. Alice Grein felt, contrary to Archer, that the unusual dialogue enhanced the climax. She wrote, "The play, finely conceived, was written in well-phrased dialogue which, by not following a natural sequence of thought, led away from, and all around, as well as towards the dramatic climax," (pp. 135–36). The account of events given in the text relies on Alice Grein, unless otherwise indicated. Other page numbers are cited in the text.

24. In succeeding years, a trilogy on the decline and fall of the Roman Empire was published at the press owned by the women's artist friend Charles Ricketts. In order of the historical sequence, these are: *The Race of Leaves* (London: Hacon and Ricketts, 1901); *The World at Auction* (London: Hacon and Ricketts, 1898); and *Julia Domna* (London: Hacon and Ricketts, 1903). It is not coincidental that these plays were written at *fin de siècle*. Other plays published by the women at this time were: a reprint of *Fair Rosamund* (London: Hacon and Ricketts, 1897), and *Noontide Branches*, a masque and their only non-tragic offering (Oxford: privately printed by Henry Daniel, 1899).

25. Jullian in *Dreamers of Decadence*, quoting from the French review *Le Decadent* (1890), finds this concept of the destructive mission of the artist, preparing for the birth of new order: "The future belongs to Decadism. Born of a Schopenhauerian civilization, the Decadents are not a literary school. Their mission is not to found but to destroy, to demolish the old order and prepare the elements of the great . . . literature of the twentieth century" (p. 258). This is the one theme of the *fin de siècle* that consistently appears in the women's work, the call for the destruction of the old, restrictive, patriarchal ordering of society.

26. Cf. Jullian, p. 161 and 156. Yeats's Byzantium poems were, of course, written well into the present century.

27. *Works and Days*, p. 97. Edith described Oscar Wilde's Salome, another character

written with the "divine Sarah" in mind, in *Works and Days*, p. 251, as "a pale, exacting virgin—thirsting for tragedy." The parallels between Honoria and Salome are somewhat obvious.

28. Preface to *Attila, My Attila*, p. iv. Jullian, p. 210, indicates that "a Byzantine play by Michael Field" was printed in the *Dial*, a short-lived magazine, published by Ricketts and Shannon, and though Jullian mentions neither date nor title, the play is most likely this one. The women in their preface also promise plenty of irony, p. iv.

29. The type was most notable in the Ibsen plays performed at the Independent, as well as in Shaw's *Widowers' Houses* and John Todhunter's Ibsenesque play *The Black Cat*. Todhunter, an Irish Quaker and feminist, active in the dramatic revival of the nineties, was known to Katherine and Edith as "Toddy," and he is mentioned in *Works and Days*, p. 183.

30. Though seemingly mild by today's standards, one need only recall the shock waves Shaw sent through his audience some years later when he used the vulgar epithet, "bloody," in his *Pygmalion*. For a description of the outcry caused by this performance at the St. James Theatre in 1913, see Hesketh Pearson, *The Last Actor-Managers* (London: Methuen, 1950), p. 26.

31. Aphra Behn's opinion of such male critics is expressed in "An Epistle To The Reader" of her play *The Dutch Lover* (1673). Cf. *The Works of Aphra Behn*, ed. Montague Summers (1915; rpt. New York: Phaeton Press, 1967), I, pp. 221–24. Addressing the reader as "Good Sweet, Honey, Sugar-Candied Reader," she writes about one man's initial response to her play:

Indeed that day 'twas Acted first, there comes me into the Pit, a long, lither, phlegmatick, white, ill-favour'd, wretched Fop, an Officer in Masquerade newly transported with a Scarf & Feat her out of France, a sorry Animal that has nought else to shield it from the uttermost contempt of all mankind, but that respect which we afford to Rats and Toads, which though we do not well allow to live, yet when considered as part of God's Creation, we make honourable mention of them. A thing, Reader— but no more of such a Smelt: This thing, I tell ye, opening that which serves it for a mouth, out issued such a noise as this to those sate about it, that they were to expect a woful Play, God damn him, for it was a woman's.

32. "Note" to *Underneath the Bough*, 3rd ed. (Portland, Maine: T. B. Mosher, 1898), n.p.

33. *Works and Days*, p. 237. This anti-rational attack on the Victorian Age contains the key to the women's ultimate conversion, like so many of their contemporaries, to Roman Catholicism. Jullian, *Dreamers of Decadence*, p. 71, indicates that the extensive list of *fin de siècle* artists who converted was due to an aesthetic reaction to the rational spirit of the age, since the Roman Church had a mystical and aesthetical basis. Edith had, years before her conversion, been attracted to the aesthetic rituals of the Roman Catholic rites, viewing this as a potential source for the renewal of her former Bacchic fervor. In *Works and Days*, p. 272, she wrote, "The Bacchic joy of Benediction was shed on me years and years ago at the Oratory—though rarely going to it, I have loved its flame-lit gratitude." The women were also fascinated with the occult as an alternative to "the rational spirit of the age." One of Katherine's nicknames was "Sim," short for Simiorg, a fabulous bird of Persian mythology, possessed of all knowledge and mentioned in the occult literature. Cf. *Works and Days*, p. 14. According to Sturgeon, *Michael Field*, p. 25, Edith was a psychic who had foreknowledge of both her parents' deaths. Eric Warner and Graham Hough have edited in two volumes, *Strangeness and Beauty:*

An Anthology of Aesthetic Criticism 1840–1910 (Cambridge: Cambridge University Press, 1983), revealing the various sources and intellectual history of this anti-rational movement, which so influenced these women.

34. The poems are collected in: *Wild Honey* (London: T. Fisher Unwin, 1908); *Poems of Adoration* (London and Edinburgh: Sands and Co., 1912); *Mystic Trees* (London: Eveleigh Nash, 1913); and *Dedicated* (London: G. Bell and Sons, 1914). Sturgeon, *Michael Field*, p. 94, points out that *Poems of Adoration* is primarily the work of Edith, Katherine contributing only two poems, while *Mystic Trees* contains two poems by Edith. Another volume, *Whym Chow, Flame of Love*, privately printed in twenty-seven copies for their close friends (London: Ergny Press, 1914), is an expression of grief at the death of their pet dog, their beloved "Whym Chow," but Sturgeon (p. 54) extrapolates on it as a philosophical discussion of the concept of sacrifice and as an *apologia*, providing insight into their conversion. Emily Fortey has selected and edited the women's unpublished religious verse, *The Wattlefold* (Oxford: Basil Blackwell, 1930). The plays were printed without attribution to author or publisher, but it is likely that they were printed at The Vale Press, a private press founded by Ricketts and Shannon, the women's artist friends. Cf. Jullian, p. 210. Two plays appeared before their conversion, *Anna Ruina* (London: 1899) and *Borgia* (London: 1905), a play which Symons prefers among their later dramas for what he calls its "abnormality," a decadent characteristic. Cf. Symons, "Michael Field," p. 1587. After their conversion, they printed *Queen Mariamne* (London: 1908), and two volumes, one containing *The Tragedy of Pardon and Dian, 'Queen of Earth and Heaven and Hell,' A Fantasy* (London: 1911), the other, *The Accuser, Tristan de Leonois, and A Messiah* (London: 1911).

35. Sturgeon, "Michael Field," *Studies of Contemporary Poets*, pp. 362–64. Sturgeon suggests that the play was not published in the women's lifetime because they did not want it misconstrued as an attack on the church. Though this, and other later plays such as *Anna Ruina* and *Borgia*, have anti-Catholic overtones, they are set in an historical epoch during which the Church of Rome was the established order. During the modern period, to which the main theme of the play applies, "science is the priestcraft," the symbol of the established, current order, and the rebel must forge an alliance, as did the women, with the anti-rational opposition, the Church of Rome. The other posthumous volume includes *Deirdre, A Question of Memory, and Ras Byzance* (London: Poetry Bookshop, 1918). The women's revision of *A Question of Memory* reveals the sensitivity with which they responded to criticism. The main characters' names are altered slightly; the dialogue is a bit more "coherent," but the major change involves the rewriting of the ending. The triad situation, to which Archer objected, is replaced by a more conventional resolution: Because of his cowardice in divulging his comrades' ambush, Lazlo (Stanislaus) is executed, while Ferencz, who has sacrificed his loved ones, is freed. Sturgeon, *Michael Field*, pp. 245–46, provides a bibliography of the women's published works, complete to 1919. Subsequently, *The Wattlefold* (1930) and *Works and Days* (1933) were published. Sturgeon had edited *a Selection from the Poems of Michael Field* (London: Poetry Bookshop, 1923).

36. Quoted by Sturgeon, ibid., p. 365, and *Michael Field*, p. 173.

37. Also quoted by Sturgeon, ibid., p. 366, and *Michael Field*, p. 177. The fact that Mary Sturgeon quotes these key lines in her article, as well as her book, strongly indicates the importance she sees in them as capsulizing their philosophy of life.

38. Ibid., pp. 365–67.

39. Austin Clarke, *The Celtic Twilight and the Nineties* (Dublin: Dolmen Press, 1969), p. 71.

40. Cf. Sturgeon, "Michael Field," *Studies of Contemporary Poets*, p. 358, and Richard Gilman, *Decadence: The Strange Life of an Epithet* (New York: Farrar, Straus, and Giroux, 1979).

41. Annis V. Pratt, "The New Feminist Criticisms: Exploring the History of the New Space," *Beyond Intellectual Sexism: A New Woman, A New Reality*, ed. Joan I. Roberts (New York: David McKay, 1976), p. 183.

42. Theodore Maynard, "The Drama of the Dramatists," *Carven From the Laurel Tree, Essays* (Oxford: B. H. Blackwell, 1918; rpt. Freeport, N. Y.: Books for Libraries Press, 1967), p. 45.

43. Sturgeon, "Michael Field," *Studies of Contemporary Poets*, pp. 347, 355, 358, 359, 360, 361, 364.

44. Maynard, p. 48.

45. Cf. Gilbert and Gubar, *Madwoman in the Attic*, pp. 617–20, for a discussion of the figure in Tennyson's poem and its relationship to the work of Emily Dickinson, with its imagery of imprisonment.

46. Schreiner, who published her novel under the obvious pseudonym 'Ralph Iron,' later became involved in South African politics and married in 1894 S. C. Cronwright, a member of the South African Parliament. She subsequently took the name of Cronwright-Schreiner.

14

Feminism and Positivism in George Eliot's *Romola*

Nancy L. Paxton

George Eliot's acceptance of positivist philosophy formulated by Auguste Comte has traditionally been seen by critics of Eliot to be antithetical to her feminism, when, indeed, that feminism is acknowledged at all. Shakur Guru Prasad, for example, sees Eliot's use of Comte as proof positive that she was "no feminist. He writes:

But her novels are full of encomiums of homespun virtues in women, the marriage bells and the fireside. Precept and example both converge; and that is a more decisive proof of her Comtean rather than feminist leanings.[1]

Like many similar criticisms of Eliot's "sentimental" view of women and the family, Prasad's comment betrays his unfamiliarity with the incipient feminist movement of the 1850's and 1860's.[2] Many of the radical intellectuals who were prominent in the Victorian women's movement were attracted to Comte's positivist philosophy for a number of reasons.

The most obvious reason why feminists found Comte's philosophy to be attractive was that he recommended that women be given an education identical to that which was to be universally provided for men, an education that embraced all branches of the positivist sciences including mathematics, astronomy, physics, chemistry, and biology as well as the social sciences which approached the more traditional subjects of women's education in a far more complete, rigorous, and scientific way. Many Victorian intellectuals and feminist sympathizers accepted this aspect of Comte's philosophy because it was not inconsistent with their goals. Harriet Martineau, for example, translated Comte's *Cours de Philosophie Positive* into English and was a dedicated positivist and feminist throughout her life.[3] Harriet Taylor and John Stuart Mill were deeply impressed with Comte's philosophy, and the latter praised him particularly for his stance on the education of women in his *Auguste Comte and Positivism*.[4] The consistency between Eliot's feminism and her acceptance of this aspect of Comte's thought is particularly clear. Throughout her career as a writer, Eliot was an ardent defender of women's right to an improved education, and her commitment to educational reforms for women finds expression in both her life and her novels. She joined feminist activist Barbara Bodichon, who was one of her most intimate friends, and Bessie Parkes in supporting Bedford College for Ladies in the early 1850's.[5] When Emily Davies began her campaign to establish Girton College in 1867, Eliot contributed generously and enthusiastically.[6] In an early essay written for *The Leader*, she paid tribute to both Mary Wollstonecraft and Margaret Fuller, two feminists she recognized as eloquent and intellectually sagacious advocates of better education for women.[7] Most of all, in her novels—particularly in *The Mill on the Floss* and in *Middlemarch*—Eliot dramatized the tragic waste of talent and intellect occasioned by women's pitifully deficient education.

A second reason that Comte's philosophy proved useful to the more radical intellectuals and feminist sympathizers was that his scientific rationalism offered a powerful and comprehensive tool for the analysis of society. Even though Comte declared himself vehemently opposed to the efforts of feminists to emancipate women by granting them legal and civil rights, radical thinkers like Martineau, Taylor, and Mill exploited the very rationalism Comte recommended in their own analysis of society in general and the family in particular. Comte's massive system of positivist methodology added intellectual respectability to the historical arguments feminists traditionally used to illustrate and protest the domestic slavery enforced by English and American law. J. S. Mill's "Subordination of Women" provides perhaps the clearest example of how Comte's social science served the feminist cause. Mill uses historical and social arguments against slavery similar to the ones that Comte cited but by unerring logic, Mill applied them to domestic slavery as well:

... for everyone who desires power, desires it most over those who are nearest him, with whom his life is passed, with whom he has most concerns in common, and in whom any independence of his authority is oftenest likely to interfere with his individual preferences.[8]

Eliot's sympathy with legal reforms like the ones feminists like Bodichon, Caroline Norton, and J. S. Mill recommended is more ambivalent. Though she signed Bodichon's petition in support of the Married Woman's Property Act in 1856, she declined to lend her support to the campaign in the 1860's to extend the suffrage to women.[9] Eliot's reluctance to support women's suffrage is interpreted by Gordon Haight as a sign of her commitment to Comte's more conservative view of politics, his preference for gradual social change rather than the comparatively sudden changes prompted by legislation. In a letter written in 1867, however, Eliot explains her position on suffrage but cautions that the social ostracism she suffered because of her choice to live with G. H. Lewes though she could not marry him "may have caused" her to have "idiosyncracies rather than an average judgment" in matters concerning the women's suffrage.[10] Her position on feminist legal reforms remains somewhat of a mystery.

Comte's perspective on women and their role in the family underwent a dramatic transformation in his later work, *Systeme de Politique Positive, ou Traite de Sociologie, Instituant la Religion de l'Umanite*. In his *Positivist Philosophy*, Comte declared that

biological philosophy teaches us that, through the whole animal scale, and while the specific type is preserved, radical differences, physical and moral, distinguish the sexes. Comparing sex with age, biological analysis presents the female sex, in the human species, as constitutionally in a state of perpetual infancy, in comparison with the other; and therefore more remote, in all important respects, from the ideal type of the race.[11]

By the time Comte wrote his second major work, however, he had experienced a moral regeneration caused by the influence of Clothilde de Vaux; in the *Polity* Comte described women not as infants but as angels. J. S. Mill provides a succinct summary of Comte's "curious" new sentimentalism about women:

Women being the *sexe aimant* represent the best attribute of humanity that which ought to regulate all human life, nor can humanity possibly be symbolized in any form but that of woman. The objects of private adoration are the mother, the wife, the daughter, representing severally, the past, the present, and the future, and calling into active exercise the three social sentiments: veneration, attachment, and kindness. We are to regard them whether dead or alive, as our guardian angels, *les vrais anges gardiens*.[12]

Though Mill and Martineau joined many other English and French intellectuals in dismissing the second phase of Comte's work, other Victorian feminists— including Eliot—found his later work more appealing perhaps because of this shift in his view of women. In fact, Comte's conversion to his "religion of humanity" offered a means of uniting the deeply divided feminist movement of the 1860's by lending religious significance to the family and the mother which would allow more radical agnostic intellectuals like Eliot to join forces with more conventionally religious feminist sympathizers from the trade union and Christian socialist movements. Comte's sentimental exaltation of women and his description of their central place in the family was echoed variously in the 1860's by feminists like Emily Davies, Bessie Parkes, and Emily Faithful. J. A. and Olive Banks comment particularly on the ideology expressed by these women,

Time and time again, these early feminists stressed that they did not want to remove women from the sphere of the home. This was the view of Emily Faithful and of Bessie Parkes, who argued that the "married household is the first constituent element in national life" and that "the immense majority of women are, and ought to be, employed in the noble duties which go to make up the Christian household."[13]

When prominent Victorian feminists repeat Comte's sentimental view of the family and speak in such enthusiastic praise of marriage and motherhood, Eliot's similar "Encomiums" cannot be seen—as they are by Prasad and many other critics—as evidence of her "anti-feminist" sympathies.[14]

Of all Eliot's novels, *Romola* provides perhaps the most interesting synthesis of her positivist and feminist philosophy. J. B. Bullen has brilliantly demonstrated how Eliot's *Romola* can be read as a positivist allegory,[15] but he, like Prasad, has failed to note how Eliot's feminism shapes her use and transformation of Comte's philosophy, perhaps because he, too, sees the two ideologies as antithetical. Eliot's view of positivism is particularly relevant to *Romola* because she commented to Frederick Harrison that she attempted to portray in it some of Comte's "normal" domestic relations.[16] Nonetheless, in her description of Romola's marriage to Tito, she focused on the problems with Comte's view of marriage implicit in his conceptions about altruism and egotism that Mill criticized in his essay on Comte:

There is only one passion or inclination which is permanently incompatible with this condition—the love of domination, or superiority, for its own sake, which implies and is grounded on, the equivalent depression of other people. (P. 145)

In *Romola*, Eliot writes that "marriage must be either a relation of sympathy or of conquest"; in this novel she presents the anatomy of a marriage of conquest.[17]

Eliot invites the reader to see the romantic relation developing between her heroine and Tito in positivist terms, for the attractive young man seems inclined to submit, at first, to what seems to him to be the superior "moral force" of his beloved, a submission Comte describes as characteristic of "normal domestic relations" between husband and wife. Tito's love for Romola is described as "subjection":

Tito felt himself strangely in subjection to Romola with that simplicity of hers. He felt for the first time without defining it to himself, that loving awe in the presence of noble womanhood, which is something like the worship paid of old to a great nature goddess, who was not all knowing, but whose life and power were something deeper and more primordial than knowledge. (P. 88)

While Tito pays homage to Romola's beauty and calls her "regina mia," "my angel," "my goddess," language that echoes Comte's, he does not ever truly submit to her in his courtship or, far less, in the marriage that ultimately results.

By the time Tito is betrothed to Romola, he has already participated in his "sham marriage" with the "little contadina" Tessa and has demonstrated his "unconquerable aversion to anything unpleasant" because he declined to tell the innocent Tessa that their marriage was a joke. Even his motives for marrying Romola are subtly transformed during their courtship: Romola becomes a "prize" that he "wished to have," she is included in a list of the accomplishments he desires (p. 109). By the time they are married, Tito has grown not only to resent but also resist Romola's moral impulses and her "primordial power." Comparing his legitimate wife Romola to his "second wife," Tito begins to feel vague resentment and faint alarm:

He had an uneasy feeling that behind her frank eyes there was a nature that could judge him, and that any ill-founded trust of hers sprang not from pretty brute-like incapacity, but from a nobleness which might prove an alarming touchstone. (Pp. 176–77)

Tito shrinks from Romola's moral censure and his role in their marriage, as it is culturally defined, allows him to do so with Romola's passive assent. After two years of marriage, he has come to regard his young wife as part of the "furniture" of his life. Though Romola "labors," Eliot writes, "as a loving woman must to subdue her nature to her husband's," she is unable to inspire Tito to the mutual submission that Comte predicted as the product of mutual love.

As she describes Tito's increasing restiveness in their marriage, Eliot generalizes about it, suggesting that the dynamic of his egotism is not particular to Tito alone, but is rather fostered by the institution of marriage as it existed in fifteenth-century Florence. She writes that Tito, when he decided to sell Romola's father's library, is uncertain how far the "revulsion" of Romola's feeling toward him might extend but nonetheless risks her displeasure because of "all that sense of power over a wife which makes a husband risk betrayals that a lover never ventures on" (p. 254). As Tito is forced to reveal his selfishness to Romola, he grows increasingly arrogant in wielding his husbandly rights. When he tells Romola that he has sold the Bardo library, he defends himself by describing Romola's desire to honor her father's dying request as "mere superstition." Reminding Romola of his prerogatives, Tito asserts his "masculine predominance" forcefully by locking Romola inside the room that used to house the library. Eliot emphasizes their formal relations in her description of how their original feelings have altered: "Such power of dislike and resistance as there was within him . . . was beginning to rise against a wife whose voice seemed like the herald of retributive fate. Her, at least, his quick mind told him that he might master" (p. 264). By repeatedly defining Tito's and Romola's reactions as those of husband and wife, Eliot deflates the idealism of Comte's theory of domestic relations by showing the dominance exercised by the husband and the submission required by the wife. Tradition and law incline the husband to assume the role of conquerer in marriage, leaving the wife the place of the conquered. Even women as strong and intelligent as Romola submit willingly in the name of love.

In her portrait of this marriage, Eliot shows that Tito is increasingly driven to exert physical "predominance" over Romola as their love disintegrates. Romola is prompted to leave Tito because of his betrayal of her father's memory, but she meets Savonarola along the road from Florence and is persuaded to return to her husband by his arguments. When Romola discovers that Tito has been instrumental in a plot to assassinate Savonarola, however, she resolves to expose him, trying first to urge him to abandon the plot by saying "if we are united, I am that part of you that will save you from crime," but when her effort to play the part of Tito's "good angel" proves ineffective, she tries more active means. When Romola meets Tito in public and urges him not to interfere with Savonarola, Tito compels her to desist by grasping her wrists and whispering bitterly, "I am master of you. You shall not set yourself in opposition to me" (p. 369). He disparages Romola's intellect, claiming that she cannot understand the details of the political games he is involved in, and asserting that she is "a fair creature who lives in the clouds" (p. 371). By showing how Tito eventually criticizes Romola for the "angelic" qualities he has cultivated in her, Eliot emphasizes the ineffectuality of Romola's altruism and illustrates what is wrong with Comte's analysis of marriage. In fact, Eliot shows that Romola's moral sensibility intensifies her powerlessness in marriage:

The grasp of her wrists, which asserted her husband's physical predominance, instead of arousing a new fierceness in her, as it might have done if her impetuosity had been of a more vulgar kind, had given her a momentary shuddering horror at this form of contest with him. (P. 370)

While Tito has permanently assumed "the husband's determination to mastery," Romola habitually responds with "self-reproof," courting ignorance of Tito's wrong doings and trying to maintain silence. The very qualities that define Romola as morally superior to her husband thus allow Tito to "master her" even more thoroughly. Ultimately, Romola's moral influence over Tito is proven to be even less effectual than Tessa's. Tito's love for his mistress becomes the only uncontaminated spring of kindness in his otherwise corrupted life; he is particularly responsive to his two children:

He was very fond of these round-cheeked, wide eyed human things that clung about him and knew no evil of him. And wherever affection can spring it is like the green leaf and the blossom—pure, and breathing purity, whatever soil it may grow in. Poor Romola with all her self-sacrificing effort was really helping to harden Tito's nature by chilling it with a positive dislike which had beforehand seemed impossible to him; but Tessa kept open the fountains of kindness. (P. 386)

Tito's love for Tessa and his children cannot reform him; he is as unwilling to submit to either wife as a leopard is liable to "lap milk when its teeth are grown" (p. 379). With this damning metaphor, Eliot insists that we see that love does not always flourish inside the bounds of conventional marriage and that even mother love cannot transform an intractable reality. Thus, Eliot discloses the false logic in Comte's theories about the power of both the angelic wife and the domestic madonna.

If we consider Romola's moral development throughout the novel we can see, n fact, that though Romola appears to resemble the angelic saint that Comte lescribed as the perfect wife and mother, she is much mcre than this.[18] Romola's dealization disguises the fact that she is a feminist heroine of great moral stature who is not unsexed by her splendid classical education but who is, in spite of her fitness, unable to find the usual woman's satisfactions in domestic life because she shares her husband with his mistress and because she has no children of her own to care for.[19] Romola finds a vocation outside the home as a secular sister of charity, a career that is strikingly similar to the one that Elizabeth Fry advocated for Victorian women.[20] Romola is impelled, in the end, because of the intolerable circumstances of her marriage to a man who has proven himself to be a traitor to both her family and Florence, to leave her husband in deliberately chosen defiance of civil and religious law.[21] Finally, on returning to Florence, Romola establishes a new and most revolutionary family, when contrary to all conventional expectations, she offers shelter to Tessa and her two children.[22] In this way, Eliot exploits the figure of the sainted wife and mother that Comte described in order to disclose the radical feminist alternative of the matriarchal family that is implicit in his description of woman's place in the history of fourteenth-century Italy and in the course of Western civilization as a whole. It is no accident that Eliot chose Barbara Bodichon as the model for Romola, and it is in consequence not surprising that Eliot's contemporaries saw this novel as an allegory of nineteenth-century life, an allegory, I contend, that demonstrated the impact of the feminist movement upon the Victorian cult of domesticity.

NOTES

1. Shakur Guru Prasad, *Comtism in the Novels of George Eliot* (Lucknow: Hindustani Book Depot, 1968), p. 172.

2. Even feminist critics make this assumption about Eliot. See, for example, Ellen Moers, *Literary Women* (Garden City, N. Y.: Doubleday, Anchor Books, 1977), p. 295.

3. W. S. Simon, *European Positivism in the Nineteenth Century* (Ithaca, N. Y.: Cornell University Press, 1963), p. 215.

4. See John Stuart Mill, *Auguste Comte and Positivism* (Ann Arbor: University of Michigan Press, 1961), p. 76.

5. Ray Strachey, *The Cause: A Short History of the Women's Movement in Great Britain* (London: G. Bell and Sons, 1928), p. 124.

6. Francoise Basch, *Relative Creatures: Victorian Women in Society and the Novel* (New York: Schocken Books, 1974), pp. 94–95.

7. Thomas Pinney, ed., *The Essays of George Eliot* (New York: Columbia University Press, 1963), pp. 199–211.

8. The "social science" movement, of course, owed far more in England to James Mill and the Utilitarians than it did to Comte. The passage from Mill shows the influence, particularly, of Comte's interest in history as a tool for studying contemporary life. See *The Subjection of Women* (Cambridge, Mass.: M. I. T. Press, 1970), p. 27–28.

9. Gordon Haight, *George Eliot: A Biography* (New York: Oxford University Press, 1968), pp. 204, 396.

10. Letter to John Morley, May 14, 1867, cited by Haight, *George Eliot*, p. 396.

11. Auguste Comte, *Positive Philosophy*, tran. and abr. Harriet Martineau (New York: Calvin Blanchard, 1858), p. 504.

12. J. S. Mill, *Auguste Comte and Positivism*, p. 150.

13. J. A. Banks and Olive Banks, *Feminism and Family Planning in Victorian England* (New York: Schocken Books, 1964), pp. 48–49.

14. Sandra M. Gilbert and Susan Gubar borrow this term from Mary Daly and apply it to Eliot in their excellent work, *The Madwoman in the Attic: The Woman Writer in the Nineteenth-Century Imagination* (New Haven: Yale University Press, 1979), p. 466.

15. J. B. Bullen, "George Eliot's *Romola* as Positivist Allegory," *Review of English Studies*, 26 (1975), 425–35.

16. Gordon Haight, ed., *The George Eliot Letters* (New Haven: Yale University Press, 1955), IV, p. 301.

17. All citations are to *Romola* in *The Complete Works of George Eliot* (New York: George D. Sproul, 1899).

18. Mill points out the contradictions concerning Comte's use of the idea of woman as "saint" on pages 142–45.

19. Perhaps one of their reasons why Eliot idealized her heroine is because she was anxious to counter the prevailing concern that women be "unsexed" by the higher education that feminists proposed. See *Letters*, IV, p. 468.

20. See Francoise Basch, *Relative Creatures*, p. 116.

21. There are interesting parallels, of course, between Eliot's own life and Romola's. By emphasizing Tito's domination over Romola, Eliot seems to indicate her agreement not only with Mill but also with more radical feminists like Wollstonecraft and Norton who saw marriage as a voluntary tie. Her comments on Charlotte Brontë's *Jane Eyre* seem to confirm her radical feminist position on marriage. See *Letters*, I, p. 268.

22. This alliance between wife and mistress seems to anticipate the coalition Josephine Butler attempted to create between middle-class and working-class women in her campaign to repeal the Contagious Disease Act.

15

George Eliot and Barbara Leigh Smith Bodichon: A Friendship

Nancy Pell

In January, 1881, less than a month after George Eliot's death, John Cross wrote to Barbara Bodichon, "Amongst all her intimate friends I know there was none she valued more or who was more to her than yourself" (*Letters*, IX, p. 325). Cross had been faulted for many things by subsequent biographers of George Eliot, but in this instance, I think, we may trust him. From their first meeting in the summer of 1852 until George Eliot's death nearly thirty years later, these two women shared a friendship that was nourished by the very differences that might otherwise have made an intimate friendship quite impossible.

Their relationship began when Marian Evans and Barbara Leigh Smith were members of the "advanced" circle that surrounded the *Westminster Review*, which was owned by John Chapman and edited almost single-handedly, and, of course, anonymously, by Marian Evans. Hester Burton tells us that in the summer of 1854 George Eliot and George Lewes invited Barbara to advise them about what to do in the face of Lewes's impossible marriage to Agnes Jervis Lewes and their own acknowledged need and love for each other. " 'What earthly right had I to advise her in such a case?' Barbara told a friend long afterwards," Burton writes; " 'her own heart must decide, and . . . no matter what her decision, or its consequences should be, I would stand by her so long as I lived.' "[1] The situation was reversed somewhat two years later, when Barbara, bruised by the breakup of a strange affair with John Chapman, who, in the words of Joseph Reed, "continually augmented his marital arrangement . . . with an ever-shifting cast of women," was invited to come and stay with the Leweses at Ilfracombe.[2] Having herself been quite nearly included in that "cast of women," George Eliot concludes her letter with generous sympathy: "I shall say nothing," she writes, "of sorrow and renunciations, but I understand and feel what you must have to do and bear. Yes—I hope we shall know each other better" (*Letters*, II, p. 255).

Although both young women were considered feminists by comparison with the more conventional women of their class, the most obvious point of difference between them was the contrast between George Eliot's lifelong equivocation about the women's movement of her time and Barbara Leigh Smith's articulate and unequivocal participation in activities designed to secure women's welfare in law, employment, and in education. In response to Caroline Norton's public campaign to gain possession of her property and the right to visit her children after her separation from her husband, Barbara published, in 1854, *A Brief Summary in Plain Language of the Most Important Laws of England Concerning Women*.[3] In some personal "Remarks" at the conclusion of the summary, she urged the benefit of the franchise for women "not as a means of extorting justice from unwilling legislators," but "simply on the general ground that under a representative government, any class which is not represented is likely to be neglected. Proverbially, what is out of sight is out of mind."[4]

George Eliot, about this time, was writing unsigned essays for the *Leader*, similarly supportive of Mrs. Norton's *Letter to the Queen*, and also sympathetic to feminists like Margaret Fuller and Mary Wollstonecraft, whose writings reflected her own view that "Men pay a heavy price for their reluctance to encourage self-help and independent resources in women."[5] Yet, although she acknowledges that women are weakened, indeed "debased," by their subjection legally and socially, she concludes cautiously that "There is a perpetual action and reaction between individuals and institutions; we must try to mend both by little and little—the only way in which human things can be mended."[6] As the years went by George Eliot's hesitations increased lest any particular cause prove to be less than an unmitigated good (see *Letters*, V, pp. 366, 390). She writes to Jane Hughes Senior in 1869:

I feel too deeply the difficult complications that beset every measure likely to affect the position of women and also I feel too imperfect a sympathy with many women who have put themselves forward in connexion with such measures, to give practical adhesion to them. There is no subject on which I am more inclined to hold my peace and learn, than on the "Woman Question." (*Letters*, V, p. 58)

Barbara, however, never wavered from her assertion that legal grievances should be removed by appropriate legislation, as a necessary, if not sufficient measure. "A little knowledge of the laws of other countries, and the changes in some of our own laws within a few years," she believed, would do much to alter the English woman's "respect of the law, as something like revelation," an attitude which tends to deny that human institutions are a "set of rules made by man" that must "as years move on, be capable of being made better, that is, more fitting" to present circumstances.[7] George Eliot, at times, seems to share this perspective. At the time of John Stuart Mill's amendment to Gladstone's Reform Bill, which would have permitted women householders to vote, Eliot writes to Mrs. Peter Taylor: "I do sympathise with you most emphatically in the desire to see women socially elevated—educated equally with men, and secured as far as possible along with every other breathing creature from suffering the exercise of any unrighteous power" (*Letters*, IV, p. 366). Yet at other times her diffidence restricts her, as when, two weeks earlier, she writes to John Morley: "I do not trust very confidently to my own impressions on this subject. The peculiarities of my own lot have caused me to have idiosyncrasies rather than an average judgement" (*Letters*, IV, p. 364).

Barbara's clear thinking on the subject of women's alleged influence in society illustrates how she was able, at times, to resolve the "difficult complications" that so beset her friend Marian on the subject of women. "An assertion often made," she writes in her *Summary*,

that women would lose the good influence which they now exert indirectly on public affairs if they had votes, seems to require proof. First of all, it is necessary to prove that women have this indirect influence,—then that is good,—then that the indirect good influence would be lost if they had direct influence. . . . I see no necessary connexion between goodness and indirectness. On the contrary, I believe that the great thing women want is to be more direct and straightforward in thought, word, and deed.[8]

"Straightforward" was, certainly, Barbara's own approach to life, art, and the "Woman Question." And with all her doubts, self-doubts, and self-consciousness, George Eliot rejoiced in the "little draught of pure air" that Barbara's energetic activity and self-confidence brought into her world, affirming that "One always gets good from Barbara's healthy practical life."[9]

Descended from several generations of wealthy English radicals, Barbara Leigh Smith published two short books on women before she was thirty: the *Brief Summary* in 1854, and an essay called *Women and Work* in 1857. Her first venture had been to establish, with Elizabeth Whitehead, the Portman Hall School, which was open to the daughters as well as the sons of the neighborhood professionals, tradespeople, and artisans, and to all denominations including Roman Catholics, Jews, and free-thinkers.[10] When she became interested in the issue of married women's property she joined the women's committee of the Law Amendment Society and drafted a petition calling attention to the hardships under the present law.[11] Two years later, with Bessie Rayner Parkes, she founded the *Englishwoman's Journal* in order to provide a newspaper forum for women to discuss legal, educational, and economic issues that vitally concerned them.[12] In later years, after her marriage to Eugene Bodichon took her to Algeria for many months of the year, she continued to be involved in the founding of Girton College, to which she bequeathed her life savings of 10,000 pounds after having given 5,000 pounds during her lifetime.

During these years of intense political activity Barbara continued as well to pursue her interest in landscape painting, which she had studied as a young girl with William Henry Hunt and Jean-Baptiste Corot. She had visited Joseph Turner's studio; her work had been praised by John Ruskin and Dante Gabriel Rossetti; and she had exhibited at the French Gallery in London (1859 and 1861) and in the United States with the traveling British Exhibition in Philadelphia and Boston in 1858.[13] Her *American Diary* of 1857–58, recently edited by Joseph W. Reed, Jr., describes how her wedding trip through the American South combined conversations with slaves and visits to slave auctions and black churches, with equally anomalous, booted expeditions into the New Orleans swamps to paint Spanish moss and alligators. Her straightforwardness and evident enjoyment of all her activities are conveyed in a letter of Rossetti to his sister Christina.

Ah if you were only like Miss Barbara Smith! a young lady I meet at the Howitts', blessed with large rations of tin, fat, enthusiasm, and golden hair, who thinks nothing of climbing up a mountain in breeches, or wading through a stream in none, in the sacred name of pigment. Last night she invited us all to lunch with her on Sunday; and perhaps I shall go, as she is quite a *jolly fellow*.[14]

Only to be "like Miss Barbara Smith" was absurdly impossible for Christina Rossetti and equally impossible for George Eliot, however desirable it might have been. "To this puzzled and self-distrustful rebel," Hester Burton wrote, "Barbara's sense of direction was not only an inspiration, but an assurance."[15] Assurance. What George Eliot and scores of other Victorian women needed, and what Barbara Bodichon had. To account for the difference we must look at their families, for there, I think, the explanation lies.

As is well known, George Eliot, as Marian Evans, grew up in the provincial milieu of the English midlands. Her social attitudes were dominated by her father's outspoken contempt for the reform movements that had grown up in England following the French Revolution and the Napoleonic Wars. According to Leslie Stephen's biography, George Eliot was transcribing the memories of her own childhood in the following passage from "Looking Backward":[16]

To my father's mind the noisy teachers of revolutionary doctrine were, to speak mildly, a variable mixture of the fool and the scoundrel; the welfare of the nation lay in a strong government which could maintain order; and I was accustomed to hear him utter the word "government" in a tone that charged it with awe, and made it part of my effective religion, in contrast with the word "rebel," which seemed to carry the stamp of evil in its syllables, and, lit by the fact that Satan was the first rebel, made an argument dispensing with more detailed inquiry.[17]

Marian Evans's personal conflict with her father formed one of the crisis points of her young life and provided an abiding theme for the later work of George Eliot, a theme that was both personal and social.[18]

Barbara Leigh Smith, on the other hand, was born into a family with a long history of radical activity. Her eighteenth-century antecedents had supported the colonists during the American Revolution and had surrendered land holdings in

Savannah, Georgia, as a result of their sympathies.[19] Her grandfather, William Smith, M. P. for Norwich, was a Unitarian and an Abolitionist who also supported the removal of religious disabilities and the introduction of parliamentary reform.[20] He made a great deal of money as head of a firm of merchant grocers, collected pictures, including Reynolds and Rembrandt, and loved to travel with all of his ten children. Barbara's father, Benjamin Leigh Smith, never married Ann Longden, the mother of his five children, apparently because he believed that married women were unfairly victimized by the laws regarding property.[21] He supported free trade, abolition of the Corn Laws, and other good radical positions, but was chiefly outstanding in his practice of educating and providing for his daughters equally with his sons. After the death of their mother, when Barbara, the eldest child, was seven years old, Ben Smith educated them all at home with the best masters he could find, encouraged their individual interests and talents, and travelled with them extensively. When they came of age, both the sons and the daughters were given an income of about 300 pounds a year, which increased as they grew older.[22] Barbara Stephen writes, in her history of Girton College, that Barbara Bodichon was fortunate in her heritage: "Freedom and responsibility, and the sympathy of her elders . . . enabled her to do things which were then unusual and unconventional with a remarkable absence of self-consciousness."[23] As a result of this supportive and liberating family situation, Barbara was apparently quite free of the internalized guilt and social pressure that distorted the development of most of her contemporaries, including her cousin Florence Nightingale as well as her friend Marian Evans.

The richly complex bonds between Barbara Bodichon and George Eliot as women, feminists, writers, and artists can best be seen, I think, in relation to the novel *Adam Bede*, which Barbara immediately recognized as having been written by her friend Marian simply from reading an excerpt in an English newspaper review. We know that George Eliot considered the germ of the novel to be the story of an unhappy girl who murdered her illegitimate child and was comforted on her way to the gallows by George Eliot's Methodist aunt, the wife of her uncle Samuel Evans.[24] Infanticide, however, was at that time much more than a provincial family story; it was a wide-spread social problem, which Barbara had addressed in an appendix to her *Summary* of English laws concerning women.

"The hideous mortality of infants among the poor, especially the infants of women who are not married, is one of the most startling facts of our day," she writes. "We will not go into figures, for hardly a weekly newspaper can be read which does not contain these details."[25] The brief, cogent essay then turns immediately to the father of the child, since "It appears that the original cause of the cases of infanticide . . . is the desertion of the child by the father."[26] "The law appears to me to be very inefficient in this case," Barbara Bodichon continues, "for though theoretically it is the father's duty to provide for this offspring, he is not compelled to do so by the fear of any penalty in case of its death. . . . The mob may duck him, but even then the police will take care he suffer no great harm."[27] She proposes two remedial measures to be implemented through changes in law: first, that the parish officers, rather than the newly delivered mother, be made responsible for collecting the sums for confinement and support due from the father; and second, that "in cases of infanticide the father should always be treated as accessory to the fact" when it can be proved that such payment was not made. Her succinct concluding argument emphasizes both the practical and moral benefits of a single standard of liability for unmarried parents; if the child's death from neglect entailed punishment on the father, his present interest in its being allowed to die would be counterbalanced, "and three good results would follow:—fewer girls would be seduced; fewer children murdered; and poor rates would be greatly lightened."[28]

Although George Eliot mentions Barbara Bodichon's later book, *Women and Work*, she does not refer to the *Summary* of laws in her letters or journals.[29] Her awareness of the prevailing situation is included in *Adam Bede*, however, in the apprehensions of isolation and beggary that beset Hetty Sorrel when she learns that Arthur Donnithorne's regiment has left Windsor for Ireland.

She thought of a young woman who had been found against the church wall at Hayslope on Sunday, nearly dead with cold and hunger—a tiny infant in her arms. The woman was rescued and taken to the parish. . . . To Hetty the "parish" was next to the prison in obloquy, and to ask anything of strangers—to beg—to lie in the same far-off hideous region of intolerable shame that Hetty had all her life thought it impossible she could ever come near. But now the remembrance of that wretched woman whom she had seen herself, on her way back from church, being carried into Joshua Rann's came back upon her with the new terrible sense that there was very little now to divide *her* from the same lot.[30]

Adam Bede was published in London on the first of February, 1859. On April 26, Barbara Bodichon sent George Eliot a triumphant letter from Algiers: "I have not yet got the book but I *know* that it is you . . . not because it is like what you have written before but because it is like what I see in you" (*Letters*, III, pp. 56–57). From her perusal of one of the first reviews "in an obscure paper," which included one long extract, she had instantly exclaimed, "that is written by Marian Evans, there is her great big head and heart and her wise wide views."

Although neither the source of the review nor the extract is identified in the *George Eliot Letters*, the subject of infanticide is clearly alluded to in Barbara's closing anecdote. Before ending her letter with a reiteration of her joy at Marian's achievement, she interjects, seemingly without antecedent, that she had cried her eyes out over a newspaper account of "a certain girl undefended, alone [and] condemned to death for killing her illegitimate infant." Bodichon closes resignedly, "Cool now, I don't think anyone can help her."[31] Her allusion to this incident seems to be an utter *non sequitur* without the context of a concern for just such girls shared over time between the two writers.

In *Adam Bede* Hetty's trial for the murder of her infant puts her in the legal position of being not the victim of Arthur Donnithorne's seduction, but a criminal agent who must be punished as a threat to the traditional forms of English atriarchy. The structure of the novel, juxtaposing Hetty's trial to Arthur's irthday feast, exhibits a highly critical social commentary on the sexual double tandard, which functions as the thematic substructure of *Adam Bede* as insis- ently as the ceremonial rhythm functions as the formal one.[32] It is the artist ieorge Eliot's own commentary "in plain language" on one of "the most nportant laws of England concerning women." And in it, her activist friend 3arbara Bodichon recognized immediately her "great big head and heart and ler wise wide views."

NOTES

1. Hester Burton, *Barbara Bodichon, 1827–1891* (London: John Murray, 1949), p. 88.

2. Joseph W. Reed, Jr., "Barbara Leigh Smith Bodichon," in *An American Diary '857–58*, ed. Joseph W. Reed, Jr. (London: Routledge and Kegan Paul, 1972), p. 32. Reed's account of the Chapman-Bodichon affair is drawn from their correspondence, which is published here for the first time from the Beinecke Library's manuscript col- ection. Gordon S. Haight's *George Eliot and John Chapman* (New Haven: Yale Uni- versity Press, 1940), also describes this relationship. In *George Eliot: A Biography* (New York: Oxford University Press, 1968), p. 205, Haight acknowledges his indebtedness to an account of one of Barbara Bodichon's letters for information about "the intimate marital relationship" between George Eliot and Lewes which revealed that they practiced contraception and intended to have no children.

3. Barbara Leigh Smith Bodichon, *A Brief Summary in Plain Language of the Most Important Laws of England Concerning Women, Together with a Few Observations Thereon*, 3rd ed., rev. with additions (London: Trubner, 1869). Hereafter cited as *Summary*.

4. *Summary*, p. 17.

5. See "Life and Opinions of Milton" (August 4, 1855) and "Margaret Fuller and Mary Wollstonecraft" (October 13, 1855) rpt. in Thomas Pinney, ed., *Essays of George Eliot* (New York: Columbia University Press, 1963). Hereafter cited as *Essays*.

6. *Essays*, pp. 204–5.

7. *Summary*, p. 26.

8. Ibid., pp. 20–21.

9. Barbara Stephen, *Emily Davies and Girton College* (London: Constable, 1927), p. 38.

10. Ibid., p. 36.

11. The text of this petition is found in Burton, pp. 70–71.

12. Ibid., pp. 91–114.

13. Reed, pp. 43–44. See also Hugh Witemeyer, *George Eliot and the Visual Arts* (New Haven: Yale University Press, 1979), pp. 15–16. Presently John Crabbe, in England, is working on a book about Barbara Leigh Smith Bodichon as a painter.

14. Reed, p. 44.

15. Burton, p. 187.

16. Leslie Stephen, *George Eliot* (London: Macmillan, 1902), pp. 2–3.

17. George Eliot, *Impressions of Theophrastus Such* (New York: Harper and Brothers, n.d.), p. 34.

18. The painful situation at the time of Robert Evans's death is described in convincing

detail by Lawrence and Elisabeth Hanson, *Marian Evans and George Eliot: A Biography* (London: Oxford University Press, 1952), p. 94: "Marian had lived virtually alone with her father for twelve years, and entirely alone with him for the last eight. Any bond of understanding between them had long disappeared—not since her childhood had she been able to pay more than lip-service to his beliefs—and for the past three or four years he had been a burden and a hindrance to nearly every pleasure, every aim."

19. Reed, p. 37.

20. Stephen, p. 32.

21. Hanson, p. 349.

22. See Gordon S. Haight, ed., *The George Eliot Letters* (New Haven: Yale University Press, 1954), I, pp. liii–liv.

23. Stephen, p. 35.

24. See *Letters*, II, pp. 502–5. "A History of 'Adam Bede' " from George Eliot's Journal.

25. *Summary*, p. 29.

26. Ibid., pp. 30–31.

27. Ibid., p. 30.

28. Ibid., p. 31.

29. *Letters*, II, p. 396 (October 30, 1857) to Charles Bray: "That passage you quote from Mrs. Bodichon's book about 'doing small things badly' is mine. She did me the honor to copy it from a letter I wrote to her." On February 1, 1853 George Eliot wrote to Mrs. Peter Taylor: "A notable book just come out is Wharton's 'Summary of the Laws Relating to Women'" (*Letters*, II, p. 86). Haight's note adds that John Jane Smith Wharton had published *An Exposition of the Laws Relating to the Women of England* in 1853; it also dealt with the subject of infanticide.

30. George Eliot, *Adam Bede* (New York: New American Library, 1961), p. 361.

31. Haight's note to this letter reads: "Mary Jones, convicted at the Kingston Assizes of the willful murder of her female illegitimate child by cutting its throat, was sentenced to death. Subsequently she received a respite during her Majesty's pleasure, and 'within the last few days, had her sentence commuted to penal servitude for life,' (*Leader*, April 30, 1859, p. 551)."

32. See Keith Thomas, "The Double Standard," *Journal of the History of Ideas*, 20 (1959), 195–216; also Francoise Basch, *Relative Creatures: Victorian Women in Society and the Novel* (New York: Schocken Books, 1974), pp. 160–261.

16

The Second Act: Emily Dickinson's Orphaned Persona

Vivian R. Pollak

"Oh Austin . . . I wish we were children now. I wish we were always children, how to grow up I dont know," (Letter 115) Dickinson wrote to her brother in 1853, shortly after he became engaged to her closest friend, Susan Gilbert.[1] Her girlhood was over, but no marriage loomed on the horizon for her, distanced as it was by her vision of union with otherness as the abdication of selfhood. Thus at the age of twenty-two she had already begun to stave off her fears of a desolate future by clinging to an idealized past. In the following year, when she rejected an invitation to visit her pious friend Abiah Root (Abiah was shortly to become a minister's wife), she called herself "your quaint, old fashioned friend." The letter reads,

My Dear Child,
    Thank you for that sweet note, which came so long ago, and thank you for asking me to come and visit you, and thank you for loving me, long ago, and today, and too for all the sweetness, and all the gentleness, and all the tenderness with which you remember me—your quaint, old fashioned friend. . . . You asked me to come and see you—I must speak of that. I thank you Abiah, but I dont go from home, unless emergency leads me by the hand, and then I do it obstinately, and draw back if I can. Should I ever leave home, which is improbable, I will with much delight, accept your invitation; till then, my dear Abiah, my warmest thanks are your's, but dont expect me. I'm so old fashioned, Darling, that all your friends would stare. (L 166)

This article was written in 1980 and reflects my views at that time. I have updated some of this article in *Dickinson: The Anxiety of Gender* (Ithaca, N. Y.: Cornell University Press, 1984), especially in chapters 1 and 4.

And still later, in 1862, addressing Thomas Wentworth Higginson, the literary critic who advised her to " 'delay' to publish" as her "Preceptor," signing herself his "Scholar," she asked, "Could you tell me how to grow—or is it unconveyed—like Melody—or Witchcraft?" "I went to school—but in your manner of the phrase—had no education" (L 261). Visiting the thirty-nine-year-old poet in Amherst in 1870, it was this impression of a vulnerable, childlike persona which Higginson carried away as his dominant impression. Writing to his invalid neurasthenic wife, he described his encounter with a saintly simpleton or wise fool:

A step like a pattering child's in entry & in glided a little plain woman with two smooth bands of reddish hair & a face a little like Belle Dove's; not plainer—with no good feature—in a very plain & exquisitely clean white pique & a blue net worsted shawl. She came to me with two day lilies which she put in a sort of childlike way into my hand & said "These are my introduction" in a soft, frightened breathless childlike voice— & added under her breath Forgive me if I am frightened; I never see strangers & hardly know what I say—but she talked soon & thenceforward continuously—& deferentially— sometimes stopping to ask me to talk instead to her—but readily recommencing. Manner between Angie Tilton & Mr. Alcott—but thoroughly ingenuous & simple which they are not & saying many things which you would have thought foolish & I wise—.[2] (L 342a)

" 'Oh why do the insane so cling to you,' " his wife inquired not long thereafter.[3] Finally, on her deathbed, just before she lapsed into unconsciousness in May 1886, writing to those same orphaned Norcross cousins some sixteen years her junior to whom she had signed herself "Uncle Emily," whom she had called "Poor Plover," "Dear Peacock," "Dear Children," "Dear little solid gold girl(s)," Dickinson concluded, "Little Cousins, Called back," but whether to plenitude or void she did not say (L 1046).

Childhood—quintessential romantic metaphor of purified beginnings, edenic freedom, unfallen organic union between self and world, self and nature, self and God; metaphor, in short, of the undivided, uncorrupted, aboriginal self— fascinated Dickinson both as woman and poet, as a number of her critics have been quick to observe.[4] Yet the conclusions they have drawn in their quest for a central idea which would unify Dickinson's boldly disparate images of child-hood have differed widely, in part because of their desire to establish a context for this child persona in the obsessions of the poet's life. I too followed this richly suggestive biographical path in my article "Thirst and Starvation in Emily Dickinson's Poetry," where I examined some of the psychosexual causes of the discontinuous cycle of privation, self-privation and qualified self-reliance Dick-inson's artistic universe delineates.[5] Her letters of the 1850's establish that her fascination with deliberately shrunken appetites and willfully stunted growth emerged as a defensive posture against the repressive mid-Victorian cult of "True Womanhood."[6] Adopting the style of the pre-pubescent child, she was intent on besting an infantilizing society whose patriarchal sexual politics were writ large in her own "home sweet home" by exaggerating its latent identification of femininity and unselfconsciousness. But what emerges even in her letters is a highly self-conscious parodic stance, best understood as a mode of passive aggression initially directed outward and intended to liberate her "free spirit" from the conformist pressures that she chronicles throughout the correspondence of the formative years before 1858 when she emerges suddenly, abruptly, elliptically as the poet whose voice we recognize.[7] A combatant posing as a noncombatant, Dickinson sought to distance "these problems of the flesh" through the renunciation of the appearance, although not the inner reality, of autonomous selfhood. But even willfully chosen roles are adopted against the heft of socially appointed fates. Masks have a way of fusing with and devouring the reality they are designed to conceal. Hence Dickinson confined to a kind of lifelong house arrest within her father's house and ground, her sexuality shrouded by the virginal white gown of the self-designated, incorporeal bride. However, the figure with whom I shall be concerned in this essay is not the biographical self who lived out a defensive strategy, at once self-protective and self-destructive, which was endemic to the female sensibility of the nineteenth century, as Ann Douglas, Elaine Showalter, Sandra Gilbert, Susan Gubar, Nancy Cott, and others have demonstrated.[8] Rather, I wish to consider the artist who worked "for Immortality" (406) in order to address the following questions. How does childhood function in Dickinson's art and why does she characteristically represent innocence as a value which collapses as soon as it is tested? What are the consequences of this vision of beginnings as subject to abrupt and wholly inexplicable interruption for her poetics, and what is the relationship between childhood and death she imagines most compellingly so that we, like the unwitting Wedding Guest, cannot choose but hear?

Charting the disruptive progressions of the human life cycle, Dickinson often declares that "Finding is the first Act / The second, loss" (870). Most poems of her child group are organized by these absolutes: faith and despair, aspiration and frustration, originating victory and terminal defeat. There is a parthenogenic moment when consciousness is uncontaminated by bereavement and an equally contextless moment when bereavement is unassuaged by the memory of an earlier bliss. Childhood in its pure or archetypal form is the moment before death—in either its ultimate or prefiguring types—violates the persona's faith in a deathless, pain-free universe. Thus I shall be speaking here both of poems in which Dickinson explicitly names herself "child," "little girl" or, more rarely, "boy," and more generally of those poems which explore crucial turning points from innocence to experience. In many poems, these turning points are inconclusive. In still others, Dickinson measures the unalterable distance between her helpless child persona's ideal of original freedom and the secondary reality of her grotesque psychic bondage. In the following poem, for example, appetites she can neither eliminate nor gratify paralyze her absolutely:

> It would have starved a Gnat—
> To live so small as I—

And yet I was a living Child—
With Food's necessity

Upon me—like a Claw—
I could no more remove
Than I could coax a Leech away—
Or make a Dragon—move—

Nor like the Gnat—had I—
The privilege to fly
And seek a Dinner for myself—
How mightier He—than I—

Nor like Himself—the Art
Upon the Window Pane
To gad my little Being out—
And not begin—again— (612)

Although the romantic ideal of childhood seldom commands her sustained attention, Joanne Feit Diehl's assertion that "Dickinson writes only songs of experience" and that "she does not recall the 'visionary gleam' lost in the process of growth, for it has never been hers" oversimplifies this poet's relationship both to her own personal past and to what R. W. B. Lewis in *The American Adam* has called "the party of hope."[9] Without some individual and cultural memory of this "visionary gleam," which, it could be argued, is encoded by her subverted hymn meters themselves, her vehement protests against the loss of faith she associates with childhood, "earth's confiding time," could never have been written. It is precisely the distance between the romantic archetype and the reality of her deviant experience around which many of her poems are structured. Because Dickinson is a steadfast adherent to neither the "party of hope" nor of "memory," her American Eve has not one but two faces. Indeed, the most characteristic poems of her child group testify to the impossibility of their temporal fusion. The Dickinsonian "I," having lost a coherent vision of its past, never solves the mystery of its origins. The primary function of her victimized child persona is not, as Clark Griffith has asserted, to reveal a universe "contaminated to the core," but rather to insist on the instability of consciousness.[10]

Exposing the vulnerability of mere unaided innocence, Dickinson is concerned with protecting her orphan-exiles both from the suicidal despair of the starvation poem just quoted and from the incurable hopefulness which the dark forces of the universe and the unconscious are compelled to destroy. This latter enterprise is complicated by her child persona's strategic withdrawals from nature and human society and from the aggressive impulses she projects onto others— masculinity, God, "heaven," nature, convention, the world—intent on her destruction. This "I-He," "I-It," "I-They" structure makes her a perfect victim, and a perfect sexual victim at that. The association between femininity and vulnerability these poems emphasize is too widespread to be missed. But such a structure also forecloses any final resolution to the psychological problem with which these poems wrestle: how to live in the world without being imprisoned by it, how to conceive a self in a landscape of absence. As Griffith implies, these strategic retreats are essential to the survival of her voice. When she takes her power in her hand and assaults the world frontally, she is invariably defeated. Poet of strong beginnings, she often concludes with a question mark. Moreover, the economy of her style enables her to pretend to more certainty about her psychological ambitions than she commands:

> I took my Power in my Hand—
> And went against the World—
> 'Twas not so much as David—had—
> But I—was twice as bold—
>
> I aimed my Pebble—but Myself
> Was all the one that fell—
> Was it Goliah—was too large—
> Or was myself—too small? (540)

Out of this self-critical dialogue between arrogance and humility, a third voice emerges: the voice of the poet mediating this conflict through language which calls attention to the instability of its ironic mode. Dickinson's ironic child persona perpetuates her profoundly ambivalent contract with the rage she tends to represent as unintegrated otherness, but the question she poses in the poem just quoted ("Was it Goliah—was too large— / Or was myself—too small?") is unanswerable. As bard, with no strong line of female "Great Progenitor(s)" to gird her for combat, she forges an uneasy alliance with her David. As a woman, Dickinson was too shrewd a social observer not to note the equally powerful alliance between the "Soft—Cherubic Creatures—," the "Gentle-women" against whose "Dimity Convictions—" she protested, and the world which preferred her " 'still.' " Thus we find a poem such as the following where the speaker's aggression is partially controlled by a series of startling metamorphoses. "Little Girl," "Bird," "Himself," "Star," she attempts to will herself into a condition of liberated orphanage. A boasting poem which fails to live up to the promise of its strong beginning, "They Shut Me Up in Prose" illustrates the tension between the romantic myth of childhood freedom and the reality of the Dickinsonian persona's powerlessness. Identifying imaginative play with childhood, play which is still accessible to the adult consciousness, the speaker brags of the ease with which she escaped from a society that wishes to immobilize her. The argument ends, however, with an unconvincing assertion of total freedom. The divorce between the speaker and her environment leaves her with no place to go. Laughing down at those others against whom she defines her strength, purging herself of any conceivable human identity, Dickinson's terminal phrase "No more have I" ends her angry *apologia* with a prosaic, skewed rhyme without resolving the conflict between feelings of helplessness and power the poem describes:

They shut me up in Prose—
As when a little Girl
They put me in the Closet—
Because they liked me "still"—

Still! Could themself have peeped—
And seen my Brain—go round—
They might as wise have lodged a Bird
For Treason—in the Pound—

Himself has but to will
And easy as a Star
Look down upon Captivity—
And laugh—No more have I— (613)

In poem after poem the fall which precipitates her child persona out of the paradisiacal garden has also left her stranded in empty space. The continuous relationships that would enable her to move beyond illusory comedy, pathos, or tragedy to maturity—to a successful accommodation between herself and her world—are ruthlessly eliminated by a nature she can neither understand nor command. Consequently, she finds herself trapped in the prison of an alien self; her memory of the liberty she knew "When Memory was a Boy" is "Avoided— like a Dream— / Too wide for any Night but Heaven— / If That—indeed— redeem—" (652).

Bereft of mentors, human or divine, Dickinson is forced to birth herself. Rhetorically, this generational compression begets irony, but her compulsion to enact all the roles in her family romance frustrates her attempts to find the enabling experiences that she associates with mature power. Representing speakers who have lost their childhood in its purely joyous form, who have been prematurely initiated into the anxieties of adulthood, a significant number of these statements are determined to provide her orphan-exiles with a second childhood after some extreme form of separation has isolated the persona from a human environment intent on killing off her "Real Me." Not surprisingly, given the evangelical religious rhetoric that informs her style (Karl Keller aptly describes her as stamping her foot "at what she stands on"), one of her orphaned persona's stock responses to privation is to imagine that she has a father in heaven who has a new home prepared for her in the sky.[11] When Dickinson's born-again tropes describe "Gates Ajar" family reunions, indulgent Victorian patriarchs, nicely naughty little girls, or any of the other domestic appurtenances of the cottage-style heaven popularized by her contemporary Elizabeth Stuart Phelps in a series of enormously successful spiritualist novels,[12] they generate that disquieting archness for which she has been so roundly spanked by critical hands over the years.

However, this hopeful Christian-derived mythology, when more thoroughly misread, also informs one of the most esthetically harmonious poems of Dickinson's child group, "A loss of something ever felt I—" (959). The sometimes distracting emphasis on other characters, whether as antagonists or allies, has been jettisoned; the speaker's isolated consciousness is the locus of conflict. Disciplined by its resistance to easy resolutions magically enacted, in this orphan's lament the persona cannot adequately name her "Missing All." The poem's theme is the relationship between self-knowledge and lost access to experience. Calling herself "the only Prince cast out," bemoaning a lost "Dominion" that she identifies with maleness, she permits the emphasis to fall on an uncertain quest which is associated with particular places ("Delinquent Palaces," "the site of the Kingdom of Heaven") that her finite vision prevents her from fully repossessing. The speaker's uncertainty about the nature of her lost paradise, perhaps the androgynous consciousness whose presence is experienced as an absence, generalizes the theme well beyond the specific autobiographical sexual context that the poem both incorporates and masters:

> A loss of something ever felt I—
> The first that I could recollect
> Bereft I was—of what I knew not
> Too young that any should suspect
>
> A Mourner walked among the children
> I notwithstanding went about
> As one bemoaning a Dominion
> Itself the only Prince cast out—
>
> Elder, Today, a session wiser
> And fainter, too, as Wiseness is—
> I find myself still softly searching
> For my Delinquent Palaces—
>
> And a Suspicion, like a Finger
> Touches my Forehead now and then
> That I am looking oppositely
> For the site of the Kingdom of Heaven—

To retain her faith in an original harmony between self and nature, self and God, Dickinson's bereaved child persona must effect some compromise between her need for sustaining temporal relationships and her need to free herself of their constricted reality. Space limitations prevent me from considering here those love poems in which an orphaned female persona is abruptly transformed into an uncourted, unhusbanded bride, married to her own phoenixlike imagination of invulnerable identity. Therefore, I should like to conclude this discussion of the two faces of Eve, looking forward toward paradise and backward toward paradise lost, with a transitional poem where the child persona's immersion in nature is delineated with greater narrative particularity than in any of the poems previously discussed:

> I started Early—Took my Dog—
> And visited the Sea—

The Mermaids in the Basement
Came out to look at me—

And Frigates—in the Upper Floor
Extended Hempen Hands—
Presuming Me to be a Mouse—
Aground—upon the Sands—

But no Man moved Me—till the Tide
Went past my simple Shoe—
And past my Apron—and my Belt
And past my Boddice—too—

And made as He would eat me up—
As wholly as a Dew
Upon a Dandelion's Sleeve—
And then—I started—too—

And He—He followed—close behind—
I felt his Silver Heel
Upon my Ancle—Then my Shoes
Would overflow with Pearl—

Until We met the Solid Town—
No One He seemed to know—
And bowing—with a Mighty look—
At me—The Sea withdrew— (520)

Although the "simple" persona's death into disillusion is narrowly avoided, in opting for the "solid town" and in resisting the sea's erotic embrace, she also loses the opportunity to clarify the moral ambiguity of her anesthetized emotional response. As Robert Weisbuch has remarked, the persona aborts a passionate dramatic contest with "experiential unknowns" and "denied irrational urges," but his formulation of this deceptively fragmented soulscape must be particularized somewhat further.[13] At the heart of the poem's insight into the complex relationship between risk and maturation lies a thanatized vision of love and an eroticized vision of death, a blinding vision of powerful mystery which the speaker cannot simultaneously experience and tell. In the end, whether the sea represents the persona's repressed sexual aggression projected onto a lascivious male universe or whether the sea is genuinely shaped as male otherness matters little. What is important here is that these "experiential unknowns" are not wholly unknown. Encountering the "man of noon," the sun god in his watery habitat, Dickinson shapes a contest her childlike persona has no chance of winning in frontal combat. Given this shrewdly politicized sensibility of unequal sexual odds, the pattern of physical advance and retreat is not accompanied by any growth in the persona's consciousness, nor can it be. Designing a drama between male-identified aggression and female-identified passivity, Dickinson is caught between self-preservation and ego-annihilating adventure.

'The shore is safer . . . but I love to buffet the sea,'' (*L* 39) she had written to ₄ friend in her nineteenth year. But by 1862, when she composed her seascape, ₃he had been further schooled in the need for renunciation, that "piercing Virtue," ₂st the "Wild Nights" of which she dreamed drown her voice in pearly silence.

NOTES

1. All texts for Dickinson's letters are from Thomas H. Johnson and Theodora Ward, ₂ds., *The Letters of Emily Dickinson*, 3 vols. (Cambridge, Mass.: Harvard University ₃ress, 1958). The letter *L* precedes such citations to differentiate letters from poems. All ₂exts for Dickinson's poems are from Thomas H. Johnson, ed., *The Poems of Emily Dickinson*, 3 vols. (Cambridge, Mass.: Harvard University Press, 1955). The parenthetical ₃umbers correspond to the relative chronological numbering in this work.

2. Neither "Belle Dove" nor "Angie Tilton" has been identified. "Mr. Alcott" is Bronson, transcendental seer and father of Louisa May.

3. As quoted in Jay Leyda, *The Years and Hours of Emily Dickinson* (New Haven: Yale University Press, 1960), II, p. 213.

4. Adrienne Rich, for example, writes that "Most of us, unfortunately, have been exposed in the schoolroom to Dickinson's 'little-girl' poems, her kittenish tones. . . . One critic—Richard Chase—has noted that in the 19th century 'one of the careers open to women was perpetual childhood.' A strain in Dickinson's letters and some—though by far a minority—of her poems was a self-diminutization, almost as if to offset and deny— or even disguise—her actual dimensions as she must have experienced them. And this emphasis on her own 'littleness,' along with the deliberate strangeness of her tactics of seclusion, have been, until recently, accepted as the prevailing character of the poet." "Vesuvius at Home: The Power of Emily Dickinson," *Parnassus*, V (Fall / Winter 1976), p. 58.

5. Vivian R. Pollak, "Thirst and Starvation in Emily Dickinson's Poetry," *American Literature*, VI, no. 1 (March, 1979), 33–49.

6. Three recent works defining nineteenth-century American attitudes toward women are Nancy R. Cott, *The Bonds of Womanhood: "Woman's Sphere" in New England, 1780–1835* (New Haven, Conn.: Yale University Press, 1977); Ann Douglas, *The Feminization of American Culture* (New York: Alfred A. Knopf, 1977); and Barbara Welter, *Dimity Convictions: The American Woman in the Nineteenth Century* (Athens: Ohio University Press, 1976).

7. Only five poems have been identified as having been written before 1858. For discussions of the difficulties of Dickinson chronology, see Johnson, *Poems*, I, pp. xvii– lxvii; and R. W. Franklin, *The Editing of Emily Dickinson: A Reconsideration* (Madison: University of Wisconsin Press, 1967).

8. Douglas, *The Feminization of American Culture*, and "The 'Scribbling Women' and Fanny Fern: Why Women Wrote," *American Quarterly*, XXVII (Spring 1971), 3– 24; Elaine Showalter, *A Literature of Their Own: British Women Novelists from Brontë to Lessing* (Princeton: Princeton University Press, 1977); Sandra Gilbert and Susan Gubar, *The Madwoman in the Attic: The Woman Writer and the Nineteenth-Century Literary Imagination* (New Haven, Conn.: Yale University Press, 1979); Nancy Cott, *The Bonds of Womanhood*, and idem, "Passionlessness: An Interpretation of Victorian Sexual Ideology, 1790–1850," *Signs*, IV, no. 2 (Winter, 1978), 219–36.

9. Feit Diehl, " 'Come Slowly—Eden': An Exploration of Women Poets and Their Muse," *Signs*, III, no. 3 (Spring, 1978), 574; R. W. B. Lewis, *The American Adam: Innocence Tragedy and Tradition in the Nineteenth Century* (Chicago: University of Chicago Press, 1955). Lewis argues that "a culture achieves identity not so much through the ascendancy of one particular set of convictions as through the emergence of its peculiar and distinctive dialogue," invoking the terms "party of hope" and "party of memory" to describe the ideological extremes from which the seminal dialogue about the nature of the American self emerged.

10. Clarke Griffith, *The Long Shadow: Emily Dickinson's Tragic Poetry* (Princeton: Princeton University Press, 1964), p. 31. Despite my quarrel with Griffith's basic assumption that Dickinson's child persona functions primarily as an ironic mask behind which she is free to attack a hostile universe, his chapter "The Post-Romantic Child" is indispensable reading on this subject. Evidently, there is some truth in his assertion that "To lie low in order to gain the freedom for striking back—here, surely, is the essence of the child poetry," p. 39. But it is ironic that, in a book which purports to emphasize tragic vision, Griffith views the Dickinsonian child as an essentially comic mask, and has her laughing "up her sleeve" at the malice and hostility of "Nature and God." Dickinson's poetry is genuinely tragic when consciousness itself is death-ridden and those others against whom she defines her strength, including Nature and God, have disappeared from view.

11. Perhaps the most interesting of these poems is "We don't cry—Tim and I" (196), where the persona also furnishes herself with a boyish alter ego. The poem is, as Rebecca Patterson argues in "Emily Dickinson's 'Double' Tim: Masculine Identification," *American Imago*, XXVII (winter, 1971), 330–62, a compelling revelation of the poet's sexual anxieties, as are all those utterances where her flight from femininity propels her into a male persona. However, Albert Gelpi's attempt to assert its artistic merit, in *The Tenth Muse: The Psyche of the American Poet* (Cambridge, Mass.: Harvard University Press, 1975), p. 249, seems to me not to withstand close scrutiny. He writes:

This early poem contains many of the motifs scattered throughout the love poems: a passion linked to religion, withdrawn into exclusive association, resistant to the death it is doomed to, uncertain of the eternity which offers the only chance for genuine union. The seriousness of the poem is no more betrayed by the witty playfulness than it would be in a poem of Robert Frost or John Crowe Ransom. The poet is employing the resources of the little-girl persona to distract us at first from what she is revealing, but the nursery-rhyme quality, the singsong rhythms, the repetitions and refrains . . . all lead up to the last lines, spaced out with dashes to heighten the recognition. How can we, Tim and I, arrange for simultaneous death? Because we are one and the same person? "I— 'Tim'—and Me!"

Gelpi's eloquence almost succeeds in rewriting the poem, but his assertion that it is "resistant to the death it is doomed to" calls for a howl of protest. If Tim and I have any passion at all, it is to quit this vale of tears for the storybook heaven they can see only if they shut their brown eye to those divisions of desire which Tim may have signified in the author's unconscious, but which he is not made to symbolize in the poem.

12. Barton Levi St. Armand's "Paradise Deferred: The Image of Heaven in the Work of Emily Dickinson and Elizabeth Stuart Phelps," *American Quarterly*, XXIX (Spring, 1977), 55–78 explores significant parallels in the work of these two writers. He argues that "*The Gates Ajar* and Dickinson's poems on spiritual marriage are products of that

more pervasive common source: the rebellion against the tyrannical Father-God of New England orthodoxy'' (p. 56).

13. Robert Weisbuch, *Emily Dickinson's Poetry* (Chicago: University of Chicago Press, 1975), p. 55.

17

The Female Alcoholic in Victorian Fiction: George Eliot's Unpoetic Heroine

Sheila Shaw

In a book about women drinkers, the following title appears in the bibliography: "Females are Different."[1] I noted it as an item that might be useful at a future time, thinking also that I'd like to ask the gentlemen who wrote the paper, which was presented in 1971, about their title, "Females are Different." Different from what? From each other? The answer, of course, is plain enough: females are different from the norm, and the norm is male. It's an old story and we've all heard it before.

One evening during that year, I was strolling through Boston's Copley Square with another woman and two men. The venerable Boston Public Library was on our right, historic Trinity Church on our left, the elegant Copley Plaza Hotel directly ahead. We had just had an expensive dinner, complete with French wines and cordials. About thirty yards away, on the sidewalk in front of the hotel, a shabby woman clutching a paper bag staggered as she moved into the shadows, where she lifted her dress and squatted. The experience was unforgettable, though I don't know what my friends thought, for we never mentioned it, then or since.

Why were the four of us unable to come to terms with what we had just seen? After all, the English language does have gender-free sobriquets to describe such a person: drunken bum, skid-row derelict. But no, somehow, for a female they just won't do, no matter how liberated we are. Although we've often seen males in degrading stages of public drunkenness, we simply are not used to inebriated females squatting in the street. The authors of that title had a point after all: females *are* different.

Almost a century earlier, Edgar Degas in 1876 painted "Absinthe," which depicts a man and a woman in a cafe. The woman, a full glass on the table before her and an empty decanter to her right, is in center foreground. The droop of her eyelids, the blotches on her puffy face, and the position of her feet, spread slightly askew and "unladylike," show her to be in an advanced stage of intoxication. If we could stand her up, we know she would fall, probably hurting herself on one of the tables. She is better off sitting down, better off immutable, hanging on her wall in the Louvre. It would never do to have the likes of her urinating in Boston's Copley Square.

Nineteenth-century England would have agreed, for when this painting was shown in London in 1893, it caused a scandal.[2] Male drunks are bad enough, the Victorians must have thought; female drunks are anathema, although the Industrial Revolution had made it impossible to ignore their growing numbers. Disraeli's *Sybil* (1845) and Kingsley's *Alton Locke* (1850), two well-known examples of the popular thesis novels, contain many references to these women. Charles Dickens also had them in mind when he produced *Sketches by Boz* (1836). Chapter 22 depicts "the bar of a large gin-shop and its ordinary customers," which include "girls of fourteen or fifteen, with matted hair, walking about barefoot . . . and women, in every variety of scanty and dirty apparel." Dickens concludes:

Well-disposed gentlemen, and charitable ladies, would alike turn with coldness and disgust from a description of the drunken besotted men, and wretched broken-down miserable women. . . . Gin-drinking is a great vice in England, but wretchedness and dirt are a greater; and until you improve the homes of the poor, or persuade a half-famished wretch not to seek relief in the temporary oblivion of his own misery . . . gin shops will increase in number.[3]

Dickens was in his early twenties when he wrote this compassionate piece. How would the mature novelist of forty-two show a broken-down, miserable, gin-drinking woman? Enter Mrs. Stephen Blackpool of Coketown (*Hard Times*, 1854):

Such a woman! A disabled, drunken creature, barely able to preserve her sitting posture by steadying herself with one begrimed hand on the floor. . . . A creature so foul to look at, in her tatters, stains and splashes, but so much fouler . . . in her moral infamy, that it was a shameful thing even to see her. (Ch. 10)

The description of Mrs. Blackpool is saturated with contempt and revulsion.

Not all of Dickens's drinking females arouse his moral indignation. Mrs. Weller (*Pickwick Papers*), Mrs. Bangham (*Little Dorrit*), Lady Tippins (*Our Mutual Friend*), and the insuperable Mrs. Gamp in *Martin Chuzzlewit* are great tipplers and not notably repulsive. Indeed, in their drinking scenes Dickens unleashes his great comic powers, and their portraits are laced with good-natured ridicule.

The message was clear enough. In order to write about females who drink, they must be 1) poor; 2) depraved; 3) comical; or 4) invisible. Grace Poole, caretaker of the mad Mrs. Rochester in Charlotte Brontë's *Jane Eyre* (1847), is not any of the first three, but she does meet the fourth criterion—she is practically invisible. Although she plays an important role both at Thornfield and in Jane Eyre's imagination, Grace Poole appears in the novel just four times, and then, only briefly. In chapter 11 we learn what she looks like ("between thirty and forty; a set, square-made figure, red-haired, and with a hard, plain face"); in chapter 12 that she drinks too much— "oh, romantic reader, forgive me for telling the plain truth!" whispers Jane; in chapter 17, Grace Poole passes before Jane to "eat her dinner . . . and go back, carrying her pot of porter with her, for her private solace, in her own gloomy upper haunt"; and in chapter 16, she is present when Rochester reveals his insane wife to Jane and members of the wedding party.

Two of the above conditions for story-book female drinkers are present in Elizabeth Gaskell's *Mary Barton* (1848): Esther is both poor and depraved. Formerly a lovely, innocent girl who had eloped with a handsome officer, Esther reappears midway through the novel in order to save her niece, Mary Barton, from her own fate: prostitution, vagrancy, and drunkenness. The following passage, where Esther rejects a kindly offer of shelter and nourishment from a family friend, proves that Gaskell understood the horrors of withdrawal associated with alcohol addiction:

"I tell you, I cannot. . . . I must have a drink. . . . If I go without food, and without shelter, I must have my dram. Oh! you don't know the awful nights I have had in prison for want of it. . . . Don't speak to me of leading a better life—I must have drink. I cannot pass tonight without a dram; I dare not." (Ch. 14)

Predictably, "the abandoned and polluted outcast" dies. Fortunately, we are spared the details.[4]

George Eliot broke all the rules when she wrote "Janet's Repentance," the third tale in *Scenes of Clerical Life* (1858), her first published work of fiction.[5] Janet Dempster, an unhappy, battered wife, is not poor, not depraved, not comical, not invisible, and not always sober. The central drama concerns Robert Dempster, a lawyer, his wife Janet, and Reverend Edgar Tryan, an Evangelical pastor. Dempster, a loud-mouthed bully and an alcoholic, ultimately dies of delirium tremens complicated by a broken, "mortified" leg. Janet Dempster, intelligent and loving, finds "every coming night more impossible to brave without arming herself in leaden stupor." As she confesses later to Mr. Tryan,

"I had never been used to drink anything but water. I hated wine and spirits because Robert drank them so; but one day when I was very wretched, and the wine was standing on the table . . . I poured some into a large glass and drank it. It blunted my feelings, and made me more indifferent. After that, the temptation was always coming, and it got stronger and stronger. . . . It seemed as if there was a demon in me always making me rush to do what I longed not to do." (Ch. 18)

Mr. Tryan becomes Janet's spiritual mentor, and with kindness, faith, and patience, leads her toward a life of sobriety and inner peace. Destined to an early

death from tuberculosis, Tryan lives just long enough to witness—Janet's
Repentance.

John Blackwood, publisher of *Blackwood's Magazine* where the tale first
appeared, exchanged letters with George Eliot from June to October, 1857, while
"Janet's Repentance" was in progress. Their correspondence is fascinating to
read—almost a social document reflecting Victorian attitudes on the relationship
between art and life.[6] On receiving the first four chapters, Blackwood thought
the picture of Milby too "harsh," and

the first scene especially I think you should shorten. It is deuced good but rather a
staggerer in an opening scene of a Story of Clerical Life. Dempster is rather too barefaced
a brute and I am sorry that the poor wife's sufferings should have driven her to so
unsentimental a resource as beer. Still it is true to nature. The case is but too common.[7]

And he advised the author to "*soften*" the picture as much as possible. Her
response was firm:

I feel that I shall not be able to make any other than *superficial* alterations. . . . Everything
is softened from the fact, so far as art is permitted to soften and yet to remain essentially
true. The real town was more vicious than my Milby; the real Dempster was far more
disgusting than mine; the real Janet alas! had a far sadder end than mine. . . . There is
nothing to be done with the story, but either to let Dempster and Janet and the rest be
as I *see* them, or to renounce it as too painful. I am keenly alive, at once to the scruples
and alarms an editor may feel, and to my own inability to write under any cramping
influence.[8]

George Eliot closed the letter by offering to withdraw "Janet's Repentance" if
"its publication in the Magazine [is] a disagreeable risk." Blackwood replied:
"I'd not fall in with George Eliots every day and the idea of stopping the Series
. . . gave me 'quite a turn'. . . . In continuing to write for the Magazine I beg . . .
that you will not consider yourself hampered in any way."[9] Finally, when the
story was completed and in proof, Blackwood praised the depiction of Janet

in spite of the unpoetic nature of her weakness. . . . It was a bold choice of a plot and
some will object to such a feature *in a heroine*, but there is no more common agent of
human misery and trial than drunkenness and consequently there can be no more legitimate
material for the writer of Fiction.[10]

Yet reservations lingered, as the next paragraph showed: "I was a little puzzled
when I came to the climax about the bottle of brandy . . . but it contributes to
the air of truth. Should there be so much of Dempster's delirium?" No doubt,
Blackwood was uneasy with these sections because they deal so explicitly with
"the unpoetic nature" of alcoholism.[11] I suspect that Blackwood was less "puzzled" than discomforted by such features "in a heroine." Even Henry James,
for all his rhetoric about granting the artist his donnée, is critical "of a heroine

stained with the vice of intemperance. The theme is unpleasant; the author chose it at her peril.''[12] The key word is *heroine*: decent women don't drink.[13]

Janet's case, to be sure, is not nearly as advanced as that of Dempster, but as James said, it was unpleasant enough that the "heroine [is] stained with the vice of intemperance." Perhaps for this reason we learn of Janet's drinking through other characters. In chapter 3, where Janet is mentioned for the first time, a Milby matron remarks: "poor thing, looking so strange, anybody passing her in the street may see plain enough what's the matter." Another says: "There's great excuses for her. When a woman can't think of her husband coming home without trembling, it's enough to make her drink something to blunt her feelings." Nor are the ladies the only ones to notice. Good-hearted Mr. Jerome comments in chapter 8 that " 'I hear sad stories about her now. But she's druv to it, she's druv to it.' "

Nowhere do we actually *see* Janet drinking. Indeed, the only time we know at first hand that she has been drinking is after the fact, and that occurs only once, at the end of chapter 4. Dempster comes home late at night, drunk, and knocks loudly at the front door. When no one answers, he uses his key, enters, and calls out angrily for his wife. Slowly, she comes toward him, her face "pale with . . . premature lines . . . lengthened by sorrow. . . . Her wide open black eyes had a strangely fixed, sightless gaze, as she paused at the turning, and stood silent before her husband." Should the reader fail to recognize the state Janet is in, Dempster clarifies: " 'What, you've been drinking again, have you? I'll beat you into your sense.' "

The only phase of Janet's addiction that we see is her recovery, although the initial withdrawal is either glossed over or dealt with metaphorically. For instance, just after Dempster in one of his rages forces Janet out of bed and into the street (chapter 16), she goes to the home of a neighbor. Mrs. Pettifer, whose home becomes a sort of halfway house for a few days, takes Janet into her bed and brings her a cup of tea. Toward morning, having just fallen asleep, "her movements became more violent, her mutterings more frequent and agitated, till at last she started up with a smothered cry . . . shaking with terror." Janet is reassured by Mrs. Pettifer and sinks back on the pillow, "still trembling." It was, says Janet, "a horrible dream." And indeed, that is the level on which this episode might have been interpreted. On the other hand, it happens to be an accurate description of what Janet's physical condition would be after six or eight hours without a drink. The next day (detoxification lasts several days), Janet has "a violent fit of weeping":

She was suffering, too, from the absence of the long-accustomed stimulus which she had promised Mr. Tryan not to touch again. The poor thing was conscious of this, and dreaded her own weakness. (Ch. 21)

And she says to her mother, "Don't let me have anything if I ask for it." But a few hours later, Janet's "imagination influenced by physical depression as well as by mental habits, was haunted by the vision of her husband's return home, and she began to shudder.'' What Janet is really undergoing should be clear to any reader who is familiar with alcoholic withdrawal pains.

On the third day of Janet's ordeal, Mr. Tryan, to whom Janet appealed and who had been visiting her at Mrs. Pettifer's, says, ''I believe a great change of feeling has begun in her.'' The obvious meaning is that Janet has begun to ''repent.'' On the other hand, it is possible that ''this great change of feeling'' is more than a palliative for Victorian sensibilities, for a ''change of feeling'' is the second stage in the initial recovery. Ask any sober alcoholic about that sense of exhilaration which comes when the tremors and, for some, hallucinations, have ended. The third stage comes several weeks after the last drink and is a combination of physical and mental forces, which George Eliot recognized. The good feeling has abated and something—it can be almost anything—happens to bring the victim within inches of the next drink. If she does slip, she may go back to drinking for a year or forever, or she may regain control in a day. If she does *not* slip, her experience will be similar to that of Janet when she comes upon her dead husband's secreted brandy bottle. In this scene, Janet, several weeks sober, finds Dempster's brandy and though terrified, she is able to overcome temptation. The crisis—and it is just that—is preceded by scenes depicting Janet's depression, craving, and loneliness, states which are now recognized as being very dangerous for a newly recovering alcoholic. In a phrase of great insight, George Eliot calls them ''states of susceptibility . . . states of excitement or depression, half mental, half physical'' (ch. 25). It is extraordinary that a nineteenth-century writer would be familiar with this phenomenon: members of Alcoholics Anonymous even have an expression for it— ''budding.'' It means, prosaically, Building Up to a Drink, and that is what seems to be happening to Janet, for shortly after this last experience she comes close to drinking Dempster's brandy.

How much did mid-nineteenth-century physicians know about alcoholism? Outside of treatment for delirium tremens, I have been unable to verify that they knew even as much as George Eliot did, probably because they viewed alcoholism as a moral weakness, not a treatable disease. In short, the kind of details George Eliot describes would be known only by one who had experienced them. It is my guess that her source was either ''the real Janet''—Nancy Wallington Buchanan—or Maria Lewis, George Eliot's first teacher and good friend. For one thing, the letters to Maria Lewis in 1839–40 suggest that Mrs. Buchanan and Marian Evans saw each other often and appeared to be on close terms. The letters show, moreover, that Maria Lewis and Nancy Buchanan, approximately the same age, were intimate companions; in fact, Miss Lewis accompanied the ailing Mrs. Buchanan to Margate, where she died in 1840 at the age of thirty-seven.[14]

After ''Janet's Repentance,'' George Eliot never again depicted a female alcoholic, although in *Silas Marner* (1861), Mollie Farren, Effie's mother, is a drug addict and dies of an overdose of opium. Eliot did, however, retain her non-judgmental attitude toward the problem of alcohol addiction. Thus, Adam Bede (1859) is blamed for being too hard on his alcoholic father, Thias. And Tommy Trounsem, the drunken bill-sticker in *Felix Holt* (1866), is treated with affection. In *Middlemarch* (1871–72), there is nothing endearing, to be sure, about Raffles, who, like Dempster, dies of delirium tremens. There is a radical difference, however, in their medical treatment, for Dr. Lydgate instructs Bulstrode not to give Raffles any liquor; yet fourteen years earlier, Dempster was spoon-fed brandy by his doctor at regular intervals. Lydgate, we're told, is familiar with "Dr. Ware's abundant experience in America, as to the right way of treating cases of alcoholic poisoning," and he is opposed to "the prevalent practice of allowing alcohol and . . . large doses of opium" (ch. 69). The care used by George Eliot in researching material for *Middlemarch* is well known, and this detail is worked out with meticulous precision: Raffles dies on March 21, 1832, and Dr. Ware's "History and Treatment of Delirium Tremens" was published in 1831.[15]

George Eliot was not a crusader. Her aim, as she told Blackwood, was to write her story as she saw it, "or to renounce it as too painful." Female alcoholism is not a subject, then or now, that people wish to confront; it may well be "too painful." For many reasons, then, "Janet's Repentance," the first detailed portrait of a middle-class, female alcoholic, is unique in nineteenth-century English fiction.[16]

The story of Janet notwithstanding, mid-Victorians viewed the woman drinker with loathing, as Dickens and Gaskell proved. Later in the century, this attitude again surfaced in Samuel Butler's portrait of Ellen, the fallen woman who married Ernest Pontifex in *The Way of All Flesh* (published in 1903 but written between 1873 and 1885). A more sympathetic study was offered in George Gissing's *The Odd Women* (1893), which contained a poignant look at an aging female alcoholic. In France and America, Zola's Gervaise in *L'Assommoir* (1876) and the mother in Crane's *Maggie, A Girl of the Streets* (1896) exemplified the naturalistic outlook.

Whether or not Victorians like Brontë, Gaskell, and even Eliot perceived the rich, symbolic possibilities of the female alcoholic is difficult to say, for the prevailing social stigma inhibited a writer's choice. Since then, society's attitude toward the flesh and blood alcoholic woman—in our homes, on our sidewalks—has not changed very much. Modern writers, it is true, have loosened the Victorian structures and have explored the self-destructive, alienated, doomed lives of female alcoholics. Thus, the alcoholic woman, a figure of profound self-despair—rootless and agonizingly lonely—has come to represent in modern literature a grotesque parody of the human condition. She is, in a way, a twentieth-century version of the madwoman in the attic.

NOTES

1. John L. Horn and Kenneth W. Wanburg, "Females are Different: Some Difficulties in Diagnosing Problems of Alcohol Use in Women," University of Denver and Fort

Logan Mental Health Center, Washington, D.C., June 25–26, 1971. Cited in Edith Lynn Hornik, *The Drinking Woman* (New York: Association Press, 1971).

2. *Degas*, Folio of prints (New York: Harry N. Abrams, 1951), p. 4.

3. In Jacob Korg, ed., *London in Dickens' Day* (Englewood Cliffs, N. J.: Prentice-Hall, 1965), p. 22.

4. Gervaise comes to mind: "Death meant to take her little by little, bit by bit, dragging her to the end along the wretched path she had made for herself. It wasn't even quite clear what she did die of . . . but the truth was that she died of poverty, from the filth and exhaustion of her wasted life. One morning, as there was a nasty smell in the passage . . . she was discovered in her hole, turning green already." Emile Zola, *L'Assommoir* (1876), trans. Leonard Tancock (1970; rpt. New York: Penguin Books, 1979), p. 422.

5. "The Sad Fortunes of the Rev. Amos Barton" and "Mr. Gilfil's Love-Story" were the first two tales, respectively.

6. See Gordon S. Haight, *George Eliot: A Biography* (New York: Oxford University Press, 1968), p. 239: "Neither George Eliot nor Blackwood was converted by this correspondence. But through it she learned to respect his practical wisdom as the editor of a family magazine and publisher of fiction that had to be kept acceptable to circulating libraries; and he learned to be chary of trying to mould her genius into the conventional pattern."

7. Gordon S. Haight, ed., *The George Eliot Letters* (New Haven: Yale University Press, 1954), II, p. 344. Hereafter cited as *Letters*.

8. *Letters*, II, pp. 347–48. Haight's note points out that the Dempsters were drawn from James William Buchanan (1792–1846), a lawyer at Nuneaton, and his wife, Nancy Wallington Buchanan (1803–40). The "*superficial* alterations" to which George Eliot alludes are explained in Thomas A. Noble, *George Eliot's "Scenes of Clerical Life"* (New Haven: Yale University Press, 1965), pp. 155–57.

9. *Letters*, II, pp. 352.

10. Ibid., pp. 386. My italics.

11. Admittedly, Dempster's delirium is a gruesome scene. One is reminded of Coupeau's more graphically detailed death from D.T. in Zola's *L'Assommoir* (1876). This connection was also made by Barbara Hardy, *The Novels of George Eliot: A Study in Form* (London: The Athlone Press, 1959), p. 23.

12. "The Novels of George Eliot," *A Century of George Eliot Criticism*, ed. Gordon S. Haight (Boston: Houghton Mifflin, 1965), p. 46.

13. Alcoholism was regarded in George Eliot's day as a vice, not an illness, and drinking to excess was viewed as especially sinful in a woman. This stigma still exists: see Marian Sandmaier, *The Invisible Alcoholics: Women and Alcohol Abuse in America* (New York: McGraw-Hill, 1980), pp. 1–23. That alcoholism is a *disease*, not a moral weakness, was endorsed by the medical establishment one hundred years after the publication of "Janet's Repentance." Yet outside of the title, which carries an implicit moral judgment, George Eliot nowhere censures Janet. Since Eliot could not have known what it took medical societies a whole century to learn, the following lines are intriguing:

. . . this tenderness of the son [Dempster] for the mother was hardly more than a nucleus of healthy life in an organ hardening by *disease*. (Ch. 7)

[Janet's] troubles had been sinking her lower from year to year, pressing upon her like heavy fever-laden vapours, and perverting the very plenitude of her nature into a deeper source of *disease*. (Ch. 15)

I have emphasized the word "disease" in both passages in order to stress this prophetic metaphor.

14. Maria Lewis (1800?–87) was principal governess at a school run by Mrs. Wallington (Nancy Buchanan's mother) at Nuneaton when George Eliot was a pupil there. See *Letters*, I, pp. lxxii, 15, 16, 31–33, 47, 53, 54, 56, 58.

15. George Eliot kept a small notebook, which she called her "Quarry," throughout the planning and writing of *Middlemarch*. (This notebook was first published in 1950 in an edition prepared by Prof. Anna T. Kitchel.) In it, Eliot made notes on the article by John Ware, M.D., published in *Transactions of the Massachusetts Medical Society* (Boston, 1831). See "Quarry for Middlemarch" in *Middlemarch: An Authoritative Text; Background, Reviews and Criticism*, ed. Bert G. Hornback (New York: Norton Critical Edition, 1977), pp. 622–23.

16. But see U. C. Knoepflmacher, *George Eliot's Early Novels: The Limits of Realism* (Berkeley and Los Angeles: University of California Press, 1968), pp. 73–88. Knoepflmacher's main emphasis is on Dempster and Tryan; Janet is discussed only as her life affects theirs. Her alcoholism is barely mentioned. Moreover, he is blithely sexist in his references to Janet's childlessness, explaining that "The parallel to George Eliot's situation is hard to miss. The illegality of her union with Lewes prevented her from bearing children. . . . Like Janet or Romola, Marian Evans had to content herself with being the loving 'Mutter' of another's offspring" (p. 77n). Would Knoepflmacher analyze Henry James's childless heroines using the same approach? Last, and least, Knoepflmacher does not know Mr. Tryan's first name—he persists in calling him Edward, not Edgar.

18

Afro-American Women Poets of the Nineteenth Century

Rennie Simson

As long ago as 1893 Dr. L. A. Scruggs in his book *Women of Distinction* (a work discussing noted Afro-American women) made the observation that it was "a painful experience to see how little is known of our great women and their works."[1] This neglect is echoed in the words of contemporary scholars. Bert Lowenberg and Ruth Bogin in their recent work, *Black Women in 19th Century American Life*, commented: "If the black male's words, before the most recent period of ferment, were recorded only spasmodically, those of the black female were still less frequently set down on paper."[2] In their introduction to *Sturdy Black Bridges*, an anthology containing works by and about Afro-American women writers, the editors state:

Only slight attention has been given to Black women in creative literature, thus evoking grave concerns among female artists and scholars. . . . Recently a number of Black Anthologies and major critical works have been published. It is unfortunate, however, that in most cases, attention accorded Black women writers is sparse.[3]

This condition of neglect is particularly true of the works of nineteenth-century Afro-American women authors. Their autobiographies, poems, short stories, and novels are not only unread today, but they are virtually unheard of. This situation becomes doubly unfortunate and absurd when we consider the rather uniform inclusion in American literature anthologies of such literary luminaries as Mary Rowlandson, Anne Bradstreet, Sarah Kemble Knight, Harriet Beecher Stowe, and Julia Ward Howe. The editors of the fourth edition of the well-known *Norton Anthology of American Literature* concluded their discussion of Anne Bradstreet by stating: "When all has been said, the principal contribution of Anne Bradstreet to posterity is what she revealed, through herself, of the first generation of New

Englanders."[4] Based on the obvious omission of nineteenth-century Afro-American women authors from our literary anthologies, we must assume that the editors of these anthologies have felt that Afro-American women did not make meaningful revelations about American society during the nineteenth-century. Perhaps Addison Gayle was correct when he made the following observation in 1975 to Roseann Bell, an editor of *Sturdy Black Bridges*.

We can go back to the eighteenth century in English literature when criticism first begins its large impetus and males always wrote condescendingly about women writers. This is historic among Black male critics and, I think, all males have probably done so. I suppose the big chance will come when women begin doing critical work of their own on women writers.[5]

Even though Gerda Lerner, when discussing the "black female literary tradition" in *Black Women in White America*, skips from Phyllis Wheatly to Frances Harper and mentions no other black female poets of the nineteenth-century, black women were making meaningful literary contributions during this period.

It seems safe to say that the earliest works written by nineteenth-century Afro-Americas were not issued primarily to create a body of literature nor to entertain readers, but rather to arouse a sentiment that would work toward the abolition of slavery. In this category can be placed many slave narratives and pre–Civil War novels such as *Clotel, The Heroic Slave, The Garies and Their Friends* and *Blake*. These works were promoted by the abolitionists of the North and thus gained a relatively large white audience. During this period relatively few blacks were educated, and so these early pre–Civil War works were initially read by more whites than blacks. The only black women to achieve widespread recognition during this period were Francis Harper and Harriet Jacobs. While none of the works just mentioned can be classified as great literature, some of them definitely qualify as good literature and are deserving of far more attention than they have received in the past. The works of these writers reflect their dual position as members of a large society as well as of a specific culture within that larger society. This dualism was best expressed by W.E.B. Du Bois in his book *The Souls of Black Folk*. Wrote Du Bois: "One ever feels his twoness—an American, a Negro; two souls, two thoughts, two unreconciled strivings; two warring ideals in one dark body, whose dogged strength alone keeps it from being torn asunder."[6] A second class of writers appeared after the Civil War. Freed from an overwhelming absorption in the institution of slavery, they were free to explore and diversify their literary approaches as well as content. Their topics ranged from humorous folk tales to bitter satires reflecting the racial climate of post–Civil War America. The white audience interested in their works was smaller than in pre–Civil War days. Many whites preferred to read about the lives of black men from the pens of white racist romanticists like Thomas Dixon. The Civil War was over and for many whites the "race issue" was settled, and the concerns expressed in the works of black Americans no longer held any interest for them. Black authors like Charles Chesnutt and Paul Lawrence Dunbar found acceptance both with the general white populace and the critics (such as William Dean Howells) as long as they focused their talents on producing folk tales and dialect verse. However, white readers and critics turned away from them in dismay when their observations about their environment become harsh and bitter. While no Afro-American woman writers of this period achieved recognition comparable to that attained by Chesnutt and Dunbar, many talented black women turned to literature as a means of presenting their views. Most of their works reached a limited audience. They faced not only the handicap of being female writers, a "d——d mob of scribbling women" as Nathaniel Hawthorne called them, but of being black. A number of them felt it expedient to establish their own journals with black women as editors and these journals formed a major outlet for the stories, poems, and essays of a number of nineteenth-century Afro-American women authors. Among some of the more notable journals of that period were *Ringwoods* (Julia Costen, editor), *St. Matthews Lyceum Journal* (M. E. Lambert, editor), *Virginia Lancet* (Lucinda Bragg, editor), *The Boston Courant* (Josephine Ruffin, editor), *Women's Light and Love* (Lidia Lowry and Emma Ransom, editors) and *Waverly's Magazine* (Victoria Earle, editor). A number of books by Afro-American women were published either privately or by small, relatively unknown publishing companies. For the most part neither the journals nor the books enjoyed a long lifespan, so when they went out of print, the works of many black women were unavailable to the general public and existed only (and still exist only) in the rare bookrooms of specialized libraries scattered throughout the country. This very lack of accessibility has helped to perpetuate the myth that black women of the nineteenth century made few if any contributions to American literature. Their works are simply not available for general study and examination.

For the most part the work of nineteenth century Afro-American women poets conforms to the poetic standards of the nineteenth century. In discussing Frances Harper, the most prolific of the nineteenth-century Afro-American poetesses, Benjamin Brawley in the *Negro's Genius* observes that her poetry distinctly shows the influence of Longfellow. But Harper's poetry, as well as that of her contemporary Clara Ann Thompson, also shows the influence of black folklore and folk legend; each poetess wrote dialect verse spoken by a wise old narrator. In general, however, most Afro-American poetesses of the nineteenth-century wrote in a style typical of traditional nineteenth-century verse.

While black poetesses concerned themselves about such issues as religion, intemperance, and women's rights, their overwhelming concern focused on racial issues and it was in this area that their poetry achieved its greatest strength. It is true that some of their poetry dealing with racial matters was either overly sentimental and / or melodramatic, but for the most part it was forceful and direct, evoking empathy rather than sympathy for the position of the nineteenth-century Afro-American. In May 1837, Sarah Forten addressed a poem to the interracial Anti-Slavery Free Women of America Society in which she appealed

to her audience's sense of sisterhood to unite blacks and whites in fighting for
the abolition of slavery.

> We are thy sisters, God has truly said,
> That of one blood all nations He has made.
> O Christian woman! in a Christian land,
> Canst thou unblushing, read this great command,
> Suffer the wrongs which wrong our inmost heart
> To draw one throb of pity on thy part;
> Our skins may differ, but from thee we claim
> A sister's privilege and a sister's name.[7]

The first book of poetry published by a black poetess in the nineteenth-century,
Ann Plato's *Essays: Prose and Poetry* (1841), contained a tribute to England
for its abolition of slavery in the poem "To the First of August."

> Lift ye that country's banner high,
>   And may it nobly wave,
> Until beneath the azure sky
>   Man shall be no more a slave.[8]

One of the earliest poems of Frances Harper, "The Dying Fugitive," appeared
in 1859 in the *Anglo African Magazine* and is a strong statement in favor of the
abolition of slavery. We can share the extreme frustration of a goal unfulfilled,
a dream forever deferred.

> He must die, when just before him,
> Lay the long'd for precious prize—
>
> And the hopes that led him onward
> Faded out before his eyes.
>
> For a while a fearful madness,
> Rested on his weary brain;
> And he thought the hateful tyrant,
> Had rebound his galling chain.[9]

It is highly unlikely that any literary critic will argue that these three poems
are literary masterpieces, but they are strong testimonials to the sentiments of
Afro-Americans in pre–Civil War America and thus are as worthy of our attention
as the poems of Anne Bradstreet as reflections on early Puritanism.

Racial injustice continued to be an issue of concern which was reflected in
the poetry of Afro-American writers after the conclusion of the Civil War. Harper,
in *Sketches of Southern Life* (1872), created a wise old ex-slave, Aunt Chloe,
who, as narrator, offers the folk wisdom of generations of slaves. Upon the
death of Lincoln, Aunt Chloe speculated upon the presidency of Andrew Johnson:

> Then we had another President—
>   What do you call his name?
> Well, if the colored folks forget him
>   They wouldn't be much to blame.[10]

Aunt Chloe felt great disgust with any man who sold his vote, and her friends shared her distress at such behavior on the part of their menfolk.

> Day after day did Milly Green
>   Just follow after Joe
> And told him if he voted wrong
>   To take his rags and go.[11]

But Aunt Chloe had only praise for men

> Who know their freedom cost too much
>   Of Blood and pain and treasure
> For them to fool away their vote
>   For profit or for pleasure.[12]

Like Harper, Clara Ann Thompson created an old character, Uncle Rube, who reflected on the society of his day. In the poem "Uncle Rube's Defense" Uncle Rube expressed his disgust with the stereotyping that white Americans directed toward black Americans.

> Ev'ry low truk dat te black man's a doing',
>   'flects right back on de race, as a whole;
> But de low co'se dat de white man's pursuin'
>   Costs not a blot on his good brudder's soul.
>
> Let de black man do somepin wuth mentionin',
>   White folks ez still and shy ez a fawn;
> Let him do somepin dat's mean and belittlin',
>   Umph! den de whole race has got it an' gone.[13]

No doubt one of the most outspoken protest poets of the nineteenth century is the little known poetess Josephine Heard, whose single volume of poetry, *Morning Glories*, was published in 1890. In her poem "Black Samson" she made a sweeping indictment of post–Civil War American society in the treatment of its black population. Her bitter words did not show the conciliatory tone of so much of the literature written during "The Age of Washington" as Robert Bone has called the period of late nineteenth-century Afro-American literature. Nor did she seek to camouflage her criticisms in the guise of folk wisdom and folk dialect. Her tone was straightforward and direct, and even the most obtuse reader could scarcely miss her sharp message:

> O, what cruelty and torture has he [the Black Samson] felt?
> Could his tears, the heart of his oppressor melt?
> In his gore they bathed their hands,
> Organized and lawless bands—
> And the innocent was left in blood to wilt.[14]

But the Black Samson of Heard was not going to lie sleeping forever; he was not a pitiful victim, but rather a courageous man ready to lose his life, if need be, fighting for what he believed in. He was not Harper's dying fugitive for whom the reader cannot help but shed tears of pity, nor was he Stowe's Uncle Tom stoically ready to die for his principles, but the Black Samson was a fighter:

> The Black Samson is awaking,
> And the fetters fiercely breaking,
>   By his mighty arm his rights shall be obtained![15]

Traditionally whites have had a harder time dealing with black fighters than with black victims, with realistic black figures than with black folk figures, so Aunt Chloe was a lot more popular with nineteenth-century audiences than the Black Samson was.

Heard had great confidence that the Black Samson would be successful and this confidence is reflected in her poem "They are Coming." At the beginning of the poem "they" (her fellow black citizens) are coming "slowly," then "proudly," and finally "boldly." In their ranks

> There are Doctors, Lawyers, Preachers;
> There are Sculptors, Poets, Teachers—
> Men and women, who with honor yet shall shine.[16]

This joy of pride in accomplishment is also reflected in Cordelia Ray's two poems "In Memoriam: Frederick Douglass" and "In Memoriam: Paul Lawrence Dunbar." Published in her collection *Poems* (1910), both poems possess a sense of triumph in accomplishments achieved in the face of what seemed to be insurmountable odds. Ray's pride in Douglass is clearly evident when she writes:

> . . . . .what matter then
> That he in chains was held, what matter when
> He could uplift himself to noblest heights![17]

Dunbar's creative genius was an equal cause of celebration of the black race.

> Who was this child? The offspring of a race
> That erst had toiled 'neath slavery's galling chains,
> And soon he woke to utterance and sang.[18]

It was a long journey from the helpless fugitive of Frances Harper to the glorious talent of Paul Lawrence Dunbar, and that journey has been well documented by the pens of Afro-American poetesses of the nineteenth-century. Surely if we can learn of the Puritans from Anne Bradstreet and of the early Native Americans from Mary Rowlandson, both of whom are routinely included in American Literature anthologies, then we can learn of the early Afro-American from early Afro-American women writers.

As stated earlier Afro-American women wrote of issues other than race. Christianity played an important role in the lives of the nineteenth-century Afro-American, but it must be clearly understood that this was not the version of Christianity promoted by the white man. Throughout the days of slavery and even after, the white man twisted the scriptures to suit his purposes. His abuse of Christianity was initiated to serve three purposes: first, to soothe his own gnawing conscience about the fact that he was enslaving his fellow man; second, to convince the world that his actions were compatible with the will of God; and third, to convince the slaves themselves that they were inferior beings. His purposes succeeded in diminishing order; he did a good job of brainwashing himself, less of a job in brainwashing the rest of the world, and a poor job of brainwashing the slaves. Even after slavery some segments of the white Christian church continued to preach the gospel of black inferiority. But blacks established their own relationship with the Christian faith. Even during the days of slavery, when it was illegal for slaves to read and write, there were those who managed to learn and they read the Bible and informed the others of the distortions that were being perpetrated by the whites. Many blacks followed the example of Frederick Douglass, becoming devout believers in the Christianity of Christ, but rejecting the Christianity preached to them by the whites.

This dual concern, devout belief in an honest Christianity and total rejection of a hypocritical Christianity, is reflected in the works of nineteenth-century Afro-American women. This dualism is perhaps best reflected in Clara Ann Thompson's poem, "His Answer:"

> He prayed for patience: Care and sorrow came
> And dwelt with him, grim and unwelcome guests;
> He felt their galling presence night and day;
> And wondered if the Lord had heard him pray,
> And why his life was filled with weariness.
>
> He prayed again and now he prayed for light
> The darkness parted and the light shone in;
> And lo! he saw the answer to his prayer—
> His heart had learned, through weariness and care,
> The patience that he deemed he'd sought in vain.[19]

The true Christian, according to Thompson, finds his spirituality through God directly and not in his relations with his fellow man here on earth. When he prays for relief from the care and misery imposed by others, his prayers appear to go unanswered, but if his prayers are for spiritual enlightenment he will be blessed. He will not perceive Christ through an intermediary, but will do so directly. It is only in such a perception that Christianity is possible, since any form of Christianity that rooted its faith in God as presented by a people who sanctioned slavery was not acceptable to a black person.

Frances Harper's poetry likewise expressed her faith in the Christian religion. Although she expressed skepticism and downright rejection of the white man's Christianity in her novel *Iola LeRoy*, she reflected a deep faith in the Christianity of Christ in her poetry. One of her earliest poems, "Gone to God," published in the *Anglo African Magazine* of 1859, is a eulogy of a woman who has died and whose soul has gone to heaven. Subsequent poems, such as "A Grain of Sane," "Go Work in My Vineyard," "Renewal of Strength," "The Night of Death" and "The Refiner's Gold" all attest to Harper's strong faith in Christianity.

This faith in Christianity is also seen in Josephine Heard's lines on the death of Abraham Lincoln in her poem "Solace":

> The grave no terror hath, and death no sting,
> For him who fully trusts in Christ the King.[20]

Nineteenth-century women were frequently the victims of alcohol abuse. Usually unable to fend for themselves economically, they were dependent on their husbands, fathers, or brothers for support. Temperance thus became a significant issue for a number of nineteenth-century women, including a few Afro-Americans. The only black poetess who devoted a considerable amount of her energies to this cause was Frances Harper. She lectured widely on the evils of intemperance, and several of her poems dealt with that subject. In "The Total Pledge," a reformed alcoholic takes a drink when asked by his bride to make a toast at their wedding; it was not long thereafter that she wept over a drunkard's grave. In "A Little Child Shall Lead Them," Harper depicted the death of a drunkard's child as the only factor which could influence him to reform. In "Save the Boys" she illustrated how it was too late to save a drunkard, but not too late to save his sons, and in "Nothing and Something" she chronicled how people become alcoholics and criminals.

Like many nineteenth-century women, black women were concerned about the position of the female in their society. Their poetry concerned itself not only with love and marriage, but also with women's rights. Frances Harper rejected the double sexual standard of her day which "excuses all in the male and accuses all in the female,"[21] and she elaborated her views in a poem entitled simply "The Double Standard."

> Crime has no sex and yet to-day
> I wear the brand of shame

Whilst he amid the gay and proud
  Still bears an honored name.[22]

Can you blame if I've learned to think
  Your hate of vice a sham,
When you so coldly crushed me down
  And then excused the man.

Alice Dunbar Nelson, wife of the famous poet Paul Lawrence Dunbar, in her poem "I Sit and Sew" drew a vivid contrast between the task of sewing, acceptable for a woman, and the task of fighting, acceptable for a man. The narrator of "I Sit and Sew" longs to participate in battle, to live the active life of the male, but her task as a female is to passively sit and sew.

I sit and sew—a useless task it seems,
My hands grown tired, my head weighed down with dreams
The panoply of war, the martial tread of men.
Grim faced, stern-eyed, gazing beyond the ken
Of lesser souls, whose eyes have not seen Death,
Nor learned to hold their lives but as a breath—
But I must sit and sew.

I sit and sew—my heart aches with desire—
That pageant terrible, that fiercely pouring fire
On wasted fields, and writhing grotesque things
Once men, My soul in pity flings
Appealing cries, yearning only to go
There in that holocaust of hell, those fields of woe—
But I must sit and sew.

The little useless seam, the idle patch;
Why dream I here beneath my homely thatch.
When there they lie in sodden mud and rain.
Pitifully calling me, the quick ones and the slain?
You need me, Christ! It is no roseate dream
That beckons me—this pretty futile seam.
It stifles me—God, must I sit and sew?[23]

Lest it be believed that nineteenth-century Afro-American poetesses did not write of themselves as lovers, such is not the case. Frances Harper, Cordelia Ray, and especially Josephine Heard wrote some very fine love lyrics. Heard's "The Parting Kiss" reflects a particular charm.

We were waiting at the station,
  Soon the cars would surely start,
Hearts beat high with love's emotion,
  For we knew we soon must part.
On dark lashes seem to glisten

> Tiny crystal tear drops shine;
> To the fond voice glad I listen,
> While teary eyes look into mine.[24]

Black women writers of nineteenth-century America in their works offer us the opportunity to explore a dimension of understanding offered by no other group. As Julia Cooper pointed out in *A Voice From the South* (1892), black women face a special dilemma in American society:

The colored woman of today occupies, one may say, a unique position in this country. . . . She is confronted by both a woman question and a race problem.[25]

Her unique position cannot be completely comprehended by either her black brother nor her white sister and certainly not by the white male. Thus if we wish to understand her unique position in American society we must study her own words as reflected in her writings. Few critics will claim literary greatness for any of the writers mentioned in this paper, but much of their writing was good if not great, and as long as we study good literature as well as great literature, our study should include Afro-American women authors of the nineteenth century.

NOTES

1. L. A. Scruggs, *Women of Distinction* (Raleigh, N.C.: L. A. Scruggs Publisher, 1893), p. vi.

2. Bert Lowenberg and Ruth Bogin, *Black Women in 19th Century Life* (University Park: Pennsylvania State University Press, 1976), p. 5.

3. Roseann Bell, Bettye J. Park, and Beverly Guy-Sheftall, *Sturdy Black Bridges* (New York: Anchor Books, 1979), p. xxviii.

4. Sculley Bradley, Richard Beatty, E. Hudson Long, and George Perkins, *The American Tradition in Literature* (New York: Grosset and Dunlap, 1974), p. 34.

5. Bell, Parker, and Guy-Sheftall, p. xxiv.

6. W.E.B. Du Bois: *The Souls of Black Folk* included in *Three Negro Classics*, ed. John Hope Franklin (New York: Avon Books, 1973), p. 215.

7. Sarah Forten quoted in M. A. Majors, *Noted Negro Women* (Chicago: Donohue and Hennebury, 1893), p. 194.

8. Ann Plato, *Essays: Prose and Poetry* (Hartford: n.p., 1841), p. 115.

9. Frances Harper, "The Dying Fugitive," *The Anglo African Magazine*, vol. I (May, 1859), 253–54.

10. Frances Harper, *Sketches of Southern Life* (Philadelphia: Merrihew and Son, 1872), p. 12.

11. Ibid., p. 15.

12. Ibid., p. 16.

13. Clara Ann Thompson, *Songs From the Wayside* (Ross Mogre, Ohio: n.p., 1904), p. 4.

14. Josephine Heard quoted in M. A. Majors, p. 263.

15. Ibid., p. 264.

16. Ibid., p. 265.

17. Cordelia Ray, *Poems* (New York: The Grafton Press, 1910), p. 161.

18. Ibid., p. 166.

19. Thompson, p. 133.

20. Josephine Heard quoted in M. A. Majors, p. 267.

21. Frances Harper, *The Sparrows Fall and Other Poems* (n.p., n.d.), p. 13.

22. Ibid., p. 13.

23. Alice Dunbar Nelson, quoted in Robert Kerlin: *Negro Poets and Their Poems* (Washington, D.C.: Associated Publishers, 1935), pp. 145–46.

24. Josephine Heard, *Morning Glories* (Philadelphia: n.p., 1890), pp. 13–14.

25. Anna Cooper, *A Voice From the South* (Ohio: The Aldine Printing House, 1892), p. 134.

19

Jane Austen's Mediative Voice

Alison G. Sulloway

A few Austenian critics have recently begun to suggest that Jane Austen's feminist perspectives are ambivalent.[1] In fact, Austen examines the great post-Augustan debate on "woman's proper sphere" far more as a conscious mediator than as a mere subconsciously ambivalent reflector. Her six finished novels all mediate among three types of contemporary advisors to women, no matter how legitimately her critics have described what else concerns her.

The most conservative advisors to women—eighteenth-century equivalents of our Drs. Freud and Spock—were usually clergymen who wrote courtesy books which minutely analyzed women's anatomical, intellectual, and spiritual inferiority to men. The conservatives almost invariably quoted the Pauline Epistles and Milton's *Paradise Lost* in order to define for women their appropriate role as post-Edenic penitential daughters of Eve. Suffering, the conservatives preached, is becoming to women: it imitates Christ's willing martyrdom; it forces women as an entire class to atone perpetually for Eve's aggression against God and man; and it suits their ordained vulnerability and therefore renders them sexually attractive and marriageable. The conservatives thus constructed unalterable connections between human welfare, women's martyrdom to men and to their own maternal flesh, and their unquestioning assumption that divine anatomy is divine destiny.[2]

Feminine education, the conservatives explained, should be deliberately sparse, encouraging women's faith in God and man and discouraging pretensions to any sustained intellect. Women should read only such histories—often written expressly for them—which stressed God's design for their subordination.

Women were expected to be silent in mixed company unless pauses in the masculine conversation indicated a need for some sprightly and unpretentious contribution to it. Women's customary silences were to serve not only as an

emblem of their willing subjection to men but also as additional penance fo
Eve's transgressions.

Women were urged to cultivate the charming arts, a little amateur music, soft
feminine water colors, and of course, serious sewing, always called "work,'
or any other gentle pursuit which would show off their figures and their docile
charms without stimulating their innately feminine vanity, which they had all
as a sex, inherited from Eve. Austen's wry but tender description of the vain
glorious Mary Crawford, playing the harp as she and her instrument are carefully
silhouetted against "shrubs in the rich foliage of summer," indicates how thor
oughly Austen understood the sexual implications of women's shallow education.[3]

Wit in women, the conservatives preached, was one of the most dangerous
feminine rebellions. Such anathemas against witty women did not entirely please
Austen, who frequently read portions of her novels to her family, accompanied
by their appreciative laughter. Yet two of Austen's last three novels contain
distinctly penitential studies of women whose articulate wit is as cruel and as
rebellious as the courtesy-book conservatives preached that wit in women invariably was. Austen's own prayers, which she composed herself for her private
spiritual guidance, often beg her "dear Lord and saviour" to forgive her the
very barbed wit which has delighted generations of readers.[4]

The conservatives commanded women to shun all professions and to limit
their public social functions as much as their husbands' positions would permit.
Even anonymous novel writing was considered very dangerous for them, since
it fostered that articulateness and that pride in achievement which was Eve's
downfall, a lapse for which the female sex must forever atone.

Austen comments caustically upon two conservative advisors to women: in
Pride and Prejudice, the pompous and callous clergyman, William Collins, reads
one of James Fordyce's *Sermons to Young Women* to the assembled Bennet
daughters. As Austen remarks, Collins intones this sermon "with very monotonous solemnity," and therefore, Austen's irony implies, in a manner not only
befitting "the very monotonous solemnity" of Fordyce, the historical courtesy-
book clergyman, but of Collins, the fictional courtesy-book clergyman.[5] Hannah
More, who was paradoxically both a conservative and a bluestocking, also earned
Austen's contempt. No doubt the spectacle of a woman leading a public life and
writing so as to silence other women was irresistible material for Austen's
wonderfully malicious irony.

Another courtesy-book clergyman earned Austen's attention. In 1797, Thomas
Gisborne had written his *Enquiry into the Duties of the Female Sex* to counteract
Mary Wollstonecraft's notorious *Vindication of the Rights of Women*. Gisborne
described dancing as "an amusement in itself both innocent and salubrious, and
therefore by no means improper, under suitable regulation." Austen herself
adored dancing, suitably regulated or not.[6] Gisborne, on the other hand, gave
his ecclesiastical approval of dancing with a solemnity and portentousness equal
to Mr. Collins's manner, when *he* recommended dancing for clergymen like
himself, under suitable regulations, of course.[7]

Another group of advisors to women who shaped Austen's novels were the meliorists, or moderate women. These writers wanted to see their sex far better educated and far more economically secure, despite women's legal and social dependencies, than women usually were. The voices of such meliorists as Maria Edgeworth, Priscilla Wakefield, Elizabeth Hamilton, Clara Reeve, Jane West, and Catherine Macaulay, three of whom appear in Austen's letters and in her bibliography, are the closest to Austen's own voice.[8] They believed, as Austen did, that women's destiny would remain largely maternal and domestic. Yet they deplored the terrible predicament of penniless widows and spinsters whose male guardians would leave them nothing, since the law of entail forbade it.[9] And the meliorists condemned even more bitterly those heads of households who had indisputable legal rights to the fortunes of their wives and daughters, and who had squandered these jointures along with the rest of the estate revenues. The pathetic genteel poverty of Mrs. Dashwood and the Dashwood sisters in *Sense and Sensibility*, of Fanny Price in *Mansfield Park*, of Jane Fairfax and Miss Bates in *Emma*, of Anne Elliot in *Persuasion*, to say nothing of Mrs. Bennet's ugly but legitimate obsession with the Bennet women's future poverty in *Pride and Prejudice*, all indicate how carefully Austen had been following the great eighteenth-century debates on women.

The radical feminists, such as Mary Wollstonecraft and Mary Hays, advocated not only greater financial security for women, and access to infinitely better education and to the professions, but changes in the property laws. They believed that only legal changes would bring about attitudinal changes between the sexes.[10] Austen and the meliorists appeared to hope that changes in the nationwide masculine contempt for women and women's contempt for themselves could take place without radical upheavals in law and custom.

Since Austen's conservative family destroyed many of her letters, we cannot be sure which radical feminists Austen read. But beneath her light, deliberately reassuring humor, her novels and her extant letters contain subtle yet distinct allusions to the feminist tracts. Her fictional themes, symbols, dialogues, and even her own authorial cadences all duplicate, in covert ways, the feminist distress over women's multiple deprivations.

There are several reasons why Austen muffled the distress she felt for her own sex. She was a devout Christian and a provincial gentlewoman, who had been taught by 2,000 years of masculine polemics that preaching does not become the woman. Furthermore, she respected the craft of fiction, and she was too tactful to preach. Obsessive polemics, after all, are not appropriate to the intelligent entertainer of either sex. She may frequently have risked the barbed, ironic tones of the late eighteenth-century feminists, and thus anticipated the feminist elements in George Eliot and Charlotte Brontë. But feminine diffidence, even more than the fantasy components in fictional tradition, shaped her plots as they shaped the plots of later women novelists. Habitually, every heroine is provided with a husband.

For Austen, there was also a compelling national reason why a woman writer's open rebellion, or any English disaffection, for that matter, would have been considered extremely dangerous to England's military security. As Warren Roberts explains, in *Jane Austen and the French Revolution*, almost all of Austen's writing life coincided with periods when England was threatened by French invasions, and when most Englishmen wished to eradicate the concomitant threat of a French-inspired petticoat rebellion at home.[11] Any overt rebellion in Austen's fiction would have been unthinkable to her; it would have disparaged the sacrifices of her beloved sailor brothers who had been guarding England's coasts against the French menace since they were young naval apprentices.

But despite Austen's loving commitment to her faith, her family, and her country, and despite her refusal to recommend all the solutions proposed by the radical feminists, each of her six mature novels studies a series of commonplace radical complaints. For example, a female character is incarcerated on the estate so as to care for a hypochondriac parent, or because male relatives have squandered the estate revenues, or because scant revenues are all reserved for the brothers' professional advancement. Women can only leave the estate for their own advancement when some rich surrogate parents rescue them and take them traveling so that they can meet potential husbands. This motif is particularly emphatic in *Northanger Abbey*, *Sense and Sensibility*, and *Pride and Prejudice*.

Women's involuntary departure from the estate, either as punishment for some disobedience to their male guardian or because the male heir of an entail wishes them elsewhere, constitutes the second commonplace threat to penniless women which the radicals and the meliorists condemned, and which appears as an obsessive threat in all six novels. We have only to think of General Tilney's sudden expulsion of Catherine Morland from Northanger Abbey, of the malicious way that the widowed Mrs. Dashwood and her almost penniless daughters were expelled from Norland, of the threatened exile from Longborn which haunted the hysterical Mrs. Bennet, of Fanny Price's punitive exile from Mansfield Park, of Jane Fairfax's involuntary journeys around England as she searched for marginal security, and of Anne Elliot's painful farewell to Kellynch Hall, to realize how women's economic and domestic insecurity troubled Austen.

Another aspect of women's lives which particularly distressed all the women writers, even the conservative Hannah More, was the way men and women played out the roles of Pygmalion and Galatea.[12] Fathers, brothers, and suitors all tended to teach marriageable women the roles proper for wives. The men in Austen's novels also tend to think of themselves as pedagogues to the women pupils. Sometimes the masculine advice is useful; sometimes it is merely patronizing. But whether the advice is beneficial or baneful, or a combination of both, every heroine undergoes a ritual courtesy-book duplication of Eve's anguished guilt after her disobedience. Sometimes these paroxysms of guilt are appropriate and sometimes not.

There is even a difference in male and female speech patterns in mixed company, just as the courtesy-book conservatives advised that there should be. The speech patterns of Austen's men are usually pedagogical-imperative; the women's speech patterns, especially of modest heroines such as Catherine Morland, Elinor Dashwood, Fanny Price, and Anne Elliot, tend to be interrogative-diffident. At one moment, even the imperious Emma Woodhouse tactfully asks a question about the management of Knightley's Donwell Abbey, so as to avert a quarrel between her incarcerating father and her testy brother-in-law.[13] But so just an incipient sociologist is Austen, and so carefully has she examined the sensible recommendations of the courtesy-book conservatives that she creates heroines[14] and subheroines[15] whose total refusal to abide by the conservative rules of decorum creates serious dangers for them, and at the worst, expels them forever from the marginally secure commonwealth of provincial gentlefolk.

In examining the whole question of "woman's proper sphere," Austen creates a distinct spatial symbology between indoors, which is largely women's sphere, and outdoors, which is largely men's. With the exception of Hannah More, the conservatives all thought that gentle gardening and quiet walks were the only appropriate outdoor exercises for women, and so does the conservative courtesy-book hero, Henry Tilney, who is the target of as much Austenian irony as is the heroine whom he constantly teases.[16] The radicals and the meliorists urged women to exercise freely and they frequently demanded feminine freedom from the starvation diets, the languid postures and conduct, and the physical restraints of corsets, wooden feet-socks, and iron backboards which were known to tear and warp bones and muscles and to rupture internal organs.[17]

Austen's novels are full of ironic spatial symbols of men hunting, fishing, and farming, and of women knitting, sewing, playing pretty songs, or cutting out colored paper. There are dozens of scenes where the men look through windows at the women engaged in their indoor pursuits; there are as many scenes where women look wistfully *out* the windows at men returning from their masculine pursuits. Yet Austen studies each heroine symbolically, according to the heroine's attitude toward fresh air and vigorous exercise: each heroine's acceptance or rejection of these masculine prerogatives represents her attitudes toward "woman's proper sphere."

Austen clearly considered marriage the one potential economic provision for women, risky as it was. But she also believed marriage for Christian love, which includes sexual attraction as well as respect, to be a sacrament. In all six novels, the poignant passing of the seasons, usually from fall to fall, symbolizes her heroines' yearning for that security and that sacrament. Her women characters who despise country seasons, such as Isabella Thorpe, Lydia Bennet, Maria Bertram, and Mary Crawford, arrogantly flout all the conservatives' commands. They prove to be unworthy of Christian marriage. Yet the solipsistic Marianne Dashwood, who hysterically adores the passing seasons, must moderate her excessive feminine sensibilities before she can marry intelligently. On the other hand, Catherine Morland, Georgianna Darcy, Anne de Bourge, and Fanny Price are so badly crippled by rigid adherence to conservative rules of decorum that they lack the feminine self-respect which radicals and meliorists alike demanded not only as a human prerogative for both sexes but as a Christian duty.[18] It is buoyant moderation in all things which Austen requires—a wonderful moral paradox which typifies Austen's discreet prescription for all human dilemmas.[19]

NOTES

1. Some Austenian critics, such as Alistair M. Duckworth, (*The Improvement of the Estate*) (Baltimore: Johns Hopkins University Press, 1972), and Avrom Fleishman, (*A Reading of Mansfield Park*) (Minneapolis: University of Minnesota Press), suggest Austen's persistent but ambivalent feminist perspectives by describing at length her obsession with women's predicament as this obsession is chastened by her sound provincial conservatism. Others, such as William Walling, implicitly describe Austen's ambivalent feminism by describing "the paradoxical coherence in both Duckworth's 'conservative' reading and Nina Auerbach's 'revolutionary' one" (William Walling, "The Glorious Anxiety of Motion: Jane Austen's *Persuasion*," *The Wordsworth Circle*, VII, no. 4 [Autumn, 1976], 336). Nina Auerbach, Sandra Gilbert, and Susan Gubar all frankly identify Austen's vision as ambivalently feminist, perhaps sometimes unconsciously so. My own persuasion is that Austen's vision is deliberately mediatory. See Nina Auerbach, "O Brave New World: Evolution and Revolution in *Persuasion*," *ELH*, 39 (1972); see also Sandra Gilbert and Susan Gubar, chapters 4 and 5 in *The Madwoman in the Attic: The Woman Writer and the Nineteenth-Century Literary Imagination* (New Haven, Conn.: Yale University Press, 1979).

2. Austen mentions three of the most popular courtesy-book writers: the Rev. Thomas Gisborne, author of *An Enquiry into the Duties of the Female Sex*, Hannah More, author of *Practical Piety* and *Strictures on the Modern System of Female Education*, and the Rev. James Fordyce, author of *Sermons for Young Women*. See *Jane Austen's Letters to her Sister Cassandra and Others*, ed. R. W. Chapman, 2nd ed. (London: Oxford University Press, 1952), pp. 169, 287, and *Pride and Prejudice*, *The Novels of Jane Austen*, II, ed. R. W. Chapman, 3rd ed. (London: Oxford University Press, 1932–34), p. 68. All citations from Austen's novels and letters will refer to the Chapman editions.

3. Jane Austen, *Mansfield Park*, p. 65.

4. Jane Austen, *Minor Works*, (*The Oxford Illustrated Works*) VI, ed. R. W. Chapman (London: Oxford University Press, 1954), pp. 452–57. Austen's two witty women are Mary Crawford (*Mansfield Park*) and Emma Woodhouse (*Emma*).

5. Jane Austen, *Pride and Prejudice*, p. 68.

6. See Austen's affectionately ironic comments about young people's love of dancing—including her own love of dancing—in *Sense and Sensibility*, pp. 44–45, 53, *Emma*, p. 247, and *Letters*, pp. 2, 4, 44, 257, and *passim*. And see also Fitzwilliam Darcy's contemptuous comments about dancing as a diversion worthy only of savages, a remark which insults the provincial company he is visiting and which confirms Elizabeth Bennet's temporary hostility toward him, as well as the temporary hostility of his creator (*Pride and Prejudice*, p. 25).

7. Gisborne, *Enquiry*, pp. 180–81.

8. *Letters*, pp. 305, 398, 405, 466.

9. See Emma Woodhouse's bitter comments about the humiliating plight of impoverished spinsters, a predicament which Jane Fairfax later echoes with all Emma's bitterness, and which Jane and her aunt, the hysterically gabbling Miss Bates, both symbolize (*Emma*, pp. 84–85, 300). See also Austen's own wry comment to her niece Fanny Knight:

"Single Women have a dreadful propensity for being poor—which is one very strong argument in favour of Matrimony, but I need not dwell on such arguments with you, pretty Dear, you do not want inclination.—" (*Letters*, p. 483).

10. Mary Hays, *Appeal to the Men of Great Britian in Behalf of Women* (New York: Garland Publishing, Inc., 1974), pp. 81, 94, 110–12, 113–16; Mary Wollstonecraft, *A Vindication of the Rights of Women*, ed. Carol Poston, Norton Critical Edition (New York: W. W. Norton and Co., Inc., 1975), pp. 18, 40, 64–65.

11. Warren Roberts, *Jane Austen and the French Revolution* (New York: St. Martin's Press, 1979), pp. 10, 29–30, 203.

12. Hannah More, *Strictures on the Modern System of Female Education* (New York: Garland Publishing, Inc., 1974), I, p. ix. See also Juliet McMasters, "Love and Pedagogy," *Jane Austen Today*, ed. Joel Weinsheimer (Athens: The University of Georgia Press, 1975), pp. 68, 69, 87.

13. Jane Austen, *Emma*, p. 104.

14. Marianne Dashwood in *Sense and Sensibility* and Emma Woodhouse in *Emma*.

15. Isabella Thorpe in *Northanger Abbey* and Maria Bertram in *Mansfield Park*.

16. See Hannah More's delightful description of the charm and health to be gained from vigorous and spontaneous feminine exercise (*Strictures*, I, pp. 86–87). And see Henry Tilney's unconsciously ironic lectures to the tomboy Catherine Morland about the worth of gentle feminine exercise (*Northanger Abbey*, p. 174).

17. Priscilla Wakefield, *Reflections on the Present Condition of the Female Sex* (New York: Garland Publishing, Inc., 1974), pp. 22, 24–25. And see also the grim descriptions of illness and death resulting from the deliberate warping of young girls' bodies in Lawrence Stone, *The Family, Sex, and Marriage in England, 1500–1800* (New York: Harper and Row, 1977), pp. 444–46.

18. It is typical of the way Austen satirizes mandatory feminine silence, as it was enjoined upon women by the courtesy-book writers, that these four young women, two of them heroines and two of them minor feminine figures, are characterized by their silences. Catherine Morland and Fanny Price customarily hold internal monologues when they disagree with male definitions of what they are and think and do, and ought to be, think, and do. Anne de Bourgh and Georgiana Darcy are completely silent whenever they appear in *Pride and Prejudice*; readers never once hear their voices. In all four cases, the young women are either wards or potential wives of people who are highly accomplished dominators of others around them, people who have awarded to themselves the privilege of defining exactly what other people are and ought to be.

19. The research for this paper was completed during my tenure (1978–79) as a Senior Fellow of the National Endowment for the Humanities. I would like to express my gratitude to the officers of NEH.

20

Margaret Fuller's *Woman in the Nineteenth Century:* The Feminist Manifesto

Marie O. Urbanski

Woman in the Nineteenth Century is the quintessential feminist treatise. Published in 1845, Margaret Fuller's work is a public declaration that women must become self-reliant and free themselves from their dependence on men. Written in eloquent language befitting the high seriousness of its subject, Fuller's *Woman in the Nineteenth Century* demands total freedom for women— "We would have every arbitrary barrier thrown down. We would have every path open to woman as freely as to man."[1] In effect, it is the feminist manifesto. Inspired by the power of Fuller's proclamation, a small group of people met three years later in Seneca Falls to draft their Declaration of Independence for women, "A Declaration of Sentiments." And yet, despite the recent revival of interest in the feminist movement, Fuller's *Woman in the Nineteenth Century* has not had the recognition it merits. Hence, my plan is first to delineate her contribution, and then to discuss why *Woman in the Nineteenth Century* has not taken its place among cardinal documents in the history of ideas.

In order to assess the importance of *Woman in the Nineteenth Century*, it is necessary to examine other pioneering feminist writing. Mary Wollstonecraft's *A Vindication of the Rights of Women* (1792) is the germinal British work which prepared the way for Fuller's publication by justifying, by means of arguments derived from "natural rights" concepts, the idea that women should even have innate rights. Although the American novelist Charles Brockden Brown debated in dialogue form feminist topics in his *Alcuin* (1798), he reached no conclusion in his early work.

It is not certain whether or not Fuller had even read Brown's piece; however, she undoubtedly was aware of Sarah Moore Grimké's *Letters on the Equality of the Sexes and the Condition of Woman*. Published in the Boston *Spectator* from July 11, 1837, in a series of fifteen, these letters were later printed in pamphlet form. Their major premise is that in the sight of God, men and women are equal, and, therefore, whatever is morally right for a man to do is also morally right for a woman to do.

To help them achieve equality, Sarah Grimké suggested that girls should be better educated for their future duties as mothers and sisters. She recognized the damage that social conditioning did to women, as girls were educated "from earliest childhood to regard themselves as inferiors,"[2] and consequently learned duplicity as their means of survival: " 'Rule by obedience and by submission sway,' or in other words, study to be a hypocrite, pretend to submit, but gain your point, has been the code of household morality which woman has been taught."[3] Another inequity she treated in straightforward fashion was the unequal pay for men and women. Complaining that a woman earned half or less than a man, often for the same job (a statistic not too dissimilar from the 59 to 100 percent ratio of the present day), Grimké called for equal pay for equal work. Moreover, she suggested that ladies' sewing societies should sew for the advancement of their own sex instead of for the education of young men for the clergy. Her bravest writing had to do with her depiction of the plight of the female slave, who was sexually exploited by her master and other white men. As did Wollstonecraft before her, she compared the lot of woman to that of the slave, but Grimké made the connection between sex and race more specifically.

Not unlike other early American writers interested in the difficulties women faced, Lydia Maria Child and Catharine Maria Sedgwick (whom both Grimké and Fuller cited), Grimké was inconsistent in her argument. Apparently, feeling the need to reassure her readers that her demands were not excessive, she wrote that she did not "approve of woman's holding the reigns of government over man."[4] She admonished her women readers to carry out scrupulously both their domestic duties and their work for moral reformation. Other topics that may be less interesting to modern readers are in letters dealing with the Bible. Her careful study of the Old and New Testaments is evident in letters, such as "Man Equally Guilty with Woman in the Fall." Grimké argued that from a scriptural viewpoint, men and women are equal. Despite some strained Biblical exegesis and occasional inconsistencies, Sarah Grimké's *Letters on the Equality of the Sexes and the Condition of Woman* were important precursors to Fuller's *Woman in the Nineteenth Century*.

By their nature, however, epistolary essays are not a unified work and tend to be fragmented, whereas *Woman in the Nineteenth Century* is unified by its spiritual vision of ultimate reality and its organic writing style within the sermon framework. At first glance, Fuller's writing might appear verbose. As with any complex literary art, it calls for active participation on the part of the reader. Then the hallmarks of the transcendentalist organic style of writing become apparent. A transcendental work of art grew out of experience and hence was organic; the spirit of a work was superior to the form. Ultimately, transcendental writing was a theory of religion as well as of knowledge, which accepted the authority of intuition.[5] The seer (writer) united his or her experience (the spectacle) into a whole, as Thoreau later did in *Walden*. Thus a writer's subjectivity became universal, as was Fuller's when she fused her experience with that of all women and spoke directly to her reader. The movement of Fuller's treatise is not one of formal rhetoric with syllogistic logic, but is circular. It soars in spiraling thought patterns in an ebb-and-flow undulation similar to waves cresting and breaking on the sea shore. Although she recognized the problems women faced—seamstresses laboring for pennies, pregnant slaves toiling in the fields— her work was visionary in its cosmic scope. Prophetic, she looked to future generations, believing that signs pointed "distinctly to the glories of that destiny; faint, but not to be mistaken streaks of the future day,"[6] when men and women would alike benefit from a just society.

Although some of the words Fuller used are outmoded, her concepts are surprisingly modern. She understood the androgynous aspects of sexuality, that there was no wholly masculine man or wholly feminine woman. In other words, she wanted to do away with sexual stereotyping: Nature "will make a female Newton, and a male Syren," she predicated. "Penelope is no more meant for a baker or weaver solely, than Ulysses for a cattle-herd." Although she deplored the double standard of morality and suggested that a man should be as chaste as a woman, she also made it clear that a woman's sexual fulfillment was as important as a man's. The time had come for "Eurydice to call for an Orpheus, rather than Orpheus for Eurydice."[7] In her outspoken plea for help for prostitutes, in which she implied that they were "victims" rather than "sinners," she sounds not unlike a modern sociologist.

Another device Fuller used that is frequently mentioned today as important for the education of girls was the "role model." She cited as examples of a life to emulate Catharine Maria Sedgwick, Lady Russell, and Madame Roland. She explained she used a plethora of examples in order to show there was no age without "a witness of the equality of the sexes in function, duty, and hope."[8] Not unlike a professor in a modern women's studies course evaluating the image of women in literature, Fuller discussed whether or not female characters in literature were heroic. She thought Edmund Spenser and Philip Massinger painted stronger female characters than Shakespeare, whose genius she nevertheless acknowledged. After examining women in fiction, Fuller turned to myth. She discussed women in the Bible, and then delved beyond patriarchal Hebrew-Christian society to a culture that valued the mythic earth mother. In her quest for the feminine principle, she turned to Cassandra, Ceres, and Sita from classical and oriental mythology.

Margaret Fuller's famous Conversations, seminar-style classes which the Boston area intellectual elite paid to attend, were a form of what is in present-day feminist terminology called "consciousness raising." Radical ideas, as no doubt first discussed in these Conversations, are crystallized in *Woman in the Nineteenth Century*. Then as now, the sensitive reader is forced to question received opinion as to the status of women. As the leaders of the women's suffrage movement, Elizabeth Cady Stanton and Susan B. Anthony, later wrote, "the precursor of the Woman's Rights agitation of the last thirty-three years, Fuller, vindicated a woman's right to think."[9]

Although her radical biographer, Julia Ward Howe, complained that people of her day were not so confident of Fuller's assumptions about the existence of the soul, it is important to note that when Fuller did discuss mundane reforms, she did so without compromise. She meant literally her most famous occupational suggestion that women should be sea captains if they wished. Some years before writing her treatise, she visited a French man-of-war, the *Hercules*, anchored in Narragansett Bay. At that time, she wrote her brother that she would "like to command such a vessel, despite all the hardships and privations of such a situation."[10] Her idea that women could command men on a ship and her pleas for help for prostitutes brought denunciation and ridicule to Fuller. Reviews of her work were sometimes bitter and sometimes ironic, although there were others that were surprisingly favorable.

The reviews, however, were not as damaging to Fuller's reputation as were the comments made by "friends" after her untimely death at sea. *The Memoirs of Margaret Fuller Ossoli* (1852), edited by Ralph Waldo Emerson, William Henry Channing, and James Freeman Clarke, established the critical canon that is still powerful today that Fuller's "pen was a non-conductor."[11] It further damaged her reputation by painting an unattractive picture of Fuller as an arrogant, irrational egotist, who mesmerized her friends and repelled her enemies. Study of the two-volume *Memoirs* indicates that it was Emerson who was the chief architect of the distortion of Fuller's reputation. Not only did he say she had a "mountainous ME," but he also faulted her for not being pretty. Nevertheless, he admitted that as a brilliant conversationalist and as a woman, she fascinated him. In fact, study of Emerson's journals and of his lengthy correspondence with her reveals a strong ambivalence in Emerson's emotions toward Fuller. His analysis was not objective. Because of Emerson's reputation as a secular guru, few subsequent writers questioned his assessment of Margaret Fuller.

Other acquaintances of Fuller joined in the chorus of denigration. Probably in retaliation for Fuller's unfavorable review of his poetry, James Russell Lowell attacked her in his *A Fable for Critics* for her spite, egoism, and reliance on the Infinite Soul. Her most malicious critic was Nathaniel Hawthorne, who portrayed Fuller as Zenobia in *The Blithedale Romance*. He recorded his obsessive curiosity about Fuller's activities in Italy in his journal, which was published posthumously. Hawthorne wrote that her husband, Marchese Giovanni Ossoli, was "half an idiot," that Margaret was ridiculous and had an "evil nature," and "fell as the weakest of her sisters."[12] In *The Bostonians*, a novel which satirized the suffragist movement, published soon after Hawthorne's journal, Henry James used fragments of the Fuller legend. Like the other novelists, Oliver Wendell

Holmes personified the threatening feminist in *Elsie Venner* (1858) and *A Mortal Antipathy* (1885) with aspects of the personality attributed to Fuller.

Twentieth-century scholars carried into the academic world the biased picture of Fuller created by the nineteenth-century literary giants. In his chapter "Margaret Fuller: Rebel," in *The Romantic Revolution in America*, Vernon L. Parrington used as his major source the *Memoirs*, from which he quoted copiously. He accepted the Emersonian view that Fuller wrote nothing of "high distinction either in thought or style." Not unlike Emerson, he was somewhat patronizing: "What she lacked in knowledge of Kant and Fichte she made up in enthusiasm."[13] Parrington's conclusion that Fuller was the embodiment of the "grandiose aspirations" of her age was later echoed by Perry Miller who wrote that Fuller had not been forgotten because she was the "only candidate" for the "role of a native champion of the Romantic heroine in the grandiose (and so, for an American dangerously close to the ludicrous) operatic manner."[14] Perry Miller, the renowned American literature scholar, gave the Harvard imprimatur to the feminist archetype created in the *Memoirs*. He chose a quotation attributed to Fuller from the *Memoirs*, "I Find No Intellect Comparable to My Own," for an article in *The American Heritage* (1957). In addition to stressing what his title suggests—her "nearsighted arrogance"—Miller concentrated on Fuller's appearance, asserting she was "phenomenally homely" with an "abnormally" large neck. In fact, although a "scholar," Miller changed recorded descriptions of her abundant fair hair to "not quite blond, stringy," and of her full figure to "angular and ailing." Miller complained of the picture he used to illustrate his article, that it made "the aging, unlovely Margaret young and beautiful."[15]

Perry Miller continued his defamation of Fuller's reputation with an anthology of her works published in 1963. He attacked her intellectualism, thus revealing his own hostility to intellectual women:

One factor in our settling a public image of Margaret Fuller is that she cannot be dissociated from the hyperbolically female intellectualism of the period, the slighted invocation of which invites our laughter.[16]

Miller joined the chorus of Hawthorne and Lowell in their attack on feminists with their deadly weapon of ridicule. He began his foreword with the anecdote in which Fuller was alleged to have told Carlyle, "I accept the universe," and he was supposed to have retorted, "By Gad, she'd better."[17] Although Miller explained she came off from this interchange "with honor," and also gave her credit for her high intellect and ability as a critic, he asserted her feminist propaganda was a slight contribution to the women's rights campaign. In his foreword, Perry Miller even blamed Fuller for her death when he described her actions as the ship was foundering as "suicidal." He concluded his introduction by denigrating Ossoli, "according to Hawthorne a boor," and by again suggesting that had Margaret "wanted to make the effort" the family might have been saved. Miller chose to disregard the fact that she had a strong young husband at her side who had just fought in a revolution. The Ossolis were the only people on board with a baby, and understandably as anxious parents probably panicked. The leading transcendentalist scholar, Perry Miller (1905–63) had absorbed the ambivalence of Emerson and Hawthorne in his unfair assessment of Fuller.

What seems clear at this point in time is that the *Memoirs of Margaret Fuller Ossoli* must be regarded as a judgmental nemesis, and should be disregarded in a study of the writing of Margaret Fuller. *Woman in the Nineteenth Century* must be read anew with the same attention that a complex work of literature merits. It needs to be read in the context of the transcendentalist writing of its time. Its philosophic framework is predicated on universals, that there is a spiritual basis to the universe, that indeed principles of right and wrong do exist, that an individual can take responsibility for his or her life. *Woman in the Nineteenth Century* recognizes the power of the human spirit to transform society. A call for action, it is the feminist manifesto—''Always the soul says to us all, 'Cherish your best hopes as a faith, and abide by them in action.' ''[18] *Woman in the Nineteenth Century* should be ranked in the history of ideas with other powerful declarations of its time, with the ''American Scholar'' address, with the ''Declaration of Sentiments,'' and with the *Communist Manifesto*.

NOTES

1. S. Margaret Fuller, *Woman in the Nineteenth Century* (1845; rpt. Columbia: University of South Carolina Press, 1980), introduction by Madeleine B. Stern, p. 26.

2. Sarah M. Grimké, *Letters on the Equality of the Sexes and the Condition of Woman* (1838; rpt. New York: Source Book Press, 1970), p. 51.

3. Ibid., p. 17.

4. Ibid., p. 33.

5. See F. O. Matthiessen, *American Renaissance* (London: Oxford University Press, 1941), pp. 24–31.

6. Fuller, *Woman*, p. 163.

7. Ibid., pp. 103, 33, 13.

8. Ibid., p. 157.

9. Elizabeth Cady Stanton, Susan B. Anthony, and Matilda Joslyn Gage, eds., *History of Woman Suffrage* (New York: Fowler and Wells, 1881–87), I, pp. 801–2.

10. Thomas Wentworth Higginson, *Margaret Fuller Ossoli* (1884; rpt. Boston: Houghton Mifflin, 1887), p. 88.

11. Ralph Waldo Emerson, William Henry Channing, and James Freeman Clarke, eds., *Memoirs of Margaret Fuller Ossoli* (Boston: Phillips, Sampson and Company, 1852), I, p. 294.

12. Julian Hawthorne, *Nathaniel Hawthorne and His Wife: A Biography* (1884; rpt. Mich.: Scholarly Press, 1969), I, pp. 255–56.

13. Vernon L. Parrington, *Main Currents in American Thought*, II, *The Romantic Revolution in America* (New York: Harcourt, Brace, 1927), pp. 418–26.

14. Perry Miller, ed., *Margaret Fuller: American Romantic* (New York: Doubleday, 1963), p. xiii.

15. Perry Miller, "I Find No Intellect Comparable to My Own," *American Heritage*, 8 (February, 1957), pp. 22–24, 97–99.

16. Miller, *Margaret Fuller*, p. xvii.

17. Thus far, I have been unable to find the source of this anecdote. On August 12, 1980, R. Buckminster Fuller (Margaret's grandnephew), told me that the Carlyle-Margaret anecdote was frequently repeated in Cambridge, Massachusetts.

18. Fuller, *Woman*, p. 163.

21

The Career Woman Fiction of Elizabeth Stuart Phelps

Susan Ward

Elizabeth Stuart Phelps (Ward) is most often mentioned in literary histories of nineteenth-century American literature, when she is mentioned at all, as the author of *The Gates Ajar*, a post–Civil War novel on the domestic comforts of heaven which brought probably much-needed solace to scores of bereaved American women and sold 100,000 copies in a few years. Phelps went on to write three sequels—*Beyond the Gates*, *The Gates Between*, and *Within the Gates*—and established herself as the leading authority on heaven among America's popular women novelists. Heaven, however, was not her only subject. An avowedly didactic writer, aware, as she records in her autobiography, that "such sympathies with the moral agitations of our day as have touched me at all, have fed, not famished my literary work,"[1] she also championed temperance, anti-vivisectionism, dress reform for women, and "[women's] right to make their own best possibilities in every department of life."[2] Her interest in women's struggle to attain equality led her to speak out on the issues of women's education and women in the professions in terms that were radical for the 1870's. Her ideas on these subjects, expressed both in non-fiction pieces and in the fiction which they fed, are the primary area of investigation of this paper.

A secondary area of investigation is the way in which Phelps's ideas on the position of women affected the form of her fiction. Phelps made her name and her living as a popular writer, and, as critics of the popular arts have pointed out, popular writers, to remain popular, must support the status quo.[3] In the America of the mid–nineteenth century, both ideology and form were well-defined for women novelists. The correct ideology was complete espousal of the Cult of True Womanhood with its principal "virtues" of piety, purity, domesticity, and obedience.[4] The correct form, an outgrowth of the "feminine novel" which flourished from 1820–50, featured a plot in which heroines might rail against the womanly virtues for a time but which demanded that they settle down, preferably with a proper Victorian hero, to practice them in the end.[5] In her fiction that deals with the issues of women's education and women in the professions, Phelps altered both ideology and form. The ways in which she did so form an interesting example of the effect the agitation for women's rights in the mid–nineteenth century had on a member of the group we call "domestic feminists," who felt it her first duty to, as she put it, "portray the most important . . . features of the world [she] lives in"[6] for a very wide, feminine audience.

Phelps made her most succinct statements on women's issues in a series of non-fiction articles she wrote for *The Independent* in the 1870's. Aside from her thoughts on the issue of dress code for women, all her thoughts on the feminist struggle may be found there. The *Independent* articles may be examined under three headings: enfranchisement, education, and professionalism.

Phelps's position on enfranchisement[7] was very clear; she considered the vote the right of women as "one-half the human race." In an article published in 1871, she outlined the factors she saw operating against the achievement of female enfranchisement: the apathy of the American woman herself and the opposition of men who did not wish to relinquish any of the power they held as superior citizens. "The real trouble at the core of this question," she wrote, "is the reluctance of men to yield the superiority which they have assumed and acquired by virtue of being the governing class to a class which, at the most which can be said, they have made the foil of their own elevation and the mirror of their own exellencies."[8] She called for women's financial independence as a first step toward breaking the "class rule."

Phelps rightly recognized that sound education for women was a vital first step in achieving the goal. Before the Civil War, Emma Willard, Catherine Beecher, and Mary Lyon had made important progress in establishing the idea that women should be educated, but all three of these pioneers in the field of women's education emphasized a curriculum which kept in mind woman's ultimate goal as housewife and mother. In the decade after the Civil War, Dr. Edward H. Clarke's influential book, *Sex in Education*, which argued that women violated their natures when they entered schools of higher education and became nervous, physically ill, and eventually unfit for motherhood as a result, gave added impetus to the notion that women should not be educated too strenuously.[9] Phelps was firmly opposed to this notion. In an 1871 article, she maintained that young women often suffered precisely because their schooling was interrupted at the point where their education was becoming interesting and that more education, not less, might be the cure for many a nervous complaint. "The powers of self-management, self-support, and self-investment are the inherent needs of the maturing man or woman," she wrote. "The best and broadest use of these powers is obligatory upon them. . . . Individuality is the birthright of each human soul."[10] In a subsequent article, she attacked "female education" and supported the growing number of coeducational institutions coming into being during the period.[11]

Phelps's final point, that women can and should have the opportunity to have
areers outside the home, is a running thread throughout the *Independent* series.
n her 1871 article on women's education, she suggested that girls be given
pprenticeships in a business which would fit them to earn their own livings.[12]
ater, she grew more specific about the "businesses" she saw them in, picturing
vomen as ministers,[13] as doctors,[14] and as "grocery store managers, engravers
n wood, druggists, [and] potato diggers."[15] At first, she sidestepped the mar-
iage issue, pointing out, "whatever may be said of married women . . . the
luties of the unmarried woman are not at home."[16] But later she reminded
eaders that even marriage did not insure financial support, since many women
vere forced to earn their husbands' keep and many more were widowed.[17] And
n 1871, she neatly disproved the argument that women did not have the physical
strength for careers by outlining, in detail, the physical demands of housework.[18]
n an interesting sidenote, Phelps did not urge that girls take up the few nine-
eenth-century occupations compatible with housework and thereby open to
women. Sewing she regarded as harmful and underpaid;[19] authorship was at best
chancy and able to offer rewards only to a talented few.[20] Her advice to most
ambitious young women was to become "refined, clear-headed, true-hearted,
and successful businesswom[e]n."[21]

In evaluating the liberal nature of these views, it is necessary to remember
that Phelps wrote immediately after the Civil War, when the feminist movement
was in a state of flux and, to some extent, of disorganization. The Civil War
had distracted the energies of the first feminists, and after the war America's
reformers turned their attention to the question of Negro suffrage. In 1869, there
was the split between the Anthony-Stanton National Women Suffrage Association
and the Blackwell-Stone-Howe-Livermore American Woman Suffrage Association. As feminist historians have pointed out, this split and the distraction of
the war itself weakened the push for the vote.[22] Likewise, in the field of women's
education, Beecher, Willard, and Lyon had made significant strides before the
war, but their stress on female education and the controversy begun by Clarke
had halted progress. And, while there had been some progress made by feminists
into the professions during the period 1850–70—Lucy Stone into the field of
public speaking, Antoinette Brown and Olympia Brown into the ministry, and
Elizabeth Blackwell and Marie Zakrewski into medicine—all had fought bitterly
against prejudice and discrimination.[23] Phelps, then, writing articles urging enfranchisement, equal opportunity in education for women, and female professionalism for a middle-class, mid–nineteenth-century female audience, was taking
a daring step.

How daring a step it was becomes even clearer when we consider some of
the assumptions behind Phelps's ideas and compare them to accepted ideology
of the time. For the purpose of this discussion, let us accept Barbara Welter's
definition of the Cult of True Womanhood as the accepted ideology. The assumptions behind Phelps's views as they are expressed in the *Independent* articles
violate at least two of the cult's "womanly virtues."

Phelps did not take issue with the prescription for purity; to do so would hav been to go against her own rather rigid Christian morality. On the face of it, a the author of one of the best-selling religious books of the period, she seeme to support the piety dictum as well. Yet in an article published in 1871, sh attacked the creed of "live for others," upheld by those she called "moralist and sentimentalists" because it "[stood] in the way of woman's progress." Christianity, she pointed out, did not originally preach self-development for me and self-depreciation for women, and businesswomen could just as well donat money as time to the poor.[24] Thus, the Christianity she espoused, though strict was tempered by her allegiance to feminism.

Phelps also refuted the notion that the home was the "proper sphere" fo women. Her suggestion that women be apprenticed in places of business arguee implicitly against the domestic ideal. In 1872, she came out explicitly agains educating girls in the "domestic sciences," maintaining that " 'the other side in a matter like this of the elevation of woman generally takes care of itself' and that "the burden of domestic care will devolve on women exclusively a long as women are ready to bear it.''[25] Her assertions that young girls could be trained to oversee a house in a few weeks or months and that "the duties of the unmarried woman are not at home" further subverted the domestic ideal.[26]

Phelps's biggest quarrel with the Cult of True Womanhood, however, came in the area of submissiveness. In an 1871 article entitled "The True Woman," she claimed that "the most palpable obstacle we meet [in the struggle for women's rights] is an enormous dummy to which has been given the title of the 'true woman.' " She went on to proclaim:

Woman is not man's ward. Man is not woman's guardian. Man is incapable, even if he were called upon to do so, of competently judging for woman. . . . Indeed, if one wisdom must decree for two, woman is far better qualified to regulate the position which shall belong to man. . . . His force is more comprehensible to her than her fineness to him.[27]

In articles published in 1871 and in 1874, she supported equality rather than hierarchy in marriage.[28] In an 1872 article addressed directly to young women, she warned that in the matter of career choice "your dearest advisers and guardians may not recognize the dawn of the day in which you live" and advised them to "draw the line affectionately between their convictions and yours.''[29] In thus urging wives to demand equal footing in marriage and girls to go against parents' wishes, Phelps was seriously at odds with one of the most commonly upheld Victorian beliefs about the role of women in society.

Though we cannot and should not class Elizabeth Stuart Phelps as a radical feminist,[30] the views she stated in the *Independent* articles of the 1870's were, for the time, fairly advanced. Further, as a successful woman author who had begun her career with a best-selling novel, she could speak and expect to be listened to by both housewives and ladies of leisure who might have turned away from a Victoria Woodhull, a Lucy Stone, or even an Elizabeth Cady Stanton.

Phelps's feminist views as expressed in these articles, then, were tremendously important to the women's movement because of the potentially wide audience to whom they spoke. They were also valuable to Phelps's own development as a writer because they made their way into some of her fiction and helped to shape both its underlying ideology and its form.

Between 1870 and 1909, Elizabeth Stuart Phelps published at least eight short stories and three novels which have as their major concern the question of women and careers. As might be expected, much of the feminist ideology of the *Independent* articles spilled over into the career woman fiction. The ideology underlying the fiction may be examined under two general headings: women and education, and women and work.

In "More Ways Than One,"[31] Phelps illustrates the desire of half-educated girls to continue their educations. The heroine, a graduate of a young ladies' school assigned to the nursery to babysit after graduation, wants to continue her education so badly that she sells silver polish door to door to pay for a baby nurse to free her for further study. Although he is not mentioned, the story is clearly an attack on Dr. Edward Clarke and his notion that higher education is unnatural for young women. Phelps's support of the notion that women should be educated on a par equal to men also become clear in her fiction. Zay Lloyd, the doctor-heroine of *Doctor Zay*, is educated at Vassar, then one of the new women's colleges, and Lois McQuentin of "Our Little Woman" is determined to become a medical student who will "know as much as some medical students I saw coming in on the horse-car today—Harvard fellows with eye-glasses." An *Independent* article in which Phelps applauded the founding of a coed medical school at Boston University,[32] and her long interest in fostering the education of more women doctors stand behind Lois's somewhat derogatory dismissal of the "Harvard fellows."

Phelps's view that women have work to do in the world as well as the home stands behind most of her career woman stories. Two of the working heroines—Jemima Jasper in "The Girl Who Could Not Write a Composition" and Miss Aura in "The Autobiography of Miss Aureola"—inherit businesses from their fathers and elect to manage them themselves rather than turn them over to male relatives. Two more—Sarah Raven, the telephone operator in "The Chief Operator," and Aunt John, the photographer in "The Day of Judgment"—work because they are widows. At least two others—Perley Kelso in *The Silent Partner* and Miss Aura in "The Autobiography of Miss Aureola"—contribute some of their business profits to the poor, living up to Phelps's suggestion that businesswomen give money instead of time to fulfill the demands of Christian charity.[33] And many of the career woman heroines work to support families. Sarah Raven supports her stepmother, Jemima Jasper runs the family business for her mother and her younger brother, Hannah Colby builds a life for herself and her mother after the loss of the family income, and Avis Ostrander's artwork pays the bills for herself, her sickly husband, and two small children.

Genteel nineteenth-century America allowed that some gentlewomen might be forced to work and singled out a few acceptable professions. But the careers which Phelps's working heroines pursue are outside the prescribed bounds. Lois McQuentin, when she tells Hannah Colby not to teach or sew, pointing out that "we all do the same things and run the wages down," eliminates the two lines of work most commonly followed by women in the nineteenth century.[34] Hannah becomes a seller of engravings and photographs; most of Phelps's other working women follow equally "unfeminine" pursuits. Jerusha Bangs is a minister, Zay Lloyd and Lois McQuentin are or would be doctors, Miss Aura runs a shoe factory, Perley Kelso is part owner of a mill, Jemima Jasper runs a furniture company, and Avis Dobell is an artist. None of the heroines in any of the fiction of Elizabeth Stuart Phelps I have read makes her living by sewing.

Most of Phelps's working heroines manage to combine careers with the exercise of some of the traditional domestic virtues. "Dr. Zay," who knows how to dress and can decorate a "homey" parlor when she has the time, is a good example. But in at least two instances, Phelps shows that too much cultivation of the domestic in woman can be counter to her nature and harmful to her other talents. The girl in "More Ways Than One," who sees her mother's expectation that she care for a younger brother as a direct threat to her studies, is one example. Avis, whose artistic energies are drained by caring for a sick husband and two children and who, in the end, can only paint one great picture, is another. Significantly, both of these heroines hate housework, even as children. Given the outcome of their stories, Phelps seems to suggest they should never have been asked to do it in the first place.

Thus, the ideology which emerges from Phelps's career women directly calls into question one of the four "virtues" of True Womanhood—domesticity. When a career heroine goes counter to the wishes of her relatives by taking over a furniture company or refusing to learn to sew and make jelly, the stories implicitly question another of the virtues—submissiveness. But by exhibiting strong signs of the other womanly virtues, the career heroines never seem too radical. Zay Lloyd, as noted, knows how to dress well and decorate a parlor, Avis is a good mother and a saintly wife, Perley Kelso and Miss Aura share their business profits with the poor. This mix of the traditional and the new in the ideological makeup of Phelps's heroines, though it may be disturbing to present-day readers, was probably precisely what made them palatable to readers of the 1870's. And their very palatability to an audience with a basically conservative ideology helped to spread Phelps's message.

Understanding the form of Phelps's career woman fiction is a complex matter which depends, first of all, on a grounding in the form of the woman's novel, written by women, about women, and for women, during the period 1820–70. Phelps, writing roughly from 1870 to 1910, published at the end of the period in which they flourished. Nevertheless, her readers' formal expectations were doubtless based partly on a familiarity with them. And, as at least one critic of the literature has pointed out, popular writers such as Alice Hegen Rice (*Mrs. Wiggs of the Cabbage Patch*, 1901), Gene Stratton-Porter (*Freckles*, 1904 and

Girl of the Limberlost, 1909), Kate Douglas Wiggin (*Rebecca of Sunnybrook Farm*, 1903), Eleanor Hodgman Porter (*Pollyanna*, 1913) worked strands of the nineteenth-century woman's novel into fiction which continued to sell well into the twentieth century.[35]

The plot of the nineteenth-century woman's novel contained, of course, many variables. Almost always, however, it features a young woman, sometimes a child, who is either an orphan or an heiress reduced suddenly to poverty and forced to make her way in the world. Often, she is surrounded by powerful adults who stand in the way of happiness and financial ease. She must learn to survive her troubles on her own through self-sufficiency of character and, if necessary, through the plying of some feminine trade such as teaching, sewing, or going out as a companion to an invalid gentlewoman. Although independent, saintly women appear from time to time, a different fate is usually reserved for the heroine. A hero appears on the scene, and, once he has proven himself trustworthy, marries her. A final chapter suggests that the marriage will be a happy one.[36]

The issue of marriage in these novels is a knotty one. Brown points out that one plot variant concerns a woman who is unhappily married and must learn to endure,[37] Cowie outlines a plot which stops with the heroine still single and resigned to a life of saintly single blessedness,[38] and Baym notes that marriage is not an end in itself, since "honest independence" is preferred to a "mercenary" union.[39] But the fact is that the majority of the heroines *do* marry, thus achieving the status of wife and mother which seemed so necessary a part of woman's identity in the Victorian era. Even those heroines whose marriages turn out badly have at least had the experience and achieved the dignity of motherhood along the way. The single state is clearly not preferred of and for itself.

The background setting of the woman's novel is almost always the home, and home and country virtues are exalted over the talents of the city-bred and fashionably educated. Housekeeping is shown to be hard work, but it is woman's work and the heroine is expected to enjoy it. There are usually more women than men in the novels, and they offer each other emotional support. Baym outlines a "cult of domesticity" which assumes that men as well as women find "greatest happiness and fulfillment in domestic relations" and that "home and the world would become one."[40]

The proper heroine of the woman's novel possesses, in sum, all four of the virtues of True Womanhood. She is pure as a matter of course; she is pious because religion, especially in Victorian America, was seen as a woman's sphere.[41] Although she may exercise "home influence" and possess self-sufficiency of character, she rarely openly rebels against those in control of her money and property (usually, male executors) or her social loyalties (husbands, fathers, and legal guardians). Instead, she is submissive and domestic because not to be would be to undercut the Victorian notion that the most exalted role for woman was the role of wife, mother, and ideal housekeeper.

There are at least two types of heroes in the woman's novel. One, modeled

on Jane Eyre's beloved Rochester, is domineering, moody, irreligious, attractive—and tries to seduce the heroine. Sometimes he is reformed, by bitter experiences or by the moral influence of the heroine herself, and allowed to marry
her. The second, solider if less interesting, is "ethical, generous, frank, hard-
working, energetic, and an admirer and respecter of women who likes the heroine
as much or more than he lusts for her."[42] He is the best bet for a happy marriage.

Phelps's career woman stories and novels depart from this formula in a number
of ways. First, although her career women heroines work toward "self-sufficiency of character," they do so at all costs, even that of undercutting one or
more of the four virtues of True Womanhood. Phelps's personal morality would
not allow her to draw heroines who were impure or impious, but domesticity
and submissiveness, as we have seen, were often swept under the rug. Some
refuse to like housework. Others—Perley Kelso and Sip Garth in *The Silent
Partner* and Zay Lloyd in *Doctor Zay*—renounce the domestic role completely
by vowing never to marry. Still others are notably unsubmissive as they go
against the wishes of parents or guardians to achieve their career goals. What
is finally noteworthy about these heroines, however, is not so much that Phelps
drew them as that she encouraged her readers to admire them. Their failure to
practice all four of the feminine virtues places them outside the standard held
up for women to emulate during the Victorian era.

The hero in Phelps's career woman fiction plays a relatively minor and almost
always a weaker role in comparison to that of the heroine.[43] Sometimes he is
dead, as in the case of Miss Aura's fiancé ("The Autobiography of Miss Aureola") or Sarah Raven's husband ("The Chief Operator"). Sometimes, as in
"More Ways Than One," "A Woman's Pulpit," "Our Little Woman," "Hannah Colby's Chance," and "The Girl Who Could Not Write a Composition,"
he is entirely absent. The weak hero, such as Philip Ostrander in *The Story of
Avis* and Maverick Hayle in *The Silent Partner*, exists to underline the nobility
of the heroine who must cope with him.[44] More interesting, the hero of the
"ethical, frank," etc. variety, the preferred hero of the Victorian woman's novel,
is often rejected by a Phelps heroine. In having her heroines reject such essentially
deserving men, Phelps both questions the validity of marriage itself ("If I married
you, sir, I should invest in life, and you would conduct it. I suspect that I have
a preference for a business of my own," says Perley Kelso in *The Silent Partner*)
and suggests that a different hero must emerge to win her "different" heroine.
("You see, Mr. Yorke, you have been so unfortunate as to become interested
in a new kind of woman. The trouble is that a happy marriage with such a
woman demands a new kind of man," says Zay Lloyd of *Dr. Zay*.) Both
suggestions lead to themes which continue to claim the attention of women
writers in the present day.

Because of her notion that women can and should be financially independent
and because her heroes and heroines differ from the standard heroes and heroines
of the earlier woman's novel, the plots of Phelps's career woman fiction also
depart from the accepted formula. If they follow the pattern of the poor or

abandoned woman who must struggle with adversity and develop self-suffi-ciency— "Hannah Colby's Chance"—the self-sufficiency is always linked with the successful launching of a professional career. Some of the plots center not on a struggle against adversity, but on a struggle against those who would keep the heroine from exercising her right to be professional— "More Ways Than One," *The Silent Partner*, "A Woman's Pulpit." These stories end happily when the heroines throw off the influence of those who oppose them and proceed toward their professional goals. In both instances, professional identity, not strength of character, is the key, though the two are undeniably linked. And in no instance is long suffering acceptable as a mark of self-sufficiency.

The love story, when it exists as part of the plot, represents a threat, rather than a salvation, for the heroine. For Avis Dobell, the one Phelps career heroine who marries halfway through the novel, marriage is a destruction of potential rather than fulfillment. Most career heroines' love stories center on the heroine's resistance to marriage, and that resistance is based on the mutual exclusivity of the Victorian ideal of wifehood with the goals of a career. "Marriage," says Avis Dobell to Philip Ostrander as she refuses him, "is a profession to a woman. And I have my work." Zay Lloyd, who finally agrees to marry a man who has vowed to help support her career, does so at the end of the novel. Phelps sidesteps the problem of portraying the happy marriage of two professionals, a problem which remains largely unsolved in contemporary woman's fiction.

In altering the form of the woman's novel to accommodate some of her ideas on feminine independence, Elizabeth Stuart Phelps thus introduced some of the very themes and experimented with some of the formal problems which still occupy women writers today. Her work is historically important because it gives us an idea of some of the problems that even non-militant domestic feminists pondered in 1870. And it is critically important because it documents and links to an ideology the beginnings of new forms of fiction by, for, and about women.

NOTES

1. Elizabeth Stuart Phelps, *Chapters from a Life* (Boston: Houghton, Mifflin and Company, 1896), p. 256.

2. Ibid., p. 250.

3. See, for example, Russell Nye, "Introduction: The Popular Arts and the Popular Audience," in *The Unembarrassed Muse: The Popular Arts in America* (1970; rpt. New York: Dial Press, Inc., 1971), pp. 1–7.

4. Barbara Welter, "The Cult of True Womanhood: 1820–1860," *American Quarterly*, 18 (Summer, 1966), 151–74.

5. Useful summaries of the "woman's novel" of the period include Nina Baym, *Woman's Fiction: A Guide to Novels by and about Women in America, 1820–1870* (Ithaca, N.Y.: Cornell University Press, 1978); Herbert R. Brown, *The Sentimental Novel in America* (1940; rpt. New York: Pageant Books, Inc., 1959); Alexander Cowie, "The Vogue of the Domestic Novel, 1850–1870," *South Atlantic Quarterly*, 41 (October, 1942), 416–24; Helen Waite Papashvily, *All the Happy Endings* (New York: Harper and

Brothers, 1956); and Fred Lewis Pattee, *The Feminine Fifties* (New York: D. Appleton-Century Company, 1940). My study of these sources and of the fiction itself supports this critical generalization.

6. Phelps, *Chapters from a Life*, p. 259.

7. Phelps's views on this subject, not discussed here, may be found published in four parts in the May, 1873, *Independent* and republished, with additions, in *What to Wear?* (Boston: James R. Osgood and Company, 1873).

8. Elizabeth Stuart Phelps, "The Gist of the Matter," *Independent*, 23 (July 13, 1871), 1.

9. See Barbara Harris, *Beyond Her Sphere: Women and the Professions in American History* (Westport, Conn.: Greenwood Press, 1978), pp. 100 and 106 for a discussion of this influential work.

10. Elizabeth Stuart Phelps, "Unhappy Girls," *Independent*, 23 (July 27, 1871), 1; and "A Word for the Silent," *Independent*, 26 (January 1, 1874), 1633–34.

11. Elizabeth Stuart Phelps, "The 'Female Education' of Women," *Independent*, 25 (November 13, 1873), 1409–10.

12. Phelps, "Unhappy Girls," p. 1.

13. Elizabeth Stuart Phelps, "The United Head," *Independent*, 23 (September 4, 1871), 1.

14. Elizabeth Stuart Phelps, "The Experiment Tried," *Independent*, 26 (March 5, 1874), 1.

15. Elizabeth Stuart Phelps, "A Talk to the Girls," *Independent*, 24 (January 4, 1872), 1.

16. Phelps, "Unhappy Girls," p. 1.

17. Elizabeth Stuart Phelps, "Too Much Conscience," *Independent*, 23 (August 3, 1871), 3.

18. Elizabeth Stuart Phelps, "Rights and Relativities," *Independent*, 3 (September 7, 1871), 1.

19. Elizabeth Stuart Phelps, "The Song of the Shirt," *Independent*, 23 (August 10, 1871), 1.

20. Phelps, "A Talk to the Girls," p. 1.

21. Ibid.

22. See Gerda Lerner, *The Woman in American History* (Menlo Park, Calif.: Addison-Wesley Publishing Company, 1971), p. 110 for a summary of these issues.

23. Harris, *Beyond Her Sphere*, p. 90.

24. Phelps, "Too Much Conscience," p. 3.

25. Phelps, "A Talk to the Girls," p. 1.

26. Phelps, "Too Much Conscience," p. 3.

27. Elizabeth Stuart Phelps, "The True Woman," *Independent*, 23 (October 12, 1871), 1.

28. Elizabeth Stuart Phelps, "The New Earth," *Independent*, 23 (September 28, 1871), 1; and "A Dream Within a Dream," *Independent*, 26 (February 19, 1874), 1.

29. Phelps, "A Talk to the Girls," p. 1.

30. See Christine Stansell, "Elizabeth Stuart Phelps: A Study in Female Rebellion," *Massachusetts Review*, XIII (Winter-Spring, 1972), 239–56. Stansell calls Phelps's work "a superb entry into an underground war against the male" but suggests that her later fiction emphasizes "manipulation through weakness." She also speculates that Phelps's life experiences left her unable to "locate the exceptional woman within herself."

31. The short stories and novels under discussion, listed with heroines, are:

NOVELS:

Doctor Zay (1882)—Zay Lloyd
The Silent Partner (1871)—Perley Kelso and Sip Garth
The Story of Avis (1877)—Avis Dobell Ostrander

SHORT STORIES:

"The Autobiography of Miss Aureola," *Century*, 46 (May, 1904), 109–24. Miss Aura.
"The Chief Operator," *Harper's New Monthly Magazine*, 119 (July, 1909), 300–308.
Sarah Raven.
"The Day of Judgment," *Our Young Folks*, 5 (May, 1869), 327–32. Aunt John.
"The Girl Who Could Not Write a Composition," *Our Young Folks*, 7 (August-
September, 1871), 467–69, 540–44. Jemima Jasper.
"Hannah Colby's Chance," *Our Young Folks*, 9 (October-December, 1873), 595–
604, 653–60, 730–40. Hannah Colby.
"More Ways Than One," *Our Young Folks*, 7 (April, 1871), 227–32. Unnamed.
"Our Little Woman," *Our Young Folks*, 8 (November-December, 1872), 654–62,
727–37. Hannah Colby and Lois McQuentin.
"A Woman's Pulpit," *Atlantic Monthly*, 26 (July 1870) 11–22. Jerusha Bangs.

32. Elizabeth Stuart Phelps, "The Experiment Tried," *Independent*, 26 (March 5,
1874), 1.
33. Phelps, "Too Much Conscience," p. 3.
34. See Louisa May Alcott's *Work*, featuring a heroine who tries all the traditional
professions open to a young woman in mid–nineteenth-century America, for a fictional
treatment of the subject. See also Harris, *Beyond Her Sphere*, for an historical treatment.
35. See James D. Hart, *The Popular Book in America* (1950; rpt. Berkley, Calif.:
University of California Press, 1963), pp. 208 ff. for a discussion of these writers and
their relationship to the nineteenth-century "woman's novel."
36. I base these and all further generalizations concerning the form of the woman's
novel on those made by Baym, Brown, Cowie, Papashvily, and Pattee (see note 5) and
on my own readings in the genre.
37. Brown, *The Sentimental Novel*, p. 290.
38. Cowie, "The Vogue of the Domestic Novel."
39. Baym, *Woman's Fiction*, pp. 38–39.
40. Ibid., p. 40.
41. For a discussion of this topic, see Ann Douglas, *The Feminization of American
Culture* (New York: Alfred A. Knopf, 1977).
42. Baym, *Woman's Fiction*, p. 41.
43. See Stansell, "Elizabeth Stuart Phelps," and Mary Angela Bennett, *Elizabeth
Stuart Phelps* (Philadelphia: University of Pennsylvania Press, 1939) for discussions of
this point and its relation to Phelps's life experiences.
44. Brown, *The Sentimental Novel*, pp. 290–95.

22

The Soul's Society: Emily Dickinson and Colonel Higginson

Anna Mary Wells

The role of Colonel Thomas Wentworth Higginson in his relations with Emily Dickinson has been consistently misrepresented and he himself maligned. Why this should be is rather hard to understand. Higginson's coeditor in the first posthumous publication of the Dickinson poems, Mabel Loomis Todd (1858–1933), tended to exaggerate her own part and denigrate his, but it should not have been necessary for later biographers to follow her lead. The primary sources of information, Dickinson's letters to Higginson, a few of his to her, and his first-hand account of their friendship have been available from the time public interest in the poet began.[1] The consistent use of secondary sources in preference to these has increasingly distorted Higginson's image.

If this were merely an injustice to the Colonel perhaps only his biographers need be concerned; he is remembered and honored for his work in many other areas. But the misinterpretation of this friendship blocks an understanding of much we might know about the poet. It was, as she said repeatedly, the single most important emotional attachment in her life. I do not mean a love affair; her family and her biographers have invented quite enough of those. The friendship with Higginson was unique; it is not easy to understand, but the effort to understand it is rewarding. In her own words:

> The Soul selects her own Society—
> Then—shuts the Door—
> To her divine Majority—
> Present no more—

The first startling fact about the friendship is that Emily Dickinson initiated it. She was thirty-one years old, and if any of the family legends about a tragic aborted romance is to be believed, she had already suffered it. She had almost entirely withdrawn from society to the shelter of her father's house, although she continued for a few years longer to make occasional visits to Springfield and Boston. She had never before sent an unsolicited letter to a stranger, and she was never to do so again.

The stranger she chose was a man of thirty-eight who had already made a national reputation as abolitionist, adventurer, feminist, orator, preacher, traveler, and writer. His record would have made him anathema to the Dickinson family. As a Unitarian minister he was no better than a heretic in the eyes of an Amherst Congregationalist. His clashes with the law in his efforts to aid fugitive slaves in Boston and Kansas made him technically a criminal, whereas Emily's father and brother were conservative lawyers. His views of women's rights must have appeared to them absurd if not indecent. Emily did not consult any of them about writing him.

She had learned about him chiefly from the pages of the *Springfield Republican*, at that time one of the leading newspapers in the United States. She had also read his essays in the *Atlantic Monthly*, then four years old and still referred to throughout New England as "the new magazine." In those years it did not carry the names of contributors with their articles, but a part of its publicity was to list them so that readers could guess who had written what. The *Republican* usually identified the authors in its review of the issue, either as a result of its own detective work or a publicity release from the magazine. Dickinson had evidently followed these identifications and satisfied herself that she could recognize Higginson's work even when it was published anonymously.

His contributions to the *Atlantic* during its first four years had included articles on health, nature, women's rights, travel, biography, and history. The article that elicited a response from her was "Letter to a Young Contributor," a rather heavy-handed and sententious piece of advice to would-be authors. This fact has led to the widespread misapprehension that she was asking for advice about publication, a misapprehension that Higginson himself shared very briefly. She soon set him right.

How carefully she had collected all the information she could about him is indicated by the fact that she sent her first letter to his home address in Worcester, not to the *Atlantic* for forwarding. The letter is brief and worth quoting in full.

Mr. Higginson,
    Are you too deeply occupied to say if my Verse is alive?

In the "Letter to a Young Contributor" he had written:

Charge your style with life, and the public will not ask for conundrums. . . . If therefore, in writing, you find it your mission to be abstruse, fight to render your statement clear and attractive as if your life depended on it; your literary life does depend on it, and, if you fail, relapses into a dead language.

The poet went on to explain why she felt it necessary to pose the question.

The Mind is so near itself—it cannot see, distinctly—and I have none to ask. Should you think it breathed—and had you the leisure to tell me, I should feel quick gratitude— If I make the mistake—that you dared to tell me—would give me sincerer honor—toward you I enclose my name—asking you, if you please—Sir—to tell me what is true?

That you will not betray me—it is needless to ask—since Honor is its own pawn—

What she would have regarded as betrayal can now only be guessed. It was not unusual at the time for a woman author to be presented for publication through the good offices of a friend, often supposedly without her knowledge or consent. Emily may have been saying that she would consider it dishonorable of Higginson to have her poems published so. If we accept the twentieth-century view that she wanted to be published, it is even possible to regard this as a double bluff—that in saying she did not want to be betrayed she was hinting that she did. (I don't think so, but it remains a possible interpretation of the line.)

The four poems she enclosed were "Safe in their Alabaster Chambers," "The Nearest Dream Recedes Unrealized," "We Play at Paste," and "I'll Tell You How the Sun Rose."

Higginson's answer has not survived. If, as seems probable, Emily kept it, her family destroyed it after her death. We know, however, that he answered promptly, for her letter acknowledging his reply and apologizing for her own tardiness is dated only ten days later than her first one.

Mr. Higginson [she was not yet ready to call him "dear"]

Your kindness claimed earlier gratitude—but I was ill—and write today from my pillow. Thank you for the surgery—it was not so painful as I supposed. I bring you others—as you ask—though they might not differ.

This sentence has been very widely quoted out of context, to Higginson's discredit. And it must be admitted—the evidence is incontrovertible—that he had attempted to advise Emily Dickinson about how to write poetry. Never mind that his intentions were good. Never mind that as an established author writing to an unknown he was generously fulfilling the normal expectations of his society. Never mind even that he may have made some useful points. (Any of us who have ever tried to teach must have *some* sympathy for him here.) He had made an irretrievable error, and posterity has made him pay for it with compound interest.

Emily Dickinson, however, was grateful if disappointed. She did not, however, have any intention of following his advice. She brought him back to the major question—is my verse alive?—with tact.

While my thought is undressed—I can make the distinction, but when I put them in the Gown—they look alike and numb.

This was a reference to a figure of speech he had used in his article:

When I think how slowly my poor thoughts come in, how tardily they connect themselves, what a delicious prolonged perplexity it is to cut and contrive a decent clothing
of words for them, as a little girl does for her doll. . . . I certainly should never dare to
venture into print, but for the confirmed suspicion that the greatest writers have done
even so.

The trick of picking up his metaphors, condensing them, and tossing the result
back at him was one she perfected over the years. Of course she always said it
much better than he had, but the original metaphor was his, and her use of it a
subtle flattery.

In this second letter she continued with a wealth of autobiographical material
cryptically expressed.

You asked how old I was? I made no verse—but one or two—until this winter—Sir—

One of the things she is saying here is that she regarded her work with the
seriousness it deserved. Her life was to be measured, as it has been, not in years
passed but in poems written.

He had asked questions a shy recluse might well have considered intrusive,
but Emily answered them fully if ambiguously. The information she offered
about her family and the mysterious trauma of the previous autumn is too well
known to require repetition here. Biographers have combed it and interpreted it
to the point of exhaustion, though they have never been able to agree as to what
she meant.

From her very wide reading she lists Keats, the Brownings, Ruskin, Sir
Thomas Browne, and the Book of Revelation. Notable among the omissions is
the name of Shakespeare, whose work she knew very well; perhaps both she
and Higginson assumed that it went without saying that everybody read Shakespeare. Of American authors she mentions only Whitman, against whom she
had been warned, and Harriet Prescott, a young lady who had been one of the
first of Higginson's literary proteges. Her coldness to Miss Prescott's work has
a faint flavor of jealousy; could she already have felt that Higginson was *her*
preceptor and should remain hers alone?

In conclusion she states quite unequivocally that she has already been approached with requests to publish, and that she values Higginson's opinion above
those of the two quite respectable editors, Samuel Bowles of the *Republican* and
Josiah Holland of *Scribner's* and *The Century*.

Two Editors of Journals came to my Father's House, this winter—and asked me for my
Mind—and when I asked them "Why," they said I was penurious—and they would use
it for the World—
I could not weigh myself—Myself—My size felt small—to me—I read your Chapters in

the Atlantic—and experienced honor for you—I was sure you would not reject a confiding question—

She does not mention the fact that two of her poems had actually been published in the *Springfield Republican*: "I Taste a Liquor Never Brewed" in May, 1861, under the title "The May Wine" and painfully edited; "Safe in Their Alabaster Chambers" as "The Sleeping" in March, 1862. Perhaps these publications constituted the betrayal of which she felt sure Higginson could not be guilty.

In his second letter, Higginson evidently abandoned the attempt to advise and was content to admire.

Her third, dated June 7, 1862, began "Dear Friend" and continued:

Your letter gave no Drunkenness because I tasted Rum before—Domingo comes but once—yet I have had few pleasures so deep as your opinion, and if I tried to thank you my tears would block my tongue—

These lines have not been quoted nearly so often as the ones about surgery. They seem to me among the most moving in all of Dickinson's letters. Anyone who has ever responded to her poetry must share to some extent in the delight that she had found in her lifetime an audience that satisfied her. Her sister-in-law Susan, her tutor Benjamin Newton, Bowles and Holland—these four had told her she was a poet, but she could not quite believe them until Higginson added his approval. With it she had all the audience she wanted or needed.

I smile when you suggest that I delay "to publish"—that being foreign to my thought as Firmament to Fin—If fame belonged to me, I could not escape her—if she did not, the longest day would pass me on the chase—and the approbation of my Dog would forsake me—then—my Barefoot Rank is better—

The refusal to publish here would seem to be unequivocal, and yet an ambiguity remains. With due apologies to the poet for reducing one of her favorite metaphors to a slangy cliche, we might paraphrase her: "In regard to publishing I'm like a fish out of water." But she goes on, showing to us who have the benefit of hindsight a remarkable prescience—"If fame belonged to me" it might well come after my death when the attendant publicity could not be a personal embarrassment.

In the remainder of this letter she discusses (and refutes) specific points of advice, but then proposes that she should send poems from time to time for Higginson's criticism "to ask [him] if [she] told it clear."

She ends the letter with a poem.

As if I asked a common Alms
And in my wondering hand
A Stranger pressed a Kingdom,
And I, bewildered, stand—
As if I asked the Orient

> Had it for me a Morn—
> And it should lift its purple Dikes,
> And shatter me with Dawn!

This stunning tribute is the first of many attempts she made to tell Higginson how much his attention meant to her.

A month later she wrote in reply to a request for a picture the description of herself too familiar to require repetition here. In the same letter she said:

You spoke of *Pippa Passes*—I never heard anybody speak of *Pippa Passes*—before.

This comment is a little unfair to her sister-in-law Susan with whom she frequently talked on literary themes. Her sister Lavinia and her mother had no interest in anything beyond the housekeeping; her brother Austin would not have considered discussing any intellectual subjects with a woman; her father "bought her many books but begged her not to read them because he feared they joggled the mind." He probably worried about Emily's brilliance; it was a widespread opinion in the late nineteenth century that superior intelligence in a woman damaged her health and threatened her sanity. This was one of the popular opinions against which Higginson battled. He always wrote Miss Dickinson as if she were not merely his intellectual equal but his superior.

A very gregarious man himself, he was concerned about her isolation, although he understood it better than we do. The choice of withdrawing from society to live close to nature was not an unusual one for nineteenth-century intellectuals. Higginson's friends Henry Thoreau, the younger William Ellery Channing, and Levi Thaxter were among those who had chosen withdrawal.

The choice was somewhat different for a woman. They had to retire to shelters provided by husband or father. Dickinson always tied her seclusiveness closely to her feelings about her father:

You ask of my Companions—Hills—Sir—and the Sundown—and a Dog—large as myself, that my Father bought me . . . I had promised to visit my Physician for a few days in May, but Father objects because he is in the habit of me . . . I must omit Boston. Father prefers so. He likes me to travel with him but objects that I visit . . . I do not cross my Father's ground to any House or town. . . .

In spite of these refusals Higginson continued for some years to try to lure her into literary circles in Boston:

It is hard for me to understand how you can live so alone with thoughts of such a quality.
. . . Yet it isolates one anywhere to think beyond a certain point— . . . so perhaps the place does not make much difference. You must come down to Boston sometimes? All ladies do. I wonder if it would be possible to lure you to the meetings on the 3rd Monday

of every month at Mrs. Sargent's 13 Chestnut St. at 10 am. . . . Next Monday Mr. Emerson
reads. . . . I have a right to invite you and you can merely ring and walk in.

It was only after seven years of this sort of exchange that he made time in
his busy schedule to go to Amherst and see her. By that time they had become
intimate friends without benefit of a personal meeting. "A Letter always feels
to me like immortality because it is the mind alone without corporeal friend,"
Emily wrote.

The seven years included the two of Higginson's military service. They were
for him perhaps the most important in his life. They gave him the title he preferred
to use for another half century and the material for the only one of his books
still in print, *Army Life in a Black Regiment*. To Emily Dickinson they meant
only separation and the fear of a final one. When she learned from the newspapers
that he had gone to war, she wrote:

Dear friend
    I did not dream that Planetary forces annulled—but suffered an Exchange of Territory,
or World—
I should have liked to see you, before you became improbable. War feels to me an
oblique place— . . .
I trust you may pass the limit of War, and though not reared to prayer—when service is
had in Church, for Our Arms, I include yourself— . . .

This tells incidentally that in 1863 E.D. was still attending church at least
occasionally.

Should you, before this reaches you, experience immortality, who will inform me of the
Exchange? Could you, with honor, avoid Death, I entreat you—Sir—It would bereave
Your Gnome.

The chapters later collected in *Army Life in a Black Regiment* appeared first
as separate essays in the *Atlantic*, where the poet read all of them. Higginson
was an unusual war correspondent; very little of his book concerns combat.
Rather it is about the recently emancipated slaves under his command, their
songs, their language and customs, and the magnificent countryside in which
they lived. Of all of this Emily responded only to the descriptions of nature and
the somewhat sentimental stories of children. Whatever it was in his work that
had attracted her to him, she never shared his interest in reform. She cared neither
for abolition nor for women's rights. She had her own private quarrel with her
Creator regarding the human condition, but within its limits the differences
between the privileged and the deprived seemed to her trivial.

Of Higginson's visit to her in 1870 we have two accounts—his own minutely
accurate factual one in a letter to his wife and an article for the *Atlantic* many
years later—and the recently popular fictional one in *The Belle of Amherst*. The
latter, it may be noted, draws some of its material from the former, though
without credit to Higginson. All the Dickinson biographers have used it; it is a
mine of information, and also in many ways so much more dramatic and ap-

pealing than *The Belle of Amherst* version that one wonders why the author didn't follow it all the way.

Higginson stayed at the Amherst Inn around the corner from the Dickinson homestead, and made two visits to Miss Emily, one in the afternoon and a second one in the evening. He sent around a note first, to which her reply survives. (Fortunately for posterity 1870 was pre-telephone although post-stagecoach.)

Higginson's letter to his wife that evening is perhaps too long to quote in full. It is available, however, and rewards the effort of locating it.

I shan't sit up tonight to write you all about E.D., dearest. . . . A large county lawyer's house, brown brick, with great trees and a garden.—I sent up my card. A parlor dark and cool and stiffish, a few books and engravings and an open piano—Malbone and O.D. Papers among other books.

Malbone was his latest publication, a first novel to which he had pinned high hopes but which had been comparatively unsuccessful. *Outdoor Papers* was a collection of his nature essays from the *Atlantic*. The omission of *Army Life* is interesting.

Higginson ended the letter to his wife with a curious comment:

I never was with anyone who drained my nerve power so much. Without touching her, she drew from me.

This matches her own acknowledgment:

The Vein cannot thank the Artery—but her solemn indebtedness to him, even the stolidest admit.

Her extravagant gratitude, however, did not prevent her asking for more.

Enough is so vast a sweetness I suppose it never occurs . . . After you went I took Macbeth and turned to "Birnam Wood." Came twice "to Dunsinane"—I thought and went about my work.

Higginson did visit her once again in December, 1873 when he was lecturing in Amherst. This time he took a somewhat facetious tone in reporting the meeting to his wife, who commented "Oh, why do the insane so cling to you?" It is possible to suspect that the intensity of the stranger's emotional attachment to her husband bothered her a little. Higginson apparently shared all of the poet's letters with her, and their tone was increasingly intimate. When Mrs. Higginson died in September 1877, Emily's letters of condolence were those of an old and intimate friend and showed, as might have been expected, a subtle knowledge of the stages of grief.

Danger is not at first, for then we are unconscious, but in the after—slower—Days.

The intimacy continued when he remarried. His second wife was one of the young lady writers whose work he had encouraged. More than twenty years younger than he, she made it possible for him to enjoy in late middle age the delight of paternity, but their first daughter died in infancy. " 'Seven Weeks' is a long life—if it is all lived' "—E. D. wrote. A year later another was born who lived to be the joy of her father's old age. Emily took the same sort of New England–maiden-aunt interest in this child as in her own niece and nephews.

She continued to follow Higginson's work in *Scribner's* and *The Century* as well as in the *Atlantic*. She even read the *Woman's Journal* for the sake of his contributions, though she never mentioned anything else in it.

Each letter included two or three or four poems. Higginson's immediate comments on them have been lost to posterity, but he kept them all and arranged for their posthumous publication. His opinion of them is recorded in the first book of poems and in an *Atlantic* article in 1891. There is every reason to believe that he expressed it first to the poet.

One of the last letters she wrote in the month of her death was to Higginson.

Deity—does He live now?
My friend—does he breathe?

She was asking the Unitarian minister the same question about God that she had once asked the literary critic about her work. It was a question which was to be answered for her within days, for him not for a quarter century. The most important task he completed in that time was the publication of Emily Dickinson's letter to the world, though he himself may not have thought so.

NOTE

1. The entire Dickinson-Higginson correspondence is reproduced in volume II of *The Letters of Emily Dickinson* in three volumes, edited by Thomas H. Johnson and Theodora Ward (Cambridge, Mass.: Harvard University Press, 1958), Letters 260, 261, 265, 268, 271, 274, 280, 282, 290, 330, pp. 403–60.

23

George Eliot and Feminism: The Case of *Daniel Deronda*

Bonnie Zimmerman

George Eliot did not generally associate herself with nineteenth-century feminism because she was profoundly troubled over the issue of women's rights. Yet her novels are equally profound studies of the pinched, confining, and repressive female role: the social corset she and all her sisters were forced to wear. Mrs. Transome in *Felix Holt* sums up the situation when she observes, "God was cruel when he made women." Any devotee of George Eliot thus must ponder the gap that exists between her portrayal of female life and her expressed political views. Although I cannot systematically analyze George Eliot's statements on feminism in this paper, I will attempt to show how her ambivalent feelings about the situation of women helped to shape her final novel, *Daniel Deronda*. I will argue that, although earlier novels indicate a belief in separate spheres of influence and separate character traits for each sex, in *Daniel Deronda* George Eliot attempts to unite the male and female spheres through a male political leader endowed with those characteristics and duties ordinarily reserved for heroines. I will also investigate why Eliot did not choose to endow a female spiritual guide like Dorothea with the attributes of a political leader. Finally, I will suggest that Eliot's choice in *Daniel Deronda* is, ultimately, a justification of patriarchy and rejection of feminism.

Eliot was certainly sympathetic to the problem—one might say the tragedy—of intelligent, passionate, and responsible women such as Maggie, Dorothea, and Romola who yearn for transcendence and power. Yet her novels are case studies of the painful education of these women into the domestic role. This is because Eliot, like the majority of her contemporaries, articulated an ideology of separate sexual spheres that delegated power and authority to women in the home, as it did to men in the world. In the home, women provided moral and spiritual guidance as well as education, love, and nurturance, while in the world men provided intellect, action, and leadership. These duties, it was argued, gave women prestige and fulfillment equal to that of men in their more exacting social and political functions. As George Eliot wrote to Emily Davies, founder of Girton College for women, women have a "peculiar constitution for a special moral influence."[1] This version of domestic feminism, as I have argued elsewhere,[2] appealed to Eliot as a moderate, careful approach to the vexing issue of women's rights. It both legitimated the traditional female role, and pointed a direction women might take in exercising their desire for power. Although Eliot can be quite caustic toward individuals who carry sex roles to extremes (think of Lydgate and Rosamond, for example), she never seriously questioned the appropriateness of sex roles and sexual spheres themselves. Human progress, in fact, requires a balance of male and female traits and functions joined together by marriage:

We can no more afford to part with that exquisite type of gentleness, tenderness, possible maternity suffusing a woman's being with affectionateness, which makes what we mean by the feminine character, than we can afford to part with the human love, the mutual subjection of soul between a man and a woman—which is also a growth and revelation beginning before all history. (*The George Eliot Letters* IV, pp. 467–68)

Consequently, a George Eliot novel paradigmatically concludes with the happy union between a man as provider and social agent, and a woman as wife and mother. Adam and Dinah, Felix and Esther, Will and Dorothea: each couple exemplifies the institutional balance of head and heart, activity and affection.

Some novels are not paradigmatic, although the basic message about the proper role for women remains the same. Maggie's tragedy is partially that her true partner is her brother, a man she cannot marry; Romola's religion and culture permits virginal heroism which did not occur to Eliot as a nineteenth-century option. The most interesting exception, however, is *Daniel Deronda*, a novel that modifies the ideology of separate sexual spheres by uniting the male and female functions and character traits in one person, rather than in an exemplary marriage. Head and heart, action and feeling are united in the ideal leader, Daniel himself. Not only is he a budding political leader in search of a cause, he also plays the role of the "heart" in the novel by converting an egoist through his sympathy and moral example.[3] Contemporaries contemptuously called Daniel a Maggie, Romola, or Dorothea masquerading in "divided skirts."[4] But the point is not that George Eliot, as a woman writer, was incapable of creating a real man. I would suggest instead that Eliot was no longer confident in the ability or willingness of women of her own era to provide the kind of moral leadership and sympathetic inspiration provided by her previous heroines. The spectre of feminism caused Eliot to focus her attention on the male hero, not only as a political leader but also as the center of sympathy in the novel.

In order to unite the separate spheres of head and heart in one person, Eliot attempts to depict Daniel as an androgyne who integrates stereotypically feminine traits, such as beauty, passion, ardency, feeling, and especially sympathy, with his masculine destiny. The phrases used by Eliot to describe Daniel are more typical of Eliot's heroines than of her heroes: "strong rush of feeling," "delicacy of feeling," "intensified inner experience," "ardent clinging nature," "newly-aroused set of feelings," "ardently affectionate nature," and "in-born loving-ness" are just a few repetitive and didactic examples. Eliot also states explicitly that Daniel is both feminine and masculine in certain characteristics.[5] She uses the phrase "practically energetic sentiment" (p. 414) to describe the object of Daniel's life search, a phrase which succinctly unites the separate sexual spheres of head and heart. "Practical energy" is precisely what characterizes Adam Bede, Tom Tulliver, Felix Holt, and Lydgate; "sentiment" characterizes Maggie, Romola, Esther, and Dorothea. Men do; women are. George Eliot, in this novel, attempts to have Deronda both be and act.

Daniel's integration of stereotypically masculine and feminine traits is similar to his social position somewhere between that of a man and a woman. He is an outsider: even before discovering his Jewish identity, he is excluded from the birthright of an English gentleman by his apparent illegitimacy. Thus, Daniel is excluded from male power, and as a result of his exclusion, he identifies with powerless groups like Jews and women. Psychologically maimed himself, Daniel sympathizes with suffering women, underdogs, and the Calibans of the earth. In both novels and letters, George Eliot demonstrated that woman's hard lot made her more susceptible to the needs of others and more sympathetic to human suffering. In *Daniel Deronda*, she extends her analysis to include other victims of "entailed disadvantage."[6] The enlarged sympathetic vision that had been reserved for her "best of women" such as Dorothea and Romola is bestowed on Daniel, a man who is also destined to be a political leader. In this way, Eliot attempts, for the first time, to bridge the gap between the political and spiritual realms—that is, between the male and the female. Although the most significant social change, she believed, occurred through the direct influence of one individual on another, change must also occur on the larger political scale. George Eliot's political leaders are typically male (Felix Holt, Will Ladislaw, and Daniel) and her spiritual leaders female (Dinah, Esther, Romola, and Dorothea). To paraphrase Milton, he works for Progress, she for Progress in him. In *Daniel Deronda*, Eliot in effect eliminates the helpmeet.

Although Daniel unites in himself the masculine and feminine, and sympathizes with suffering women, he does not address himself to the issue of women's oppression. Rather than challenging the biases of patriarchy, he eagerly embraces its authority. When he discovers his identity and his cause, he turns his "practically energetic sentiment" toward political leadership in the cause of Zionism, guided by the spirit of his patriarchal and tyrannical grandfather. According to Daniel's mother, about whom I will have more to say, "such men [the grandfather] turn their wives and daughters into slaves. They would rule the world if they could; but not ruling the world, they throw all the weight of their will on the necks and souls of women" (p. 694). Accordingly, she had attempted to break the patrilineal link by denying Daniel his Jewish heritage. Nevertheless, Daniel eagerly accepts his grandfather's "trust," which his mother calls a "yoke," because it is, in Eliot's words, "knit into the foundations of sacredness for all *men*" (p. 727, italics mine). In accepting his heritage as a Jew, Daniel also accepts the role of a patriarch. He repudiates his mother and her anger over the treatment of women. His first words after her famous cry that "a woman's heart must be of such a size and no larger" are, "Was my grandfather a learned man?" (p. 694).

Nor does Daniel's sympathy with the oppressed sensitize him to the fact that Judaism oppresses its own women. Not only does he ignore his mother's anger, he treats Mirah, his future wife, as an angelic housefrau. Although Eliot anticipates contemporary Jewish feminists in her appraisal of Judaism's male bias, she ultimately minimizes its significance. For example, when an objection is raised against sex segregation in the synagogue, the narrator blandly comments that "[Mirah's] religion was of one fibre with her affections, and had never presented itself to her as a set of propositions" (p. 410). In other words, Mirah is all heart, and very little head. Even the Jewish man's prayer, thanking God he was not born a woman, did not temper George Eliot's admiration of Judaism, any more than the patriarchal Cohen family tempered her approval of the Jews as a kinship group.

Daniel's failure to acknowledge the oppression of women within his own kinship and religious group is only symptomatic of George Eliot's own refusal to acknowledge female leadership. The issue is not that she ignores the oppression of women as a political fact. She suggests, for example, some interesting comparisons between the position of women and that of the Jews. When Mordecai says, "What wonder that multitudes of our people are ignorant, narrow, superstitious?" (p. 591) and that "there is hatred in the breasts of Jews who are the children of the ignorant and oppressed" (p. 597), we might think of Mary Wollstonecraft's cry, "The passions thus pampered, whilst judgment is left unformed, what can be expected to ensue: undoubtedly a mixture of madness and folly!"[7] Mordecai's belief that "the world will gain as Israel gains," (p. 595) is virtually borrowed from Fourier: "The extension of women's privileges is the general principle of all social progress."[8] George Eliot was certainly aware that women, like Jews, form a biological group whose "entailed" disadvantages subject them to oppression and inspire them to rebellion; nevertheless, she refuses to allow to women the same political vision she allows to Jews.

Thus we must ask why Eliot does not suggest that sympathetic women might become active political leaders. Although her era offered her outstanding models of activist women such as Barbara Bodichon, Octavia Hill, Emily Davies, Josephine Butler, and, had she looked to the American movement, equally striking exemplars, Eliot quite consciously did not choose to write about female political leadership. We might note that there is not even a Dorothea or Romola in this final novel. Instead, the female characters in *Daniel Deronda* are either throwbacks to the drooping lilies or little women of popular novelists, or they are

nnatural, "unsexed" women like the Alcharisi or Gwendolen Harleth (who is
orn again into a tired, spiritless, self-sacrificing femininity).[9] If Eliot could
reate an androgynous male who combines in himself masculine and feminine
irtues, and who becomes a leader of the oppressed and despised Jews, why did
he not address the issue of women who incorporate traditionally male virtues
f activism and independence, and dedicate themselves to improving the con-
lition of women? Lest I be accused of asking artificial questions about a novel
hat was never written, let me say that I see the issue of women's political
eadership as integral to the conception of *Daniel Deronda* and to George Eliot's
olitical philosophy as a whole. Furthermore, female leadership, especially in
he nineteenth century, necessarily raises the issue of feminism and George Eliot's
mbivalence toward it.

A partial and preliminary analysis of why Eliot rejected female leadership and
eminism is suggested by the characterization of Daniel's mother, the Alcharisi.
She functions in the novel as a contrast to Daniel's androgynous humanism and
as a warning to women like Gwendolen Harleth about the dangers inherent in
anger, hatred, and what Eliot might have called feminist subjectivism. George
Eliot was concerned that those who take the wrongs of women as unique "frustrated claims" rather than "as one among a myriad" (p. 215) could not, to use
her characteristic moral vocabulary, exchange a subjective feminist vision for
an objective humanist vision. She wrote that "[The "woman question"] seems
to me to overhang abysses of which even prostitution is not the worst. Conclusions seem easy so long as we keep large blinkers on and look in the direction
of our own private path" (*GEL* V, p. 58). Although Eliot never specifies what
these abysses might be, the novels, particularly *Daniel Deronda*, suggest that
one at least is the rejection of the traditional female role which would entail the
loss to society of love, sympathy, tenderness, affection, and nurturance. The
Alcharisi embodies Eliot's fear through repeated utterances of intensely militant
and almost contemporary feminist rhetoric. She disentangles herself from the
connecting web of the family; as she tells Daniel, "I have not felt exactly what
other women feel—or say they feel for fear of being thought unlike other. . . .
I was glad to be freed from you" (p. 691). To Daniel's cry of "Mother! Take
my affection," she counters, "you owe me no duties" (p. 697), thus freeing
him for the wider social duties resting in the metaphorical relationship between
him and Mother Israel. The Alcharisi also denies the power of romantic love,
which was sacramental to George Eliot: "I am not a loving woman . . . I was
never willingly subject to any man. Men have been subject to me" (p. 730).
Finally, the Alcharisi, like Gwendolen, is intensely conscious of her position as
a woman and rebelliously determined to run her own life. In their egoism, both
women defy the patriarchal power that stands in their way, whether it be man-
ifested in an individual man or in social institutions. George Eliot, I believe,
identified this hatred and intolerance, as well as the rejection of feminine sympathy and nurturance, as a potential danger in the emerging feminism of her
day.

George Eliot's fear was neither abstract moralizing nor self-righteous conservatism. Quite the contrary: she is both sympathetic to women's suffering and conscious of its incendiary potential, because of her own experience as a woman in the nineteenth century. Again, it is through the Alcharisi that Eliot explores her ambivalent feelings toward feminism and traditional femininity. Although the Alcharisi is clearly meant to be a bitter, unnatural, selfish woman, her magnificent, heart-felt rhetoric can hardly help but elicit the reader's unqualified compassion. Indeed, Eliot seems to have placed her most intensely feminist outcries in the mouth of this "unnatural" woman precisely in order to protect herself at the same time that she exposes deep resentments. The Alcharisi's cry— "I hated living under the shadow of my father's strictness. Teaching, teaching for everlasting—'this you must be,' 'that you must not be'—pressed on me like a frame that got tighter and tighter as I grew" (p. 693)—might have been inspired by the years Mary Anne Evans spent tending her father's house in Coventry. Similarly, the Alcharisi's protest— "You may try but you can never imagine what it is to have a man's force of genius in you, and yet to suffer the slavery of being a girl" (p. 694)—may also express Eliot's long pent-up resentment of female socialization. The Alcharisi's words could be dismissed as the bitterness of a dying, unhappy woman. Yet her oratory—staged and deliberate as it might be—has the convincing flash of lived experience that eludes the rest of the theoretically interesting but dramatically stultifying Jewish plot.

Thus, George Eliot's emotional sympathy with feminism is not completely shrouded by her philosophical rejection of it. In fact, it may have been the very depth of Eliot's own anger, suggested through the Alcharisi, that led her to protect society as she learned to protect herself from what she called "women's unsatisfied, diseased longings" (*GEL* III, p. 403). According to this analysis, Eliot foresaw that alleviating the causes of women's oppression would require more than colleges and the vote. It would require fundamental alterations in marriage, family, and access to power—in other words, revolution rather than reform. Feminism in fact might threaten the very evolution of the race, which, as I have pointed out, depended for her on the heterosexual union. George Eliot found this too high a price to pay for the amelioration of women's wrongs. Unequivocally committed to the social order of England and to the primacy of familial relations, she would not brave the abysses of violent change, hatred of men, and the destruction of the family. In dismay at the violent tremors she felt in the distance, she edged away from the abyss of revolutionary feminism to a steadier terrain illuminated by the humanist vision of an androgynous male political leader.

NOTES

1. Gordon S. Haight, ed., *The George Eliot Letters* (New Haven: Yale University Press, 1954), IV, p. 467. Hereafter cited as *GEL*.

2. See particularly Bonnie Zimmerman, "*Felix Holt* and the True Power of Womanhood," *ELH*, 46 (1979), 432–51.

3. See the very interesting article by Carole Robinson, "The Severe Angel: A Study of *Daniel Deronda*," *ELH*, 31 (1964).

4. William Henley, "On George Elliot," in *A Century of George Eliot Criticism*, ed. Gordon S. Haight (Boston: Houghton Mifflin, 1965), p. 161.

5. For example, Daniel shows "the same blending of child's ignorance with surprising knowledge which is oftener seen in bright girls" (p. 205). Also, he is "moved by an affectionateness such as we are apt to call feminine, disposing him to yield in ordinary details, while he had a certain inflexibility of judgment, an independence of opinion, held to be rightfully masculine" (p. 367). All references are to the Penguin edition of the novel, edited by Barbara Hardy.

6. "The sense of an entailed disadvantage—the deformed foot doubtfully hidden by the shoe, makes a restlessly active spiritual yeast, and easily turns a self-centered, unloving nature into an Ishmaelite. But in the rarer sort, who presently see their own frustrated claim as one among a myriad, the inexorable sorrow takes the form of fellowship and makes the imagination tender" (p. 215).

7. Mary Wollstonecraft, *A Vindication of the Rights of Women* (New York: W. W. Norton and Co., 1967), p. 105.

8. Charles Fourier, *Theorie de quatre mouvements et des destinees generales* (Paris: n.p., 1967, c. 1808), p. 147.

9. See my article, "Gwendolen Harleth and the 'Girl of the Period,' " in *George Eliot: Critical Essays*, ed. Anne Smith (Edinburgh: Vision Critical Studies, 1980), pp. 196–217.

Bibliographical Essay

Rhoda B. Nathan

The title of this anthology can only suggest the broad scope of the subjects addressed by the individual papers. While many of the essays mark the achievement of women as writers, others examine the representation of women in the literature itself. "Women Authors" and "Women in Literature" are both distinct and overlapping topics as dealt with in these articles. Ethnic, minority, and regional issues are touched on within the two dominant subdivisions; some attention is given to Australian and Canadian authors who were emerging at about the same time that their British and American counterparts were gaining recognition for their more prolific literary output. Individual writers of acknowledged genius, novelists such as the Brontës, Jane Austen, and George Eliot, and poets such as Emily Dickinson, are scrutinized in this volume in a number of lights: their relationship with their respective male mentors; their pre-occupation with conventional female roles of the period; the influence their rearing had in shaping their art; and their dawning awareness of "sisterhood," a relationship not yet articulated in political terms. Finally, the evocation of women in the novels of a small number of male authors at the time is the focus of some attention in this collection.

The following bibliography, organized according to the major subjects of the essays, is offered to provide the reader with some useful books and journals for the purpose of pursuing the issues and studying the individual authors in greater depth and from a variety of perspectives.

WOMEN AUTHORS

These far-ranging studies trace the development of individual writers against the nineteenth-century background of male-dominated society: Marjorie Bald,

Women Writers of the Nineteenth Century (New York: Russell and Russell, 1963); Nina Baym, *Women's Fiction: A Guide to Novels by and about Women in America, 1820–1870* (Ithaca, N.Y.: Cornell University Press, 1978); Sandra Gilbert and Susan Gubar, *The Madwoman in the Attic: The Woman Writer and the Nineteenth Century Literary Imagination* (New Haven: Yale University Press, 1979); Ellen Moers, *Literary Women* (Garden City, N.Y.: Doubleday and Company, 1976); Patricia Meyer Spacks, *The Female Imagination* (New York: Alfred M. Knopf, 1975); and Cheryl Walker, *The Nightingale's Burden: Women Poets and American Culture Before 1900* (Bloomington: Indiana University Press, 1982). Of the books cited, Baym's best illustrates the double focus of most of the essays in this anthology.

The studies in this category demonstrate a philosophical indebtedness to earlier landmark books on the subject of the historical female role in literature and on its political and social implications for succeeding generations of women. The most influential of these are Germaine Greer's *The Female Eunuch*, 1971, Kate Millet's *Sexual Politics*, 1970, Simone de Beauvoir's *The Second Sex*, 1953, and Vivian Gornick's *Women in Sexist Society: Studies in Power and Powerlessness*, 1971. Even though the bias of these books is explicitly feminist, they are useful for the light they cast on nineteenth-century attitudes toward the female "scribbler." Further, although their thrust is polemical, they provide the necessary historical background against which the woman artist's struggle may be assessed. Millet's study, for instance, clarifies the two conflicting points of view in Victorian society as typified by John Ruskin's condescending attitude toward "the angel in the house," and John Stuart Mill's bold championing of women's rights in his essay, "The Subjection of Women," in 1869. Beauvoir's book is valuable in its shrewd analysis of the "myths" attached to the female, which originated in antiquity and persist into the present day.

WOMEN IN LITERATURE

The representation of women in fiction is the subject of the following studies, some highly acclaimed and widely quoted, and others recent and offering fresh insights: Nina Auerbach, *Women and the Demon: The Life of a Victorian Myth* (Cambridge, Mass.: Harvard University Press, 1982); Rachel Brownstein, *Becoming a Heroine: Reading about Women in Novels* (New York: Viking, 1982); Gail Cunningham, *The New Woman and the Victorian Eve: Women in the Nineteenth Century American Novel* (New York: Oxford University Press, 1976); Carol Pearson and Katherine Pope, *The Female Hero in American and British Literature* (New York: Bowker, 1981); Patricia Stubbs, *Women and Fiction: Feminism and the Novel, 1880–1920* (New York: Barnes and Noble, 1979); and Mary Vanderwoude, "The Myths of Childhood and the Realities of Womanhood in Nineteenth Century American Fiction" (Ph.D. diss., Hofstra University). An interesting, if somewhat outdated, account of the roles of women by a prominent American author of realistic fiction is William Dean Howells's *Her-*

oines of Fiction (New York: Harper and Brothers, 1901). The sympathetic if limited insight into the ''plight'' of women by the writer who gave the American reading public its first novel of divorce, *A Modern Instance*, offers an illuminating contrast between a turn-of-the-century liberal male view of the female and the more militant views in current literary criticism.

DOMESTIC ROLES

Wifehood, motherhood, and homemaking are the subjects of some of the papers in this anthology. The omission of Kate Chopin's revolutionary short novel, *The Awakening*, is regrettable, but is justified on technical grounds. Written in 1899, the book is disqualified from the temporal boundaries of this study, but it foreshadows the dramatic rebellion against marriage and home-making during the coming century by women conditioned by nineteenth-century values for their destined roles. Although the book appeared at precisely the turn of the century, it reflects the standards of the previous century in a particularly tradition-bound part of the United States. For critical studies of this subject the following books are recommended: Patricia Beer, *Reader, I Married Him: A Study of the Women Characters of Jane Austen, Charlotte Brontë, Elizabeth Gaskell and George Eliot* (New York: Barnes and Noble, 1974); Jennie Calder, *Women and Marriage in Victorian Fiction* (New York: Oxford University Press, 1976); Mary Kelley, *Private Woman, Public Stage: Literary Domesticity in Nineteenth Century America* (New York: Oxford University Press, 1984). This last has a slightly different dimension than the others. In addition to portraying women in their domestic roles, the study also surveys the lives of twelve best-selling American authors—Harriet Beecher Stowe and Catharine Maria Sedgwick among others—who were reared to lead conventional lives, but found themselves increasingly public and powerful figures in a world dominated by men. Another recent book, which does not fit precisely into this category because it deals with actual historical figures—five couples containing one famous writer in each—is nonetheless a study of domesticity in nineteenth-century life: Phyllis Rose, *Parallel Lives: Five Victorian Marriages* (New York: Vintage, 1984). The merit of this carefully researched multiple biography of Ruskin, Carlyle, Mill, Dickens, and Eliot and their mates, is its conclusion that famous people were plagued by the same domestic conflicts as were the fictional characters they created.

INDIVIDUAL AUTHORS

Recent critiques and biographies of some of the major authors included in this volume have direct bearing on the writers under scrutiny. Of the two recommended Dickinson biographies, Vivian Pollak's *Dickinson: The Anxiety of Gender* (Ithaca, N.Y.: Cornell University Press, 1984) is related to her paper on Dickinson which is included in this volume. Shira Wolosky's *Emily Dickinson:*

A Voice of War (New Haven: Yale University Press, 1984) is an original linguistic analysis of the poet's metaphysics and sexual psychology. Two recent Jane Austen biographies are worth noting: John Halperin, *The Life of Jane Austen* (Baltimore: Johns Hopkins University Press, 1984), and Margaret Kirkham, *Jane Austen: Feminism and Fiction* (New York: Barnes and Noble, 1983). Both studies reinforce some contemporary feminist readings of Austen's novels. As the following titles suggest, two critical studies present aspects of Austen's and Eliot's fiction not fully covered in the conference: Felicia Bonaparte, *Will and Destiny: Morality and Tragedy in George Eliot's Novels* (New York: New York University Press, 1975); and Judith Wilt, *Ghosts of the Gothic: Austen, Eliot and Lawrence* (Princeton: Princeton University Press, 1980). Edward Wagenknecht's *Eve and Henry James: Portraits of Women and Girls in his Fiction* (Norman University of Oklahoma Press, 1978) is an appropriate addition to this list, because, although James is a male author, his fiction is discussed in Mary Edwards's article and is alluded to in other essays in this anthology.

REGIONAL, ETHNIC, AND FRONTIER LITERATURE

The books in this category illuminate the character of the women who helped to create America. They are minorities, pioneers, and settlers of the remote regions of the country. Canadian women are a subject of one study, and is a useful adjunct to the essay in this collection: M. G. McClung, *Women in Canadian Literature* (Toronto: Fitzhenry and Whiteside, 1977); Trudier Harris, *From Nannies to Militants: Domestics in Black American Literature* (Philadelphia: Temple University Press, 1982); Kristin Herzog, *Women, Ethics and Exotics: Images of Power in Mid-Nineteenth Century American Fiction* (Knoxville: University of Tennessee Press, 1983); Anne Goodwyn Jones, *Tomorrow is Another Day: The Woman Writer in the South, 1859–1936* (Baton Rouge: LSU Press, 1981); Annette Kolodny, *The Land Before Her: Fantasy and Experience of the American Frontiers, 1630–1860* (Chapel Hill: University of North Carolina Press, 1984); Lillian Schlissel, *Women's Diaries of the Westward Journey* (New York: Schocken, 1982).

JOURNALS AND LIBRARIES

Legacy: A Newsletter of Nineteenth Century Women Writers (Amherst: Department of English, Bartlett Hall, University of Massachusetts at Amherst), established in spring, 1984, appears to be the most promising source of forthcoming information. *Sigma: Journal of Women in Culture and Society* has a broader range of interests. The Arthur and Elizabeth Schlesinger Library of the History of Women at Radcliffe College, 10 Garden Street, Cambridge, Mass., 02138, was founded in 1949 as The Women's Archives, and houses the letters of Harriet Beecher Stowe as well as an enormous variety of documents pertaining to literary women in nineteenth-century America. The correspondence of Lydia

Maria Child and Charlotte Perkins Gilman are among the Library's holdings. Finally, The New-York Historical Society has a vast collection of papers, documents, and manuscripts, among which are the many literary clubs which flourished in the past century and engaged the creative interest of women of letters.

NINETEENTH CENTURY WOMEN WRITERS' INTERNATIONAL CONFERENCE

November
7, 8, 9, 1980

Eliza Acton
Juliette Adam
Bettina von Arnim
Jane Austen
Fredrika Bremer
Charlotte Brontë
Germaine de Staël
Emily Dickinson
Annette von Droste-Hülshoff
George Eliot
Michael Field
Charlotte Forten
Margaret Fuller
Elizabeth Cleghorn Gaskell
Sarah Grimké
Josephine Heard
Mary Jane Holmes
Harriet Jacobs
Anna Korvin-Krukovskaia Jaclard
Sophia Korvin-Krukovskaia Kovalevskaia
George Maldague
Ely Montclerc
Susanna Moodie
Adelaida Muñiz y Mas
Louise Otto
Elizabeth Stuart Phelps
Christina Rossetti
George Sand
Catherine Parr Traill
Flora Tristan
Frances Milton Trollope
Rahel Varnhagen
Catherine Fenimore Woolson

HOFSTRA UNIVERSITY

HEMPSTEAD, NEW YORK 11550

CONFERENCES AT HOFSTRA UNIVERSITY

George Sand Centennial - November 1976	Vol. I - available
Heinrich von Kleist Bicentennial - November 1977	Vol. II - December 1980
The Chinese Woman - December 1977	
George Sand: Her Life, Her Works, Her Influence - April 1978	Vol. III - 1981
William Cullen Bryant and His America - October 1978	Vol. IV - 1981
The Trotsky-Stalin Conflict and Russia in the 1920's - March 1979	Vol. V
Albert Einstein Centennial - November 1979	Vol. VI
Renaissance Venice Symposium - March 1980	Vol. VII
Sean O'Casey - March 1980	
Walt Whitman - April 1980	Vol. VIII
Nineteenth Century Women Writers - November 7, 8, 9, 1980	Vol. IX
Fedor Dostoevski - April 9, 10, 11, 1981	Vol. X
Gotthold Ephraim Lessing - November 12, 13, 14, 1981	Vol. XI
Johann Wolfgang von Goethe - April 1, 2, 3, 1982	Vol. XII
Twentieth Century Women Writers - November 5, 6, 7, 1982	Vol. XIII
Jose Ortega y Gasset, 1883-1983 - Centennial Celebration Spring 1983	Vol. XIV
Romanticism in the Old and the New World - Celebrating the Bi-Centennials of Washington Irving, Stendhal, and Vasilii Andreevich Zhukovskii -- 1783-1983 - Fall 1983	Vol. XV

"Calls for Papers" -- available upon request

NINETEENTH CENTURY WOMEN WRITERS' INTERNATIONAL CONFERENCE

November 7, 8, 9, 1980

PROGRAM

CONFERENCE DIRECTORS: Avriel Goldberger
                                     Rhoda Nathan

CONFERENCE COORDINATORS: Natalie Datlof
                                     Alexej Ugrinsky

CHAIRMAN OF CONFERENCE COMMITTEE: Robert N. Keane

CONFERENCE COMMITTEE: Joseph G. Astman   Nora McNair
                                     Diana Ben-Merre   Maureen O. Murphy
                                     Edwin L. Dunbaugh   Robert B. Sargent
                                     Arthur Gregor   Wilbur S. Scott
                                     Denis-J. Jean   William S. Shiver
                                     William A. McBrien   Miriam Tulin

COOPERATING INSTITUTIONS: Consulate General of the Federal Republic
                                        of Germany
                                     New York, NY

                                     Country Art Gallery
                                     Locust Valley, NY

                                     Cultural Services of the French Embassy
                                     New York, NY

                                     Goethe House
                                     New York, NY

                                     Nassau County Office of Cultural Development
                                     Roslyn, NY

UNIVERSITY CENTER FOR CULTURAL & INTERCULTURAL STUDIES

HOFSTRA UNIVERSITY
HEMPSTEAD, NEW YORK 11550

Joseph G. Astman, Director
University Center for Cultural & Intercultural Studies

The Conference on Nineteenth Century Women Writers

is dedicated to

GERMAINE BREE

--in grateful admiration of her life's work as master teacher-
scholar, inspiring generations of students -- many of whom have
become noted teachers and critics in their own right -- with the
understanding that literature is central to human experience;

--in grateful recognition of her scholar's discipline and her
breadth. of imagination which have been applied to the question
of literature by women: her skill and her reputation have made
a major contribution to the intellectual legitimizing of such
studies as well as to our understanding of the writers and works
involved;

--in grateful appreciation of her generosity over the years to us
at Hofstra in the Department of French and to the whole University
community.

In Praise of the Woman Writer

The title of this conference has been formulated to reflect a broad spectrum of distinctive talents and nationalities. Our purpose is to explore and pay homage to the creative genius of nineteenth century women writers. However, in the process of organizing the individual panels, we encounter a problem inherent in so ambitious an undertaking: will it be possible for the twentieth century scholar to bring Jane Austen's satire, Emily Dickinson's wit, George Eliot's intellect and George Sand's passion into a coherent cultural framework for the purpose of drawing instructive conclusions about women in the nineteenth century? From the biographies of these writers, their poems, novels and letters, and the reliable histories which deal with their contributions, we learn that they were alternately and sometimes simultaneously encouraged, ignored, relegated to the kitchen and elevated to the salon. They wrote in secrecy, reigned in public, served some men and were served by others. Their subjects were personal, social, political and philosophical. In short, they represented no single point of view, nor shared any common overriding preoccupation. What characterized nineteenth century women writers was the intensity of their commitment to their craft and the excellence of a large proportion of their work. Although the peripatetic Margaret Fuller, the reclusive Brontë sisters and the sedentary Mrs. Browning led diverse lives, they shared the qualities of courage, devotion to their art and persistence. They were, to a woman, high-minded and dedicated, remarkable as personalities and formidable as writers.

The directors, conference committee and coordinators have gone beyond the familiar major authors of the period to encourage papers about minor figures such as Mary Jane Holmes, Continental and Afro-American poets of distinguished but minor reputation, and even some curiosities, such as two

women writing under a single male <u>nom de plume</u>. Themes central to nineteenth
century domestic life, such as education, marriage and mental health, have been
grouped in panels devoted to questions of culture. Our moderators are professors
and authors of distinction, men and women who have taught and written about the
subjects under discussion. All the events and entertainments and celebrations
of this three-day conference are dedicated to women writers of the nineteenth
century, to their integrity as artists, and to their pioneering role in the
world of letters.

Rhoda Nathan, English Department
Avriel Goldberger, French Department

GREETINGS

All good fortune to your Conference.

                              Joseph Jay Deiss
                              Positano, Italy

With all good wishes for the success of your program.

                              Gordon S. Haight, General Editor
                              The Clarendon Edition of the Novels of
                                George Eliot
                              Woodbridge, CT

Best Wishes to the Women Writers' Conference. I wish I could be with you.

                              Julie Harris

Greetings from Higginson Press, especially the Dickinson Studies section, for a
successful sesquicentennial conference at Hofstra University. It is a deep
satisfaction to know that Dickinson is considered on a par with George Eliot.
My two Dickinson journals, after thirteen years, now reach all continents, including Japan, India, Africa, and Australia. Her "letter to the world" is truly
taking place.

                              Frederick L. Morey, Editor-Publisher
                              Higginson Press
                              Brentwood, MD

To the Conference on Two of Our Greatest:

When I said I couldn't come, Natalie Datlof and Alexej Ugrinsky, in a joint
communiqué, asked me if I'd write a paragraph of greetings, to include some of
my "thoughts and feelings about Emily Dickinson and her place and significance
as an American woman and poet." (How can one resist a joint communiqué?) The
greetings are easy -- and here they are, warm and (because I can't be with you)
envious. It should be a memorable occasion.

As to my thoughts and feelings: we're gaining all the time. When I was in college,
her name was never even mentioned -- and I majored in English. And now, just a
few weeks ago, the Washington Post, no less, called her "the great, arguably the
greatest, American poet." (I'll argue for her any time). That's the focus I like.
Certainly we must try to understand her position as a woman in her time, though
I'd warn against extrapolating late 20th century tensions into the mid-19th. But
the overarching aim of all our endeavors is to make her poetry -- and those mar-
velous poetic letters -- live and breathe (those are her metaphors) for all people
who can read English, so that never again will an English major leave his Alma
Mater without having at least tasted that immortal wine!

                              Richard B. Sewall
                              Professor of English, Emeritus
                              Yale University
                              New Haven, CT

Thursday, November 6, 1980   Hofstra University Library, David Filderman Gallery
                                  Department of Special Collections - 9th Floor

Pre-Conference Event   Art Exhibit:

7:30 - 9:30 P.M.   Women Artists of the Berry Region - France

                                 Marie Ebbesen - Eguzon, France
                                 Christiane Sand - Gargilesse, France

                                 Wine and cheese Reception

Friday, November 7, 1980

9:00 - 11:00 A.M.   Registration David Filderman Gallery
                                               Dept. of Special Collections
                                               Hofstra University Library - 9th Floor

11:00 - 12:00   Greetings from the Hofstra University Community

                                 Joseph G. Astman, Director
                                 University Center for Cultural & Intercultural Studies

                                 James M. Shuart
                                 President

                                 Opening Address: Germaine Greer
                                                   Director, The Tulsa Center for the Study
                                                   of Women's Literature
                                                   University of Tulsa
                                                   Tulsa, OK

                                 "'Infinite Riches in a Little Room': Suggestions
                                 Toward an Alternative Aesthetic."

12:00 - 1:00 P.M.   Opening of Gallery Exhibit and Reception

                                 Greetings: Marguerite Regan
                                             Assistant to the Dean of Library Services

                                 "Nineteenth Century Literary Women"

1:00 - 2:00   Lunch Main Dining Room, Student Center, North Campus

                                 Dining Rooms ABC, Student Center, North Campus

1:30 - 2:00   Film: "The World of Emily Dickinson"
                                        starring Claire Bloom

2:00 - 3:30   PANEL I: EMILY DICKINSON AND T. W. HIGGINSON

                                 Moderator: Rhoda Nathan
                                             Dept. of English, Hofstra University

                                 "T. W. Higginson and Emily Dickinson in Feminist
                                  Perspective."
                                 Tilden G. Edelstein, Rutgers University
                                 New Brunswick, NJ

Friday, November 7, 1980 (cont'd.) - Dining Rooms ABC, Student Center, North Campus

2:00 - 3:30   "The Soul's Society: Emily Dickinson and Colonel
                                 Higginson."
                            Anna Mary Wells
                            Douglass College - Rutgers University
                            New Brunswick, NJ
                            Professor Emerita

                "A Second Look at 'The Belle.'"
                Howard N. Meyer
                Rockville Centre, NY

3:30   Coffee Break

3:45 - 5:15 P.M.   PANEL II: GEORGE ELIOT

                Moderator: Virginia Tiger, Dept. of English
                                 Director of Women Studies
                                 Rutgers University-Newark
                                 Newark, NJ

                "Feminism and Positivism in George Eliot's Romola."
                Nancy L. Paxton, Rutgers University
                New Brunswick, NJ

                "George Eliot and Feminism: The Case of Daniel Deronda."
                Bonnie Zimmerman, San Diego State University
                San Diego, CA

                "George Eliot and Barbara Leigh Smith Bodichon:
                   A Friendship."
                Nancy Pell, University of Michigan
                Ann Arbor, MI

5:30   Dinner Dining Rooms ABC, Student Center, North Campus
                                  $4.25 - Prix fixe   (unlimited)

8:00   Evening Program - Student Center Theatre, North Campus

                Greetings: Robert C. Vogt, Dean
                                 Hofstra College of Liberal Arts & Sciences

                                 Marcia E. O'Brien, Director
                                 Nassau County Office of Cultural Development

---

                Margaret Fuller - "Still Beat Noble Hearts."
                             Part II - The European Years, 1846-1850

                             Laurie James
                             Actress and Dramatist

                Sponsored by: Hofstra College of Liberal Arts & Sciences
                            Robert C. Vogt, Dean

                            Nassau County Office of Cultural Development
                            Marcia E. O'Brien, Director

**HOFSTRA UNIVERSITY'S
NINETEENTH CENTURY WOMEN WRITERS'
CONFERENCE**

proudly presents

LAURIE JAMES as MARGARET FULLER
in

Still Beat Noble Hearts

Part II

THE
EUROPEAN YEARS
1846 - 1850

**A Dramatic Portrait written,
directed, and produced by
Laurie James**

FRIDAY, NOVEMBER 7, 1980 8:00 PM
STUDENT CENTER, NORTH CAMPUS

Sponsored by:
Hofstra College of Liberal Arts & Sciences   Nassau County Office of Cultural Development
Robert C. Vogt, Dean   Marcia E. O'Brien, Director

Saturday, November 8, 1980   Dining Rooms ABC - Student Center, North Campus

8:00 - 9:00 A.M.   Continental Breakfast

                                David Filderman Gallery Exhibit
                                "Nineteenth Century Literary Women"

                                Gallery hours: Saturday, Nov. 8 - 9:00-1:00 & 2:15-4:00 p.m.
                                                Sunday, Nov. 9   - 9:30-2:00 p.m.

9:00 - 5:00 P.M.   Book Fair - Student Center Mezzanine

9:00 - 10:30   PANEL III A: EMILY DICKINSON

                                Moderator: Wilbur S. Scott
                                            New College, Hofstra University

                                "The Bride of the White Election: A New Look at
                                   Biblical Influence on Emily Dickinson."
                                Peggy Anderson
                                Virginia Beach, VA

                                "The Second Act: Dickinson's Orphan-Child."
                                Vivian R. Pollak, Cheyney State College
                                Cheyney, PA

                                "'Oh, Susie, it is dangerous': Emily Dickinson and
                                   the Archetype of the Masculine."
                                Joanne A. Dobson, SUNY - Albany
                                Albany, NY

9:00 - 10:30   PANEL III B: GENERAL EUROPEAN: RUSSIA, SPAIN, & SWEDEN

                                Moderator: Myroslava Znayenko, Dept. of Foreign Langs.
                                            Rutgers University-Newark
                                            Newark, NJ

                                "Fredrika Bremer: Sweden's First Feminist."
                                Doris R. Asmundsson, Queensborough Community College
                                Bayside, NY

                                "Adelaida Muñiz y Mas: Maruja Carmela, a Spanish Parody."
                                Patricia Bentivegna, Saint Francis College
                                Loretto, PA

                                "A Nigilistka and a Communarde: Two Voices of the
                                   Nineteenth Century Russian Intelligentka."
                                Isabelle Naginski, Bard College
                                Annandale-on-Hudson, NY

10:30 - 11:00   Coffee Break - Student Center Mezzanine

11:00 - 12:30   PANEL IV A: GENERAL ENGLISH

                                Moderator: Carole Silver, Dept. of English
                                            Stern College - Yeshiva University
                                            New York, NY

                                "Christina Rossetti: A Reconsideration."
                                Robert N. Keane, Hofstra University
                                Hempstead, NY

Saturday, November 8, 1980 (cont'd.)   -   Dining Rooms ABC - Student Center, North Campu

11:00 - 12:30   "The Price of Love -- Eliot and Gaskell."
                                 Coral Lansbury, Rutgers University
                                 Camden, NJ

                                 "'Michael Field' (Edith Cooper and Katherine Bradley)
                                    and Their Male Critics."
                                 David J. Moriarty, Hofstra University
                                 Hempstead, NY

11:00 - 12:30   Special Panel under the Auspices of the Consulate
                                    General of the Federal Republic of Germany:

                                 PANEL IV B: ANNETTE VON DROSTE - HÜLSHOFF

                                 Moderator: Ulrike Woods
                                              Goethe House
                                              New York, NY

                                 "Annette von Droste-Hülshoff and Her Critics."
                                 Maruta L. Ray, Rider College
                                 Lawrenceville, NJ

                                 "Inwardness and Creativity: Privacy and Artistic
                                    Commitment in Emily Dickinson and Annette von
                                    Droste-Hülshoff."
                                 Edith Toegel, University of New Hampshire
                                 Durham, NH

                                 "Feminism and the Feminine in Annette von
                                    Droste-Hülshoff."
                                 Friedrich Ulfers, New York University
                                 New York, NY

12:30 - 1:15   Lunch Main Dining Room, Student Center, North Campus
                                            A la carte

1:15 - 2:00   Special Presentation:

                                 Lucille and Walter Fillin
                                 Hofstra Library Associates

                                 "Nineteenth Century Women Cook Book Writers."

2:00 - 4:00   PANEL V A: GENERAL NORTH AMERICAN

                                 Moderator: Margaret Vanderhaar Allen
                                              Bethlehem, PA

                                 "Sisters and Survivors: Catherine Parr Traill
                                    (1802-99) and Susanna Moodie (1803-85)."
                                 Ann Edwards Boutelle, Suffolk University
                                 Boston, MA; Mount Holyoke College, S. Hadley, MA

                                 "Nineteenth Century Afro-American Women Poets."
                                 Renate Simson, Syracuse University
                                 Syracuse, NY; SUNY at Morrisville, Morrisville, NY

2:00 - 4:00   "Margaret Fuller's Woman in the Nineteenth Century:
                       The Feminist Manifesto."
                       Marie O. Urbanski, University of Maine
                       Orono, ME

2:00 - 4:00   PANEL V B: GENERAL FRENCH

                       Moderator: Erica Abeel, Dept. of Foreign Languages
                                    John Jay College - CUNY
                                    New York, NY

                       "Juliette Adam: She Devil or Grande française."
                       Jean Scammon Hyland, University of Rhode Island
                       Daniel H. Thomas, University of Rhode Island
                       Kingston, RI

                       "Flora Tristan: A Woman's Struggle for Equality
                          and Justice."
                       Mary Lee Morris, Cathedral College
                       Douglaston, NY

                       "George Sand's View of the English."
                       Patricia Thomson, University of Sussex
                       Brighton, England

                       "George Sand and the Puppet Theatre at Nohant."
                       Julia Bloch Frey, University of Colorado
                       Boulder, CO

4:00 - 4:30   Coffee Break and Book Fair - Student Center Mezzanine

                       Student Center Theater, North Campus

4:30 - 6:15   PANEL VI - WOMEN AND EDUCATION

                       Moderator: Vivian Gornick
                                    New York, NY

                       "Education for Wifehood in the Courtesy Book Novels
                          of Mary Jane Holmes."
                       Lucy Brashear, Appalachian State University
                       Boone, NC

                       "Minerva in the Shadows: Women and the American
                          Intellectual Tradition."
                       Berenice A. Carroll, University of Illinois at
                          Urbana-Champaign, Urbana, IL

                       "Lewis Carroll and the Education of Victorian Women."
                       Morton N. Cohen, The Graduate School of CUNY
                       New York, NY

                       "The Career Woman Fiction of Elizabeth Stuart Phelps."
                       Susan Ward, St. Lawrence University
                       Canton, NY

6:30   <u>Conference Banquet - Dining Rooms ABC, Student Center</u>

<u>Greetings</u>: James M. Shuart, President
                   Hofstra University

<u>Guest of Honor</u>: Germaine Brée
                       Wake Forest University
                       Winston-Salem, NC

<u>Keynote Address</u>:

"The Unpredicted Double: Nineteenth Century Women
  Writers as Twentieth Century Mirrors."

<u>Award Ceremony</u>:

                       Avriel Goldberger, French Department
                       Cultural Counselor of the French Embassy
                       James M. Shuart, President

PROGRAM

Sonata in F Major   George Philipp Telemann
   Vivace   (1681-1787)
   Largo
   Allegro

Variations on a Theme by Rossini   Frédéric Chopin
                                                      (1810-1849)

Offertoire, Op. 12   Johannes Donjon
                                                    (19th century)

Divertissement No. 2, Op. 68   Friedrich Kuhlau
                                                      (1786-1832)

INTERMISSION

Gigue   Jean-Marie Le Clair
                                                      (1697-1764)
                                                 arr. Georges Barrère

Syrinx   Claude Debussy
                                                      (1862-1918)

Baroque Suite   Ellen Levy
   Allegretto   (1954-   )
   Andante
   Moderato

Concertino, Op. 107   Cécile Chaminade
                                                      (1857-1944)

                   Martha Tunnicliff, Flute
                   Mary Elizabeth LaTorre, Piano

Sunday, November 9, 1980   Dining Rooms ABC - Student Center, North Campus

8:00 - 9:00 A.M.   Continental Breakfast

David Filderman Gallery Exhibit - 9:30 - 2:00 p.m.

"Nineteenth Century Literary Women"

9:00 - 11:00   PANEL VII - MME DE STAEL AND WOMAN AS ARTIST

Moderator: Avriel Goldberger
French Department, Hofstra University

"Corinne and the 'Yankee Corinna': Mme de Staël
and Margaret Fuller."
Paula Blanchard
Lexington, MA

"Woman as Mediatrix from Rousseau to Mme de Staël."
Madelyn Gutwirth, West Chester State College
West Chester, PA

"Mme de Staël on the Position of Women in France,
England and Germany."
Eve Sourian, The City College of CUNY
New York, NY

"Henry James and the Woman Novelist: The Double
Standard in the Tales and Essays."
Mary P. Edwards, Randolph-Macon College
Ashland, VA

11:00   Coffee Break

11:15 - 1:00 P.M.   Special Panel under the Auspices of the Cultural
Services of the French Embassy:

PANEL VIII - GEORGE SAND AND INTERTEXTUALITY

Moderator: Michael Riffaterre, Chairman
French Department
Columbia University
New York, NY

"Intertext and Sexuality in George Sand's Lélia."
Sherry A. Dranch, Wheaton College
Norton, MA

"Lélia: An Intertextual Perspective."
Shelley Temchin Henze, Tufts University
Medford, MA

"Intertextuality: George Sand and Flaubert -- An
Exchange of Letters as an 'art poétique.'"
Gérard Roubichou, Cultural Attaché
Cultural Services of the French Embassy, New York, NY

"Alfred de Musset and George Sand: An Intertextual
Literary Liaison."
Alex Szogyi, Hunter College/CUNY
New York, NY

Sunday, November 9, 1980 (cont'd.) - Dining Rooms ABC, Student Center, North Campus

1:00 - 2:00   <u>Brunch</u>   Main Dining Room
                                        Prix fixe (unlimited)
                                        $3.95

2:00 - 4:00   PANEL IX A - GENERAL EUROPEAN: FRENCH PANEL

                               Moderator: Beth Brombert
                                            Princeton, NJ

                               "George Sand et Frances Trollope."
                               Marie-Jacques Hoog, Douglass College-Rutgers University
                               New Brunswick, NJ - Presently at Université de Tours
                               Tours, France
                               Read by Marie M. Collins, Rutgers University-Newark
                               Newark, NJ

                               "Regards sur le 19ème siècle - le témoignage au féminin."
                               Marie-Claire Hoock-Demarle, Sorbonne-Nouvelle
                               Paris, France

                               "Les femmes auteurs de romans populaires dans la
                                  Grande-Presse française à la fin du 19ème siècle."
                               Evelyne Diebolt, Université de Paris VII
                               Paris, France

2:00 - 4:00   PANEL IX B - GENERAL EUROPEAN

                               Moderator: Robert N. Keane, Chairman
                                            Department of English
                                            Hofstra University

                               "The Rediscovery of Nineteenth Century Women Waiters:
                                  The Contribution of Ellen Moers."
                               (This talk is in honor of the late Ellen Moers)
                               Ruth Prigozy, Hofstra University
                               Hempstead, NY

                               "Toward a New Freedom: Rahel Varnhagen and the German
                                  Women Writers Before 1848."
                               Doris Starr Guilloton, New York University
                               New York, NY

                               "An Introduction to the Life and Times of Louise Otto."
                               Ruth-Ellen Boetcher Joeres, University of Minnesota
                               Minneapolis, MN

Sunday, November 9, 1980 (cont'd.) - Dining Rooms ABC, Student Center, North Campus

4:00   Coffee Break - Dining Rooms ABC

4:15 - 5:45   PANEL X - GENERAL ENGLISH

                              Moderator: Rachel France, Drama Dept.
                                          Lawrence University
                                          Appleton, WI

                              "Jane Austen's Mediative Voice."
                              Alison G. Sulloway, Virginia Polytechnic Institute &
                                State University
                              Blacksburg, VA

                              "Once More to the Attic: Bertha Rochester and the
                                Pattern of Redemption in Jane Eyre."
                              Gail P. Griffin, Kalamazoo College
                              Kalamazoo, MI

                              "Jane Eyre and Poverty."
                              Barbara Gates, University of Delaware
                              Newark, DE

                              "The Alcoholic Female in the Fiction of George Eliot
                                and Her Contemporaries."
                              Sheila Shaw, Wheaton College
                              Norton, MA

6:00   Wine and Cheese Reception

Nineteenth Century Women Writers Conference
Book Exhibition

Participants

AMS Press
56 East 13th Street
New York, NY 10003

Canadian Women's Studies
Toronto, Canada

Farrer, Straus & Giroux
19 Union Square West
New York, NY 10003

The Feminist Press
Box 334
Old Westbury, NY 11568

Hofstra University Publications
Hempstead, NY 11550
   George Sand Newsletter
   Twentieth Century Literature

Irvington Publishers, Inc.
551 Fifth Avenue
New York, NY 10016

The New American Library, Inc.
1633 Broadway
New York, NY 10019

New Sibylline Books, Inc.
Box 266 - Village Station
New York, NY 10014

Paulette Greene Rare Books
140 Princeton Road
Rockville Centre, NY 11570

Paulette Rose, Ltd.
Fine and Rare Books
3 North Lake Circle
White Plains, NY 10605

Wantagh Rare Book Company
18 East Sunrise Highway
Freeport, NY 11520

Nel Panzeca
Director, Book Exhibition

CREDIT for the success of the Conference goes to more people than can be named on
    this program, but those below deserve a special vote of thanks:

HOFSTRA UNIVERSITY OFFICERS: James M. Shuart, President
                               Harold E. Yuker, Provost
                               Robert C. Vogt, Dean, HCLAS

ARA Slater: Richard Adler

DAVID FILDERMAN GALLERY: Department of Special Collections
                           Marguerite Regan, Assistant to the Dean of Library Services
                           Nancy Herb
                           Anne Rubino

DEPARTMENT OF COMPARATIVE LITERATURE & LANGUAGES: Alice Hayes, Senior Executive Secretary

ENGLISH DEPARTMENT: Barbara Stroh, Senior Executive Secretary
                      Nancy Mumolo, Secretary to the Faculty

FRENCH DEPARTMENT: Colette Bailey, Senior Executive Secretary

HOFSTRA LIBRARY ASSOCIATES: Walter Fillin, President

HOFSTRA UNIVERSITY LIBRARY: Charles R. Andrews, Dean

OFFICE OF THE SECRETARY: Robert D. Noble, Secretary
                           Armand Troncone
                           Doris Brown and Staff

SCHEDULING OFFICE: Margaret Shields

UCCIS: Marilyn Seidman, Conference Secretary
         Conference Assistants: Karin Barnaby
                                  Alexander Lake
                                  Nel Panzeca

UNIVERSITY RELATIONS: Harold Klein, Director
                        Brian Ballweg, Assistant Director

THE WOMEN'S CENTER

STUDENT AIDES: English Department

Name Index

Subject Index

About the Contributors

PEGGY ANDERSON, a Tidewater, Virginia, free-lance writer, has published material on Emily Dickinson in *Explicator* and *Dickinson Studies*. Her poetry and articles have appeared in *Christian Century, The Lyric, Kansas Quarterly, Piedmont Literary Review, An & Q, Commonwealth Magazine* and others with an article forthcoming in *Presbyterian Survey*. She is listed in the Directory of Virginia Writers published by the Virginia Center for the Creative Arts. She holds a graduate degree in English from Old Dominion University, Norfolk, Virginia.

ANN EDWARDS BOUTELLE is Visiting Lecturer at Smith College. She is author of *Thistle and Rose: A Study of Hugh MacDiarmid's Poetry*, in addition to numerous articles on women writers, Canadian literature, and health issues. She is currently at work on a novel.

LUCY M. BRASHEAR is a Professor of English at Appalachian State University of North Carolina. While her specialty is sixteenth-century drama, in recent years she has become interested in women writers and has done extensive research on women poets of the seventeenth and eighteenth centuries in England and Wales. She has published articles on Shakespeare; D. H. Lawrence; Emily Dickinson; Anne Finch, Countess of Winchilsea; and Katherine Philips, the "Match-less Orinda."

MORTON N. COHEN, Professor Emeritus of The City University of New York, is the editor of *The Letters of Lewis Carroll*.

TILDEN G. EDELSTEIN is a Professor of History and Dean of the Faculty of

Arts and Sciences at Rutgers University, New Brunswick, New Jersey. He is the author of *Strange Enthusiasm: A Life of Thomas Wentworth Higginson* and has written about the American Civil War as well as about race and ethnicity. His essay, "*Othello* in America: The Dream of Racial Intermarriage," recently appeared in a collection of articles honoring C. Vann Woodward.

MARY P. EDWARDS KITTERMAN is on the faculty of Randolph-Macon College, Ashland, Virginia, where she chairs the Education Department and also teaches English and Women's Studies courses. During 1985–86 she has been on sabbatical leave in order to work on a book about Henry James's attitudes toward women writers. She serves as Secretary-Treasurer of the Ellen Glasgow Society, has co-edited the *Ellen Glasgow Newsletter*, and has lectured extensively on Glasgow as part of a public library series of programs on Southern writers.

LUCILLE FILLIN and WALTER FILLIN have been collecting cookbooks and related materials for many years. They write as a team. They helped to organize the Exhibition on Cookbooks for the Hofstra University Library, with a display of books from their personal library. They wrote the article on *Collecting Cookbooks* for the Time-Life Encyclopedia of Collectibles and *Feasting in Literary Cookbooks* for Imprint, the publication of the Stanford University Libraries Associates. They have written articles for the Journal of Long Island Book Collectors, and contributed material for the Conference on Women Writers and for the Victorian Studies Association at Hofstra University.

BARBARA T. GATES is Associate Professor of English at the University of Delaware. Her published work includes articles on a wide range of Romantic and Victorian writers and has appeared in journals such as *Criticism*, *Victorian Poetry* and *The Victorian Newsletter*. Currently she is completing a book-length study of suicide and the Victorians.

GAIL B. GRIFFIN is Associate Professor of English and Coordinator of Women's Studies at Kalamazoo College in Michigan. She has written and published on nineteenth- and twentieth-century women writers, as well as on women's educational history.

ROBERT N. KEANE is Professor of English at Hofstra University. He has written a number of articles and given papers on Dante Gabriel Rossetti, Christina Rossetti, William Morris, and the Pre-Raphaelite movement. He is currently working on a book, *Dante Gabriel Rossetti as Poetic Craftsman*.

CORAL LANSBURY is Professor of English and Dean of Graduate Studies at Rutgers University, Camden, New Jersey. She has published five books on Victorian themes and is also a novelist. Her most recent study is *The Old Brown*

Dog: Women, Workers, and Vivisection in Edwardian England (University of Wisconsin, 1985). Her latest novel is *Ringavia* (Harper and Row, 1985).

HOWARD N. MEYER, an independent scholar, is a civil rights historian and student of related literature. Former Special Assistant to the U.S. Attorney General and labor attorney, he serves as a court and labor Arbitrator. Meyer wrote the Pulitzer-nominated *The Amendment that Refused to Die*, a lay history of the 14th Amendment (civil rights) to the U.S. Constitution and is a biogrpaher of Thomas Wentworth Higginson. He is editor of Higginson's recently reissued *Army Life in a Black Regiment*, as well as other books and articles.

DAVID J. MORIARTY is Adjunct Professor of English at both Hofstra University and Long Island University (C. W. Post College). He has a Ph.D. from the University of Wisconsin–Madison, where he has also taught, and has done research on nineteenth-century poetry and drama at the University of Reading, England, and Trinity College, Dublin. A Vietnam veteran, he has acted as consultant on Vietnamese refugee education for the Wisconsin Department of Public Instruction, coauthoring with Thuy Pham *English for Vietnamese Students in Wisconsin*. He has also written on William Cullen Bryant and extensively on John Todhunter, Irish poet and playwright.

RHODA B. NATHAN is an Associate Professor of American Literature at Hofstra University, where she is also the resident Shavian. Among her publications are *The American Vision*, a study of individual and collective modes of thought in American society, and articles contributing to the study of the plays of George Bernard Shaw. She has published widely in American literature, most recently in an article and scholarly papers on the subject of Henry James. Professor Nathan is an officer of the Bernard Shaw Society and a lecturer at The New-York Historical Society, where her special interest is the Hudson River Landscape painters and their relationship to the nature poetry of the nineteenth-century poets. She is currently engaged in writing a biography of the New Zealand writer Katherine Mansfield.

NANCY L. PAXTON is an Assistant Professor of English at Northern Arizona University, where she teaches Victorian and modern British literature, feminist theory, and Women's Studies. She has published several articles on George Eliot and on feminist literary theory and is completing a book entitled *George Eliot and Herbert Spencer: Feminism, Evolutionism, and the Reconstruction of Gender*.

NANCY PELL is Instructor in English at the Cranbrook Kingswood School in Bloomfield Hills, Michigan, and previously held teaching positions at the University of Michigan and the State University of New York at Buffalo. She has published articles on George Eliot's *Daniel Deronda* and Charlotte Brontë's *Jane*

Eyre. Her current research includes the American-owned paintings of Barbara Bodichon, as well as the work of the contemporary writer Harriette Arnow.

VIVIAN R. POLLAK is Professor of English at Cheyney University in Pennsylvania. She is the author of *Dickinson: The Anxiety of Gender* (Cornell University Press, 1984), which examines sexual identity themes in the poet's life and work. Her articles on Dickinson have appeared in leading scholarly journals and she is currently preparing an edition of Dickinson family letters for publication as a book.

SHEILA SHAW is Professor of English at Wheaton College in Norton, Massachusetts. Her publications include articles in *PMLA* and *CEA Critic*. The present essay is part of a longer study on the female alcoholic in English and American fiction.

RENNIE SIMSON is Professor of English at the State University of New York, Morrisville, and also teaches in the Afro-American Studies Department, Syracuse University. Her articles have appeared in numerous publications, including the *Review of Afro-American Issues and Culture*, *Obsidian*, *College Language Association Journal*, *College English Association Critic*, and in the book *Powers of Desire: The Politics of Sexuality*. She has been the recipient of a National Endowment for the Humanities grant and an American Philosophical Society grant.

ALISON G. SULLOWAY is the Senior Victorian in the Department of English at Virginia Polytechnic Institute. She is the author of the Ansley Prize–winning book, *Gerard Manley Hopkins and the Victorian Temper*, of a finished manuscript, *The Province of Womanhood: Jane Austen and the Conduct Books*, and of essays on Hopkins and Austen. Her principal scholarly pre-occupation is nineteenth-century literary history, especially the history of masculine education, of the feminine predicament, and of national and international events shaping the lives of both sexes.

MARIE OLESEN URBANSKI is Associate Professor of American Literature at the University of Maine at Orono. She is the former editor of the *Thoreau Journal Quarterly*. Her book, *Margaret Fuller's Woman in the Nineteenth Century*, has caused a revaluation of Margaret Fuller's place in nineteenth-century American literature.

SUSAN WARD is Associate Professor of English at St. Lawrence University in Canton, New York. Her research interests include nineteenth-century popular American writers and American women writers. She is the author of several articles on Jack London and has also written on Elizabeth Stuart Phelps, Helen Hunt Jackson, Mary Gordon, and the female bildungsroman.

ANNA MARY WELLS is Professor Emerita of English at Rutgers University's Douglass College. She is the author of *Miss Marks and Miss Woolley*, a joint biography of two distinguished Mount Holyoke women, and of *Dear Preceptor, The Life and Times of Thomas Wentworth Higginson*. She has contributed articles on Emily Dickinson to *American Literature, Dickinson Studies*, and *The Mount Holyoke Alumnae Quarterly*. She has also published five murder mysteries and a number of stories and articles in popular magazines.

BONNIE ZIMMERMAN is Professor of Women's Studies at San Diego State University. She has published articles on George Eliot and on lesbian literature and critical theory in many journals and anthologies. She is currently writing a study of the contemporary lesbian-feminist novel.